PARANORMAL BRITAIN

PARANORMAL BRITAIN

Belief in the Uncanny in England, Scotland, and Wales

Tom Clark

Christopher D. Bader and

Joseph O. Baker

BLOOMSBURY ACADEMIC
LONDON • NEW YORK • OXFORD • NEW DELHI • SYDNEY

BLOOMSBURY ACADEMIC
Bloomsbury Publishing Plc, 50 Bedford Square, London, WC1B 3DP, UK
Bloomsbury Publishing Inc, 1359 Broadway, New York, NY 10018, USA
Bloomsbury Publishing Ireland, 29 Earlsfort Terrace, Dublin 2, D02 AY28, Ireland

BLOOMSBURY, BLOOMSBURY ACADEMIC and the Diana logo are trademarks of Bloomsbury Publishing Plc

First published in Great Britain 2026

Copyright © Tom Clark, Christopher D. Bader, and Joseph O. Baker 2026

Tom Clark, Christopher D. Bader, and Joseph O. Baker have asserted their right under the Copyright, Designs and Patents Act, 1988, to be identified as Authors of this work.

For legal purposes the Acknowledgements on pp. x–xii constitute an extension of this copyright page.

Cover design: Ben Anslow
Cover images © AdobeStock

This work is published open access subject to a Creative Commons Attribution-NonCommercial-NoDerivatives 4.0 International licence (CC BY-NC-ND 4.0, https://creativecommons.org/licenses/by-nc-nd/4.0/). You may re-use, distribute, and reproduce this work in any medium for non-commercial purposes, provided you give attribution to the copyright holder and the publisher and provide a link to the Creative Commons licence.

No part of this publication may be used or reproduced in any way for the training, development or operation of artificial intelligence (AI) technologies, including generative AI technologies. The rights holders expressly reserve this publication from the text and data mining exception as per Article 4(3) of the Digital Single Market Directive (EU) 2019/790. Bloomsbury Publishing Plc does not have any control over, or responsibility for, any third-party websites referred to or in this book. All internet addresses given in this book were correct at the time of going to press. The author and publisher regret any inconvenience caused if addresses have changed or sites have ceased to exist, but can accept no responsibility for any such changes.

A catalogue record for this book is available from the British Library.

A catalog record for this book is available from the Library of Congress.

ISBN: HB: 978-1-3505-6165-6
PB: 978-1-3505-6164-9
ePDF: 978-1-3505-6167-0
eBook: 978-1-3505-6166-3

Typeset by Newgen KnowledgeWorks Pvt. Ltd., Chennai, India
Printed and bound in Great Britain

For product safety related questions contact productsafety@bloomsbury.com.

To find out more about our authors and books visit www.bloomsbury.com and sign up for our newsletters.

CONTENTS

List of Figures	vi
List of Photos	viii
List of Tables	ix
Acknowledgements	x
INTRODUCTION	1
Chapter 1 THE INNER LIGHT	13
Chapter 2 INTO THE DEPTHS	35
Chapter 3 MOST HAUNTED	55
Chapter 4 MYSTERIOUS WORLD	85
Chapter 5 AROUND IN CIRCLES	105
Chapter 6 MYSTERIOUS UNIVERSE	129
Chapter 7 THE DEVIL'S BARGAIN	151
CONCLUSION	173
Notes	181
Bibliography	209
Index	225

FIGURES

1.1	The paranormal, religion and science	18
1.2	Enlightenment beliefs in Britain, by gender (CASPAR, 2021)	33
1.3	Enlightenment practices in Britain, by gender (CASPAR, 2021)	33
2.1	The Loch Ness Monster exists (CASPAR, 2021)	38
2.2	Cryptid belief in Britain (CASPAR, 2021)	42
2.3	Belief in Bigfoot in Britain (CASPAR, 2021)	42
2.4	Paranormal clusters	49
2.5	Cryptid believer profile (CASPAR, 2021)	50
2.6	Magic and spirits believer profile (CASPAR, 2021)	52
3.1	Belief that places can be haunted by spirits (CASPAR, 2021)	62
3.2	Belief in ghosts and religious identity in Britain by year	68
3.3	Popularity of Google searches related to 30 East Drive (2011–12)	74
3.4	Ghost-related beliefs by year of birth (CASPAR, 2021)	75
3.5	Ghost-related experiences by year of birth (CASPAR, 2021)	75
3.6	Ghost-related consumption by year of birth (CASPAR, 2021)	76
4.1	Percentage of LTLAs with regular ghost tourism available (November 2023)	92
4.2	Map of ghost tourism in England and Wales	93
4.3	Percentage in the UK who have already done or plan to do paranormal tourism activities	101
5.1	Crop circles are created by nonhuman forces or energies (CASPAR, 2021)	108
5.2	Mapping paranormal beliefs	115
5.3	Correlogram of beliefs and experiences associated with Earth Mysteries	122
6.1	Belief in ancient and modern alien visitations (CASPAR, 2021)	135
6.2	Paranormal beliefs in Britain, by number held (CASPAR, 2021)	136
6.3	Additive belief in components of David Icke's narrative (CASPAR, 2021)	142
6.4	Consumption of paranormal media, by type (CASPAR, 2021)	146
6.5	Consumption of multiple paranormal topics by media type (CASPAR, 2021)	147
7.1	Average number of paranormal beliefs and experiences by religious identity	163
7.2	Number of predicted paranormal beliefs by levels of religious belief, practice and experience	164
7.3	Predicted number of paranormal experiences by levels of religious belief, practice and experience	165

7.4 Curvilinear relationship between composite measure of religion and paranormalism 165
7.5 Predicted probability of reading *The Da Vinci Code* 168
8.1 Paranormal beliefs in Britain, ranked by popularity (CASPAR, 2021) 175

PHOTOS

2.1	Steve Feltham at Dores Beach, Loch Ness, on 16 January 2023	37
3.1	Outside 30 East Drive in Pontefract, England, at night	56
3.2	Some of the Retford Ghost Hunters' equipment in the kitchen of 30 East Drive	60
3.3	Sensory experiment in the coal shed at 30 East Drive	72
4.1	Nessieland exhibit	96
5.1	Crop circle in Roundway Down, Wiltshire, 2023	106
5.2	Tom explores a crop circle	107
6.1	A horse-headed 'Egyptian Pharaoh' alien encountered by Russell Kellett	133

TABLES

1.1	Identification with 'Magical' Religions and Identities in the UK (2001–21)	30
6.1	The Syncretists (CASPAR, 2021)	148

ACKNOWLEDGEMENTS

There are many people who contributed to this project in ways big and small. Various combinations of the authors, family, and friends participated in different events, so we will simply use 'we' rather than specify each time.

First, we must thank the people who allowed us to join them on investigations, tours or for interviews and visits. We greatly appreciate Steve Feltham for meeting with us at his investigation centre and shop at Dores Beach on the shores of Loch Ness. Steve was a gracious host and very willing to answer questions about his lifetime looking for Nessie and the culture of monster hunting around the loch. His insights greatly contributed to Chapter 2. For those interested in Nessie, we suggest a visit in person or to his website (https://www.nessiehunter.co.uk/). We are also extremely grateful to Donald McLennan, owner of Donald's Highland Tours (https://www.donaldshighlandtours.com/), for taking us on a custom tour of Nessie landmarks and expertly navigating us out of a snowstorm that threatened to strand the group at a rest area overnight. Donald is a wonderful and amiable guide whose services come highly recommended to anyone visiting the Inverness or Loch Ness region. Special thanks go to Marisa Quezada and Anika Manuel for visiting Nessieland and providing their photographs and notes.

Many thanks to the Retford Ghost Hunters (RGH) for agreeing to join us at 30 East Drive in Pontefract for investigating the legend of the 'Black Monk'. The group was very generous with their time and our questions as they demonstrated their various pieces of ghost-hunting equipment and conducted experiments throughout the evening. Our thanks to founder Rachel Parsons who organized and led the proceedings and the other RGH members and investigators who participated, including Ron Simpson, Trevor Bailey, and Gary Brumby. The RGH holds regular events that they advertise and livestream via their Facebook page (https://www.facebook.com/retfordghosthunters).

Our thanks to Rolf White, owner of Rolfs Rides (https://rolfsrides.com/), for taking us to the Rosslyn Chapel on two occasions. In January of 2023, while giving us a ride to a purportedly haunted castle, the amiable Rolf pointed out the road to Rosslyn Chapel. Upon seeing our excitement at this unforeseen synchronicity, Rolf changed his plans to take us to Rosslyn, telling jokes, informing us of his fascination with the show *Ancient Aliens*, and sometimes singing along the way. When we decided to return the following October to attend a service at the chapel (see Chapter 7), Rolf again took us and joined the service, dressed in a sharp vest and kilt. If in Edinburgh or its environs, look up Rolf for an entertaining ride about town.

The drawings included in Chapter 6 were generously provided to us by Russell Kellett, who kindly invited us into his home to discuss his intense experiences with aliens and his interest in other paranormal topics. Russell has a website where one can buy his book and learn about his experiences and investigations (https://ufo-paranormal.com/).

We greatly enjoyed meeting Monique Klinkenbergh, founder and director of the Crop Circle Research Centre & Exhibition in Wiltshire. Monique hosted us for high tea, took us on a tour of the Centre, and was generous with her time and patience as we peppered her with questions. The Centre is highly recommended for those visiting Wiltshire and maintains a list of current crop circles in the area (https://www.cropcircleaccess.com/).

Many thanks to the Aetherius Society (atherius.org) for allowing us to join them at the fiftieth anniversary of Operation Prayer Power at Holdstone Down. The experience was very important in helping us to understand the place of the Aetherius Society in the British religious landscape. We are especially grateful to Darren Ball of the Society for answering our many questions, both before and after the event.

Unfortunately, due to space considerations, there are many people who gave us their time and energy whose efforts did not make it into the book. The staff at Dalhousie Castle in Bonnyburg (https://www.dalhousiecastle.co.uk/) took us on an evening tour of their wonderful castle turned hotel and told us of its resident spirits. Mike Covell (https://www.instagram.com/amazinghulltours/) guided us through the back streets of Hull and the brambles around Barmston Drain, regaling us with the history of modern werewolf sightings in the area.

Tom spent much of 2023 and 2024 traveling around the country to different events and spoke to a great many people along the way. Among others, haunted evenings were spent at Chillingham Castle, the Ancient Ram Inn (with 'Mark the Medium'), The Museum of Curiosities, Cannock Chase (with some of the team from Haunted Happenings), and The Poltergeist House Haunted Museum at Rotherham. Many days were also spent listening to a variety of speakers and chatting with attendees at various events. Highlights include Megalithomania, Origins Conference, Paracon, Awakening, the UFO and Spirituality Conference, A Night of Crop Circling, and various events organized by The Bases Project. The College of Psychic Studies offers many courses in various aspects of spirituality and runs regular open days for the curious. Thanks also to the usually very friendly and helpful people at Mind Body Spirit events at different locations around the country who offered their insights into their practices. Special thanks to Claire Cunnington for helping us to navigate the world of Tarot. Thanks also to Samuel Clark for building the index for the book.

A number of academic colleagues helped in the development of this project. Dr. Pete Simi of Chapman University joined us at Loch Ness, Dalhousie Castle, a ghost tour in Edinburgh, Rosslyn Chapel, and 30 East Drive. His notes were helpful in the development of several chapters. Thanks to Dr. David Clarke of Sheffield-Hallam University for giving advice on several matters and joining us for the evening at 30 East Drive. David's bemusement at the proceedings provided energy throughout a long evening. The Sociology and Anthropology Seminar Series at Chapman University provided valuable feedback on Chapter 3 and the Conclusion. Many thanks to Steven Pfaff, Karen Snedker, Ashley Kranjac, Peter Simi, CK Magliola, Ed Day, Nancy Rios-Contreras, Monique Charles and Mohammad Isaqzadeh for their valuable feedback. Thanks also to Prof. Richard Bentall at the University of Sheffield for many productive conversations about the psychology of the paranormal and religion. In joining Tom at a number of MBS events, Prof. Richard Jenkins also provided great company and offered much insight into many aspects of social identity and belief that we witnessed. Joseph's work on the book was generously supported by a research sabbatical in the spring of 2024. Thanks to in the Department of Sociology and Anthropology and the College of Arts and Sciences at East Tennessee State University for this support.

And of course, we could not have completed this project without the patience and support of our partners and families. Christopher would like to thank his wife, Sara, for putting up with years of strange adventures. Tom would like to thank Lydia, Betsy, Idha and the late Arfur C. Whiskerson. Joseph would like to thank Lindsey, Hazel, and Eleanor.

INTRODUCTION

I'm Nobody

Late into a chilly winter night, we are sitting in the upstairs bedroom of 30 East Drive in Pontefract, England. We are waiting for a ghost to speak.

In the late 1960s, the previous owners of this unassuming council home, Joe and Jean Pritchard, reported an assault by a violent spirit. Dubbed 'Mr. Nobody' by the local press, the entity tossed small items about the house and manifested pools of water, before escalating to more frightening behaviours. In response to an exorcism attempt, the spectre scratched inverted crosses into the walls. It destroyed a grandfather clock and dragged the Pritchards' daughter, Diane, up the stairwell by her throat. Joe was viciously attacked by an unseen force in the home's coal room.

In recent years, it has become a rite of passage for ghost enthusiasts to spend an evening at 30 East Drive with the 'world's most violent and relentless poltergeist'.[1] The site's current owner rents the home by the evening to interested parties, with an active social media community chronicling their exploits.[2] We reserved it for an evening, and a local paranormal investigation team, the Retford Ghost Hunters, graciously agreed to join us on the hunt.

The ghost hunters tried a number of experiments utilizing their host of electronic equipment. By 10.30 pm we were sitting in an upstairs bedroom watching Trevor, the resident tech expert, set up a laptop running a piece of software called 'Alice Box'. On occasion, Alice Box beeps as a word or phrase appears on the screen. Users believe that nearby spirits can manipulate the software to speak by making meaningful words appear.

Trevor attempted to entice Mr. Nobody to speak through the Alice Box.

'My name's Trevor. Our friends are here with us'. The laptop beeped. 'Can appear', read Trevor. A promising start. It beeped again. 'Ropes'. Not as meaningful. This was followed by 'figurine'. This also seemed of little import.

Then Will, another ghost hunter, took over mediumship (via technology) duties.

'Could you tell us your name on this box?'

The laptop beeped immediately.

'I'm Nobody', read Trevor.

Why Would You Do This?

Had a violent ghost decided to make an appearance? Vicariously, via spiritual software ventriloquism?

In Chapter 3, we dive deeper into the mysteries of 30 East Drive, exploring its complicated history at greater length. But readers may well be disappointed by our lack of a definitive answer as to whether a ghost was speaking through the Alice Box. After all, most books about the paranormal present an implied conclusion as to the objective existence of paranormal phenomena. A wide range of sceptics, scientists, journalists, and enthusiasts have written passionately about paranormal topics, trying to establish 'fact' or 'fiction' (or 'psychology'). We have little desire to reproduce those debates here. Frankly, we have little to add to them. Unlike most people who pursue the paranormal, we are not even concerned with the question of whether paranormal beliefs and experiences are objectively 'true' or 'false'.

When we told colleagues of our plans to visit locations such as 30 East Drive for research, one friend was horrified at the thought of wilfully entering such a notoriously haunted house. She simply asked: 'Why would you do this?' It's a fair question. Why go to a 'violently' haunted house if we did not intend to collect evidence for or against the existence of its spirits? Why explore the shores of Loch Ness if we have little to say about the existence of Nessie? Or why visit psychics if we don't seek insights into our future and personal relationships? Or, in contrast, why not put our scientific backgrounds to work and at least test the predictions we receive from psychic readings?

Rather than participating in debates about the objective reality of the paranormal, we are interested in these kinds of beliefs, experiences, and practices because, as sociologists, it is the *social* reality of the paranormal that interests us. That reality is undeniable, regardless of whether or not you think ghosts exist, psychics can tell the future, or aliens are regularly visiting Earth.

Over the past two decades, there has been a dramatic increase in public interest in UFOs, Bigfoot, ghosts, clairvoyance, and advanced ancient civilizations.[3] At the same time that paranormal beliefs have grown, there have been sizable *decreases* in both religious affiliation and participation. In 2021, for example, census data for England and Wales revealed that less than half of the population (46.2 per cent) now reported their religion to be 'Christian', down from 59 per cent just a decade prior.[4]

There is clearly an ongoing shift in how and what people in Britain believe. But the movement away from conventional religion is not necessarily resulting in a rising tide of atheism.[5] Rather, many people still desire to reach beyond the mundanity of life (and death), and if they do not find convincing answers in conventional religion, they go looking elsewhere. Many of those drifting away from organized religion are creating personalized, syncretic belief systems that combine conventional religious concepts, sometimes from multiple faiths, with the paranormal.[6] For example, an individual may believe that Jesus is the son of God but also find wisdom in the teachings of Buddha, all while thinking that extraterrestrials have visited the Earth and wildmen inhabit the forest.[7] Regardless of what they may be, beliefs about the nature of reality are also tied to our notions of good and evil and, therefore, influence our conceptions of morality, and even our social and political orientations.[8]

As sociologists, it is clear to us from the data we have collected that the paranormal plays an increasing, if often indirect, role in British culture and public life. As a result, it is important to have a better understanding of how the paranormal appeals to and influences people, regardless of whether you are a believer or a sceptic or whether or not there is any objective truth to specific paranormal claims. Given that our expertise is in social scientific methods and theories, we use the tools of our trade to generate data and analysis about the social dynamics of paranormalism in Britain.

Introducing CASPAR

To examine how people experience the paranormal, we used two different (but related) types of investigation: quantitative survey research and qualitative field research.

The first thing we needed was a rigorous and accurate way to estimate and explore patterns in paranormalism among the British public. Years ago, Britain used to be at the vanguard of polling about paranormal beliefs and experiences. As far back as the late nineteenth century, the Society for Psychical Research surveyed British citizens about belief in ghosts, mediums, psychics, and related experiences. Conducted between 1889 and 1895, the 'Census of Hallucinations' elicited over 17,000 responses.[9] Finding current data proved more difficult.[10] We did learn that as of 1984, 36 per cent of people from Great Britain had experienced telepathy, 26 per cent reported contact with the dead, and 14 per cent reported a clairvoyant experience.[11]

From *British Religion in Numbers* (BRIN), a reliable online resource that consolidates data from a wealth of polls, we learned that belief in flying saucers grew from 15 per cent of the population in 1973 to nearly a quarter (24 per cent) in 1995.[12] Belief in astrology remained steady, with 22 per cent of citizens believing in 1985 and 25 per cent in 2007. In contrast, belief in ghosts has grown substantially – from an estimated 10 per cent in 1950 to 39 per cent in 2008. Another survey of 4,000 British adults in 2009 found that nearly one-fourth of respondents (24 per cent) claimed an incidence of precognition, and one in ten reported contact with the dead.[13] These studies show that the paranormal has long been prevalent among the British public, and further, that public interests have grown on many topics, such as UFOs and ghosts.

Ultimately, our exploration of existing surveys told us that we needed to conduct our own. Available data could not speak to the contemporary era and were not suitably comprehensive in coverage. From a variety of surveys, one might piece together data on belief in black magic, ghosts, ESP, communication with the dead, and other paranormal beliefs or experiences. But nobody has recently asked about *all* these subjects together, nor asked about them in combination with measures of other relevant types of beliefs and attitudes. We also wanted to get an accurate, representative sample of the public. Learning about how different beliefs are held simultaneously can tell us much about the paranormal as well as its relationship to other social phenomena, such as religion, politics, and commerce.

To achieve these goals, we designed and fielded the most comprehensive survey of paranormal beliefs, practices, and experiences ever conducted in Britain. In the late summer of 2021, the Chapman and Sheffield Paranormal and Religion Survey (CASPAR) collected a nationally representative sample of 2,100 adults from across the United Kingdom (Wales, Scotland, Northern Ireland, and England).[14] We asked British adults if they believe in faeries, the UK Wildman, the Abominable Snowman, and Nessie. We asked if curses have power and if ley lines connect ancient structures. We found out if people believe in ghosts and if they think aliens visited in our ancient past (and if they are currently still around). We also asked about related experiences. We know if people have seen a UFO, experienced a past-life regression, or used a Ouija board, among many others. We know how often people read about the paranormal, visit related websites, go to conferences, or seek out forms of paranormal tourism. This wealth of information about the paranormal was combined with a host of questions about more conventional forms of religious beliefs and practices. We asked respondents if they were members of a religious organization, how often they attended worship services (if ever), and what they believed about God and the devil.[15]

We did not believe, however, that a survey was sufficient to appreciate the full picture of the paranormal in British culture. We needed to get out from behind our screens and out of the office. Mr. Nobody is not the first, nor the last, malevolent entity we visited while writing this book. We attended UFO conferences and talked to abductees about what it was like to be captured and taken to other galaxies. We had our palms read, auras photographed, and futures foretold by psychics. We visited churches that worship aliens and embrace conspiracy theories (in the name of tourism). We talked with cryptozoologists on the shores of Loch Ness. We visited crop circles and talked to 'croppies' about their extraordinary experiences. We went on vision quests and learned to read tarot. Our time experiencing paranormal subcultures provided insights into alternative beliefs and into how these beliefs influence other aspects of social life. Surveys can only take us so far, which is why we have combined our statistical analyses with actively studying different paranormal subcultures on the ground.

Perhaps disappointingly, even as we take you to locations steeped in paranormal lore, we will not be running Electronic Voice Phenomena recordings through spectrum analyses, looking at genetic sequencing of purported cryptid hair samples, or paying photographic experts to examine UFO images. There are, however, many topics we *will* address, including:

- How popular is belief in the paranormal?
- Who believes in the paranormal? Are there demographic patterns to these beliefs?

- Which paranormal beliefs tend to cluster together? If someone believes in Nessie, do they also tend to believe in ghosts or psychic powers?
- How common are paranormal experiences such as UFO sightings and ghost encounters? Are there certain types of people who are more likely to have these experiences?
- How does modern technology influence paranormal practices and experiences?
- How common is paranormal tourism, in terms of both supply and demand? Is there room for continued growth in paranormal tourism?
- What kinds of locations are the most likely to support organized paranormal tourism?
- What motivates people to participate in paranormal subcultures?
- How do people understand their own paranormal experiences? How do these experiences shape their lives?
- What makes some paranormal entrepreneurs or enterprises successful?
- How does the paranormal relate to organized religion? Does religious belief tend to encourage the acceptance of other types of supernatural claims?
- What happens when paranormal beliefs are turned into a religion? Or when organized religion welcomes the paranormal? Are 'magical' religions growing in Britain?
- What makes the paranormal so appealing in contemporary, technologically advanced societies?

By combining information from high-quality surveys with extensive fieldwork, our goal was to gather and analyse reliable data – both quantitative and qualitative – about the paranormal in Britain. This will allow us to accurately document and assess the social realities of the paranormal in contemporary British culture.

It is also worth clarifying what we mean when we refer to Britain. Great Britain is generally taken to refer to the countries England, Scotland, and Wales. The UK, on the other hand, is a term given to the nations of England, Scotland, Wales, and Northern Ireland (and other affiliated territories). Our survey was directed toward the UK. However, we did not have the opportunity to do any fieldwork in Northern Ireland; so while the survey data does include respondents from Northern Ireland, the main focus of our study is on Great Britain – hence the title of the book.

The Journey Ahead

Britain has a long history of esoteric practices, and many established organizations continue to provide opportunities to explore the latest developments in the paranormal world. Founded as the London Spiritualist Alliance in 1884, the College of Psychic Studies still has its headquarters in South Kensington, London, for example. Meanwhile the Spiritualists' National Union continues to operate the Arthur Findley College in Stansted, Essex. Between these two venues alone, you can take workshops on channelling your archangels, using crystals for healing and psychic self-defence, communicating with the spirits of plants, palm reading, tarot, contacting the dead, and a host of other topics. Elsewhere, the Association for the Scientific Study of Anomalous Phenomena (ASSAP) runs an accredited program for 'paranormal researchers', which trains budding investigators on forty-five topics including ghosts, UFOs, mysterious animals, possession, crop circles, out-of-body experiences, mediumship, and teleportation.[16] With various conferences, bookshops, local groups, and YouTube channels offering additional opportunities for training, improvement, and exploration, a truly bewildering array of paranormal possibilities is readily available.

It is this astounding variety that Chapter 1: The Inner Light addresses. To begin our in-depth exploration of the paranormal, we must first clarify what we are talking about. What is the paranormal? Is it the same thing as the occult, the supernatural, the 'New Age' or spiritualism? How is it related to science? How is it related to religion? Indeed, we found it a common claim amongst paranormal enthusiasts that their endeavours utilized the principles of science. Similarly, we have heard about demons from the pulpit *and* from ghost hunters telling us about demons prowling the rooms of numerous haunted houses. Chapter 1 discusses the affinities between these different social phenomena and attempts to do the impossible: define the paranormal. In doing so, we will learn that people approach the paranormal in two very different ways. Some use the paranormal to seek personal *enlightenment*, to better themselves by learning about their past, present, or future, or by engaging in forms of healing. Others engage with the paranormal in hopes of being part of a great new *discovery*, such as proving the existence of extraterrestrials or documenting the reality of Nessie. To help aid in our attempt to understand these differences, Chapter 1 takes us to Mind Body and Spirit fairs where we learn to read tarot, receive psychic readings, and undergo a shamanic healing.

Chapter 2: Into the Depths turns our attention to another vibrant tradition within Great Britain: monsters. In 1934 the *Daily Mail* published a mysterious photograph of a long dark neck rising from the depths of Loch Ness. Supposedly taken by a London gynaecologist named Kenneth Wilson, everything about the iconic photograph has since been called into question, from the size of the object in the image and the date it was taken to the identity of the photographer.[17] Whatever the truth behind it, the so-called 'surgeon's photograph' helped introduce the Loch Ness Monster to the world and earned Nessie a place in the triumvirate of world-famous 'cryptids' that includes Bigfoot and the Abominable Snowman.[18]

Scotland's remnant plesiosaur is certainly Britain's top monster attraction, but others are abundant, in both modern and historic times. Dragons feature prominently in legend.[19] The 'Black Shuck', a giant, spectral dog, left its claw marks on the door of a church in Blythburgh and is still seen today. Formerly a common motif in medieval art, the Wildman or Woodwose, has also morphed into the British Bigfoot, said to roam Cannock Chase, Thetford Woods, and the Cotswolds.[20] Nessie's less famous cousins, Morag, Morgawr, and Muc-sheilche, suggest that it is not just Loch Ness with a famous monster. Meanwhile, panther-like, anomalous big cats (ABCs) are regularly spotted in the countryside across the length and breadth of the British Isles. Cornwall even has its own 'Owl Man'. It is fair to say that Britain's landscape is crawling with mysterious beasts. To learn more about how these legends arise and inspire, we will hear from a professional Nessie hunter. As we explore the menagerie of British cryptids, we will also find out how many people believe in the Loch Ness Monster, the British Wildman, and other fantastical beasts.

One of the first things we found when talking to those interested in monsters is that they tended to be sympathetic to claims about *other* cryptids. In other words, someone who expressed belief in Nessie also tended to express belief in ABCs or Bigfoot, more so than they might believe in UFOs, ghosts, or other paranormal subjects. Chapter 2 explores this clustering of paranormal beliefs in greater detail. We find four significant groups of beliefs within the paranormal: aliens, cryptids, Earth mysteries, and magic and spirits. This allows us to look at the characteristics of different types of paranormal believers. For example, we find that women are more likely to believe in magic and spirits and Earth mysteries in all their forms, but that gender tells us little about someone's interest in aliens or cryptids. Further, one of the most common stereotypes about paranormal believers is that it is only marginalized people who engage with the strange and unreal, either out of social frustration or because they have less at risk in doing so. Chapter 2 addresses this 'marginalization hypothesis' to determine which of the stereotypes we hold about paranormal believers have some merit and which we should drop to the bottom of Loch Ness.

Chapter 3: Most Haunted explores ghosts and spirits. We look at the extent to which British adults believe in ghosts and hauntings, and how those beliefs have changed over time. We learn how often people consume ghost-related media, what percentage of them have personally experienced a haunting, and which social characteristics make people more likely to have spectral encounters. We return to The Black Monk of Pontefract for an in-depth examination of the history of the site and to see what ghost enthusiasts do when they visit 30 East Drive.

Of particular interest in this regard was that the Retford Ghost Hunters opened up our investigation to an online audience. As we wandered the house hoping to encounter Mr. Nobody, an army of fellow online ghost hunters provided advice, watched for shadows, and dared the ghost to touch us; all remotely from their mobile phones and laptops. What we saw at 30 East Drive was extraordinary, if not supernatural. The paranormal has moved from being the province of television shows and gentlemen 'experts' into grassroots, participatory events. This ability to vicariously experience the supernatural in real time is, dare we say it, not unlike some forms of church attendance and may be a sign of things to come as the paranormal grows in popularity. We also find that interest in ghosts is substantially higher among younger generations, indicating that the future of Britain looks increasingly haunted.

To these ends, Chapter 4: Mysterious World discusses an increasingly important aspect of the British economy: paranormal tourism. Indeed, any number of budding entrepreneurs and town councils have transformed the British Isles into a place where one is never far away from paranormal-themed adventures. Starting at the aforementioned Blythburgh church where the Black Shuck caused a ruckus, the enterprising visitor could reach the official 'UFO trail' at Rendlesham forest in about thirty minutes, built at the location of a historic encounter discussed below.[21] From there, one could arrive at the village of Woolpit in under an hour, the location of a twelfth-century encounter with two green children who emerged from a hole in the ground, speaking an unknown language. The 'Green Children of Woolpit' are still proudly featured on the village sign. If timed properly, you could end the day by driving forty minutes to Felixstowe for an evening ghost hunt at Landguard Fort, home to a spectral wailing woman and spirits that enjoy pushing unsuspecting visitors.

We provide the first systematic estimates of the prevalence of the 'supply' of ghost tourism, finding that 71 per cent of local areas across England and Wales provide some form of regularly available events and experiences. Further, those who live in a local community without ghost tourism are still an average of only twenty minutes away from a ghost-themed tourist activity. We also find that consumer demand for these activities is high. Our surveys find that nearly one-fourth of respondents (23 per cent) have already been on a paid ghost walk, and another 30 per cent say they intend to do so in the future. The commoditization of the paranormal is of course not limited to ghosts. As an example, we return to Loch Ness and visit the recently refurbished Loch Ness Centre & Exhibition that has been the recipient of a £1.5 million investment by an entertainment firm hoping to take advantage of the 'globally renowned Scottish brand' that Nessie has become.

Chapter 5: Around in Circles explores that most English of paranormal mysteries, the crop circle. We visit recently formed crop circles in person and tour the Crop Circle Visitor Centre & Exhibition in Wiltshire. Here we learn how the crop circle mystery is a hub that connects with many other paranormal phenomena. A popular theory for the origin of crop circles is that they are created by extraterrestrials, but others believe they may be created by Gaia herself, nature spirits or fae, psychic energy, or perhaps even ghosts. Due to their narrative flexibility, crop circles act as a gateway into a wider world of mysticism, whether that be a deep dive into sacred geometry, New Age spirituality, UFOs, or all of the above.

Beyond the temporary temples of wheat and barley, Britain has many more permanent reminders of the ancient past within its sacred landscape. Perhaps most notable are the monuments at Stonehenge and Avebury, but stone circles are actually very common if you know where to look. A huge white horse carved into a hillside in Uffington, Oxford, is one of several prehistoric hill figures dotted around Britain, while any number of ancient hill forts and barrows are part and parcel of the landscape. These markers of ancient faiths have long sparked the British imagination, and they continue to inspire paranormal researchers and enthusiasts. For some, they are evidence of advanced, ancient civilizations; for others they are alien landing spots or markers on a system of ley lines charged with mystical power.

Crop circles, stone circles, and other sacralized landscape sites function similarly. Their uncertain origins provide an opening for a variety of imaginative paranormal theories. They also provide an extensive variety of options for tourism and modern, ritualized spiritual pilgrimages. As an example, we go on a psychic quest at Avebury, showing how the stones have become a modern pilgrimage destination for all manner of paranormal purposes. We also use a unique statistical analysis that allows us to visually map how different paranormal beliefs are connected to one another, demonstrating that both crop circles and stone circles act as hubs connecting the wider world of paranormal subjects.

Chapter 6: Mysterious Universe enters the realm of UFOs and extraterrestrials to examine the tendency towards syncretism in many paranormal narratives. We compare two different paranormal entrepreneurs and researchers, Russell Kellett and David Icke. Both have incorporated extraterrestrials into wider narratives that involve, in the case of Kellett, time travel, psychic powers, government conspiracies, and super soldiers. Icke's theories are even more expansive, combining ancient astronauts, modern aliens such as reptilian shape-shifters, conspiracy theories of every kind, spirit guides, claims that the world is a simulation, and a host of other ideas, all into a heady mix.

There is an argument to be made that mixing so many different paranormal ideas into a single narrative will limit its appeal. As we discuss in Chapter 6, our survey respondents tended to be fairly restrictive in their paranormal beliefs, with comparatively few believing in lots of different phenomena simultaneously. Yet David Icke has built a successful paranormal business empire by selling a unifying theory of the paranormal that incorporates nearly everything. A large part of Icke's success has to do with a tendency we have noticed amongst paranormal believers to develop their own, personal, and idiosyncratic worldviews. In doing so, paranormalists combine bits and pieces from many topics and narratives, freely rejecting those parts they do not believe in, without rejecting the whole. A key to Icke's success is that, by providing a veritable host of potential entry points, nearly anyone can find a paranormal subject that intrigues them within his expansive narrative. People can take the parts they like and ignore the rest. David Icke has experienced much more monetary success than Russell Kellett, and a variety of factors, including Icke's pre-existing celebrity and some lucky timing, played a role in making this happen. But as Chapter 6 explores, in the modern paranormal world, part of Icke's greater success also has to do with how his narrative is much more syncretic and wider in scope than Kellett's.

Key to both Kellett's and Icke's narratives, however, is a reliance on conspiracy theories. Indeed, sometimes it is difficult to disentangle conspiracy theories from the paranormal, particularly since theories about government cover-ups of UFO evidence are quite popular.[22] As with paranormal believers, conspiracy theorists often mix and match ideas from across different conspiracies into larger worldviews. We conclude Chapter 6 by examining 'syncretists'; those who tend to believe in multiple paranormal beliefs, multiple conspiracy beliefs, and consume media about multiple paranormal subjects. Only one characteristic crosses all three groups: describing oneself as 'spiritual'. Being released from the constrictions of conventional religion liberates people to freely combine supernatural beliefs.

Consequently, we expect to see many more paranormal success stories such as David Icke if organized religion continues to decline.

While some UFO enthusiasts such as Icke and Kellett devote their lives to trying to convince others of the reality (or danger) of extraterrestrials, others have taken the subject of UFOs in quite a different direction, turning aliens into religion proper. In 1954, London taxi driver George King received an interplanetary message while washing dishes in his Maide Vale flat: 'Prepare yourself! You are to become the voice of interplanetary parliament'. Two years later, King formed a new religious movement called the Aetherius Society after claiming that a 'Master of Yoga' had helped him develop the ability to communicate with a Venusian named Aetherius.[23] Ultimately, King channelled messages from a variety of 'cosmic masters', including Mars Sector 6 and Mars Sector 8. No less than Jesus himself (a Venusian according to King) provided an endorsement for King's book *The Twelve Blessings*.[24] Although King passed into the spiritual realm in 1997, the Aetherius Society remains active, with headquarters in Los Angeles and London.

King's invention is but one of many attempts to create an organized religion out of flying saucers.[25] Chapter 7: The Devil's Bargain examines the contested ground between religion and the paranormal in more detail. What is the difference between an angel and a ghost? Or between organized religion and the paranormal? Neither religious claims nor paranormal claims can be 'proven'. Christians can no more prove the resurrection of Jesus to sceptics than UFO abductees can prove that aliens visit their bedrooms at night. So perhaps paranormal claims can be easily merged with conventional religion, since they both occupy liminal epistemological spaces, at least relative to mainstream science? History tells us otherwise.

To get a better sense of the dynamic interplay between organized religion and the paranormal, we participate in a high ritual for 'Operation Prayer Power', organized annually by the Aetherius Society, on the spot where George King met Jesus on the coast of England. Aetherius provides an interesting example of how paranormal beliefs and experiences can evolve into an organized religion.

But despite these potential synergies between religion and the paranormal, many conservative Christian groups and authors continue to make the claim that paranormal interests draw people away from biblical teachings. Some claim that the paranormal is, therefore, inherently Satanic and dangerous.[26] Consequently, religion and the paranormal may well be partners *or* enemies, depending on the context.

Returning to our survey data, we find that this complex dynamic between religion and the paranormal is also reflected in patterns among the population. We find that there is an overall positive but also curvilinear relationship between conventional religiosity and the paranormal. Those who are not religious are similarly uninterested in ghosts, UFOs, and the like. It is those at *moderate* levels of conventional religiosity – infrequent attenders and those who think there is flexibility in the interpretation of religious doctrine – who are the most open to alternative beliefs. We discuss the implications of these patterns in a world where participation in conventional religion is on the decline.

We close Chapter 7 by exploring Rosslyn Chapel just outside of Edinburgh, a historic site that played a pivotal role in Dan Brown's plot for *The Da Vinci Code* series. In the wake of the popularity of the novels and adapted films, Rosslyn has become a tourist destination for those interested in divine conspiracies. At the same time, it remains an operational church, providing a provocative example of the potentially symbiotic relationship between (some forms of) organized religion and the paranormal. If conventional religion continues to decline, will it be replaced by entirely new religions? Shall God be replaced by Aetherius? Or will believers of the future treat religion and the paranormal as a great spiritual cafeteria, piling onto their proverbial trays any metaphysical beliefs that appeal to them? As with all things paranormal, we find that the answer is complicated; although in this case, the answer is also somewhat estimable.

The Conclusion: The (Eternal) Return of Nobody brings us full (crop) circle by returning one final time to 30 East Drive in Pontefract. In our quest to understand the paranormal in Britain, our research has allowed us to answer many questions. By the end of this book, you should have a clearer understanding about what British citizens believe about the paranormal, who believes, the extent of paranormal tourism, why interest in the paranormal is growing, how the paranormal varies by religion, and why the paranormal is simultaneously both normal and deviant in contemporary British society. In addition, we hope that our detailed profiles of different paranormal believers and sites will help fill in some of the human stories that make up the kaleidoscope of paranormalism available in Britain.

But there is one question for which you will not find a satisfactory answer. So it is best to be up front about it. We do not know whether Mr. Nobody lurked the halls as we roamed 30 East Drive. If he did, he stayed out of view. However, we did witness something extraordinary. The meaning of 'truth' is changing as the paranormal is gripping hold of us. People are finding new (or renewed) ways to experience the supernatural and transcendent. We conclude by mapping the way forward, outlining how we expect the paranormal to fare in the future (spoiler: quite well). In particular, paranormal beliefs and experiences are well-suited to thrive alongside other ongoing societal trends, including secularization, greater focus on subjective truth, increased use of digital technology, and the growth of experience-based economies.

But before we can properly address such questions about changes to contemporary British society, we first need to do some aura work.

Chapter 1

THE INNER LIGHT

The Spiritual Buffet

The paranormal is a notoriously complicated subject. In many ways it is easier to recognize the paranormal intuitively than it is to define it formally.[1] Some use 'paranormal' to refer to anything that is outside the natural world, in which case both a belief in the resurrection of Jesus and a belief in ghosts would be paranormal. For some, 'New Age', 'occult', 'supernatural', and 'metaphysical' are all synonyms for the paranormal. For others these terms have distinctly different meanings. Before we dive further into the world of the paranormal in Britain, we must first understand exactly what it is we are diving into. This chapter is focused on clearly defining the paranormal, at least in terms of how we will use the concept for the remainder of this book.

We address this most complicated of topics by exploring one of the most diverse settings for doing so – a Mind Body Spirit (MBS) event (formerly known as a psychic fair). By grappling with the wide variety of services, beliefs and practices present at such events, we can begin to understand both how wide ranging the paranormal is and how it can be approached in different ways by different people. For some, embracing the paranormal is a means to personal enlightenment, while others are more interested in gathering evidence that will prove the reality of a particular phenomenon.

A little after 10.00 am on a late spring day, I (Tom) navigated through an energetic crowd to enter a reconditioned hall in a former industrial landscape. The room was simply buzzing with positive energy, and the air was thick with the sounds of a bustling marketplace. I was somewhat overwhelmed by the dazzling array of stalls and their contents. Customers leant over tables, examining strange and colourful objects, and chatted excitedly with the store owners. At some booths, there were people sitting across from one another, looking intently at curious arrangements of cards, stones, or charms. Bright, colourful crystals were everywhere, each with their own exotic sounding names – like selenite, obsidian and citrine.

But soon the predominant activity came into focus. An astounding range of 'seers,' 'healers,' and 'psychics' were offering their services to eager customers all about the cavernous space. A Reiki healer hovered her hands over a customer lying on a white sheet, seemingly in a state of complete relaxation. A Shamanic therapist was lightly tapping a drum as they tiptoed around their client who was sitting in a chair with their eyes closed. A clatter of pebbles on a stone board attracted my attention. I turned to see a reader rearranging some stones and talking to a customer about his 'runes'. Elsewhere, there were banners selling me on a host of other services: past life regression, tarot, palmistry, mediumship, auras, astrology, animal communication and something called 'holographic energetic structuring'.

Nearby, a marquee full of people was listening intently to a speaker. With standing room only, I took a position on the back wall. The presenter spoke with great animation about positivity, confidence and experiences in her personal life. She is leaving energy vampires behind and has chosen to 'live beyond the third dimension and retune negative vibrations'. She left the stage to thunderous applause.

All of this was occurring at a regional MBS event. It offered fifty+ exhibitors, twenty+ presenters and workshops during its two days. With a maximum daily capacity of at least 1,000 visitors, tickets were priced at £7 per day or £10 for the entire event. Such events are held across the depth and breadth of Great Britain, usually in the spring and summer months. Some are aimed at a local community level, with possibly a few hundred attendees; events like this one are more regional in scope and might attract numbers in the low thousands; and some are held in the very largest convention centres in the country.[2]

Years ago, such an event would have been called a 'psychic fair'. This title seems far too limiting to what one experiences today. The promotional material for an event by 'White Light' promised 'psychics, crystals, books, mediums, spiritual art, pagan goods, complementary therapists, CBD, tarot, jewellery, essential oils' and even a 'witchy emporium'. The London MBS Festival in 2023 advertised 'Bioresonance GB', 'Psychedelic Integration Support', 'King Yoga' and 'Vulva Casting', amongst many, many other products. While some of these products and services are probably best described as 'self-help', others make claims that are distinctly supernatural in nature, scope, and orientation. Mediumship is common, as are divinatory practices like tarot, runes, and palmistry. Past life regression, channelling, and all manner of practices such as Reiki, sound therapy, and crystals are similarly frequent. Animal communication is also a recurrent theme – both before and after death. Such modern day 'spiritual cafeterias' allow believers to assemble personalized combinations of practices and services that uniquely suit their own idiosyncratic pursuits.

The Cultic Milieu

The paranormal is a confusing topic with little agreement as to what it constitutes. Modern-day MBS fairs are a window into this complicated world. For example, one will almost certainly experience phenomena at an MBS fair that might best be labelled as 'psychic' *and* practices that might best be labelled as 'magic'. The term 'psychic' generally refers to a person who can see, hear, or sense things usually considered to be beyond the scope of normal human perception. It is typically used to describe someone who provides spiritual or emotional guidance – as in a 'psychic healer', for instance – or in a more general way to describe someone who has extrasensory ability relating to the mind, like telepathy or extra sensory perception (ESP). It also includes things like telekinesis, remote viewing, astrology, and divination, as well as channelling and hypnotic regression.

Magic, on the other hand, is often used to describe the manipulation of supernatural forces or entities to achieve particular goals. This can include the use of spells, rituals or objects that are thought to possess supernatural properties. Again, there are many variations on this theme. A broad distinction is often made between white magic and black magic – with white magic being used for positive or constructive purposes, whereas black magic is usually considered to have a much more malevolent quality. However, this binary distinction vastly underestimates the number of different systems of magic being practiced today. Some of these draw on ancestral traditions (Ancestral Magic), some relate to particular practitioners (Thelemic Magic), while others, such as Chaos Magic, are highly eclectic and designed to be individualized.

Partly due to the myriad variations that are associated with both terms, there exists a host of more all-encompassing headings used as a shorthand to capture this inherent elasticity. For example, the term 'occult' has sometimes been used to describe practices or beliefs that involve the supernatural, paranormal, or mystical but is now often avoided by practitioners due to the negative ways it has been used by those opposed to such practices. Similarly, words like 'pagan', 'New Age' and 'mysticism' are also used as general headings to describe beliefs and practices that sit outside of so-called convention.

Sociologist Colin Campbell coined the phrase 'the cultic milieu' to describe the wide range of unconventional beliefs and practices that exist within Western societies.[3] Often bubbling under the surface as undercurrents in urban and metropolitan settings, these subcultures are only very loosely organized. Instead of the rigid organizational structures of more conventional religions, they are composed of fluid networks of people and groups who share an interest in spiritual or esoteric practices that are not typically associated with mainstream Western cultures.

While helpful at the time, Campbell's ideas are now over 40 years old, and the communities he identified are much transformed. A more recent study by sociologists Paul Heelas and Linda Woodhead was conducted in the early 2000s and used Kendal in Cumbria (population 28,000) as a case study.[4] The 'Kendal Project' – examined the spiritual lives of two key groups: 'the congregational domain' of organized religion, and the more invisible activities of what they termed 'the holistic milieu', which was marked by the rejection of organized religion and often less formal in operation:

> Instead of congregations meeting in churches and chapels, there are group (yoga, tai chi) or one-to-one (spiritual aromatherapy, massage) activities, which often take place in less formal settings: a rented hall, somebody's house, even, perhaps, a glade in a Lakeland wood. Activities to do with holistic body-mind-spirituality

were found, for example, through contact details posted on noticeboards in shops or in the town's library, or by word-of-mouth information.[5]

Campbell, Heelas, and Woodhead all recognized that there exists in Britain a vibrant marketplace of beliefs, ideas, and practices that, while often spiritual in orientation, fall outside the boundaries of major, organized religions. Absent the doctrinal and organizational restrictions of conventional religions, these beliefs may be more easily combined into a variety of idiosyncratic and individualized forms. Indeed, these spiritualities are often taken to be part of a wider move towards secularization in that they enabled both subjective experience and self-authority to thrive. The changing religious and spiritual tendencies of Kendal were effectively a microcosm of a wider society in which 'the turn toward subjectivity' was an emerging, and driving, force.[6]

The Paranormal: Doubly Damned

While we are in agreement with the observations of Heelas, Woodhead, and others that spiritual aromatherapy, psychic readers and similar phenomena are partially understood by their relationship to religion, we believe they are also best understood in terms of their relationship to *science*.

In his seminal *Book of the Damned* (1919), American author Charles Fort gathered accounts of anomalous phenomena such as psychic powers, strange creatures, unidentified objects in the sky, mysterious disappearances and a host of others. He saw such phenomena as unified by their damnation by science.[7] While the major, organized religions have long served as the cultural arbiter of what constitutes the (proper) supernatural world, science is the arbiter of what constitutes the material world. Fort viewed the scientific establishment as being as equally dogmatic as religion in its rejection of certain, unexplained phenomena. 'Positivism is Puritanism,'[8] he argued, lorded over by a 'Scientific Priestcraft.'[9] Embracing the paranormal, he continued, necessitates the rejection of both 'Christ and Einstein.'[10]

What makes the paranormal unique is that believers and practitioners must navigate and manage the rejection of two dominant societal institutions, as expressed in our definition:

The *paranormal* consists of those beliefs, practices, and experiences that are not recognized as legitimate by science *and* not recognized as legitimate by conventional religions (within the culture in question).

Scientific authorities and institutions determine what topics and methods are considered legitimate within their boundaries. Religious beliefs fall, for the most part, outside of those boundaries.[11] The idea that Jesus was resurrected on the third day after his crucifixion is viewed as a medical impossibility by contemporary science. Indeed, it is the belief in this apparent, scientific impossibility that helps define Christian communities – primarily because they view the resurrection as evidence of the power of God over and above the materiality of this world. That is not to say that Christians are, therefore, necessarily occluded from believing in science and medicine, nor that scientists do not sometimes hold conservative, religious beliefs. However, belief in the physical resurrection is a distinct point of demarcation between believers in Christianity and non-believers.[12]

For topics that lie outside the recognized material world, organized religion will also play a role in the demarcation of phenomena. Key to the maintenance of an organized religious tradition is the ability to adjudicate between what constitutes legitimate doctrine and heresy; what is 'true' and what is 'false'. Supernatural beliefs and experiences that are not 'doctrinal' will be considered illegitimate or false, at best, and in extreme cases labelled as evil or the 'the work of the Devil'.[13]

We will discuss at much greater length the complicated relationship between religion and the paranormal in Chapter 7, but it is not difficult to see how the activities at a MBS fair occupy cultural spaces that are not part of either science or religion – although some are more likely to be of concern to one or the other. For example, auras are believed to be energy fields that surround the body. Some therapies available at the events we visited were premised on the assumption that in certain circumstances, auras can become contaminated with negative energy leading to physical, emotional, or spiritual imbalances. Aura cleansing, therefore, involves the use of things like meditation, visualization, or sound healing to remove the negative energy and restore balance to the aura. While many attendees clearly found such therapies helpful (judging by the lines at the tables offering these services), there is no scientific evidence to suggest that auras even exist, let alone that they can be manipulated by the sound of repetitive drumming. Scientists would be similarly sceptical of the use of runestones as a way of 'seeing' the future. Religious leaders would also be wary, as the Bible warns against engaging sorceresses, divination, soothsaying, fortune telling, and mediums.

While auras, divination, ESP, mediumship, telepathy, and most of the other topics covered at the MBS fair would live within our definition of the paranormal, that definition is broad enough to also include phenomena that were not the focus of the fair. Ghosts and hauntings would be paranormal, as would UFOs and 'cryptids' such as the British Bigfoot and the Loch Ness Monster.

Defining the paranormal negatively via its stigmatized relationship to science and religion allows the status of a particular phenomenon to change. For example, if the scientific community were ever to retrieve a flying saucer, then UFOs would move from the misty backwaters of the paranormal into the domain of science.[14] The past several decades have witnessed the emergence of a number of small, fringe religious groups centred around the concept of extraterrestrials, such as the Aetherius Society and Raëlism (see Chapter 7). In the unlikely event that such a group would ever grow large and influential enough to become a major, organized religion in Britain, UFOs would migrate from the paranormal to religion.

Figure 1.1 visualizes the relationship between the paranormal, religion, and science.

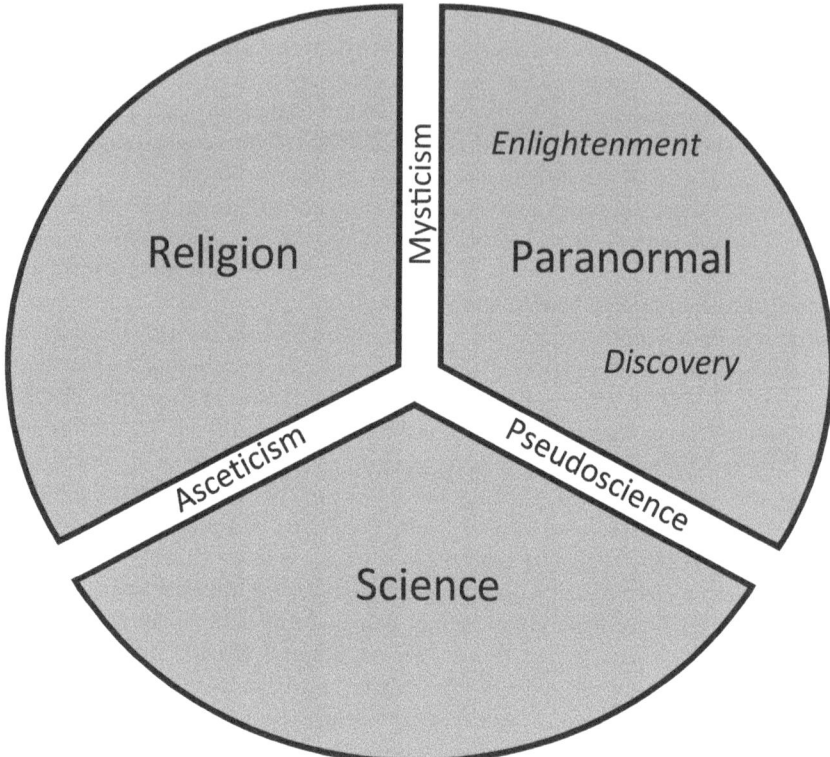

Figure 1.1 The paranormal, religion and science.

Enlightenment versus Discovery

We have engaged with the paranormal in many ways doing research for this book.[15] During this time we have noticed that topics that fall within the realm of the paranormal tend to be pursued by advocates in different ways. Some view the paranormal as a source of personal *enlightenment*. Such people are not particularly interested in 'evidence' or worried about convincing others of the truth of their claims or experiences. That 'truth' is ephemeral and internal; the focus is to better oneself or learn about one's fate. *Enlightenment* pursuits often lean on the mystical and magical and, hence, lie closer to the boundary between religion and the paranormal. As such, enlightenment practices are precisely what can be found at a psychic fair because its offerings are largely directed towards the maintenance, balance, and understanding of the (internal) self. Obviously, a psychic reading might include information about other people, but any information that is presented will be for the consideration of the person receiving the reading, who decides how to make sense of the information presented to them.

While enlightenment lives on the border of the paranormal and religion, other pursuits inhabit the murky waters nearer science. Some are drawn to the paranormal because they hope to be a part of a major *discovery* that proves to the world at large that a disputed phenomenon exists, or they are at least interested in learning about the efforts of others who are engaged in such pursuits. Topics such as UFOs, ghosts, and cryptids lend themselves to the collection of 'evidence'. As the next chapter addresses, Nessie enthusiasts are keen on collecting, presenting, and debating evidence about the monster's existence and its nature. Bigfoot hunters hope to capture photos of the beast, take plaster casts of its supposed footprints, pick hair samples from trees, and capture recordings of mysterious howls in the woods. Ghost hunters are especially keen on discovery. Every ghost 'investigation' of which we have taken part has involved ghost hunters wielding an impressive array of equipment that they believe entices spirits to communicate, facilitates that communication, and provides evidence of the presence of spirits. Indeed, discovery paranormalism often makes reference to science and scientific methods, with practitioners engaging in a form of populist, amateur science.[16] The conventional scientific community tends to reject and stigmatize such endeavours as 'pseudoscience'.[17]

But the borders between discovery and enlightenment pursuits can be porous. The aforementioned, emergent UFO religions focus upon a spiritual connection with extra-terrestrials, as opposed to searching for evidence of downed saucers. Some Bigfoot enthusiasts believe the creature to be extra-dimensional in origin and are more interested in psychic communication than gathering hair samples. In a similar vein, some of those interested in phenomena such as ESP or mediumship hope to gather evidence that would convince others that such powers exist. Nevertheless, absent such edge cases, anyone who spends time at both a MBS fair or goes on a typical ghost hunt will appreciate the profound difference between the orientations of these two endeavours.

In the MBS fairs that we have attended we noticed that the available enlightenment practices, products, and services tended to be of three types. Some of the offerings focus upon *divination* – developing a better understanding of one's past, present, and future. Others are focused more upon *healing* by cleansing the aura, grappling with past lives, or using a host of other spiritual practices. A third pillar of the psychic fair is *magic*, or the attempt to manipulate the physical world via supernatural means. As we might expect, given the general resistance of the paranormal to simple classification, the boundaries between these three major offerings were permeable. We grappled with the unique nature of MBS fairs by experiencing each of these phenomena in turn. I (Tom) began my quest for enlightenment by learning how to read the tarot.[18]

The Art of Divination

Divination practices are a very common form of enlightenment paranormal pursuit. Divination refers to the practice of interpreting signs or symbols to gain insight into one's past, present, or future. Certainly, one goal of divination is to try to predict one's future, but it is also commonly directed towards reinterpreting past events or resolving dilemmas of immediate concern. There are many different forms of divination. This includes the multitude of different systems of astrology, runic magic, the reading of tea leaves (tasseography), and the method I chose to utilize: tarot cards (cartomancy). All of these 'spiritual technologies' make use of specific tools or objects, which are presumed to be activated by the intuition or psychic ability of the practitioner.[19]

There are an enormous variety of tarot-related resources available at MBS fairs. Of course, one option was simply to sit down with an experienced tarot card reader and let them determine what enlightenment their deck could provide. Equally available were guidebooks and materials designed to self-teach the tarot. Determined to experience self-directed enlightenment, I elected to train myself. I then grappled with the bewildering variety of tarot decks on offer.

With the help of some sellers, I learned that decks were primarily variations on two types – Rider-Waite-Smith and Thoth. Both decks are composed of seventy-eight cards with two parts – the major arcana and the minor arcana. The major arcana has twenty-two major cards that begin with the fool (usually numbered 0) and contains twenty-one other characters and symbols. The Rider–Waite deck includes, amongst others, the Wizard, the Wheel of Fortune, the Hermit, the Devil, and, of course, Death. The cards of the minor arcana consist of four suits – Swords, Batons, Cups, and Coins – with each suit containing the cards ace through ten, as well as the Knave, Queen, Knight, and King. With some naming differences, such as the 'knight' referred to as the 'prince', the Thoth deck follows the same structure. A classic Rider–Waite–Smith deck utilizes Christian imagery, with Adam and Eve appearing on the 'Lovers' card, for example, and the 'Hierophant' card originally depicting a Pope. The Thoth deck, named after the Egyptian God of wisdom, was developed by Aleister Crowley. It contains much more abstract symbolism drawing upon a number of occult traditions, including alchemy and the Kabbalah. But any number of variations on these classic themes can now be found at an MBS event. Some decks depicted Norse gods and demigods, while others were entirely devoted to angels. There were tarot cards for 'witches' and decks branded with intellectual properties such as *Lord of the Rings*, Disney, *Star Trek* and many, many others.

As I grappled with the variety of cards available, the personal and intuitive nature of the practice immediately became apparent. Sellers instructed me to find a deck that suited me and that 'felt right'. Ultimately, I purchased a standard Rider–Waite deck; best to keep things as simple as possible at first, I thought.

The next few weeks were a haze of audiobooks, online classes, and internet websites, each with a variety of recommendations about learning the cards. If understanding the seventy-two cards was not difficult enough, the meaning of each card is complicated by the fact that it can be drawn in upright or in reversed format, and that individual meanings need to be understood in relation to the position of other cards that have been drawn from the pack.

The most straightforward method is to ask a question and draw a single card to divine the answer. This is usually recommended for beginners. A slightly more advanced version of this is the three-card spread, in which the position of each card is given a meaning – let's say past, present and future – with the card that is placed in the relative position acquiring that meaning. This type of spread is often used by more intermediate practitioners. From there, things get significantly more complicated, and a litany of books is dedicated to different shapes and arrangements. Crosses, rectangles, horseshoes, and astrological circles are just a few of the formations that can be used in conjunction with the cards, all of which can be further adapted with respect to what is being asked of them. There are versions that examine relationships, decision-making and wellbeing, while others use the calendar to understand particular timelines (a seven-card spread for each day of the week, for example). For the time being, however, I concentrated on the standard upright meaning of the cards, and used a single draw, with the aim of building up to a standard three-card spread.

I devised a grid system to help me remember the meanings I developed for the cards. This involves cross-referencing the number and picture cards of the minor arcana with the meaning of their suits. The ace card, for example, is generally considered to be a trump card that very broadly signifies abundance, success, or significance. This can then be cross-referenced with the meaning of a particular suit. Cups, for example, are generally concerned with love, so the Ace of Cups is all about successful relationships. Pentacles are concerned with things like finance and career, so the ace of pentacles symbolizes significant opportunities coming to fruition.

Attempting to memorize the tarot cards is a big undertaking – and I'm struggling with the volume of information. I soon find myself following the wisdom of an acquired mentor and try to use the images in the Rider–Waite deck as a device to help me 'read' the cards. I practice by pulling a card from the deck and telling stories to myself about the image. Sometimes I'm quite reserved in terms of the things that come to mind. At others, I throw myself into the task and deliberately elaborate on what I see, often crafting ornate narratives around the pictures.

A few weeks later, I'm chatting to a friend who is something of a 'dabbler' in the psychic realm. I mention that I've been learning tarot. The conversation quickly leads to repeated encouragement to give her a reading. After some resistance on my behalf, I give in and fetch my Rider–Waite deck. I quickly decide that if I'm going to give the reading, then I'll go 'all in' and run with my intuition as much as possible. I ask my 'client' to choose three cards from the deck – and they place them face down on the table. I then turn over the cards, one by one: the six of swords, the seven of pentacles, and the ten of swords.

'That's interesting', I say with a quizzical but authoritative tone as I stare intently at the cards. 'Are you feeling a bit restless?', I ask. Without pausing for an answer, I continue with some firmness: 'You're thinking of doing something – taking something on – but you are not quite making the move'. I now look at my client in the eyes directly and speak with calm reassurance. 'And that's making you feel restless. You want to move forward, but you are afraid of leaving something behind?'

My newfound client tilts her head slightly and looks at me with renewed interest. It's an inquiring look, and I feel like I've made a connection.

'It's not your job', I say, openly acknowledging the fact that we'd spoken about her career before the tarot came up in conversation. 'So, you're thinking of trying something new? Trying to open up a new path somewhere else?'

By now, my client is smiling.

I return my attention to the cards. 'The six of swords – you're travelling restless waters. It's movement – you want to sail with the wind, you feel like this is something you are meant to do, but you are worried that you might go against the tide? That it might be too difficult, too costly. So, you are floating, restlessly.'

I'm now in full flow and running entirely on intuition. 'But the seven of pentacles', I say as I focus my attention towards the card, 'teaches us patience. Waiting is good; it's about making sure; thinking things through. You don't have to do everything at once – let the idea sit a little bit, get used to it', I say reassuringly.

My stream of consciousness had come fairly naturally with the first two cards. I did not really have to 'think' about what to say. I just said whatever came to mind and relied on my intuition. The final card – the ten of swords – was a different proposition. The Rider–Waite card depicts a prostrate figure on a beach, speared by ten swords. In the background there are still waters and a black sky. It all looks a bit bleak.

I pause and move my finger towards the final card. 'The ten of swords', I say in a ponderous tone as I struggle to think of what to say next. 'It looks a bit menacing, doesn't it?' Again, without pausing for an answer: 'but it's not'. 'It's about recognizing change; creating space in your life to 'do' new things.' I pause for thought. 'See how the seven of pentacles is in the middle? You're thinking about things – and you're caught between moving on with something on one hand, and what you might leave behind on the other. It's all part of the process', I say, with some finality. 'The cards are telling you that what you are feeling is normal – thinking about what you want to do, where you want to go; it's all part of the process. So stick with it. Think things through. Make sure it's right for you at this point.'

'How did you do that?', she says excitedly. 'How did you know that?', she repeats. She then turns towards her partner who is busy with the kids. 'Have you told him?', she demands. 'Told him, what?', he responds with disinterest. 'That I'm thinking of doing Reiki?', she replies. He looks at me with a resigned disbelief, shaking his head: '£400 hundred quid. If she does that, it's going to cost me £400 quid – and that's just for starters'.

The Popularity of Enlightenment

What was clear from my education with the tarot was the inherent appeal of such practices. For someone who seeks personal enrichment, or to provide that enrichment to others, with an added spiritual layer, the benefits were obvious. With a deck of cards, I could learn about my past, present and future, or tell others about theirs. It was also quite clear that someone with the same set of cards, the same arrangement, and the same draws could have reached very different conclusions as to their meaning. But herein lies a great strength for believers. The reader and the client can develop a deeply personal narrative and a unique social relationship, one that is not prescribed by the strict dictates of a church, but rather is a malleable belief system and a collaborative spiritual practice. Should one not like the answers they receive, simply try another deck, another type of draw or another method of divination altogether. Practitioners can also use a client's resistance to a particular reading as a cue for further reflection, as any good therapist would.

Responses to our national survey tell us that enlightenment-related paranormal beliefs are quite popular in Britain. When asked if 'fortune tellers and psychics can foresee the future', nearly one-fifth of our respondents either 'tended to agree' or 'strongly agree' (19.8 per cent). One-fifth of respondents also believe that some amulets and charms can offer protection (21 per cent). Nearly one-fourth of residents believe that astrology 'impacts one's personality' (23.8 per cent). This is all good news for MBS fairs, as a substantial portion of the public has at least potential interest in their offerings.

The practice of divination using cards, numbers, and even auras relies entirely on verbal information – often because the client cannot 'see' what is happening without being told what is happening. This is most evidently the case with mediums in that the client cannot (usually) see, hear, or feel the spirits, but it is also the case with other forms of divination. It is possible to observe the cards in tarot, for example, but to understand what they mean requires interpretation on behalf of a skilled practitioner. Regardless of explanation, and although some might put more weight on one or the other, it is true enough to say that prescribed symbolic meanings need to be combined with the intuition of the practitioner for a reading to take place – and for a reading to be effective, there also needs to be a narrative that makes sense *in context*. This is to say, presentation is central to contemporary forms of divination. One of the primary functions of the MBS Fairs was clearly centred around presenting potential clients with the value of particular enlightenment practices.

The point of a reading is to convince the client that they have gained insight into something that they did not already know, *and* that the reading helped them know it. Indeed, the more successful readers are confident in their delivery and dynamic in their content. Confident in that their verbal narrative seems to flow effortlessly from whatever is being used for divination, but dynamic in that there is also a responsive interaction between readers and the clients. This interaction is directed towards shaping the substance of the reading, while serving to confirm that the reading is working and providing space for any repair strategies that are necessary, should anything appear to compromise the presentation.

To these ends, the workshops and talks that often run alongside a psychic fair are an integral part of dissemination for divinatory practitioners. Usually lasting for thirty minutes to one hour – often with room for questions and answers – these talks are part introduction, part demonstration, and part promotion and advertisement. They provide a crucial outlet for stall holders to narrate their 'product', whether it be what they do as a practitioner or whatever it is that they are selling at their stall.

For instance, a medium whose offering also covered hypnotherapy, past life regression, and mind healing, in addition to one-to-one readings on the day, suggested that '[e]veryone is a medium', but most just don't recognize it, because 'we don't hear those signals'. Mediumship, he suggested, is about getting guidance for yourself. You can get it for other people if you want, but it's harder because other people won't necessarily want to hear what you have to tell them. Instead, he advises people to 'put the practice in, put the time in, and gain that insight for yourself'. Although he did not explicitly mention it at the time, his website offers mediumship training – and it costs around £1,500.

As might be expected, the substance of these talks and workshops varies in both style and content. However, they tend towards being didactic in nature with the substance directed towards personal experience narratives (how I came to be involved), product placement (what I offer), and demand generation (why it might be useful for you). Any direct mention of cost is usually avoided, and the pitch is generally positive and supportive in tone. Critique of other practice is generally absent, and any notion that this might be a competitive marketplace is studiously avoided.[20] This is evident in one vendor 's suggestion that reading runes isn't for everyone and 'if it doesn't work for you, move on to what does work for you'. This avoids placing responsibility for the lack of success on the practice in question, the reader, or the individual being read.

These talks and workshops not only reproduce and reinforce the position of the presenter as 'expert' but also offer a valuable opportunity for targeted promotion. This is confirmed by one host who, at the end of his talk, asks the crowd to make a huge noise so 'I'll look like the most popular show here and those who booked me will ask me back next year'.

Indeed, those who are attending an MBS event are much more likely to be receptive to whatever product is on offer than a more general audience on social media. In a 'behind the scenes' video of one of the events I attended, the manager of a popular medium commented that promotion 'is a relentless task – I always think of it like painting the Forth Bridge – you know, once you've got to one end you have to start again and carry on painting'. He continues, 'no matter how many times you put things out on Facebook and social media, you've never done it enough. You can never, never do it enough'.

All of which is to say that the presentation of narrative in context is a crucial aspect of divination in the enlightenment milieu. Not just in the actual reading itself, but also in how people come to understand and use spiritual technologies for themselves, *and* how practitioners talk about what they do in order to convince people that their products are worth paying for. It is worth underlining that these are all, more or less, spiritual entrepreneurs who are operating on an individual basis in a competitive marketplace. There is not a readily identifiable organized movement – in other words, a captive audience – associated with the variety of divinatory practices that you might see at an MBS fair. Narration is crucial for selling these products to consumers.

And the sale appears to be working. While we have already presented evidence of the considerable level of belief in psychic practices in Britain, belief does not necessarily translate to action. Someone may believe that psychics have extraordinary abilities but still refuse to take the time, or spend the money, to visit one. Our national survey found, however, that a significant percentage of British citizens are willing to directly engage with enlightenment practices.

We asked our respondents about three practices related to using the supernatural for personal enlightenment, including whether or not they have ever consulted a horoscope; called or consulted with a medium, fortune teller, or psychic; or been to a tarot card reading. The most popular of these was consulting a horoscope, with nearly one-third of respondents (29.4 per cent) reporting that they have done so. Given the ready availability of horoscopes in printed media and online, there is comparatively low cost involved in viewing a horoscope, both in terms of time and money. It is not surprising that more people are willing to give their horoscope a quick glance. It is a significantly greater investment of time and money to directly consult with a psychic practitioner. Yet one-fifth of our respondents (20 per cent) report having consulted with a medium, fortune teller or psychic. A bit more than one-fifth of respondents (21.1 per cent) have been to a tarot reading. There is clearly substantial and steady demand in Britain for gaining otherworldly insight into one's past, present and future.

The Art of Healing

While the predominant products on display at MBS fairs were various forms of divination, running parallel to this was a vibrant marketplace devoted to spiritual healing.

Spiritual healing and other forms of holistic therapy are directed towards the well-being of the mind, body and spirit. However, there is an immense amount of diversity in the nature and scope of what this means in practice – and some therapies are distinctly more paranormal than others. Acupuncture and massage, for instance, are relatively mainstream practices with well-established health benefits. On the other hand, Reiki is a Japanese therapy that is based on the assumption that disruptions in the flow of the body's energy can lead to physical and emotional imbalances. Treatment involves the practitioner placing their hands near the client and channeling what is referred to as 'universal energy' back into the body to relieve any blockages.[21]

The concept of 'energy' is used quite flexibly within the MBS community to describe any number of spiritual techniques and specialisms. It is probably the closest the community comes towards having a unifying concept. Crystal therapy, sound therapy, past life regression, shamanic healing, chakra balancing, and channelling, amongst many others, also typically emphasize the idea that our physical bodies are not just made up of physical matter. Instead, our bodies are thought to have energetic fields that are interconnected with our emotions, thoughts, and beliefs. Imbalances and blockages in these energies can affect the physical functioning of the body and mind. Regardless of their exact form, healing therapies are largely directed to the removal of negative energy and/or the promotion of positive energy flow – with positive energy being associated with the health and wellbeing of the mind, body and spirit.

As the name suggests, negative energy is perceived to be detrimental to physical, emotional, and spiritual wellbeing. The presence of negative energy can be detected by feelings such as anxiety, fear and self-doubt. Or, by the experience of more physical aches and pains – regardless of whether these things have prescribed medical diagnoses. Positive energy, on the other hand, is defined by the presence of feelings such as love, peace, joy, and fulfilment. 'Universal energy' of the positive variety is generally assumed to be the natural state of being.

Of course, the notion of a 'universal energy' that can be channelled for the purposes of healing is actively rejected by conventional science.[22] Similarly, while ideas like 'prana' and 'qi' have their roots in Hinduism and Taoism, respectively, these are highly nuanced concepts that are part of much wider and more complex religious systems. Although they do not necessarily mention 'universal energy' specifically, the Abrahamic faiths reject the use of amulets, charms, and other ephemera typically associated with energies, largely because they are associated with 'other gods'. Consequently, the notion of 'universal energy' is a very good example of something that has been damned by both religion and science – which makes it distinctly paranormal in nature. Within this milieu, 'the importance of "energy" is that it provides a common denominator in terms of which types of relationships can be discussed and compared, and the contrasts with the mainstream made clear.'[23]

These broad definitions of both 'healing' and 'energy' were readily apparent as I explored their varieties at the MBS fairs by visiting a variety of healers, beginning with a shaman.

Owls, Crystals and Robin Hood: Healing at the MBS Fair

Shamanic healing is based on the assumption that negative energies can force the soul to become damaged or blocked, leading to a host of both physical and psychological problems. Shamanic healers use ritual ceremonies to travel into the spiritual realm to repair or retrieve the parts of the soul that have become unbalanced or detached. Although practitioners tend to prefer the term 'healer' to 'therapist', the host of a shamanic healing workshop I attended at an MBS fair describes herself as 'a medicine weaver'. She also has expertise in Usui and Karuna Reiki, plant spirit medicines, and Cacao Ceremonies.

As I settle into an uncomfortable chair in a room full of other participants, the healer, Karla, takes the stage.[24] 'Everything holds a memory', she exclaims, 'and everything has an energy'. Stones and crystals are alive, apparently, and our host is going to take us on a healing journey that will involve meditation and relaxation to calm the spirit. She looks up to the roof above: 'Can you feel that? Can you feel the lovely aura of the room?' I look around. 'Can you feel it? That's the stones!', she continues.

I have in my hand a pinkish crystal that is nose-shaped. I'd been given it at the start of the workshop, and as I looked at it quizzically, I had no idea what to expect. The idea that stones and crystals were alive with energy *and* were capable of memory had taken me somewhat by surprise.

Karla next pulled out a drum that had been painted bright white and blue with an image of herself as a swan. Where we go on our healing journey will be up to us, she explains, but if we are lucky, we might meet our spiritual guides. The point, she reminds us, is to go where our mind takes us. She slowly begins to beat the drum.

Karla then asks us to close our eyes and imagine that we are at the top of a cliff overlooking the sea: 'See the sea far beyond the horizon.' In our minds, she tells us, we are to walk down the cliff towards the beach. She starts to count: '10, 9, 8, 7, 6, 5, 4, 3, 2', and as she reaches one, she whispers just loudly enough for everyone to hear – 'go'.

The drum droned in 4/4 time, with an idiosyncratic emphasis, haphazardly thumping more heavily on the first, second, third, or fourth note. Occasionally, Karla made a noise somewhere between a chant, a howl and a song. It included three or four notes that ascended and descended at different pitches. Over time, there was a slight and gradual change in the pace of the beat – either faster or slower – and I listened intently.

After about five minutes, I endeavoured to let go of my inherent scepticism and to stop taking mental notes about the event. I tried to embrace the intuitive moment that I had learnt using the tarot and followed Karla's instructions to 'go on a journey'. But a long day and the rhythm of the drum as she walked up and down the hall were putting me in that mental space just before sleep. I felt myself nodding off and tried to concentrate on the drum. I firmly shut my eyes and saw colourful shapes morph and change on the back of my eyelids.

Suddenly, the outline of a white owl appeared in my mind's eye, and I imagined myself floating above the sea. I looked down and saw a whale breaching the surface of the water. More whales soon joined, rising and falling in vast currents. The owl flew in front of me, swooping further away into the distance as I tried to follow it across the sea. The pink, orange horizon was bathed in a colour much like that of the stone that I held in my hand. I felt a sense of peacefulness as I glided through the air, watching the owl as it moved into the horizon.

I'm startled by the nod of my head as I begin to fall into sleep. I had to steel myself against the sides of my bucket chair to remain awake. The sound of the drum began to quiet, and Karla directed us to return to the cliff. She counts from one to ten, quietly at first, louder with each number, and tells us to open our eyes. She then asks people about their journeys, and the focus of the audience frays as people talked excitedly to each other. As the doors opened and people started to leave the room, Karla shouted: 'You can keep your stone as a reminder of your journey!' I gripped mine firmly and tucked it snugly into the corner of my pocket.

It was wise to keep that stone. The healing powers of crystals and stones were a continual theme throughout the fair. Another practitioner at the workshop who specialized in crystal therapies, Beverly, detailed how crystals can be used for healing.[25] She identified her method as CPR – 'cleansing, protection, and replenish'. Cleansing refers to the practice of removing negative energy from the body. Selenite quartz works best for this, Beverly informed me. 'Just wave it around yourself when you get up and go to bed'. 'Fill yourself with white light', she suggested, 'because if you are taking something out, you need to fill it with something'. Protection refers to guarding the body against incoming negative energy. Tourmaline, obsidian, and black crystal help to guard against negativity and allow the positive energy to come through. For Beverly, 'replenishment' referred to the restoration of positive energy into the body. Rose quartz works especially here. 'It's love', she said. Rose quartz will remind you to 'treat yourself nicely, that you deserve better, and that you are worth more'.

Positive and negative energy are amorphic enough concepts within enlightenment circles that they need not be confined to present circumstances. At another workshop, a healer named Jane told the audience that energy has a memory. Bad things that have happened in previous lives can cause problems in the present. As a past life therapist, she aims to discover long-past experiences that are the source of current maladies, whether those maladies be physical, psychological, or psychic in nature. Once she discovers the source, she can cleanse that negative energy. She told us of a woman whose migraines were cured once Jane helped her to recover a past life memory as a knight who was betrayed and killed by someone close to them. She follows with the story of a man who was petrified of boats and open water. After performing a body scan, Jane discovered that this was because he had previously died on a plague ship in the 1700s. The memory of slow, traumatic death in *that* life, she said, still haunted him in *this* one – causing his fear of everything aquatic. Realizing this helped Jane's client come to grips with his phobia, she said.

At a different MBS fair, I was examining a pinboard overloaded with information about 'Atlantean healing' and 'Angelic Reiki' when a woman dressed in a dark blue tunic told me that she intuits past lives with help from Atlantean spirit guides. Scanning my face, she gets a serious look and tells me that there is 'absolutely no doubt' that I have lived before. Her guides tell her something about 'Sherwood'. She wonders whether I might have a past life having something to do with 'Robin Hood; but not the Merry Men, perhaps', she pauses, 'you have a lot of women in your past lives'. I decline to tell her that I live on the bottom edge of what is referred to as Loxley Common, which some believe was the actual home of Robin Hood.[26] She quickly goes on to tell me that '[t]here's Egyptian in your face', probably something Camelot, perhaps Native American too. 'You have a very bright aura'.

None of these encounters would convince the sceptic, but their appeal is clear for someone without concerns about how outsiders might view such 'evidence'. Enlightenment healing practices are a form of therapy that utilizes creative role play and narrative. The imaginative work of thinking about one's own fears or struggles in the context of past lives, as amenable to cleaning via crystal, or subject to the beat of a drum, provides an indirect but potentially effective way for people to address their insecurities and problems. It was also clear at such events that one is encouraged to find and shape an idiosyncratic narrative that best suits them, by combining possibilities out of the host of available options. I was free to choose between being Native American, Egyptian, or Maid Marian as I wished, and as felt best to me.

Based on our experiences at MBS fairs, we were surprised by the findings of our national survey. Judging from the booths, workshops, and materials available at the events we visited, we would have assumed that enlightenment healing practices were just as, if not more popular than, enlightenment practices related to divination such as tarot card readings and psychics. This may be the case within the halls of a psychic fair, but amongst the general public, such practices are considerably less popular.

While one-fifth or more of our national respondents had read their horoscope, consulted a psychic or medium or had a tarot reading, far fewer had engaged in some of the various forms of enlightenment 'healing' practices. Most popular was using crystals for the purposes of healing, with 14 per cent of the respondents reporting having done so. Nearly 8 per cent had consulted a faith healer. However, the percentage that experienced that faith healing within an enlightenment context is likely far lower than this. Faith healings can, of course, take place within the context of organized religions. Protestants have a particularly rich history of faith-based healing practices.[27] And it seems that relatively few people in Britain are addressing their current ills by delving into their past lives, with less than 6 per cent of respondents having done so.

The Art of Magic

The third pillar of the MBS fairs that we attended was magic. If anything, magic is more difficult to define than the paranormal itself. Scholars have been so frustrated by attempts to get a handle on exactly what magic is that some have called these efforts a 'conceptual mess'.[28] Part of the problem is that magic necessarily crosses many cultural boundaries. At times, magic drifts close to the border between the paranormal and science. Some magical practices and rituals involve complex rules, specific sets of required ingredients and required gestures and phrases, making magic akin to 'occult science' in some regards.[29] At other times, magic has become the basis of loosely organized religious groups, despite Émile Durkheim's edict that: '*There is no Church of magic.*'[30]

Indeed, 'magical' religions – that is, religions that embrace magical thinking and practice – are becoming much more popular in Great Britain. Using data from the UK Census for England and Wales, Table 1.1 shows the relative growth of religions that explicitly incorporate magical thinking and practices between 2001 and 2021.[31]

These figures are taken from what people write in as further information when they tick the 'other religion' box. We cannot be certain from such responses whether the person is truly affiliated with a 'Pagan' religion, for example, or simply prefers the label 'Pagan' to describe themselves. Consequently, these estimates are clearly inflated upwards, at least in terms of organizational involvement. With such caveats in mind, the biggest 'magical' religion in 2021 was Paganism, with 73,737 followers in 2021, followed by Wicca, with 12,819. The number of Pagans more than doubled between 2001 and 2021, growing by 141 per cent. Between 2001

Table 1.1 Identification with 'Magical' Religions and Identities in the UK (2001–21)

	2001	2011	2021	% Change 2001–21
Animism	401	541	798	+99.0%
Druid	1,657	4,189	2,489	+50.2%
Heathen	278	1,958	4,722	+1,598.6%
Mysticism	158	204	147	−7.0%
New Age	906	698	387	−57.3%
Occult	99	502	501	+406.1%
Pagan	30,569	56,620	73,737	+141.2%
Pantheism	1,603	2,216	2,299	+43.4%
Satanism	1,525	1,893	5,039	+230.4%
Shamanism	n/a	650	7,889	—
Thelemite	n/a	184	232	—
Wicca	7,227	11,766	12,819	+77.4%
Witchcraft	n/a	1,276	1,056	—
Total	44,423	82,697	112,115	+152.4%

and 2021 the fastest growing 'magical' religions were Heathenism, Satanism and Shamanism. Of course, the relative growth in these specific religions is influenced by the comparatively small number of people who identified with them in the first place. It is also worth remembering that, in 2021, all these religions added together still made up well less than 1 per cent of the population of England and Wales.[32]

Still, an increase in the popularity of identification with magical religions is clearly evident over time. If we concentrate on affiliation with all magical religions, between 2001 and 2021, the increase was 152 per cent in the number of people who identified with these traditions, with a total value of just over 112,000 adherents. This means that there is a potential population of magical practitioners that is bigger than the city of Lincoln, which was 103,900 in 2021.

It is worth highlighting, however, that the types of magic presented at an MBS event are constrained by the context. The magical practices that we encountered at events primarily involved the attempt to influence the physical realm using supernatural forces. These forces may or may not be connected to particular gods or deities. The school of magic in play was subsidiary to the service being provided. A Pagan might be reading one's tea leaves; a Wiccan might be casting runes. At times the connection to a particular magical school, if any, was clear; at other times it was not. Magic simply flowed through and around the event, presented as a spiritual technology for personal use more than as an attempt at conversion. In the context of an economic marketplace in which workshops are designed to support the products and services that can be bought, this makes good sense. The stalls at MBS events are usually quite busy, and the workshops are crowded. There is little time for the extended metaphysical exposition or explanation that would be required for deeper spiritual connections to be made.

For example, elemental magic is used in both modern Wiccan and Pagan traditions but resonates with many other spiritual practices. A workshop I attended on 'working with elements' was led by a self-described Wiccan, Denise.[33] The specifics of Wicca were of little importance to the proceedings, and I would not have known that Denise was Wiccan, Pagan, Heathen or anything at all, had she not briefly introduced herself as such as the workshop opened.

As the name suggests, elemental magic draws on the elements of nature to perform magical rituals and ceremonies. This usually involves earth, air, fire and water. Each element has different characteristics – or energies – that can be harnessed by the intention of the practitioner. Denise instructed the attendees to invite earth energies into the circle. She turned to the North and shouted, 'Elements of the earth, help us with our grounding, come to us now!' Followed by: 'Feel the energy; Hail and Welcome'. At her instruction, the audience chanted in unison – 'Hail and Welcome!' And with that, we had 'called the fire element in', and could now begin to work with it.

We then worked through each element in turn – East for air and breath; South for fire, passion, and soul; and West for water, emotions and feelings. The audience chanted along until all the elements were in the room. Our host asked us: 'Can you feel that? Can you feel that the room has got warmer? That's because of the elements'.

Now that we had all energies in the room, Denise told us that we could ask them for help. This took the form of a chant that could take a variety of different directions based on our intentions. Helped by Denise, the audience reached a collective agreement to focus upon 'abundance, security, prosperity, and protection'. Again and again, louder and louder, we chanted in unison, 'abundance, security, prosperity, protection'. The chant continued for a while but became softer and softer over time as the audience seemed to exhaust their energy. Finally, it extinguished completely. 'Did you enjoy that?' Denise asked. 'Yes', came the collective response.

'What we need to do now is to forget about the spell. We have to let it do its work', said Denise. She adds that we must now close the circle as 'we don't want to let anything in'. To do this, we must say goodbye to the elements and the energies that they possess. She shouted, 'Hail and Farewell!' Followed by: 'Elements of water, thank you for bringing emotions and feelings, I bid you Hail and Farewell.' The crowd intuitively responded in unison. Working counterclockwise this time, we did the same for fire, air, and earth – 'Hail and Farewell'. With this the circle was closed, as was a long day at the MBS fair.

The Gendered Spiritual Marketplace

MBS events do not exist in isolation, and there are many permanent shops and retail outlets scattered throughout Britain that cater to 'alternative' interests. One of the more well-known shops of this type is 'The Atlantis Bookshop'. Located near the British Museum in Bloomsbury, London, it was 'established in 1922 by magicians, for magicians' and advertises itself as 'the birth-place of modern witchcraft, with Gerald Gardner holding regular coven meetings in the basement of the Shop'. It offers a huge range of occult books, magicware, and tarot cards and continues to hold a range of events in the basement.

Elsewhere, there are numerous local variations on this theme. These outlets might specialize in books, crystals, candles or other magical items, while also operating as something of a hub for local groups of Pagans, witches and alternative spiritualities. Similarly, many towns will have 'wellness centres' where more mainstream treatments for the mind and body exist alongside more complementary and alternative therapies. Whether someone is seeking counselling, hypnotherapy or looking to connect with their past lives, clients simply choose the therapy they think might help them, select their favoured therapist, and make a booking.

In addition, we can see how the dynamics of late modern capitalism direct these spiritual offerings towards both expressive individualism and marketplace pressures. These marketplaces are horizontally, vertically, and regionally segmented. Indeed, although it does not typically present itself as such, the holistic milieu is a highly competitive marketplace. The market is regionally segmented in terms of what is offered in different geographical areas, horizontally segmented in that vendors offering quite different services are in competition with each other, and vertically segmented, with a clear status hierarchy between vendors. The goods and services on offer at a local community event are below those offered at a regional event, which are again different from what can be accessed at a more national event.

Indeed, a number of scholars have highlighted how, rather than enabling the authority of subjective experience, 'New Age spiritualities' actually construct equally constraining versions of 'the self', usually for the purposes of consumptive capitalism.[34] Alternative spiritualities have become commodified marketplaces where spiritual products and services are sold to consumers as a means of achieving a set of ideals – wellbeing, personal growth, and spiritual development – that are themselves constructed through the wider lens of market-based economics.[35] To put this more crudely, why sell one religion to a small group of people when you can sell bits of them all to everyone?

In terms of *who* is most attracted to enlightenment products and services, our survey found a pronounced gender gap. As Figures 1.2 and 1.3 demonstrate, women are far more likely to hold enlightenment-related paranormal beliefs and twice as likely (or more) to have engaged in enlightenment-related practices. Women are nearly twice as likely as men to believe in the abilities of psychics and fortune tellers (25.8 per cent vs. 14.7 per cent), astrology (30.1 per cent vs. 17.6 per cent), and the power of charms (26.6 per cent vs. 15.2 per cent).

Nearly two out of five women have consulted a horoscope, compared to one out of five men. Nearly three out of ten (29 per cent) women have consulted a psychic, compared to only 11 per cent of men. Women are nearly twice as likely to use crystals for healing. Similarly, nearly three in ten (29 per cent) women report having a tarot reading, compared to only 14 per cent of men. In predictive models that included a wide range of sociodemographic characteristics such as age, education level, social class, and marital status, as well as multi-item measures of different aspects of religiosity, gender was by far the strongest predictor of consulting horoscopes, psychics, and tarot readers.[36]

Notably, such gender effects are not present when it comes to paranormal beliefs and practices that are *discovery* oriented, for example, those focused more

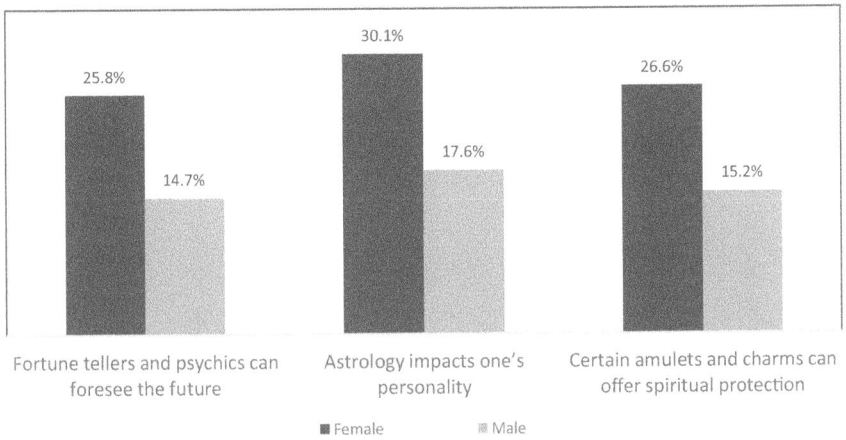

Figure 1.2 Enlightenment beliefs in Britain, by gender (CASPAR, 2021).

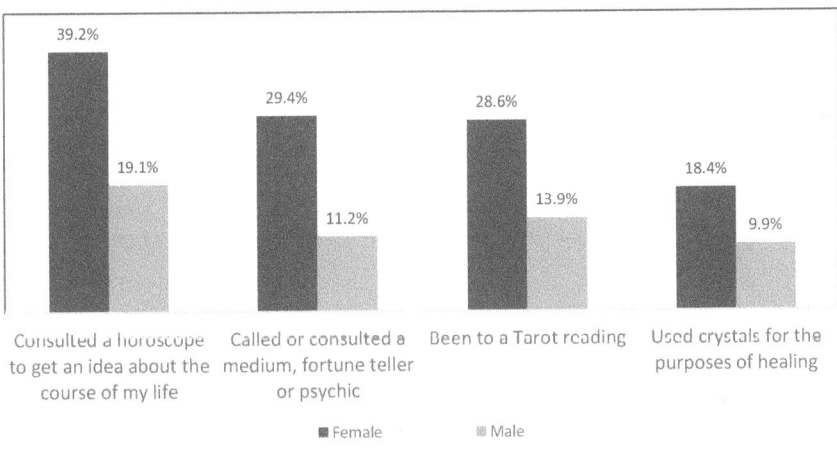

Figure 1.3 Enlightenment practices in Britain, by gender (CASPAR, 2021).

upon proving the reality of a paranormal phenomenon to others. Gender is *not* a significant predictor of belief and interest in subjects such as modern UFOs and ancient aliens, the possible existence of big cats, the Abominable Snowman, Bigfoot, or other mysterious creatures. In Britain, women are far more interested in enlightenment than discovery.

The gender gap we find regarding interest in enlightenment paranormal practices is well-documented in other surveys.[37] It is also well-documented in ethnographic research on practices such as tarot readings.[38] There are a number of different factors leading to the greater levels of interest in these practices among women. First, spirituality and related practices are culturally coded as feminine and intimately tied to the social labour of caring for others.[39] With regard to alternative practices, this often extends to providing feminist alternatives to the patriarchal structures of organized religion. In this way, alternative religious practices can sometimes become sites of resistance to the masculine control modelled and perpetuated by mainstream religions. In addition to the cultural meanings of alternative spiritualities, the integration of healing practices into these views is also an important factor in the feminization of enlightenment paranormalism. Men are less likely than women to seek care, particularly therapeutic care.[40]

An Enlightened Britain

Within Britain, magical religions are on the rise; a substantial portion of the public reports interest in and experiences of enlightenment paranormalism; and such practices are readily available in the spiritual (and commercial) marketplace. Events such as MBS fairs provide but a glimpse into the kaleidoscopic world of alternative beliefs, practices, and therapies that are available to help facilitate personal and spiritual growth. We also find that the wider social context is critical to understanding the popularity of such events and experiences. In particular, the cultural coding of spirituality as feminine is reflected in substantial gaps in patterns of interest in enlightenment paranormalism between men and women.

In sum, the cultic/holistic milieu is alive, well, and growing in contemporary Britain. We suspect that an ever-increasing drift away from organized religion by the British public will accelerate that trend. That said, enlightenment paranormalism is just one dimension of the paranormal landscape operating in Britain today. In the next chapter we turn to discovery and join the quest to find the Loch Ness Monster.

Chapter 2

INTO THE DEPTHS

Legend Come to Life[1]

'Nice big target I've just picked up near the bottom of the loch.'

It's the type of message that Loch Ness Monster hunter Steven Feltham waits for. Steve has been fascinated by reports of a long-necked, reptilian beast, nicknamed Nessie, since he was a child. He has been looking for Nessie for over thirty years. Other than a brief glimpse of an unexplained disturbance in the water in 1993, he has had no luck capturing conclusive evidence himself.

On 30 September 2020, Feltham's friend Ronald Mackenzie was on his boat and using a sonar depth metre. At 4.20 pm, in 620 feet of water off the highland village of Invermoriston, a large blue blob appeared at a depth of about 580 feet. It was moving and too large to be any fish known to inhabit the loch. Mackenzie took photos of the sonar images and sent them to Steve immediately.

Feltham enthusiastically summarized the incident on his 'Nessie Hunter' blog:

Is there large unidentified animals swimming about in Loch Ness?
BOOM!
There's one.
Right there.[2]

For Steve, such events keep hope alive that one day the Loch Ness mystery will be solved. Perhaps the sonar recording could be the piece of evidence that proves to the world that all those people who claim to have seen Nessie over the years were not mistaken, liars or simply crazy. Unfortunately, Mackenzie's recording did not have this effect. If lucky, it will join the body of eyewitness accounts, photographs and other sonar readings that Nessie enthusiasts trot out when they hope to convince others.

And herein lies the profound difference between *enlightenment* and *discovery* forms of the paranormal. At the MBS fairs we attended, there was little concern for gathering external-facing evidence. The enlightenment focus is inward. If something works for you, then it is valid. If something does not work for you, it may simply be a matter of incompatible energy; try something else.

In this chapter we will use Nessie as our entry point into the world of discovery, where evidence and theories are paramount. Chakras and auras give way to sonar readings, water samples and photographs. After exploring the world of British monsters, we will then examine how the panoply of paranormal beliefs clusters together. In other words, if someone believes in one monster, such as Nessie, are they more likely than others to believe in another, such as the British Bigfoot? Does belief in one type of psychic phenomena predict belief in others? Or is the paranormal a large, unpredictable stew, where one belief tells us little about the others someone might hold? By categorizing paranormal beliefs into clusters, we can compare enlightenment- and discovery-oriented people and explore if some common stereotypes have any merit. Do people who believe in paranormal things tend to have lower levels of education? Does religion open one up to other forms of supernatural belief? We can begin to answer such questions, with monsters as our entry point.

The Nessie Ecosystem

Setting aside the issue of whether Loch Ness's natural ecosystem could even support an undiscovered population of large animals, Steve has become a vital part of the *social* ecosystem supporting 'Nessie.' His 'NessieHunter.com' research centre, a former mobile library parked permanently at Dores Beach on the northern shores of the loch, has become a clearinghouse for new reports. When residents or visitors recount new sightings at local bars and hotels, the owners refer them to Steve. His frequent appearances on television shows and podcasts, and his ability to recount recent sightings, help maintain Nessie as a vital, going concern. And the economy of Nessie is clearly thriving. Steve funds his efforts with the sales of Nessie models; each one is a custom-crafted clay figure affixed to a rock he has pulled from the loch. On a bitterly cold, snowy day when I (Chris) visited in January of 2023, nobody else was around, and Steve had prearranged our meeting.[3] During the tourist season and warmer months, he comes to Dores Beach every day and does a brisk business selling the models.

Nessie and commerce are inexorably linked around the loch. Every shop is stocked with Nessie stickers, t-shirts, plushies, candies, books, coffee mugs and anything else upon which one might plaster a serpentine neck. Across the loch from Steve is Drumnadrochit, home to the Loch Ness Centre, which is packed with exhibits about the history of the Nessie legend and purported pieces of evidence. After buying a treat at Nessie's Gelato and taking a photo with its costumed mascot, any children present can be unleashed upon the dinosaur-themed playground equipment at Nessieland. From there it is less than a thirty-minute drive to Fort Augustus, where one can purchase a ticket from Cruise Loch Ness, owned by Ronald Mackenzie. He was entertaining a boat filled with tourists when the mysterious blob appeared on sonar.

As he carefully packed the three Nessie models I had purchased into bags, Feltham told me that quality sightings and experiences are few and far between, and have been declining over time. Most of the reports he receives from both visitors and locals are 'obvious hoaxes or misidentifications'. For example, he has been shown countless photos of 'shadows in the lake that are clearly the wakes of passing boats'. One visitor even tried to claim a photo of a rock that protrudes from the waters off Dores Beach was Nessie; admittedly, the rock did look quite like a snake's head.

New reports produce short-lived excitement, but a visit to the loch and its environs leaves the distinct impression that the legend and commerce of Nessie could persist for a very long time without new sightings. Nessie seems impervious to the slings and arrows of sceptics as the next bit of 'evidence' may be just around the corner, and the extant evidence provides plenty of fodder for discussion. All of this raises the question: Do people actually believe in the Loch Ness Monster? Or does the creature now occupy the same cultural space as Santa Claus and the Easter Bunny?

We asked our respondents if they think 'the Loch Ness Monster exists' and found that Nessie has some life in her yet (see Figure 2.1 below). About two out of five (38 per cent) choose 'definitely not' when asked if the monster exists. But the remaining 62 per cent leave the possibility at least a little open. Forty per cent said 'probably not'. About 12 percent of Scottish respondents said that Nessie 'probably' exists, compared to about 16 percent of respondents from England, Wales and Northern Ireland. About 6 percent think Nessie 'definitely' swims Loch Ness. Scots are somewhat more sceptical in their attitudes towards their home-grown monster and are less likely than those from the rest of the UK to agree that Nessie exists.

Photo 2.1 Steve Feltham at Dores Beach, Loch Ness, on 16 January 2023.

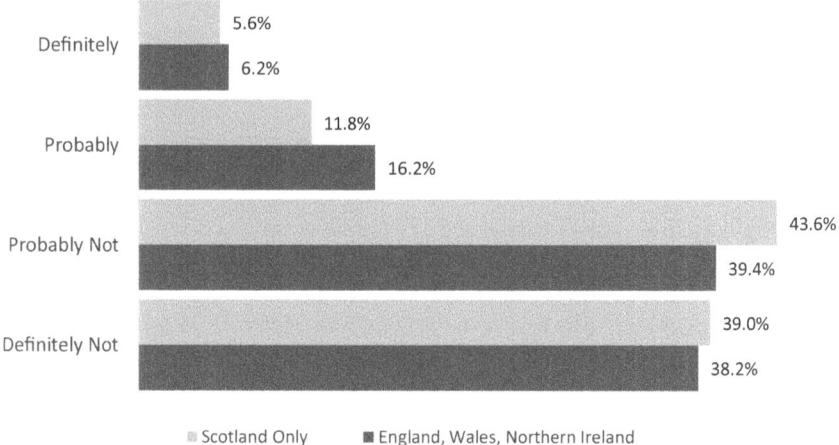

Figure 2.1 The Loch Ness Monster exists (CASPAR, 2021).

Within the paranormal realm there are countless examples of the repurposing of age-old legends to suit modern sensibilities. Believers will claim that folklore, myth and/or religious texts provide evidence that a particular phenomenon is not merely a modern invention, pointing to all manner of historical evidence to support their beliefs. For example, some UFO researchers claim that the angelic chariots of the Bible and Vimana of the Hindu gods were extraterrestrial craft misidentified by observers of the time.[4] Others point to flying saucers in artwork, such as the fifteenth century *The Madonna with Saint Giovannino* and Crivelli's *Annunciation* from 1486.[5]

Nessie represents a similar development. The folklore of Scotland includes two species of 'water horses', temperamental creatures with horse and snake-like characteristics that drag the unwary into the depths. The *Kelpie* lives in streams and rivers, while the *Each-Uisge* haunts the lakes and sea.[6] These mystical creatures were sometimes attributed the ability to change into human form. When modern Nessie mania began with newspaper reports of a sighting in 1933 (and other sightings and purported photographs that quickly followed), this folklore was reimagined. Popular media posited that the loch was home to a remnant species of dinosaur, perhaps a plesiosaur. Extant folklore became evidence of previous sightings, and Nessie morphed from a magical beast to be feared and appeased into a 'cryptid' that can be chased by sonar and photographed by lucky tourists.[7]

Big Hairy Monsters

The Woodwose or 'wild man of the woods' has undergone a similar transformation from folkloric entity to modern, undiscovered creature. Medieval art, heraldry and architecture are rife with images of hairy, man-like figures that often carry clubs and are usually depicted as walking upright.[8] *The Fight in the Forest* by German artist Hans Burgkmair I, *c.* 1500/1503, includes an armoured knight in battle with a large hairy man holding a club.[9] The entryway of St. Michael's church in Peasenhall, Suffolk, includes two mythological entities. To the left of the doorway is an image of the dragon-like Wyvern. To the right is an entirely hair-covered, bearded man, holding a club and shield.

Place names also speak to legends of the Wildman. In Northern Wales (the Nant Gwynant valley), local folklore tells of a huge man covered in reddish hair who stole from local farms until one evening when it climbed through the wrong window and a farmer's wife chopped off its right hand with a hatchet. The beast fled, leaving a trail of blood that led to a cave underneath a waterfall. The Wildman was never found, nor bothered the community afterwards. The cave was thereafter branded Ogof y Gwr Blewog or 'Cave of the Hairy Man'.[10]

Scholars speculate that the Wildman is an archetype, a symbol that originally represented the dangers of the wilderness or lack of civilization and its restraints. He is a glutton – promiscuous, savage and unconcerned with Christian notions of sin and morality.[11] By the Romantic age, the Wildman changed again. It transformed from something to be feared and tamed into an object of nostalgia for a simpler time.[12]

English mountaineers played a key role in the next evolution of the Wildman into an extant, undiscovered creature. In 1921, a British-Irish Lieutenant Colonel named Charles Kenneth Howard-Bury led a reconnaissance mission to Mount Everest, paving the way for the 1922 attempt to reach its peak. Upon reaching the top of a mountain pass, his group spotted human-looking tracks. Howard-Bury theorized that the tracks were created by a 'loping' grey wolf. But in his 1922 memoir about the mission, he notes that his porters held a different opinion: '[They] jumped to the conclusion that this must be "The Wild Man of the Snows", to which they gave the name of Metohkangmi, "the abominable snow man" who interested the newspapers so much.'[13]

British explorers visiting the Everest region continued to fan the flames of snowman excitement over the next few decades. During his 1935–6 expedition to find the source of the Salween river, mountaineer Ronald Kaulback discovered five sets of tracks that 'looked exactly like the prints of a bare-footed man', but at 16,000 feet.[14] On 13 November 1937, *The Illustrated London News* published photos of snowman prints found by English explorer Francis S. Smythe, although a follow-up article on November 27 reported that Smythe believed them to be of a bear.[15] After taking a backseat to Second World War, the Yeti returned with a vengeance in the 1950s. In 1951, climber Eric Shipton came back from an expedition to Mount Everest with photographs of large, human-like tracks on the Menlung Tsu Glacier. The December 15, 1951, issue of the *Illustrated London News* trumpeted the 'Reappearance of the "Abominable Snowman"' with a dramatic picture of a large, human-like footprint alongside a hiking boot.[16] When French zoologist Bernard Heuvelmans saw the 1951 Shipton photos, he became convinced they were evidence of a surviving population of *Gigantopithecus*, a long-thought extinct species of ape.[17]

The theory that an undiscovered ape explained Yeti encounters underscored the tensions between Western notions of scientific discovery and the stories of local folklore and myth.[18] In her book recounting folk tales of the *Migoi* (Tibetan for Wildman), Bhutanese author Kunzang Choden argues that the English expeditions took the wrong approach:

> The expeditions were aimed at getting hard core evidence to prove its existence. Most *migoi*-human encounters are purely chance encounters; they happen when least expected. These conditions, far from being deliberate are predetermined by a persons [sic] basic human qualities which in turn are influenced by each individual's astrological forces .... The *migoi* has powers beyond our comprehension; the Bhutanese respect that and therefore regard it as a *lhaende*, a being possessing all the supernatural and phantasmagoric attributes of gods and demons.[19]

Nevertheless, by the early 1950s, the British version of the Yeti lay primarily within the cultural category of an undiscovered animal for those who were open to its existence, or the category of misidentified animal or hoax for those who were not. The press worked to capitalize on and enhance the excitement. In 1954, the *Daily Mail* sponsored an expedition specifically designed to find evidence of the Yeti. The team, led by journalist Ralph Izzard, found tracks and investigated a supposed Yeti scalp held at a monastery.[20] Snowman enthusiasm faced a setback when Sir Edmund Hilary concluded that the creature did not exist after his 1960 expedition. But the cryptid never lost its position as a prevalent fixture in popular culture.

The development of the Western notion of the Yeti was closely timed with and, no doubt, influenced in the gestation of modern Bigfoot, which followed a similar path into the public consciousness. A series of large tracks found by a Northern California road crew in August of 1958 led to local coverage and the coining of the moniker 'Bigfoot'. Frequent sightings of the creature itself and national media coverage soon followed. Again, native lore of similar beings was repurposed. As noted by anthropologist David Daegling, Native American tales of hairy, man-like creatures were 'marshalled in support of the animal's zoological reality'.[21]

It took some time for the Woodwose to follow the example set by the Yeti and Bigfoot to complete its transformation from mythic archetype to modern-day cryptid. In their 1981 book on mysterious animals, influential British paranormalists Janet and Colin Bord were sceptical that 'big hairy monsters' (BHMs) roamed the Isles:

> [W]hat is the situation in the UK? So far as we know, there have been no reports of sightings of creatures *exactly* resembling the BHMs we have been describing,

but a study of UK folklore has revealed some intriguing legends which may indicate that the BHM did once have a home in Britain.[22]

By the early 2000s the situation had changed considerably. In January of 2003, the Centre for Fortean Zoology of Devon investigated recent sightings at Bolam Lake County Park in Northumberland. Members of the group reported witnessing an 'enormous humanoid' run through the woods and noted that the creature left footprints and tee-pee like structures, similar to American reports of Bigfoot.[23] By the time paranormal author Nick Redfern published his 2007 book *Man-Monkey*, he was using the term 'British Bigfoot' and promoted the term through his related blog.[24] In 2015, the popular American TV show *Finding Bigfoot* again drew attention to Northumberland with an episode about a photograph of the purported creature taken at Harwood Forest.[25] After visiting a chapel to gaze in amazement at carvings of the Woodwose, the stars of the show entered the woods to demonstrate the techniques used by American Bigfoot hunters. They roamed around with night vision cameras and attempted to elicit vocal responses from the creature by mimicking Bigfoot screams and knocking pieces of wood together.[26] Today the British Bigfoot scene is alive and well.[27] Britain is home to a number of amateur research groups, including the UK Bigfoot Research Group, the British Bigfoot Association, British Bigfoot Research, and the Irish Bigfoot Research Organisation.[28] Blogs and breathless stories in the tabloids provide blurry photos, eyewitness reports and footprint castings, fully evolving the Woodwose from folkloric archetype into a phenomenon virtually indistinguishable from Bigfoot and the Yeti.[29]

The growth of the Bigfoot phenomenon in Britain made us curious about the extent to which people believe in the creature and its cousins. Our survey asked about all three types of BHMs: the UK Wildman, the Abominable Snowman and Bigfoot. Respondents were asked to indicate if they thought 'The UK Wildman, sometimes known as "the British Bigfoot", exists'. They were also asked if 'The Abominable Snowman exists'. Finally, we asked if 'Bigfoot is a real creature'.

We expected respondents to be more open to the possibility of undiscovered hairy monsters in the vast wilderness of the Himalayas and Pacific Northwest than at home but were surprised to find that location did not matter much. There were no significant differences between belief in the British Bigfoot and the Yeti.[30] Less than 4 per cent of respondents are certain that these creatures exist. Fewer than 15 per cent think that the Yeti (14.2 per cent) or British Bigfoot (12.3 per cent) probably exists. The level of scepticism about these beasts is nearly equal; a bit over 40 per cent of respondents say 'definitely not' when asked about the existence of a British Bigfoot (44.2 per cent) and the Abominable Snowman (42.4 per cent) (see Figure 2.2).

Although asked in a slightly different way with a 'neither' response option, respondents showed similar tendencies regarding the American Bigfoot. Again, about 4 per cent were certain of the creature's existence (strongly agreed), and only about one in ten (11.9 per cent) 'tended to agree' (see Figure 2.3).

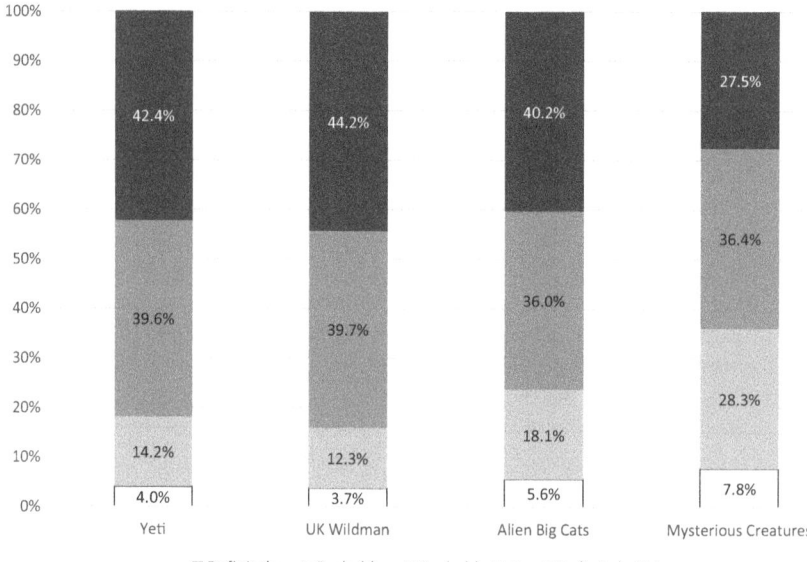

Figure 2.2 Cryptid belief in Britain (CASPAR, 2021).

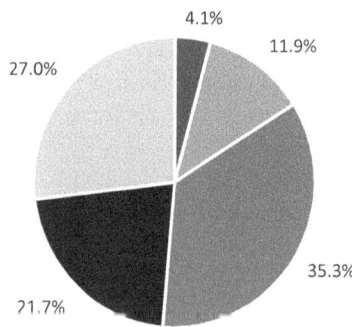

Figure 2.3 Belief in Bigfoot in Britain (CASPAR, 2021).

Alien Big Cats

Just as there are three pillars to the modern psychic fair (divination, healing and magic), the world of British cryptids primarily consists of three major categories. First, Nessie, the superstar, holds a status far above the rest. The second pillar, the British Bigfoot, is the young upstart, still fairly obscure, but emboldened by the fame of its cousins, the Yeti and Bigfoot. The third major form of British cryptid is a different type of beast altogether, the so-called alien big cats (ABCs).

Nessie and the British Bigfoot share similarities. Both appear to be the repurposing of extant legends and folklore into modern cryptids. And neither Nessie nor the British Bigfoot should exist *anywhere*. If either were to be discovered, it would cause a seismic shift within modern science.

The British big cat phenomenon, on the other hand, consists of sightings of large, predatory cats that *are* known to exist in other parts of world, just not in Britain. The 'alien' in 'alien big cats' is used in the non-paranormal sense here.[31] If the existence of ABCs were to be conclusively proven in Britain, the scientific community would have to accept that the British woodlands can support such a creature, at least in the short term. This is a far smaller change than the paradigm shift that British Bigfoot would require of scientists.

While there are earlier sightings and older legends about phantom cats across Britain, the ABC phenomenon truly took off in the early 1960s. Between 1962 and 1964, the police force of Godalming, a market town in southwest Surrey, logged 362 sightings of the 'Surrey Puma'. It was described as sandy coloured with large paws.[32] In 1983, farmer Eric Ley of Drewstone Farm in South Molton, just south of Exmoor National Park, reported that he had lost dozens of lambs to an unidentified predator.[33] Other nearby farmers reported their own losses and sightings of a black, panther-like animal poured into police agencies and newspapers. Attacks attributed to the 'Beast of Exmoor' slowed, but encounters never stopped. The 2021 pilot for the TV show *Cat Hunters* focused on Exmoor.[34] In December of 2021, wildlife photographer Sam Aston made headlines after posting a picture of the beast he captured while walking his dog.[35]

As with the British Bigfoot, clusters of big cat sightings often result in local nicknames, such as the Cotswolds Big Cat, Cornwall's 'Beast of Bodmin Moor', and Aberdeenshire's 'Beast of Buchan'.[36] Unlike Bigfoot, there has actually been hard, physical evidence of big cats. For example, on 28 October 1980, Ted Noble captured a puma that had been preying on the livestock of his farm twelve miles west of Loch Ness.[37] Frustrated by the lack of official response, Noble had baited a large steel cage with meat. Post-capture, 'Felicity' lived at Highland Wildlife Park until her death in 1985 and remains on display at the Inverness Museum and Art Gallery.[38]

Felicity is evidence that at least one exotic cat roamed Britain for a time, but she did not solve the ABC mystery. First, nobody was sure where she came from. In 1976 the UK legislature passed the Dangerous Wild Animals Act, which tightly regulated the keeping of large cats and other exotic pets. Perhaps Felicity was a former pet, released by owners unable or unwilling to deal with the new rules. If she was an escapee from a zoo or wildlife park, no such losses had been reported. There have been other exotic cats either captured or killed in Britain since Felicity, but the numbers are not sufficient to account for the volume of the continued sightings of ABCs across the UK.

Besides outright hoaxes and the misidentification of common cats, a number of theories have been offered to explain ABC sightings.[39] Some argue that the various escapees and released pets managed to develop a breeding population of big cats in the UK. In her book *Cat Country*, Di Francis speculated that Britain might be home to its own species of undiscovered big cat.[40] As always, others offer more supernatural explanations. Artist and big cat researcher Merrily Harpur likens ABCs to otherworldly, shapeshifting beings known as daimons.[41] Paranormal author Nick Redfern claims that a witch named Mother Sarah informed him that black cats (and other mysterious creatures) are summoned from another dimension by magic users.[42]

Whatever the explanation, the ABC phenomenon shows no signs of stopping any time soon.[43] Indeed, reaching out to academic colleagues from the UK quickly produced a first-hand report:

> I was on vacation in the town of Ullapool on the west coast of Scotland and did quite a bit of hiking in the area. One day I was hiking on land around the mountain Suilven north of Ullapool when I saw a shape moving in the distance. I was walking towards Suilven and the shape came in from my right-hand side. I stopped to watch and saw what I think was a large black cat. I was some distance away, but I remember being scared it might see and attack me. It stood still for a while, probably not very long, but it felt like ages, then walked away slowly and vanished out of sight. I'm aware that there are claimed sightings of animals like this and that might have impacted me, but I have a clear memory of what I saw.[44]

Our review suggests that sightings of ABCs are far more common than those of other 'monsters'. ABCs also inspire the most support among cryptids with the British population. Nearly one-fourth of those in the UK (23.7 per cent) believe that ABCs probably or definitely roam the British countryside. By comparison, a similar proportion of the population believes in Nessie (22 per cent).

The Menagerie

The British Isles are home to more strange creatures than we had the space to ask about on our survey, which required difficult choices. Scotland's Loch Lochy and Loch Urabhal have their own monsters. Loch Morar's monster has been sighted enough to earn a nickname, 'Morag' and a book.[45] Auna, Graney, Fadda, Leane and Nahooin are but a sampling of the Irish Loughs with their own lake beasts.[46] Faced with so many lake beasts, we elected to ask only about Nessie, the most famous amongst them.

Some mysterious beasts appear enough to cement themselves into local lore but too rarely (and with too little press coverage) to breakthrough into general awareness. For example, in 1976, two young girls on holiday in Mawnan, Cornwall, encountered a man-like being with large wings that flew over the tower of the local church. A different pair of young girls on holiday saw a similar thing the next morning. The creature earned a name, 'Owlman', but has been seen only sporadically since.[47] In 1984 and 1985, Brentford played host to a 'griffin'. Described as a 'dog with wings', it was seen flying over town.[48] Werewolves also make the occasional appearance. There's the 'Old Stinker' of Hull, the Cannock

Chase Werewolf and Shetland's Wulver, amongst others.[49] We did not ask about these rarely seen creatures for fear of receiving a host of 'don't know' responses.[50]

More widely known are the canine cousins of the ABCs – black dogs. There is a rich tradition in Britain regarding the sighting of large, menacing, black, spectral canines, often with glowing eyes. Going by many names, including 'Black Shuck', 'Shug Monster', and the 'Barguest', the creature inspired Sir Arthur Conan Doyle's *The Hound of the Baskervilles*. It is often associated with bad luck and assumed to be in league with the Devil.[51] It is also often taken as a harbinger of death.

As discussed in the Introduction, legends (and a strangely marked door) tell of a black dog attacking a church in Blythburgh in 1577. Just a few days earlier, one appeared to the congregation of the church of Bungay in Suffolk after a thunderstorm. While the occasional report still filters in, modern Black Shuck are comparatively rare.[52] Today the black dogs are most commonly found in alcohol marketing. Norfolk's Wagtail Brewery provides the Black Shuck stout.[53] Elgood's Brewery in Wisbech, Cambridgeshire, produces 'Black Dog' beer and utilizes the creature as its logo.[54] Those seeking a stiffer drink can visit Black Shuck Distillery (also in Norfolk), which offers a variety of rums, gins and schnapps, along with a helpful overview of the legendary beast on its website.[55] Since our focus is upon contemporary paranormal beliefs rather than basic awareness of folklore, we left Black Shuck out of our survey.

While we could not ask about every mysterious creature, we did get a sense of general attitudes towards them. When asked if they think 'mysterious creatures, previously thought extinct, still inhabit this world', fully one-third of people in the UK think they probably or definitely do (see Figure 2.2).

Alien Animals

Within the realm of mysterious creatures there is a distinct divide between those who believe their cryptid of choice is 'merely' an undiscovered creature and those who espouse more exotic explanations. ABC enthusiasts who favour the escaped pet theory are understandably leery of claims of extradimensional daimon cats.[56] In a similar vein, Bigfoot researchers in the United States who argue for a surviving population of Gigantopithecus have little patience for tales of creatures jumping through inter-dimensional portals or climbing onto UFOs.[57]

Nessie has always seemed to straddle boundaries. For every Roy Mackal, a University of Chicago biologist who argued that the Loch Ness Monster was a surviving zeuglodon (ancient whale),[58] there is a priest attempting to exorcise the evil spirit of Nessie or a wizard psychically raising her from the depths.[59] English journalist F. W. Holiday personally exemplified these two camps and transitioned between them. In his first book on the subject, 1968's *The Orm of Loch Ness*, he posited that Nessie was a giant form of an invertebrate species long thought extinct.[60] Just two years later, Holiday had changed his mind.[61] He found that the creatures always managed to avoid cameras or cause them to malfunction, never leaving any concrete evidence. He also came to believe that their presence caused toothaches and other maladies. Holiday also experienced several UFO sightings and noted that both monsters and UFOs move at high speeds, change appearance, and avoid leaving traces. His next book, *The Dragon & the Disc,* posited that lake monsters and UFOs are intimately connected and form the basis of ancient religions, with lake monsters being a manifestation of evil.[62]

Were Steve Feltham and F. W. Holiday to have met, it would surely have made for an interesting conversation. Over the years, Feltham has become convinced that the Loch Ness Monster is a Wels catfish, which is not native to the UK. In 1880, the Duke of Bedford imported seventy specimens and released them into Mutton Lake in Bedfordshire for sport fishing purposes. While there is no evidence that any Wels catfish were ever released into Loch Ness, Feltham believes it could have happened without people knowing. At up to fifteen feet in length, the fish are big enough to account for monster sightings, he argues.

As we stood by his research van looking across the Loch, Feltham told me about some of the more exotic theories he has heard. He was, of course, familiar with Holiday's theories, which he curtly dismissed. He told me more of the aforementioned 'wizard', a character named Anthony 'Doc' Shiels, who used magic to summon a squid-like Nessie to appear for photographs in 1977. Shiels self-narrates his own exploits in *Monstrum! A Wizard's Tale.*[63] Shiels was a hoaxer, Feltham said; his photos were merely paintings on glass plates. Feltham has also been told that Nessie is a dinosaur from the Jurassic period that leaps into our time via portals that occasionally open in the lake. A man who lives across the lake from where we stood once informed Steve that there is an alien spacecraft resting on the bottom of the loch. Whenever the spaceship flies on an errand, it provokes Nessie sightings as it rises to the surface. Clearly exasperated by such claims, Feltham expressed annoyance with those who 'think they can explain one mystery by bringing in another'.

Paranormal Stereotypes

We have encountered many stereotypes about paranormal enthusiasts during our studies. Chief amongst them is that people who believe in UFOs, Nessie, psychic powers and the like are gullible, credulous and willing to accept anything. Amongst the most fervent sceptics, increasing belief in the paranormal is a bellwether sign of a dangerous move towards general irrationality, and so such beliefs should be most prevalent amongst the uneducated.

Reality is more complicated than simple arguments about gullibility though. In our studies we have also noticed a tendency towards *paranormal particularism,* wherein believers in some mysterious phenomena show little interest in or explicitly dismiss others.[64] Steve Feltham exhibited this trait. His extraordinary enthusiasm for Nessie is tempered by the dismissal of any theory that posits she is not an undiscovered or out-of-place animal. We have also encountered paranormal particularism amongst ghost hunters who tell us of their encounters with spirits while decrying those who believe in demonic entities, and UFO theorists who are irrepressibly irritated when others point out similarities between alien and faerie encounters.

There are many reasons why people might develop bounded interests in paranormal topics. One is simply reputational 'damage control'. After all, to claim a paranormal obsession or experience is to risk one's conventional credibility. Most believers and experiencers are well aware that the general public perceives them as gullible, eccentric or even delusional.[65] One way to minimize that damage to one's credibility is to paint others as even more credulous than oneself and to limit one's interest to one paranormal sphere. Having an anomalous experience may also prompt deeper levels of engagement with a specific phenomenon. A person who witnesses a flying saucer, or is closely acquainted with someone who did, is likely to form an interest in UFOs and related subjects. Or a particular television show or movie may leave a lasting impression. Some people live in areas tied to specific paranormal lore. Growing up surrounded by flying saucer tales in Roswell, New Mexico, or the monster tourism of Loch Ness may prompt specific interests.

We also see evidence of particularism in our survey. In addition to the questions about monsters, we fielded questions about twelve other types of paranormal phenomena, including black magic, dowsing, ley lines, crop circles, curses, Atlantis, faeries, telekinesis, ghosts, fortune telling and visitations from aliens in modern times as well as the ancient past. About one-fifth of respondents (22 per cent) rejected all of these beliefs.[66] Less than one-fifth of respondents (19 per cent) accepted half or more of them (holding nine or more beliefs). Thus, relatively few people reject all paranormal claims, and fewer still accept lots of them. Most fall somewhere in between, and on the lower end, with the median number of paranormal beliefs being four. To hardened sceptics, all paranormal beliefs are one and the same. Most of the general public, however, picks and chooses. When it comes to cryptids, the best predictor of belief in one monster is belief in another; someone who thinks the UK Wildman is real is significantly more likely to also believe in Nessie, and this connection is substantially stronger than the link to other paranormal beliefs, such as aliens.[67]

However, there are some reasons that we might expect education to be related to paranormal beliefs. It is possible that paranormal beliefs would be more prevalent amongst those who live on the margins of society, as a coping mechanism. Karl Marx, for example, argued that belief in the unseen and unprovable was a means by which those struggling in the material sense could seek comfort in the immaterial.[68] Perhaps the desire to experience the supernatural is a response to the uncertainty that comes with a lack of social capital. Those who have higher levels of social achievement, whether this be an advanced education or a stable occupation with opportunities for advancement, do tend to feel more in control of their lives.[69] Members of status positions with lower average levels of social capital, including women, the poor, those with low levels of education, and ethnic minorities, might feel significantly less in control of their own lives.[70] And rightfully so. The fewer socio-economic resources one has available, the more difficult and stressful any unforeseen hardship will be.

Other research has found that those who lack the resources to change their own worldly circumstances are indeed more likely to seek out the supernatural.[71] Put another way, if our lives feel out of control and at the whim of outside forces, it may provide comfort to attach agency to those sources, or to seek them out. Taken together this means that if there is merit to this marginalization hypothesis, we should expect to see higher levels of paranormal belief amongst those with lower education or lower income, as well as amongst members of status groups with comparatively less social capital, including ethnic minorities and women.

X Factors

In order to properly assess what drives paranormal beliefs, we need to account for the tendency of people to have clustered sets of beliefs. It is possible that those who believe in mysterious animals are different than those convinced by claims of psychic phenomena, UFOs or witchcraft.

We performed statistical analyses to determine the patterns of survey responses to our eighteen questions about paranormal beliefs. In other words, if someone answered that they believe in visitations from aliens in Earth's ancient past, how likely were they to also indicate belief in Atlantis? To what extent was that likelihood greater or less than their likelihood of also believing in faeries or ghosts? When determining these clusters, we excluded questions that related to traditional religious beliefs. We did not do this because we deem conventional religion more credible. Rather, as discussed in Chapter 1 and explored in greater depth in Chapter 7, religion and the paranormal occupy distinctly different (though sometimes also overlapping) cultural niches. Psychologists have long noted that paranormal beliefs tend to cluster separately from conventional religious beliefs, such as belief in God or religious conceptions of life after death.[72]

Our analyses determined that, within the British public, the paranormal segments into four major categories (see Figure 2.4).[73] Questions about aliens and claims of advanced, ancient civilizations are grouped together. Someone who believes that aliens visited Earth in our ancient past is likely to also express belief that Atlantis exists and that aliens are currently visiting.[74] The Earth mysteries cluster included the belief that dowsing can be used to detect water, minerals and other elements that are underground and that structures and landmarks are connected by invisible lines of energy (ley lines). Two beliefs thwarted our best attempts to corral them. The belief that some crop circles are created by nonhuman forces or energies did not strongly group with others, even though it seems to fit well with the Earth mysteries conceptually or with belief in alien visitation. True to their liminal nature, fae folk stood off on their own too, as the belief that faeries can influence the human world did not cluster well with other beliefs either. When someone believes in faeries or crop circles, we cannot make confident predictions about what other paranormal things, if any, they might believe in.

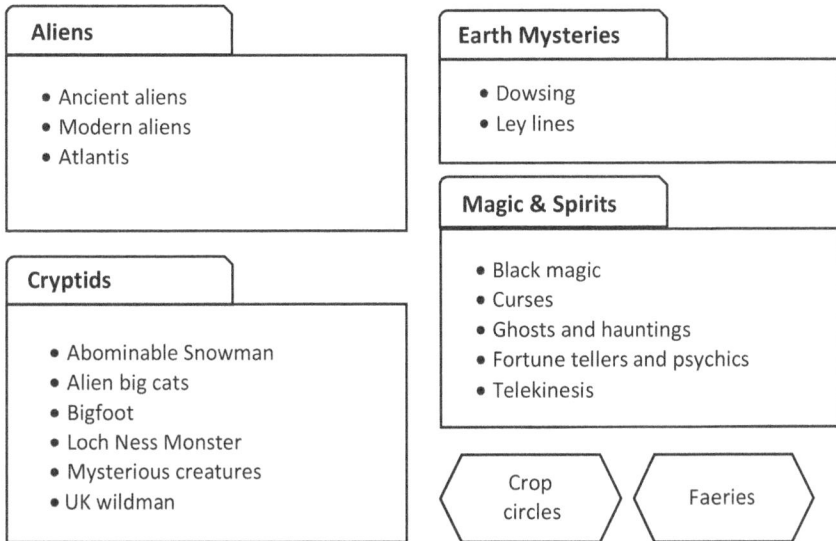

Figure 2.4 Paranormal clusters.

Some clusters align closely to our concepts of *enlightenment* and *discovery* paranormal orientations. For example, belief in the Abominable Snowman, ABCs, the American Bigfoot, British Bigfoot, Nessie, and the general belief in mysterious creatures clustered together. These beliefs all typically align closely with what we would call a *discovery* orientation. We also found a cluster we label Magic and Spirits that includes belief in black magic, curses, the ability of fortune tellers and psychics to foresee the future, and the ability of some people to move objects with their minds (telekinesis). While this cluster also includes the belief that homes can be haunted, which often crosses into the realm of discovery, the Magic and Spirits cluster more closely aligns with an enlightenment perspective on the paranormal. By examining who seems to align with each cluster, we can gain further insight into who believes in the paranormal in general and also whether discovery and enlightenment perspectives are attracting different types of people.

Paranormal Profiling

We conducted a series of analyses that allowed us to gauge the extent to which ethnic identity, number of children, educational attainment, income, marital status, age, region of the country, and gender are related to clusters of paranormal beliefs, when all are considered simultaneously.[75] We also assessed the relative impact of a number of measures related to personal religiosity. This included whether someone identified as Catholic, Protestant, Church of England, Muslim, some other religion, atheist or agnostic. Respondents also reported how often they attend religious services (if at all), and what they think about the Bible. Is the Bible simply a book of stories, or the actual word of God? Those with more 'literalist' views of the Bible believe that it is a holy book written by God, and it should be taken as literally true, word-for-word. Our analyses allowed us to determine how all of these personal characteristics, practices and beliefs related to paranormal beliefs, as well as the relative strength of those effects.

Discovery: Cryptids

Consider our profile of a typical believer in cryptids (see Figure 2.5).

People who scored very high on the cryptid factor believe in more creatures with greater certainty. The lower someone scored on the cryptid factor, the less certainty that they had about cryptids, or the fewer of them they believed in.[76] Each of the factors presented in Figure 2.5 was significantly related to higher levels of cryptid belief. Personal characteristics that are not significantly related to cryptid beliefs are not listed.

Some of the personal characteristics presented are statuses, meaning that people of a certain *type* had higher cryptid scores. Respondents who were currently separated from their spouse or partner had higher levels of cryptid belief than people of other marital statuses, for example. Sometimes the relevant status is *not* being something. People in our sample who reported a marital status as something

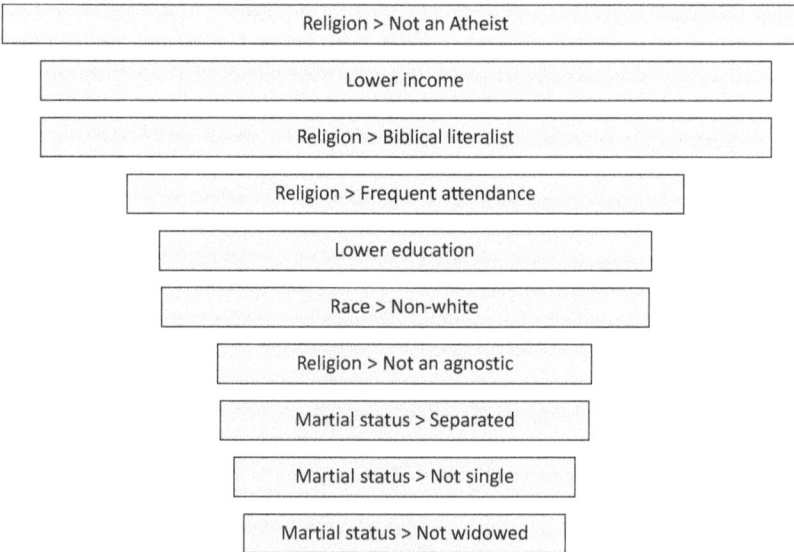

Figure 2.5 Cryptid believer profile (CASPAR, 2021).

other than single or widowed had higher levels of cryptid beliefs than single or widowed respondents.

Other characteristics range from lower to higher, such as education. The lower a person's level of education, the higher their average level of belief in cryptids tended to be. Put another way, people who did not complete their secondary education were more likely to believe in mysterious creatures than those who have a college degree. We also found that religious attendance was positively related to cryptid belief. The more frequently people report attending religious services, the higher their average scores on the cryptid belief scale. There is, however, a limit to this positive effect, as we document in Chapter 7.

The wider the bar in Figure 2.5, the greater the effect a particular personal characteristic had upon cryptid belief.[77] Assume that one desires to predict if a British citizen believes in cryptids. If allowed to ask only one question about a personal characteristic, it would be best to ask the person if he or she is an atheist. Atheists were half as likely as non-atheists to believe in monsters. For example, nearly one-fourth (24 per cent) of our non-atheist respondents believed in Nessie. Only 12 per cent of atheists believed the same. The Yeti fared just as poorly amongst atheists. Ten per cent of atheists believe in the Abominable Snowman compared to twice as many (20 per cent) non-atheists. ABCs fared slightly better, with atheists lagging only six points behind non-atheists in levels of belief (18 per cent atheists/24 per cent non-atheists). But the pattern is clear – atheists are less likely to suffer a monster.

The more of the characteristics noted above that a person possesses, the more confident we can be that they are cryptid enthusiasts.

As discussed in the previous chapter, gender is a very strong predictor of enlightenment-oriented beliefs and practices, but it is not predictive of the discovery oriented beliefs in cryptids. Knowing if someone is male or female will not help you guess whether or not they believe in Nessie. Gender *does* help us, however, when it comes to Magic and Spirits.

Enlightenment: Magic and Spirits

Since the paranormal clusters into distinctive groupings (see Figure 2.4), it is possible that cryptid believers are considerably different than those who believe in other types of things. After all, believing in out-of-place big cats does not seem particularly similar to thinking it is possible that fortune tellers can see the future.

When it comes to Magic and Spirits, a more complicated profile emerges than for cryptid believers, with twelve personal characteristics associated with belief (see Figure 2.6). There were two key differences between the clusters. Age was *not* associated with cryptid belief, but when it comes to Magic and Spirits, younger people expressed higher levels of acceptance. As we will see in the next chapter, younger people are particularly more attracted to ghosts than older people. Also, consistent with our expectations and from what we found at the psychic fair, women were more likely to believe in black magic, curses, psychic phenomena and ghosts than were men. Someone's gender will not tell you much about whether

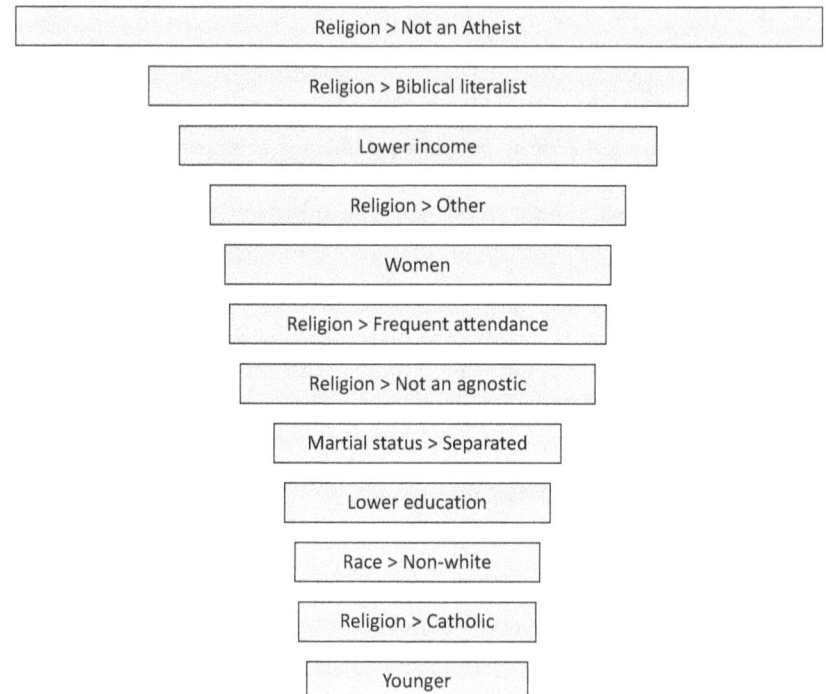

Figure 2.6 Magic and spirits believer profile (CASPAR, 2021).

they believe in Bigfoot, but women are far more likely to believe in phenomena such as fortune telling than are men.

Other than gender and age, however, the two profiles were very similar, telling us that some things are predictors of paranormalism in general. One of those characteristics is religion. As with cryptid belief, non-atheism again emerges triumphant as the single largest predictor of belief in Magic and Spirits. It seems a person must believe that something exists outside of the material world in order to engage with the paranormal. Further, biblical literalists, those of minority religions, frequent religious service attenders, non-agnostics and Catholics all showed higher levels of belief. Also consistent with the belief in cryptids, both education and income made an appearance, with higher levels of either associated with lower levels of belief in ghosts and magic. The fact that people with lower levels of income and education tend to embrace the paranormal, as do those with religious orientations, aligns with previous research and theory. For example, sociologists have long speculated that religion and the paranormal might be interconnected.

A Small Step?

In 1978, influential American sociologist of religion Robert Wuthnow published *Experimentation in American Religion*. Subtitled 'The New Mysticisms and Their Implications for the Churches', the book explored the impact that growing interest in the paranormal might have upon established, organized church groups. Wuthnow assumed that religious people would find the paranormal heretical and was surprised to find belief in God to be positively associated with both belief in ESP and related experiences. Further, more than half of Catholics and Protestants in his sample claimed to have experienced ESP themselves. Ultimately, Wuthnow concluded that 'one kind of belief in supernatural phenomena reinforces another'.[78] The argument that religion and the paranormal should be associated because of their inherent similarities became known as the small step hypothesis.[79]

Our survey findings clearly indicate that conventional religion is a key part of the story of the paranormal in the UK. The most important personal characteristic predicting both Cryptids and Magic and Spirits was belief in God. Atheists are much less likely to believe in the paranormal. These findings suggest that some level of conventional religiosity opens one up to other forms of supernatural expression. Church attendance and biblical literalism showed up in both profiles. If we want to know about a person's paranormal proclivities, it is best to know what they think about the Bible, how often they attend religious services and their religious affiliation. There is more to the story of religion and the paranormal than a simple positive relationship, and we will detail the complicated dynamics between conventional religion and the paranormal in greater depth in Chapter 7.

Unlike Wuthnow, Karl Marx did not distinguish between organized forms of religious belief and paranormal beliefs. For him, the supernatural, in all its forms, operated in the same way. Believing in something unseen and beyond the trials of material existence provided comfort to those on the margins of society, he argued. Supernatural belief is merely the 'sigh of the oppressed creature'.[80] Marx's perspective would suggest that indicators that someone is on the margins of society, such as having a lower level of income or education, should be related to both religion and paranormality. Such arguments have become known as marginalization hypotheses.

The profiles of Cryptid and Magic and Spirit believers do lend some support to marginalization arguments. Having a lower level of income was significantly related to higher levels of both types of paranormal belief, as was having a lower level of education and identifying as a racial or ethnic minority. This is evidence that, whatever one's preferred explanation, those with less social power do indeed drift towards culturally marginalized beliefs. This pattern held with all the different belief clusters.

But we do not find strong evidence for generalist marginalization arguments that have focused upon gender.[81] With lower average levels of social capital, women tend to have lower levels of perceived control and, so the argument goes, might be more likely to engage with the paranormal to find it. Perhaps the desire for control is indeed a reason that women are more attracted to enlightenment forms of the paranormal, but gender is not an effective predictor of non-enlightenment forms of paranormal expression. Instead of a general effect, it seems that the 'feminization of spirituality' is a key explanation for why women are more drawn to enlightenment paranormal beliefs, but not discovery beliefs.[82]

Our finding that younger people are more attracted to magic and spirits, however, proved to be both unexpected and important. Ghosts, for example, are a thriving area within the paranormal and one that is particularly attractive to younger people. To learn more about why that is the case, we must return to the home of the dreaded Black Monk of Pontefract.

Chapter 3

MOST HAUNTED

The Evolution of a Haunting

Britain is a 'ghost-ridden nation', and it abounds with locations that simply *look* haunted.¹ Imposing fortresses cover hillsides. Ancient graveyards and abandoned churches shrouded by trees dot the landscape. Old battle sites, bridges curving over dark rivers and stone circles of unknown purpose seem designed for housing spirits. When we started looking for notoriously haunted sites for this project, we searched for the 'most haunted locations in the UK'. We expected to visit an ancient castle, a darkened crypt or maybe a decrepit estate.

But one place kept turning up in our searches: 30 East Drive in Pontefract, England. It was none of these things.² Perhaps the most remarkable thing about 30 East Drive is how unremarkable it is.³ This simple, two-story, brick, semidetached council house has no crumbling stone walls, ancient graves or rolling fogs hiding unseen horrors. It sits amongst other council homes near a primary school, a four-minute walk from a chippy and an Indian restaurant. Other than its castle, the market town of Pontefract (population about 30,000) outside Wakefield in West Yorkshire, offers little in the way of tourist attractions. Those unaware of the home's supposed spectral occupant would pass it by without a second thought. But the current owner asserts that the property is inhabited by 'one of the most violent poltergeists in the world'. That claim has been heavily publicized on television, in film and on the internet, and it has turned 30 East Drive into a major tourist attraction for would-be ghost hunters.

Several things had to happen for an average-looking council house to become 'the most spine chilling and evil place … in the world', as television presenter Yvette Fielding once called it.⁴

All purportedly haunted houses benefit from increasing belief in ghosts over time, particularly amongst younger people. The inherent flexibility of ghost narratives helps to maintain their popularity, while the enduring ritual power of ghost hunts is also attractive to thrill-seekers and the curious. However, 30 East Drive has especially benefited from these trends due to the creation of a highly marketable villain, the 'Black Monk of Pontefract' – who is now situated within a narrative that remains flexible enough to allow alternative interpretations for those disinclined to believe in a demonic clergyman *and* those who are willing enough

Photo 3.1 Outside 30 East Drive in Pontefract, England, at night.

to seek him out. This flexible narrative has proved to be powerful enough to draw widespread media coverage and was effectively publicized by an entrepreneurial owner with close ties to the media. It was all of these factors combined that resulted in us standing in front of an otherwise unremarkable council house on a cold winter night, searching for one of Britain's most notorious ghosts.

This chapter will explain how it all happened. We are not going to tell a ghost story exactly, but rather the story of a ghost story.

The Ghost

In August of 1966, Jean and Joe Pritchard of Pontefract took their daughter, Diane, away on a bank holiday weekend. This left their son, Phillip, in the care of his grandmother, Sarah Scholes, at the family home on 30 East Drive.

That afternoon Phillip returned from the backyard to find his grandmother, Sarah, enveloped in a cloud of greyish-white powder as she sat knitting in a chair. There was no obvious source for the chalky haze, which did not seem to originate from the ceiling.[5] Assuming a natural explanation at first, Phillip, Sarah, her daughter Marie, and some neighbours investigated further.[6] It quickly became clear that something strange was going on. The group found pools of water in the kitchen. Tea and sugar began pouring from a dispenser, a potted plant moved by itself, and crockery rattled in the drawer. When Sarah saw the wardrobe in the corner of Phillip's room swaying from side to side, she had had enough. Sarah gathered Phillip and the two went to spend the night with her daughter Marie Kelly, who lived opposite with her husband Vic.

Vic was perturbed by the events. He called the police, who were unable to find an intruder or signs of forced entry. Vic then remembered that another neighbour up the street, a Mr O'Donald, was a ghost enthusiast.[7] It was after midnight, but O'Donald was still awake and came to 30 East Drive to investigate, alongside Vic and Marie. O'Donald did not witness anything himself but was convinced by what he heard. He informed Vic and Marie that 30 East Drive had a poltergeist. If this was the case, they would experience more strange happenings soon. He had an oddly specific warning in this regard: 'They're very fond of tearing up photographs, I believe.'[8] Shortly after O'Donald had left for the evening, Marie and Vic were locking up the home when they heard a crash. Sure enough, when they went to investigate, they found a wedding photograph of Jean and Joe Pritchard slashed from end to end, as if with a knife.

Ghost Stories

Given that ghosts exist in a liminal state and are believed to haunt particular places, it is not surprising that the living have always speculated about the identity of spirits and tried to discern the reasons why they might be here. People like to tell and hear stories about ghosts, and British fiction is filled with dramatic spectres, such as Jacob Marley and the ghost of Hamlet's father.[9] Of course, outside of fiction, spirits rarely appear to specify that 'I am thy father's spirit'.[10] Rather, a ghost's story is often cobbled together over time, based on the history of a location, rumours, and purported phenomena experienced at that location, all guided by prevailing cultural theories about the nature of ghosts.[11]

If a property attracts would-be ghost hunters, they will play a vital role in evolving the ghost narrative. As ghost hunters attempt to interact with the spirits at a haunted property, events will occur that require explanation. The ghost hunters will hear strange noises. Someone will feel they have been touched by unseen hands or see something moving out of the corner of their eye. The group must then discuss the events in real time and try to come to an agreement as to whether they have experienced a ghost or if there is a natural explanation instead.[12] The plethora of technology used by ghost hunters vastly expands the possibilities for perceived anomalous events to occur. When a K2 meter detects an electromagnetic fluctuation, has a ghost moved by? Or was the ghost hunter just too close to an electrical outlet? Ghost Boxes, which cycle through radio stations and stop long enough to hear a word or two, along with software like Alice Box, which continually tosses out words and phrases, add further evidence to be interpreted. Those present can decide if 'banana,' 'bank' or 'death' have anything to do with the haunting at hand. Wandering about a creaky, dark, old house provides plenty of sensory material for an emergent ghost tale. Once the constant beeps, flashing lights, and random words from ghost hunting equipment are tossed into the mix, there is a surplus of available stimuli from which to shape a narrative of spiritual contact.

The inherent ambiguity of ghostly evidence allows for multiple interpretations of the identity and purpose of the ghost. Contested lore also sets multiple possible expectations as to what one might experience in a location.[13] When evidence involves banging on the walls, the beeping of electronic equipment or the movement of objects, how are we to know if there is evil or good intent? It is up to the ghost investigators to decide what they are dealing with. Ghosts could be the shades of humans with unfinished business on Earth, desperate to communicate their reasons for not 'passing over.'[14] Or the phenomena experienced in a home may simply be a psychic 'recording' of past events, lacking intelligence or motivation.[15] Those open to religious interpretations can ascribe particularly violent hauntings to demonic entities. There is even a ghost for those of a more Freudian bent: the poltergeist.

The Poltergeist

'Poltergeist' refers to a spirit from Germanic folklore that delights in making loud noises and moving objects; 'rumble spirit', in direct translation.[16] Early references to poltergeists assumed them to be raucous spirits or demons, but in the Victorian era, theories emerged that did not rely upon religious concepts for explanation. Ghost investigators noted that poltergeist phenomena often happened in homes with teens of pubescent age. The theory was that the angst and uncertainty suffered by kids who are maturing sexually or living in distressed households might somehow produce psychic energy that projects itself as poltergeist phenomena; the emergent libido manifests as a ghost.

This is the theory that O'Donald expressed to Vic and Marie – that the true 'cause' of the strange phenomena was Phillip, the fifteen-year-old son of Jean and Joe Pritchard. Despite sitting at 30 East Drive until 1.45 am, O'Donald had not witnessed any phenomena himself and suspected this was because Phillip was not present. He did not think that Phillip was hoaxing. Rather, he argued that the bizarre mist, pools of water, moving objects and banging sounds were manifestations of psychic energy unconsciously released by the teen.

Phillip and his grandmother moved back to 30 East Drive the next day. The home was quiet. No more objects moved. No pools of water appeared, nor did any strange mists. When Joe and Jean Pritchard and their daughter Diane returned from holiday the following day, Joe was astonished, and sceptical, about what he heard. He asked what kind of knocking Phillip and Sarah had experienced, and 'as if in reply, there came three loud, distinct bangs, followed by a rattling of the window frames.'[17] But then there was silence for a long time after.

Mr O'Donald played a vital, early role in the evolution of what was to eventually become the 'Black Monk of Pontefract' by providing the earliest supernatural narrative to 'explain' what was happening. In telling Marie and Vic that 30

East Drive had a poltergeist, he labelled and organized otherwise disconnected phenomena. If Mr O'Donald was right, perhaps Phillip had released his pent-up psychic energy and now the phenomenon was over.

The fact that we still found ourselves in front of 30 East Drive on a cold winter night nearly sixty years later suggests there was far more to the tale.[18] Long departed psychosexual energy would provide little for subsequent visitors to encounter over half a century later. Yet again, the tale had evolved, adapting to its ever-changing cultural environment. Indeed, the wide variety of forms that ghosts can take ensures that any believer can find a home, with an accompanying narrative that suits their preferred explanation. East Drive has especially benefited from the ability of ghost narratives to incorporate everything from psychic energy to demonic manifestations. It turns out there was much more than a poltergeist at 30 East Drive.

The Retford Ghost Hunters

It was about 6.30 pm when we pulled up to 30 East Drive. The sun had already set.

We saw little purpose in visiting the property alone, other than, perhaps, to say that we did it. Our expertise is in studying people after all, not ghosts. Rather, our goal was to see how ghost investigators react to such a location, how such groups attempt to gather evidence of spirits, and ultimately enact and embody the practices of ghost hunting. We located a nearby ghost hunting group called the Retford Ghost Hunters (RGH) and asked them to spend the evening with us. They enthusiastically agreed.

RGH is an example of the increasingly popular subculture of ghost hunting groups. Many such teams are scattered about Britain. Some of them appear to be little more than a couple of members and an outdated web page. Others are quite active, with dedicated members, an organizational structure and frequent events and investigations. RGH is an example of the latter. The group is led by Rachel Parsons and at the time had twenty-six team members, including a business manager, a well-being specialist, a head moderator, a historian, and many dedicated ghost investigators with different areas of spiritual expertise.

We arranged to meet the team in Pontefract at 6.00 pm, but unexpected traffic delayed us, so the RGH members were already inside the house when we arrived. We knocked on the door and were warmly greeted by Rachel, who beckoned us to enter. During the evening, we learned that Rachel has always been able to 'see' spirits. She was once a born-again Christian but lost that faith. The time and effort she devotes to her ghostly pursuits have led to tensions with her close family, who remain religious, but she recites the story without melodrama or malice. There is a quiet and very purposeful authority in all that she does.

Our first impression of the home was that of an ordinary 1960s era, compact council home. A small water closet is to the right of the front door. Directly past that was another small room. This was a former coal shed. In front of us was the door to what was now the 'smoking room'. According to Rachel, neighbours had become irritated by ghost hunters talking outside late into the evening as they took smoke breaks. The current owner asks visitors to take those breaks in this back room, the walls of which are plastered with news clippings and anomalous photos taken at the property.

Rachel steered us to the left and into a small kitchen. At one end was a sink and some cupboards. Running along another wall were more cupboards and a counter on which RGH had arrayed an impressive collection of equipment they planned to use that evening.

Rachel's team was milling about the kitchen. Tonight, it was composed of four members besides her: Ron, Gary, Trevor and Will.

Ron describes himself as a 'sensitive' who can sometimes see spirits. He almost always has a smile on his face and a confident, if somewhat self-deprecating, humour. He has a particularly close relationship with Rachel (who also sees spirits), and they have a seamless, natural rhythm to their interactions. Gary suggests he is the group's sceptic. With an inquisitive and curious nature, he is quite happy to talk about his love of history and does all the research on sites the group visits. Trevor looks after a number of hotels at his day job and brings a 'no nonsense' approach to ghost hunting. He has an intensity about him and frequently berates and goads the spirits he interrogates. Will is much more circumspect. He suggests that he wasn't

Photo 3.2 Some of the Retford Ghost Hunters' equipment in the kitchen of 30 East Drive.

really into 'the paranormal' before he joined the group and is somewhat coy as the rest of the team teases him about being scared of his own shadow.

The camaraderie that exists between the team is palpable. Constantly making and sipping tea, they talk about stopping smoking, vaping, diets, food, and their future plans as a team. Ron is even making the thirty-mile move to Retford to be closer to the group. 'It just makes sense' because 'this is where [his] life is now'. Will suggests that the team is 'the best it has ever been'.[19] Each member clearly brings a different emotional character to their ghostly encounters.

The team enthusiastically told us of our plans for the evening and showed off its extensive ghost hunting equipment. Ron was both excited and wary. It seems that, as they awaited our arrival, the group had 'heard growling from upstairs, and something was walking around up there.' We asked Ron if he had gone upstairs to investigate the noises, to which he replied, 'There is no way I am going up there alone'.

Whether or not ghosts exist, and independent of what spirits may do, their true power is predicated upon humans' belief in their existence. After all, there are many available alternative explanations for hearing a growling noise and movement from the upstairs of an ageing council home. The RGH team may have heard a television in the attached home next door, or a dog outside. Maybe a heating system turned on, making strange noises when heard from downstairs. For Ron, these sounds had taken on a sinister air though because (a) he believes in ghosts, and (b) he was standing in a place notorious for ghost activity. This is not to suggest Ron is gullible just because his pre-existing beliefs happened to colour his interpretation of his experiences. That is the case for all of us, regardless of what our specific beliefs may be. Ghosts are just especially dependent upon our belief in them, as by their very nature, the identification of a ghost requires the assessment of ambiguous phenomena.

Thankfully for ghosts, belief in them continues to demonstrate cross-cultural popularity as one of the most common types of paranormalism (see Figure 3.1).[20]

We asked our random sample of British adults the extent to which they agree with the statement 'places can be haunted by spirits'. More than one-third of respondents (over 37 per cent) either strongly agreed or 'tend to agree' that places can be haunted. Nearly another third (29 per cent) are uncertain about the issue (neither agree nor disagree). Only one-fifth (20 per cent) of the respondents write off the possibility of hauntings entirely by strongly disagreeing. It seems that in Britain, ghosts have a good chance of being noticed.

If we choose to believe in ghosts, as many people do, we might also assume that the growling heard coming from upstairs by RGH members did not have a natural explanation. But what could it be then? Why would the frustrated psychosexual energy of a teenager be growling at ghost hunters nearly sixty years later? It seems the narrative had indeed evolved. The spectral phenomena returned to 30 East Drive and morphed into an entity – something that could torment the Pritchards in the 1960s *and* still linger around to growl at Ron and his fellow ghost hunters more than half a century later.

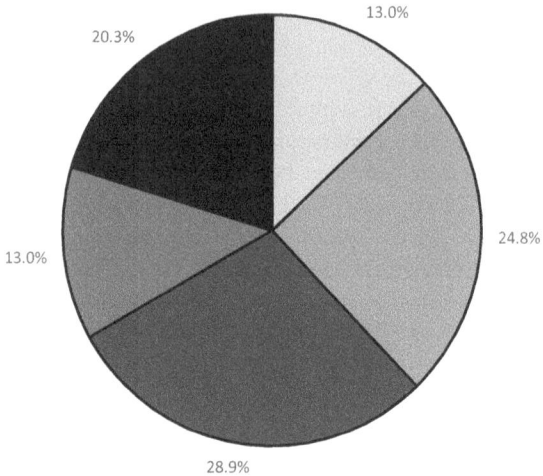

☐ Strongly Agree ☐ Tend to Agree ■ Neither Agree Nor Disagree ■ Tend to Disagree ■ Strongly Disagree

Figure 3.1 Belief that places can be haunted by spirits (CASPAR, 2021).

The Ghost (Returns)

In August of 1968, Jean was unable to sleep and decided to go downstairs. As she made her way onto the landing, a paintbrush and a paste bucket flew past her head, and a roll of wallpaper levitated like a snake in front of her. This was accompanied by a brush that swung violently from side to side in the air. When Jean cried out for help, Joe, Phillip and Diane appeared, only to be besieged by paint brushes themselves. Whatever its cause, the activity had resumed. According to the Pritchards, in the months that followed, a grandfather clock was thrown down the stairs, a cupboard full of china was smashed, and something threw a jug of milk at a family member.

Diane increasingly found herself the centre of attention. One night she was pinned to the stairs by a piece of oak furniture and an electric sewing machine. Despite her mother's attempts to free her, she remained stuck until she stopped fighting, and the force holding her down seemed to ease. When she went to bed that night an unseen force pulled off her blankets, levitated the mattress, and dumped Diane to the ground. She once again found herself pinned to the ground, this time by the mattress. As before, the pressure eventually released, and Diane could go back to bed, but the same thing happened four more times that night. During these events, Diane felt a presence in the room but could not see anyone.

By this point, the Pritchard family felt they were dealing with an entity that had an independent personality, not simply an amorphous, psychic energy. Sometimes this 'entity' was playful. At other times it seemed angry and determined to frighten. They took to calling it 'Mr Nobody,' although Jean Pritchard preferred the friendlier sounding label of 'Fred.'

It did not take long for this renewed activity to attract media attention. The *Yorkshire Evening Post* published a story on 11 September 1968, that introduced 'Mr Nobody' to readers.[21] Police were called to investigate on at least two occasions without success, while would-be ghost hunters camped out on the front lawn hoping to catch a glimpse of an apparition.

Diane initially thought Mr Nobody/Fred intended no harm. However, one evening as she entered the kitchen, the door closed behind her, and the lights suddenly went out. Jean heard her daughter scream. Jean and Phillip rushed into the hallway, where they witnessed Diane being dragged up the stairs by a disembodied hand holding her throat. They ran up the stairs after her and tried to pull her back down. When Mr Nobody finally let her go, they all tumbled to the floor. Diane's neck was covered in red finger marks.[22]

Rituals of Ghost Hunting

The evolution of the phenomena at 30 East Drive into Mr Nobody was an extremely important development for its ongoing viability as a pilgrimage location for ghost hunters. Unlike a poltergeist, 'Mr Nobody' seemingly had its own motivations and desires, inscrutable as they might be. This provided a shared focus for ghost hunters, someone or something with which they might try to communicate.

When a group of people get together with a shared focus to their interactions, it can result in a sense of greater purpose, positive emotional energy, and a 'we' feeling.[23] Sociologist Émile Durkheim labelled group interactions with a shared purpose as 'rituals', and noted their importance in generating and maintaining group solidarity.[24] Ghost hunters/investigators engage in many collective ritual activities designed to communicate with spirits. Throughout the course of a typical ghost hunt, investigators will enact various types of ritual practices using different equipment or props in the hopes of soliciting communication with spirits.

Whatever the means used, there is a general pattern to each communication attempt, perhaps best described as a call-and-response cycle. A ghost hunter acts as 'expert host'. They lead the call by providing instructions to those assembled on how the communication technique will work, setting the questions, and deciding the tone and intensity through which questions are delivered. The host will then ask those assembled to 'listen for' and interpret any responses. Claimed responses from spirits take different forms in relation to the technology being used. The simplest technique is to simply 'call out' and ask a spirit to respond to a question by making a noise – perhaps a bang on the wall, or to actively move something – such as a ball or toy car. Alternatively, the ghost hunter might use an Ouija board (or other 'spirit board') to capture any responses, or ask the ghost to manipulate dowsing rods held in the hands of a participant.[25] The more technical approaches build on this basic structure according to the communicative capacity of a technology. An electromagnetic field (EMF) meter shows a light reading; radiating electromagnetic (REM) pods sound an alarm; a spirit box will cycle through radio signals and stop long enough to produce words.[26]

Obviously, a loud pounding on a wall or a response from a spirit box that seems directly related to a question asked will produce much excitement amongst those present. But there is power in ghost hunting rituals, even when the results are subtle or seemingly random or contradictory. For ghost hunters, there is always the *possibility*, but not certainty, that they will be able to coax an interaction from a ghost.

But even if that interaction does not happen, it does not mean that ghosts do not exist or are not at the property. Rather, the ghost itself may have been uninterested in appearing that evening, or the group may have brought the wrong 'energy' to the proceedings, or they may have angered the ghost by asking the wrong questions, or perhaps there was simply bad luck.[27] The ambiguity of ghost evidence ensures that a ghost hunt can never truly fail from their standpoint.

From a sociological standpoint, ghost hunting rituals provide a combination of both structure and improvisation that tends to produce positive, emotional energy, at least in terms of the feelings between group members, if not always between members and perceived spirits. By locking into the same beliefs and rituals together, team members create strong group cohesion, a shared sense of identity, and are highly likely to engage in such ritual practices again with group members in the future.[28]

RGH's goal for the evening was to contact any ghosts present, preferably Mr Nobody/Fred. The night proceeded through a series of unscripted activities. RGH members would frequently confer and decide what type of communication technique they would try and in what part of the house particular experiments would take place. Small groups would then spread throughout the home. All of us were rarely together in the same spot. In each location, RGH members would tell all those present how the particular technique would work and then begin the call-and-response practices.

The group made frequent use of a software program called 'Alice Box', which was running on a laptop. Alice Box uses a word bank. On occasion, the software will beep, and a word will appear on the screen. To the viewer it appears that the program is randomly drawing a word from its bank at varying intervals to display on the screen. The developers of the software claim that spirits, in fact, manipulate the software in response to questions, somehow compelling it to display a meaningful word or phrase. At times the Alice Box sat quietly for long periods. At others, words and phrases would appear in quick succession. This technique provides a built-in interpretive dimension, as it was up to the ghost hunters to determine what the spirit meant by each word.

We joined Trevor and Will in one of the bedrooms upstairs at 30 East Drive. The room had little furniture in it. A twin bed was against one wall. A chair and a small dresser were next to the bed. Trevor placed a laptop running Alice Box on the chair. He also placed a toy car on the floor that would light up and make sounds when it sensed movement, along with a small ball that would light up when touched.

This offered the spirit multiple potential lines of communication. It could use the Alice Box if it wanted, or if it preferred, announce its presence by touching the car or ball. Trevor sat on the bed next to the laptop. The rest of us found places to sit as Trevor and Will began the call and (hopefully) response:

> So, spirits of 30 East Drive, we are coming to this next bedroom now. We really want to start talking to you tonight. We want you to talk to us, actually. If you could come forward to give us a sign just to let us know that you're here. Could you make a knock for us?
> We are going to be quiet for you. We want you to make as much noise as possible.
> We have a little ball on the floor. Just give it a little roll and it'll flash.
> And if you come close to this car here it'll flash green.

After each call, there would be a long pause as the group waited quietly for something to happen. Once some time had elapsed, Trevor or Will would try another prompt, or on occasion, and more frequently as time passed, goad the spirit into action. For Trevor, this included using the name of the presumed ghost.

> Is Fred here? If Fred's here, come on …
> *[Long pause]*
> I don't think Fred's here if he can't touch one of these toys.
> *[Long pause]*
> Fred if you want us to leave and don't want us here, if you have had enough of people like us coming to talk to you, set one of these off and we'll go.
> Move one of these pieces of equipment and make it flash.

The Alice Box beeped intermittently, and Trevor would read the displayed word or phrase in a deadpan voice. If that word seemed somehow related to the most recently asked question, Trevor or Will would comment, and perhaps ask a follow-up. If the word seemed unrelated, Trevor would simply speak it aloud and move on:

Alice Box	[Beeps and displays 'Can Appear']
Trevor	Can appear.
Will	We would love for you to appear!
Trevor	Can you show yourself by touching one of these [referring to the ball and car on the ground] and let us know you are here?
Alice Box	[Beeps and displays 'Ropes']
Trevor	Ropes.
Alice Box	[Beeps and displays 'Figurine']
Trevor	Figurine.
Will	Can you tell us your name on this box?
Alice Box	[Beeps and displays 'I'm Nobody']

This pronouncement obviously produced excitement. The Alice Box had name dropped 30 East Drive's resident ghost.

Trevor	Come on Mr. Nobody! You've told us you're here, so I'm sure you can do some more for us.
	[Long pause]
Will	Come on Fred! I'm gonna call you by your actual name. Use all that energy tonight. I'd love you to touch that ball on the floor just to confirm that you're here.

Trevor and Will then accused Fred of horrible crimes in the past, trying to anger the spirit and prompt some action. By this point, co-author Tom began reading what appeared on the Alice Box, allowing the ghost hunters to tag team their interrogation of the spirit.

Trevor	Fred do you know about the well? Come on. Tell us.
Will	We've heard about you being thrown down the well after you did all that horrible stuff to those women in the woods. You was hung for your crimes wasn't you? And it's believed that your body is now underneath this house. Could you confirm that for us?
Alice Box	[Beeps and displays 'Thoroughly trained']
Trevor	Thoroughly trained.
Alice Box	[Beeps and displays 'Can't breathe']
Trevor	Can't breathe.
Will	You can't breathe when you're being hung! Don't you have something to prove? That you exist? You have not shown yourself for a very long time. Surely you'd like to be seen again? Or heard again?
Alice Box	[Beeps and displays 'Stirred']
Tom	Stirred.
Alice Box	[Beeps and displays 'Heart failed']
Tom	Heart failed
Will	Heart failed!
Alice Box	[Beeps and displays 'Malevolent']
Tom	Malevolent
Trevor	Come on malevolent spirit! Show us what you got!

Unfortunately, or fortunately, depending on your perspective, no malevolent spirit appeared. What was ultimately the most meaningful to RGH was the appearance of 'I'm Nobody' on the Alice Box. This led Trevor and Will to focus their efforts on communication with Mr Nobody/Fred.

Yet, they also taunted Fred by referring to a series of murders and implying that the ghost had been hanged for his crimes in the distant past. To understand these accusations, we must go back to the 1980s, when author Colin Wilson helped to popularize a full backstory for 'Fred', transforming him from a literal nobody into the demonic Black Monk of Pontefract, propelling 30 East Drive further down the road towards 'most haunted' status.

An Evil Spirit

Despite significant local coverage in the late 1960s, the 30 East Drive tale did not come to immediate wider public attention. In fact, we might not know about the haunting as anything more than local folklore were it not for the 1981 publication of Colin Wilson's *Poltergeist! A Study in Destructive Haunting*.[29] Wilson was a prolific author of both fiction and non-fiction across a variety of genres, perhaps best known for his books on the metaphysical, including *The Occult: A History* (1971) and *Mysteries: An Investigation into the Occult, the Paranormal, and the Supernatural* (1978). Like much of Wilson's later output, *Poltergeist!* is mostly a collection of second-hand stories, littered with idiosyncratic commentary. But the account of 30 East Drive is something rather different.

Wilson first learned about the Pontefract case from a local historian named Tom Cunniff and was sufficiently intrigued by the details to visit in August of 1980 to interview witnesses. Given the novel content, the story of 30 East Drive ended up receiving a chapter of its own in Wilson's book, including many events we do not have the space to cover here.[30]

Poltergeist! unintentionally highlights the great malleability and flexibility of ghost tales, for Wilson and Cunniff developed very different theories as to the cause of the haunting. Wilson's preferred theory was similar to what Mr O'Donald had told the Pritchard family. He believed that a poltergeist had manifested, drawn by conflict in the home and the psychosexual energy of a pubescent Phillip.[31] Unlike O'Donald, Wilson attributed intelligence to the poltergeist, labelling it 'some kind of elemental' that was drawn to the psychic energy of the household and empowered by an underground stream running beneath the home.[32] Diane had ultimately become the focus of the poltergeist's attentions, he argued, because she had latent psychic powers. Once that energy was no longer available to it, the poltergeist 'again became inactive'.[33]

Cunniff's theory was quite different from Wilson; he believed the haunting was caused by the ghost of a murderous monk, dressed in black. The Pontefract area had been home to a priory inhabited by Cluniac monks until 1539. One of the Pritchards' neighbours had discovered records at the local library indicating that a monk had raped a young girl in the time of Henry VIII and been hanged for his crimes. Further, the local gallows were located on a site called 'Priest's Bridge' – apparently where 30 East Drive now stood. Was the spectre at 30 East Drive the evil spirit of a murderous monk? In fact, several people associated with the case had seen something that resembled a monk. Jean and Joe briefly witnessed a figure in a dark robe outside their bedroom door one evening.[34] Phillip and Diane had seen a similar figure standing in the kitchen. On another morning, a neighbour felt a presence behind her and turned to find a tall, lurking figure dressed in a black, monk robe that vanished upon being seen.

Wilson was sceptical of the 'Black Monk' narrative and could find no records of a rapist monk at the local library.[35] Wilson's scepticism and the historical truth of the Black Monk are of little importance, however, to its narrative power. The tale provided the property with a marquee ghost: a named villain with whom future visitors could match wits.

Right Ghost, Right Time

The flexibility of ghost narratives, the ambiguity of the related evidence, and the ritual power of ghost hunting lend power to all haunted locations, not just 30 East Drive. But sometimes a place gets lucky and gets the right ghost at the right time. Cunniff provided the property with an evil clergyman as its spirit, at a time when belief in ghosts was rising, and simultaneously faith in organized religion was waning.

The website *British Religion in Numbers* (BRIN) is a resource that provides a wide array of statistics about topics related to religion and spirituality, gathered from government and historical sources, as well as public opinion polls. BRIN gathers data from multiple polls to show how specific beliefs or affiliations have changed over time. They provide one such figure tracking ghost belief.[36] BRIN located national polls that asked the British public if they believed in ghosts that were administered between 1951 and 2008. As the site warns, we must be cautious when interpreting changes from these numbers, as exact question wordings varied slightly between surveys, as did sample sizes and the mode of survey collection (face-to-face vs. telephone, etc.).[37] With such cautions in mind, these numbers still allow us to estimate general trends (see Figure 3.2).

In March of 1950 the Gallup Organization surveyed the British public and asked them 'Do you believe in ghosts?' At the time, only 10 per cent said 'yes'. But by 1981, the year that *Poltergeist!* was first published, nearly one-fourth of

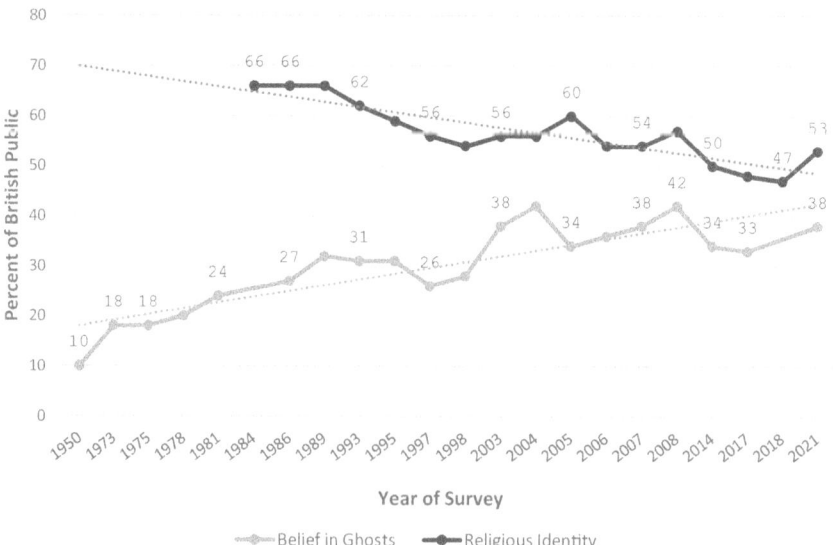

Figure 3.2 Belief in ghosts and religious identity in Britain by year.

the population (24 per cent) were expressing belief in ghosts. Levels have only increased from there. The numbers provided by BRIN end at 2008, so we appended data to the chart taken from two additional surveys in 2014 and 2017, as well as our CASPAR data from 2021.[38] Belief in ghosts grew over the 1980s and then stabilized to about one-third of the population by the millennium. It is an upward trend, but may have plateaued. Only time and, hopefully, more consistent surveys about the paranormal, will tell.

As a contrast, we have also included data in Figure 3.2 about the percentage of citizens who claim affiliation with an organized religion. In 2019, sociologists David Voas and Steve Bruce collated data on religious affiliation from the British Social Attitudes Survey (BSAS) for the years 1983 through 2018. We have added to their data the most recently available wave of the BSAS (2021).[39] While numbers for ghost belief have climbed since the 1980s, conventional religious participation has steadily declined. In 1984, two-thirds of British citizens reported that they had a religious identity, meaning they claimed affiliation and membership with a religious organization. By the time we conducted CASPAR in 2021, just over half (53 per cent) of citizens claimed a religious identity.

We discuss the complicated relationship between conventional, organized religion and the paranormal in more depth in Chapter 7, but these mirrored, opposite trends are suggestive. As more individuals are losing their faith in conventional religions, many are continuing their relationship with the supernatural by pondering existential questions via ghosts. The developing 30 East Drive narrative clearly benefited from this fortuitous timing. Wilson and Cunniff introduced the wider public to what had mostly been a local story at a time when the public had become significantly more likely to be interested in the tale. Further, Cunniff provided a spectre that aligned well with the times. Who better to haunt a home in a time of religious scandals and declining confidence in organized religion than an evil, spectral monk?

Movie Star Monk

A commercial artist named Pat Holden recognized the power of the tale of an evil monk tormenting a family. Holden was born in 1965, just a five-minute walk from 30 East Drive. His mother Rene was a friend of the Pritchards who had, herself, witnessed a black-robed entity in the home. Holden was fascinated by this local legend and became determined to bring the story to theatres. In 2010 he teamed with an ad executive named Bil Bungay to secure financing.[40] A lot of compromises followed. Rather than being a docudrama, the final movie became a heavily fictionalized version of events. The story was moved to the 1970s and involved the fictional 'Maynard' family, as opposed to the Pritchards. Its title became *When the Lights Went Out*. The film was only a modest success, bringing in under £1 million worldwide.[41]

As it turns out, it was not the box office that turned the Black Monk into a spectral celebrity but rather the creative way that the producers marketed the film. During production, 30 East Drive came up for sale. The opportunistic Bil Bungay decided to buy it and organized a screening of the film there for the cast, crew, and two competition winners. That screening received little attention, but Bungay saw future potential in owning 30 East Drive. In 2014, Bungay launched the website, 30EastDrive.com, and started offering brave souls the opportunity to spend the night with the Monk. Bungay promoted the 'Black Monk' interpretation of events, as stated on the nascent site's intro page back in 2014:

> 10 years after the hauntings stopped … a young amateur historian, with an interest in the Cluniac Monks of Pontefract, heard about the case and became the first person to formally investigate.
>
> What he uncovered from the local newspaper reports sounded almost too good to be true: poltergeist phenomena apparently caused by the ghost of a Cluniac monk who had been hanged for rape in the time of Henry VIII.[42]

Bungay's savvy marketing elevated 30 East Drive from an out-of-the-way place where a haunting had once happened to a site where the daring could test their mettle against an evil spirit.[43]

Into the Coal Shed

Well into our evening with RGH, Trevor and Will had failed to rile up the Monk in the upstairs bedroom. Some meaningful words appeared on the Alice Box, but otherwise nothing much happened. RGH members often sorted themselves into different locations, hoping that a different room or a different technique might produce stronger supernatural results.

As we wandered the home, we often commented to one another about the vintage décor. The upstairs room we had just left had a poster of the Osmonds on one wall and Sergeant Pepper's Lonely Hearts Club Band on another. The drapes and furniture remind of council homes of the 1960s–70s era, lending the impression that the Pritchards had walked out the door that morning.

Unfortunately, it all quickly falls apart under any sort of rigorous examination. Richard Clayderman and Neil Diamond LPs from the 1980s are used to enhance the feeling of 'oldness', while videos that include 'F/X: Murder by Illusion' inhabit the glass cabinet. A DVD player lies behind a fairly new LCD television, which is itself draped with a very specially made cover that depicts the old 'BBC test card F'. The kitchen and associated utensils are old, but not old enough. We were, in fact, in a paranormal-themed attraction.

RGH member Gary asked one of us (Chris) to participate in an experiment in the coal shed downstairs. According to some recountings of the haunting, Joe Pritchard entered the coal shed one day and was 'attacked by some invisible force or malevolent entity'.[44] He reportedly emerged from the shed terrified. Subsequent ghost investigations at the home had reported similar 'attacks'.[45] Nowadays the tight space is occupied by a single chair. Two small shelves at the back hold a mirror, a hard hat, and a candle. A coat hangs on a hook on one of the side walls.

I was directed to sit in the chair and put on a blindfold and headphones (see Photo 3.3). Those headphones were connected to an iPad running a ghost hunting app called 'Necrophonic.' Gary, who would be overseeing the experiment, explained it to me. He would start the Necrophonic app. At that point I would hear the sounds from it and be unable to hear what he was saying. I was to concentrate on these sounds. If they somehow formed into a word, I was to say it aloud. As I was doing this, Ron would be asking questions that I could not hear. The hope was that the Monk would somehow manipulate the stream of white noise playing in my ears to communicate. If there was a clear answer to a question that I could not hear, this would be evidence of spirit communication, according to the group.

It was Gary's job to determine if the words that I said somehow related to the question he had asked and then react to that word by taking the questioning in a new direction. In effect, I had become the Alice Box, playing the role of a word generator providing clues for the team to interpret. At one point, I heard an assemblage of noises that reminded me of 'Tom', shortly after Gary had asked a question I could not hear. Co-author Tom Clark happened to be standing behind Gary watching the proceedings. Thus, Gary found the mention of his name meaningful:

Gary	What help do you need? How can we help you?
Chris	Tom!
Gary	Tom ... Tom ... well Tom's behind me. What do you want with Tom?
Chris	Bob.
Gary	Tom ... Tell me what you're gonna do to Tom.
	[Long pause]
Chris	Face.
Gary	Are you gonna touch his face? Please touch Tom in the face.
Chris	Face.
Gary	Yes! Yeah. His face. That's perfect yeah?
Chris	Bob.

Despite our best efforts, we had failed to entice the Monk to do anything truly impressive or frightening. If Mr Nobody was speaking to me as I sat in the coal shed, I could not hear him. If the Black Monk touched Tom, he did not feel it. We did not hear growls, nor see shadows. Thankfully for 30 East Drive, a bunch of underperforming academics will not make or break its reputation.

The property has directly benefited from the boom in popular paranormal television shows since the 2000s, which have focused on 30 East Drive several times. The dramatic events depicted in these ghost hunting shows at the property helped popularize and seal its sinister reputation.

'It's the most spine chilling and evil place I have ever experienced anywhere in the world'.

- Yvette Fielding on 30 East Drive[46]

Photo 3.3 Sensory experiment in the coal shed at 30 East Drive.

Yvette Fielding first achieved fame as a presenter on the children's television favourite *Blue Peter*. Today she is best known as the host of the popular, reality-based paranormal investigation program *Most Haunted*. Since premiering in 2002, the show has filmed over 300 episodes in a variety of purportedly haunted locations throughout Britain.

In 2015, the first two episodes of season 18 of *Most Haunted* were dedicated to a seemingly hair-raising investigation of the property. *Most Haunted* is well known for being quite dramatic in presentation. Even so, the results from 30 East Drive stand apart. A mysterious knife appeared between the cushions of a sofa; an apparition was seen in the bathroom window; a cross was captured by the camera as it flew across a bedroom; ping pong balls moved across the floor; a shadow appeared on a door; the spirit of a priest called 'Carl Anthony' told the team to 'get out'; dolls moved; the team felt increasingly queasy, and one of them collapsed; growls were heard; taps turned on by themselves, and two of the team received rope burns. Seemingly exhausted by these events, Fielding would close the second episode by suggesting: 'in over 350 investigations for *Most Haunted*, 30 East Drive takes the crown as being the most violent, most evil, and most haunted place we've been to date. We know many of you will follow us here, but be careful and please be safe'.[47]

A follow-up special, *Most Haunted Live! A Nightmare on East Drive*, attracted over half a million viewers, reportedly the largest ever audience for the channel *Really*.[48] This time the team heard laughing on an EVP recording; a table jumped during a séance; and said knife reappeared after being locked in a box. The most memorable scene is captured by the static camera at the bottom of the stairs. When the group hears a loud noise on the stairs, they rush to see what is happening. The director (and Fielding's husband) Karl Beattie appears and excitedly tells the crew that he was just pulled up the stairs. His neck is glowing red as if he had been strangled, and the static camera seemingly supports his version of events.[49]

The significant media attention garnered by 30 East Drive certainly helped it to become a central site of interest for any would-be ghost hunter. We used Google Trends to examine internet searches conducted in the UK for either the 'Black Monk of Pontefract', or '30 East Drive' from 2004 to 2022 (see Figure 3.3). The numbers represent how popular a Google search was in a given month, compared to all other searches. The higher the score (from 0 to 100), the more frequent that search was among users. A value of 100 means that the item was amongst the most popular. A score of 0 indicates that searches at the time were rare.[50]

The trend is clear. Despite the attention the case received from Colin Wilson, 30 East Drive was long forgotten by 2011. There is no wider interest until the release of *When the Lights Went Out* in 2012. In the aftermath of the film, there is a dramatic uptick in Google searches, particularly for the 'Black Monk of Pontefract.' Once *Most Haunted* broadcast its dramatic escapades in the home in 2015, searches for '30 East Drive' were amongst the most popular on Google in the UK. Since that time, interest in the site has remained relatively steady.

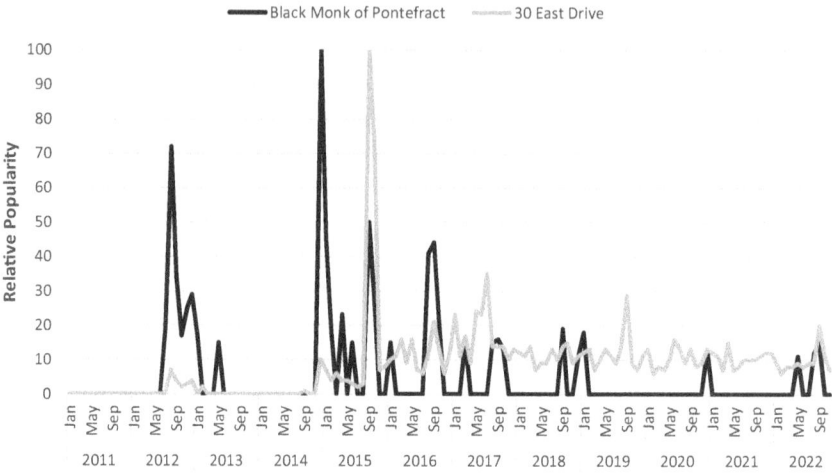

Figure 3.3 Popularity of Google searches related to 30 East Drive (2011–12).

Ghosts as Youth Movement

The fact that belief in ghosts and ghost-themed media are both on the rise leads to an obvious question: *Who* is most attracted to the concept of ghosts? We conducted a series of analyses designed to predict what types of people were most likely to believe in ghosts. People are complicated, and beliefs and behaviours never boil down to singular factors. But in our statistical models that predicted ghost-related beliefs, experiences and media consumption – which included a host of personal and social characteristics such as educational level, income, race/ethnicity, religiosity, region of residence, marital status, employment status and many others – the age of respondents kept appearing as a strong predictor (see Figure 3.4).

In addition to asking if they believe that places can be haunted, we asked respondents to the CASPAR survey if they thought that it was possible to 'communicate with the dead', which is clearly the goal of any proper ghost hunt.[51] Younger people are significantly more likely to believe in both hauntings and communication with the dead. Only about 12 per cent of respondents who were born between 1947 and 1956 (65–75 years old) believe that it is possible to communicate with spirits. Our youngest respondents (between 16 and 24 years old) were nearly *three times* as likely to believe in communication with the dead compared to the oldest respondents, with over one-third reporting this belief (36 per cent).[52] We see a similar pattern with belief in hauntings. The lowest level of belief was amongst the oldest respondents, 28 per cent of whom believe in hauntings. By contrast, more than two out of five (42 per cent) of the youngest respondents think hauntings are real.

There is a similar relationship between age and claiming ghost experiences (see Figure 3.5). We asked respondents if they had ever seen or experienced a ghost or

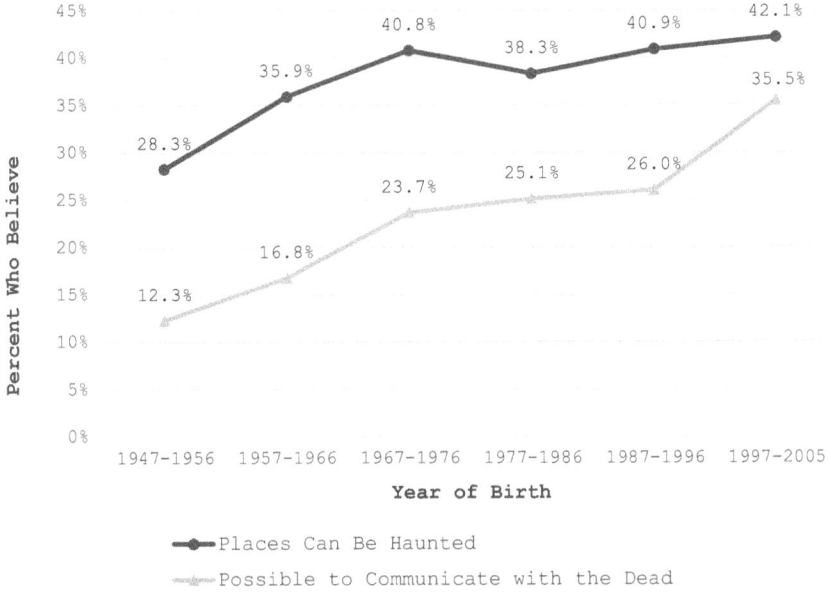

Figure 3.4 Ghost-related beliefs by year of birth (CASPAR, 2021).

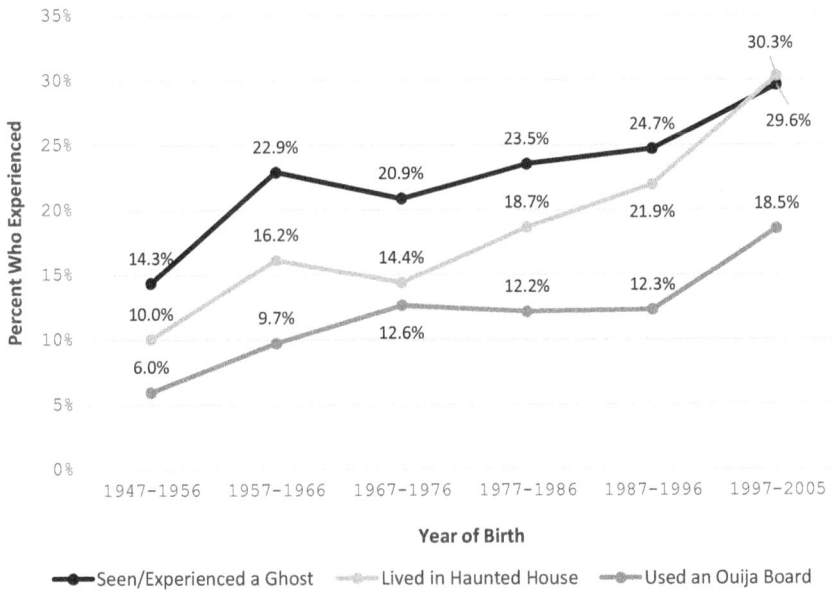

Figure 3.5 Ghost-related experiences by year of birth (CASPAR, 2021).

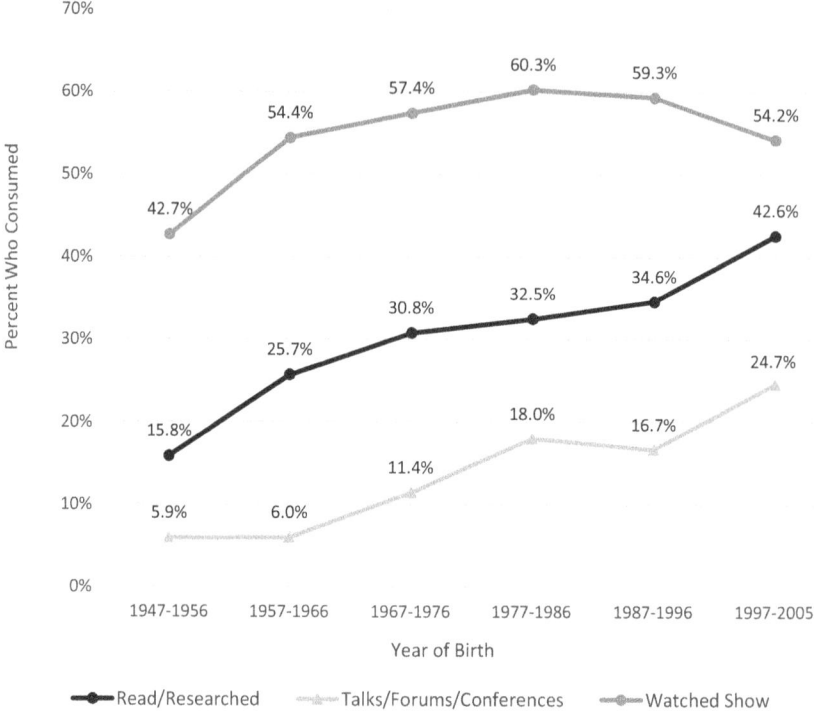

Figure 3.6 Ghost-related consumption by year of birth (CASPAR, 2021).

lived in a house that they believed to be haunted. Only 14 per cent of respondents born between 1947 and 1956 believe they have experienced a ghost. The youngest respondents are twice as likely to believe they have experienced a ghost (30 per cent). Only one in ten of the 65- to 75-year-old respondents thinks they have lived in a haunted house. Britons aged sixteen to twenty-four were *three times* as likely (30 per cent) to believe they had lived in a haunted house.[53] The youngest respondents were also three times as likely (19 per cent) to have used an Ouija board to try to contact spirits when compared to the oldest (6 per cent).

Finally, younger people were also more likely to have consumed media related to ghosts (see Figure 3.6). We asked CASPAR respondents if they had read non-fiction books, consulted websites, or otherwise researched the topic of ghosts. Once again, the youngest (43 per cent) were nearly three times as likely to have researched ghosts compared to the oldest respondents (16 per cent). There was a similar linear effect of age on the likelihood of connecting with others interested in ghosts by watching a talk, participating in an online forum, or attending a conference. Less than 6 per cent of the 65- to 75-year-old respondents have ever interacted with others on the subject of ghosts. The youngest respondents were four times as likely to report having done so (25 per cent). The relationship between age and having watched television series, documentaries, or online videos about ghosts is a bit less linear by age. Our oldest respondents are the least likely to watch ghost-related programming (43 per cent), and, generally, the younger someone is, the greater the likelihood they have watched such programming. But the very youngest respondents (16–24 years) show slightly lower levels of ghost-themed visual media consumption compared to older contemporaries, with middle-aged respondents being the most likely to watch spectral TV shows.

This multifaceted engagement with ghosts, particularly amongst youth, is increasing as affiliation with conventional religion is declining. Ghosts are filling a void by allowing people, particularly younger people, a way to maintain a connection to spiritual concerns even as conventional religion declines.[54] This matches patterns identified in the United States, where organizational religious affiliation has fallen in conjunction with younger generations reporting greater beliefs in, experiences with, and media consumption about ghosts.[55] Researchers have found similar age patterns in other European countries, such as Ireland and Italy.[56]

All of this is happening as the media landscape continues to rapidly evolve, yet again. Broadcast networks and movie theatres are struggling as people drift towards streaming platforms. Social media is taking off across all groups, but younger people are using social media platforms to communicate at a much higher rate. Therefore, how people learn about, interact with and experience ghosts is bound to change too. Consequently, the fact that the youngest respondents to our survey *were not* the most likely to watch classical visual media about ghosts but *were* the most likely to engage in online forums about ghosts is telling. Indeed, at 30 East Drive, we saw the Retford team chart the future of ghost hunting: livestreaming.

The Black Monk Joins Facebook

As it happened, the RGH team planned to stream our entire investigation to its Facebook followers. RGH does three livestreamed shows a week on average, one of which is pay-per-view, at a cost of £6.99 to join the feed. The entire night for RGH revolves around this livestream – the central pivot of which is the camera (a mobile phone housed in a handheld device with a strong light to illuminate the action). The phone is logged into Facebook and livestreamed to the audience through the team's account. Two moderators, not present, monitor the feed and privately message the team if anything goes wrong. Hundreds of people were able to join in on our ghost hunting rituals remotely and help cocreate a narrative for the evening.[57]

Rachel directs the action. She takes centre stage, acting as presenter, participant, and commentator. There is no script. Rachel directs the action according to the rhythm of whatever happens. Consequently, the 'improv' dimensions of ghost hunting, already a key aspect of spirit investigations, become heightened.[58] That is not to suggest that any of this is an act for the participants. Rachel is just as welcoming, inclusive, and affable in the livestream as she is in person, but she is also very aware of her audience and cares about their enjoyment. The group works seamlessly together, each one moving into and out of the picture as required. When they take a break from the action, they will often sit with an eye on the stream to see what is happening, continually checking in for audience feedback in real time.

The use of livestreaming technology opens a new frontier in spirit investigation. Viewers can consume ghost-themed content in a way that is similar to, but also more immersive than, reality TV ghost shows. The viewers become part of the action. The audience plays a direct role in the proceedings. They comment, provide possible interpretations of any events that have occurred, and offer suggestions for what the group might do next.

Indeed, the live audience was actively involved throughout our night at 30 East Drive. Over 8,000 comments were made by the 866 viewers who joined the livestream.[59] Team members continually monitored the stream and would often say hello to audience members or read comments aloud. We curated and thematically analysed these comments. They took several general forms.

Some comments were about mundane matters. For example, many were related to the strength of the livestream/feed. Audience members would inform the moderators if the feed did not seem to be working. Members of the RGH team would tell people who reported a bad connection to ('go off and come back on'), or provide a confirmation that the feed would return ('it'll come back') or that it has returned ('back on again guys'). Other comments concerned discussion about the members of the team, usually when they were leading the hunt. For example, when Gary was giving a tour of the house to the audience, there were a number of good-natured comments directed towards him such as 'We love ya Gary!' and 'your [sic] the man Gary!'

More important to the shaping of a narrative for the evening was that Rachel and the other RGH members continually encouraged audience members to participate directly in the proceedings. Participants did so in several ways that we noticed: by providing *suggestions* on how the group should proceed, by aiding in the *interpretation* of events as they occurred, and by the *creation* of independent forms of 'evidence'.

Suggestion

Many comments from the online audience were recommendations about something the group should do. Sometimes the participants would suggest things that an RGH member might ask or say to the ghosts. 'Ask him if he likes music', said one participant. 'Ask how many are we in the room', said another. Sometimes such requests were humorous such as: 'Ask him if he like Cadburys chocolate'. During quieter spells of the evening, audience members would want RGH to antagonize the monk: 'Tell him he's pathetic' said one. Another participant offered: 'GET RACHEL TO INSULT HIM AND TELL HIM SHES NOT SCARED OF HIM. TOTALLY BELITTLING HIM'.[60]

At other times the audience attempted to instruct the group directly as to what they should do. The following are a small sampling of the instructions RGH received from online participants during the evening.

> Go to the room Rachel and Ron were in.
> Try and do a seance.
> Get the others to call out, Will.
> Get someone to sit in the bath.
> Turn the light off or down.
> Please check the kitchen there's something in there I can sense it.[61]

The team did not act on every instruction – the volume of comments was simply too large. However, the team did react to *some* of them, and this variable success ratio seemed to encourage the audience to comment more, rather than put them off. The audience felt that they could help with and perhaps influence the investigation.

Interpretation

As discussed above, when a perceived paranormal event occurs in a haunted location, those present must develop a shared narrative about its meaning. The livestream audience was an active participant in this process, sometimes providing the context necessary to label an event as supernatural. For example, the livestream audience was crucial to the interpretation of events that occurred in an upstairs bedroom, as we joined Trevor and Will for an experiment with the Alice Box.

When the Alice Box beeped and presented the phrase 'I'm Nobody,' Trevor and Will paid little attention at first. Trevor stated the phrase dispassionately and appeared ready to move on. A flurry of comments on the livestream effectively told Trevor and Will the importance of the term.[62]

> He's now as Mr nobody
> Will … cupboard behind you … knock on door
> Mr nobody
> Mr nobody
> He's called Mr Nobody
> Omg! He's known as Mr Nobody
> They call Fred mr nobody
> Mr Nobody
> Fred are you there☺
> They call Fred Mr Nobody
> They call Fred Mr nobo
> Hey will
> That was awesome they called Fred mr nobody
> Didn't someone say he was called Mr nobody
> People call him mr nobody
> Fred was called Mr Nobody
> Mr Nobody??
> WOW THEY CALL HOM MR NOBODY. WENDY MOD XX

Try with light off
The monk is known as mr nobody 🕯️🕯️🕯️
Come on spirits talk to this group please ❤️❤️
are u sleeping here will x
Fred is known as Mr Nobody Will 😊
Ask guests if they want to shout out
Someone said earlier the monk was known as mr nobody
He is Known as my nobody
Mr nobody is the name of the munk
Ohhh they call Fred, Mr nobody
Calm before the storm it will happen there's more people they a bit shy ☺ 👍
They call Fred mr nobody
will Fred was called Mr Nobody
His nickname is mr nobody and I'm nobody has come up
OHH GOT SHIVERS THEN!! <3 KERRY MOD xxx

Will saw the flurry of livestream comments. He excitedly told us what the audience was telling him.

Will   Fred! Everyone is commenting. Fred – his nickname … everyone's going mad … is 'Mr. Nobody' … and that says 'I'm nobody.'
Trevor OK Mr. Nobody … if you're really here tell me what I just put on the floor or touch that equipment. Otherwise we don't believe you. Come on Mr. Nobody!
Will   Everybody's commenting Fred is Mr. Nobody! He's Mr. Nobody! His nickname is Mr. Nobody!

By incorporating a livestream into their investigations, the RGH team greatly increased the likelihood that meaningful events would occur. Instead of relying upon the knowledge base of the handful of us who were sitting in the room at 30 East Drive, they were drawing upon the beliefs, knowledge, and experiences of hundreds. We were not aware of the importance of 'Mr Nobody' (at the time) and neither, apparently, were Trevor nor Will. But the viewing audience was well aware.

This is not to say that the team would never have recognized the importance of 'I'm Nobody.' Its meaning would likely have been discovered as members shared stories and evidence after the investigation. But the active participation of a viewing audience brings immediacy. There is an excitement to the proceedings when connections are made in real time by the audience.

Creation

At times, the audience itself generated 'evidence' that would not have existed at all without their participation. For example, similar to what the *Most Haunted* team had done, the RGH often had two livestreams going: one that followed the primary action, and another placed in a stationary position at the bottom of the stairs. The group relied upon the audience to keep an eye on the secondary camera and report interesting activity. The livestream audience reported seeing things on the stairs throughout the evening.

For example, the audience produced a narrative that an 'Emily/Emma' was present.[63] An 'Emily' is not part of the original tale of 30 East Drive as told by the Pritchard family or Colin Wilson. She is a later addition to the site's lore, for which we have failed to discover the origin. Supposedly she is the, or one of the, victims of the Black Monk.[64] She is still trapped at the property, perhaps because the Monk will not allow her to cross over.[65] As those of us present at 30 East Drive were engaging in experiments, the livestream audience was watching both feeds and began reporting that a girl was on the stairs. Without any direct participation from the RGH members, who were busy elsewhere, the audience began reporting Emily sightings.[66]

I've seen the shadow on the stairs!!!
She is by the bannister on stairs
There is a girl on stairs
Stairs are good alot of activity x
Go out by stairs she out by stairs watching you all
Its Emily

The livestream audience also helped to build Emily's character by fleshing out a backstory:

Emily she is 9
He pushed Emily downstairs
He pushed Emily downstairs he tripped on her dress and broke her neck

Orbs: The Ultimate Audience Participation Phenomena

A major means by which a livestream ghost hunting audience can create evidence is by taking screen captures and sending them to the ghost hunters. RGH received several such pictures, both during and after the investigation, most of them 'orbs'. Orbs are a well-documented, albeit highly contested, feature of paranormal investigations. They are usually detected through photographs or film and tend to appear as small balls of light floating in a picture. Some consider them to be the soul or energy of a spirit. Others dismiss them as dust or moisture particles reflecting off a light source.

Regardless of what causes them to occur – and to be clear, there were a huge amount of them visible on the livestream – orbs have an inbuilt function in the context of an online audience. Since orbs generally do not appear to the naked eye, *only* the audience can detect them and comment on them. In most cases, the comments were positive identifications, but there were also some that pointed out that they may be due to a technical issue, such as a dirty lens. As comments about orbs build up, however, the team can use that feedback as evidence that 'there's a lot of activity in here tonight'. Essentially, orbs give people something to talk about and a way to vicariously experience the paranormal. Over 600 of the comments throughout the night were about orbs. In a livestreamed environment, viewers are effectively engaging in a remote, interactive ritual with ghost investigations, actively contributing the process of experiencing ghosts and constructing narratives about such encounters. In these terms, the audience are a crucial part of the hunt.

Making Sense of Ghosts in Contemporary Britain

Let us return to the question that opened this chapter.

How did 30 East Drive, a nondescript council home, become one of the most notoriously haunted locations in Britain considering its landscape is filled with seemingly more suitable castles, graveyards and ancient battlegrounds? It has done so by capitalizing on broader social trends, clever marketing and some well-timed lucky breaks.

First, *any* place can join the ranks of the most haunted locations. Modern ghost hunting techniques and reality-style investigation shows have democratized the search for the paranormal.[67] One need not be a credentialed scientist to search for ghosts. With a small investment in electronic equipment and access to a possibly haunted location, or by joining a ghost hunting group that has these things already, one is off and running. Livestreaming is the ultimate democratization of paranormal investigation. A large audience can join the ritual of communing with spirits without having to own the equipment or travel, all from the comfort of their own home. We anticipate that this form of participation will only increase the hold that ghosts have on the popular imagination going forward, particularly for younger generations, who are more likely both to believe in ghosts and to consume livestreamed media.

The tale of 30 East Drive has evolved during the same time as belief in ghosts has been on the rise, and conventional religious beliefs have been on the decline. This rising popularity of ghosts in post-secular contexts may be because they do not require a complex religious architecture. They are relatively free-floating and malleable, and are therefore also highly syncretic and durable.[68] The more secular or agnostic ghost enthusiasts can focus upon documenting the 'residual energy' that may attach itself to places of tragic events, without specific references to souls or an afterlife. Others who see themselves as scientific in orientation can focus on using various pieces of ghost hunting technology and on learning to interpreting its voluminous output. The more spiritually inclined can emphasize communing with spirits via psychic powers and séances. Religiously-oriented ghost enthusiasts may help the spirits to 'cross over' to an afterlife. And whether or not they frame it in religious terms such as 'demonic', ghost enthusiasts vary in whether they believe spirits can be evil. Such flexibility allows the same haunted space to be used effectively by people with different orientations and belief systems.

The 30 East Drive narrative has benefited from being *particularly* flexible. Its evolving tale includes all types of phenomena. Those with a more agnostic bent can focus upon theories about psychokinetic energy originating from an underground river. Those who believe in mischievous ghosts can try to communicate with 'Fred.' Those who believe in evil, either in a secular or religious sense, can dare to taunt the dreaded 'Black Monk', the demonic serial killer who attacks visitors.

Luck has been on the Black Monk's side as well. Had the case not attracted the interest of a local historian, Tom Cunniff, who then contacted Colin Wilson, it is unlikely that 30 East Drive would have evolved into a major haunting site. Wilson's book exposed 30 East Drive to an international audience. Cunniff's theory that the Pritchards' troubles were caused by the ghost of an evil monk provided the location with a marketable villain. Without the 'Black Monk' it is unlikely that the case would have spawned its own film, *When the Lights Went Out,* nor attracted the interest of *Most Haunted*. Both of these developments firmly added 30 East Drive to the ranks of famous, haunted locations, as we could clearly see in both internet searches and news stories from these time periods.

Even then the Black Monk's luck was not over. The entrepreneurial filmmaker of *When the Lights Went Out*, Bil Bungay, purchased the home and opened it up for paranormal tourism with overnight ghost investigations. As a result of such fortuitous events, what started as a frightening, personal experience from over a half-century ago has evolved into a cottage industry of media and tourism, offering believers the opportunity to chase their own spiritual encounters across varying levels of intimacy, from vicariously watching the exploits of others on shows to remote participation via the internet, or for the more adventurous, their own chance to personally encounter the Black Monk.

Evidence from multiple surveys over time, as well as analyses of age cohorts within our CASPAR data, shows that interest in ghosts is increasing over time among the UK population. The ever-expanding universe of opportunities for paranormal media consumption, along with the declining influence of organized religion, has created a circumstance within which ghosts are not just surviving but thriving. We are only seeing the beginnings of the hold that ghosts have on the popular imagination.

Perhaps it is no surprise that savvy entrepreneurs have noticed these same trends and looked for ways to monetize public interest in ghosts via related tourism. As we show in the next chapter, there is both a strong demand for and an ample supply of paranormal tourism in the UK.

Chapter 4

MYSTERIOUS WORLD

The Black Monk's Calendar is Booked

We did not personally encounter the dreaded 'Black Monk' of Pontefract. We avoided the transformative experience of being dragged up the stairs, bitten or scratched, as the malevolent spirit is reported to do on occasion. But the Monk did reveal to us his greatest power – marketing. An otherwise nondescript council house in a town with few other attractions has become a hotbed of media attention and tourism. And our education into how paranormal claims can evolve into lucrative commercial enterprises began well before we even stepped inside 30 East Drive.

We first contacted 30EastDrive.com in June of 2022 with a reservation enquiry and learned that only three dates remained open for the entire remainder of the year. Unable to travel on those specific dates, we booked the first available evening in January of 2023. As it turns out, we were competing for space with a host of ghost enthusiasts and professional ghost tour operators.

A current search for availability (in 2024) reveals similar, heavy usage. Three major ghost tour companies had 30 East Drive booked for ninety-eight nights between them. Haunted Happenings has forty-eight evenings reserved, Haunted Houses UK has forty, and Haunted Rooms has ten.[1] A number of smaller operators also advertised on 30 East Drive's Facebook page. For example, Veritas Paranormal had three night-time investigations and a 'lunch time tour' available.[2] JDH Books Paranormal had two evenings. Each paid event offered groups of up to ten people some time at the property with ghost hunters and their equipment, with prices ranging from £55 to £85 a person. Most tickets sold out months in advance. If you want to book an evening at 30 East Drive to meet the Black Monk, you might be in for a long wait.

The Business of Ghosts

We are not the first to notice the burgeoning interest in the spectral as a tourist draw.[3] The commodification of 30 East Drive is part of a trend in private businesses and local communities actively promoting their spectres as part of structured, paid activities. A growing number of scholars have begun to focus on this subcategory of dark tourism, often labelled 'ghost tourism'.[4] While 'dark tourism' can include visitation to a notorious site of murder or genocide, a war memorial, or places where major disasters have occurred (such as Chernobyl), ghost tourism is explicitly marketed around the haunted nature of the destination.[5]

It might seem that businesses and locales should downplay their potential haunts, for fear of scaring off customers. But there are many benefits to welcoming ghosts. Promoting local spirits can draw people to areas otherwise lacking histories that are notable, exciting or salacious enough to attract tourists on their own merits. This does not mean that such places have to ignore their history. Indeed, *most* sites of historical interest are tied to existential matters of life and death. Ghosts can provide a window into those histories and make them accessible as narrative, experiential entertainment.[6]

Further, since most ghost-related events occur in the evening, they can, ironically, bring life to places that would otherwise be closed to the night-time economy. With little other than pubs open after dark in many villages, ghost-related events can provide evening activities for families with children and others less inclined to pub hopping.[7] This focus also allows interested businesses to maximize their utilization of space. A museum can allow ghost events late at night in their building, when there otherwise would be no revenue. A restaurant that closes in the evening can rent out its facilities to ghost hunters overnight. Such businesses may even see an uptick in visits during normal hours if they gain notoriety within paranormal subcultures.

The cost of embracing one's local ghosts is minimal. Any ageing town centre with older buildings and a ghost tale or two may be able to capitalize.[8] A dated hotel or run-down restaurant may find that its spirits help it compete with more luxurious offerings. For a purportedly haunted location, expensive remodelling or modernizing would be counterproductive beyond what is required for safety or insurance reasons. Ghost enthusiasts tend to perceive age and decay as signifiers of an 'authentic' haunting.[9]

Villages and cities across Britain are recognizing these benefits. In our travels we encountered more opportunities for ghost-related tourism than we had time to explore. A near-endless supply of private businesses, heritage sites and city centres market the dead and ghoulish. Unfortunately, academic interest in ghost tourism suffers from a near-complete lack of available data or metrics, and we needed to see if our impressions of the healthy state of ghost tourism in Britain were correct.[10]

Without available data with which to compare our findings, we could not aspire to chart growth or increases in profits. That left us with trying to gauge the current state of the market, with the hope that future scholars can compare their findings to ours to check for growth or decline. It also quickly became clear that we could not hope to conduct a complete census of ghost-related business. No matter how hard we looked, we could never be certain that we had not missed some instances of ghost tourism. There is no listing of 'ghost tourism operators' to reference (yet, anyway), and no association collecting its economic data.

A key sign of the economic health of a product is its ubiquity. For example, Space Invaders and Pac-Man led to an explosion in video game arcades in the 1980s, with examples popping up in cities big and small. By the mid-1990s, home video game consoles decimated storefront arcades, which are now difficult to locate, outside of aging examples in boardwalks and amusement parks.[11] A walk through any shopping centre or city centre will speak to the current economic power of coffee.[12] With 6,417 locations between them, one would never need travel far to reach a Costa, Greggs or Starbucks. So, one way to measure the economic power of ghost tourism is to ask a simple question: if a ghost enthusiast was dropped at any given location in Great Britain, how far would they have to travel to chase a spirit?

Forms of Ghost Tourism

We excluded some forms of ghost-related entertainment from our attempt to enumerate ghost tourism. For example, adolescents and other thrill-seekers have long engaged in 'legend tripping', wherein they visit the purported site of supernatural phenomena or other sinister activities seeking to have a fright, test their mettle, or challenge the truth of the reported claims.[13] This spontaneous, sometimes inebriated behaviour may bring some commerce to its destination when the group stops for fuel or food. But there is no way for us to track such trips, which may only be known to the participants. In a similar vein, the members of ghost hunting clubs frequently engage in private investigations. As with legend tripping, ghost clubs might bring some revenue to the event location when they order pizzas to bring to the haunted castle or stop by Tesco for an extra flashlight. But it is not possible to accurately enumerate such activities.[14] Some ghost clubs announce the results of investigations on their webpages or social media; others do not report them.

Ghost-related activities that are designed as for-profit enterprises are much easier to track. If a business seeks customers, it needs to advertise. This usually means that we can find ghost events in internet searches, if we know what to look for. Certainly, we will miss activities that are only advertised via word-of-mouth or posted fliers, but with the advent of social media and free sites where businesses can advertise, events that lack an online footprint will likely be rare.

There are two major types of organized, paid ghost tourism that we found operating in Britain: ghost walks and ghost hunts.[15]

Ghost Walks are guided tours, usually of historic city centres and coastal towns, wherein the guides tell customers ghost stories and legends at multiple stops along the route. A sprinkling of other dark forms of history and related deathlore such as murders, witch trials and grave robbing is also common. These are typically walking tours, but in York, London and Edinburgh tourists also have the option of viewing haunted locations from a special effects-laden bus, offered by 'Ghost Bus Tours'.[16]

Ghost Hunts are typically late-night or overnight stays at a single, notoriously haunted location.[17] The organizers usually bring equipment such as EMF meters and spirit boxes that can purportedly be used to contact spirits or capture evidence of their existence and coach customers in their use.

As anthropologist Michelle Hanks notes in her study of ghost tourism, ghost walks and ghost hunts have different business models and, therefore, appeal to different clientele.[18] In order to participate in a ghost hunt at a famously haunted location such as 30 East Drive, people must purchase a ticket in advance and travel to a place that they might not otherwise visit, such as Pontefract. Ghost hunts often require spending all night at the event – a significant time commitment from participants.

But vendors also incur significant costs. They must rent a haunted location, maintain insurance, provide ghost hunting equipment, and pay for staff time and travel expenses. Consequently, ticket prices are considerably higher for ghost hunts than ghost walks. For these reasons, ghost hunts will most appeal to people with a pre-existing interest and enthusiasm for ghost lore; ghost hunts are often the primary reason for travel, and consumers may leave the area immediately after its conclusion.

Ghost walks, on the other hand, require less planning on the part of the consumer. Such businesses typically advertise themselves with brochures in gift shops, other tourist hubs, and posted fliers, all of which usually include instructions for purchasing tickets. The ghost walks themselves also act as an advertisement. The hosts are often colourful characters dressed in some sort of ghoulish costume. The frightening stories they tell, in booming voices so their customers can hear, attract the attention of passersby. Someone stumbling across such a walk may end up booking tickets for another time. Further, since expenses are much lower for the vendors of ghost walks, ticket prices are significantly lower than those for a ghost hunt, generally less than £15. For these reasons a ghost walk is much more likely to attract the spontaneous and opportunistic consumer – one visiting the area for other attractions.

'Thy Bones Are Marrowless; Thy Blood Is Cold'

Before we could begin counting ghost hunts and ghost walks, we had to figure out where to look.[19] England and Wales are divided into 318 administrative/council areas known as Lower Tier Local Authorities, or LTLAs, that provide services such as rubbish/trash collection, road maintenance, council housing, and park development and maintenance.[20] For example, Halton is an LTLA in Cheshire, near Liverpool, about two hours away from London by train. Nearly thirty-five square miles in size, its borders include the towns of Runcorn and Widnes and civil parishes such as Daresbury and Preston Brook. As of February 2023, the population of the entirety of the Halton LTLA was 128,577.[21] Southwark, an LTLA and borough of London across the Thames from the inner city, includes the districts of Peckham, Walworth, and Bermondsey. It is less than one-third the size of Halton at 11.14 square miles in size, but it boasts a much larger population, with 307,600 as of 2021.[22]

LTLAs vary in their size and population, but they provide a reasonable approximation of what might be experienced as 'local' and therefore accessible, were one dropped in a random location in England or Wales. Further, LTLAs contain the necessary people to make particular forms of enterprise financially sustainable (or not). Our analysis here provides a baseline estimate for the relative dispersion and availability of ghost tourism in the UK, which will make it possible for researchers in the future to chart its growth (or decline).

Armed with this list of LTLAs, we conducted internet searches for each of them looking for 'ghost walks', 'ghost hunts' and 'ghost tours'.[23] We immediately confirmed that in most tourist hotspots, ghost tourism appears to flourish alongside that area's main attractions.

Consider the Stratford-on-Avon LTLA/district in Warwickshire, West Midlands.[24] This mostly rural district includes the towns of Alcester, Southam, and large villages such as Bidford-on-Avon and Studley, but the primary draw is the district's namesake, Stratford-upon-Avon, birthplace of William Shakespeare. Tourists enjoy charming towns set along the River Avon and beautiful natural scenery, including a section of the Cotswolds. Most come to visit Shakespeare's birthplace, the site of a later home, and the former dwellings of his wife and other family members. Those less interested in Shakespearean history can visit a butterfly farm, cross the river in a historic chain ferry, view hundreds of examples of automata at the Mechanical Art & Design Museum – or they can engage with ghosts. Two different ghost walks compete for tourists. On Saturday evening, one can purchase a £10 ticket for the Stratford Ghost Walk, a ninety-minute ghost tour of historic downtown. One of three guides, Vincent, Edward, or the mysterious 'Man in Black', meets ticket holders at the Swan fountain. They promise a 'magical walk', wherein customers will:

> Discover the ancient creaky buildings seeping with tales of ghosts, witches, murder and misery. Hear about the witch who lived in a slum, a 17th century haunted tearoom, the theatre ghost and a jilted bride. Don't go home alone![25]

The 'Sinister Side of Stratford Walking Tour' offers a similar experience. It is available most days of the week at 3.00 pm, 5.00 pm, and 7.00 pm. Tour guide Joe Rukin undercuts his competition slightly by charging £9.99 for his ninety-minute tour that provides tales of 'plague, murder, ghosts, beatings, witches, sewage and grave-robbing'.[26]

Both walking tours stop outside the most well-known, haunted location in Stratford-upon-Avon, the Tudor World Museum.[27] It is purportedly haunted by the ghosts of a young pickpocket, a seventeenth-century serial killer, and a dark, robed figure with red eyes (that sounds quite like the Black Monk of Pontefract). The building's owners have expressed some consternation at the fact that other businesses are freely capitalizing on their haunted reputation. They have their own designs upon the spirits.[28] Tudor World fully embraces ghost tourism.

Opening at 10.30 am, the museum offers interactive displays of life in Tudor times. Visitors can try writing with a quill and ink, read about a witch trial, dress in a suit of armour, and learn about the plague. At 5.30 pm, the Tudor World's normal business shuts down, and, a half-hour later, it transforms into a playground for ghost enthusiasts. The museum offers a one-hour ghost tour at 6 pm, with tickets costing £8.50. Its website promises no jump scares and warns customers that the museum's interactive exhibits will be unavailable as an employee leads them through the building to 'relate the sighting of paranormal activity with each room'.

The museum's own tour ends at 7.00 pm. A few hours later, one of several outside businesses may rent the building for paid, late-night ghost hunts. Haunted Happenings had Tudor World booked for three nights in 2024: April 13, July 19, and September 13. For between £49 and £55 per ticket, ghost enthusiasts can roam the property from 10.00 pm to 2.00 am, alongside Haunted Happenings staff. Customers will have access to EMF meters, K2 meters, and other equipment; join experiments in table tipping and the use of an Ouija board; and participate in a séance.[29] A different company, Haunted Houses UK, had the museum hired for four evenings in 2024: May 24, July 26, September 6, and October 18. Their events start at 10.00 pm, end at 3.00 am, and cost £49 per person. Similar to Haunted Happenings, Haunted Houses UK offers its customers a variety of paranormal equipment to try out and leads the group in experiments throughout the night. Two other companies, Paranormal Eye UK and UK Ghost Hunts, have rented the property for paid investigations in the past.

While most of the ghost-related tourism in the Stratford-on-Avon district occurs in its largest tourist draw and namesake, there were also activities available in less frequented locations. Three companies offer late-night ghost hunts at the town hall in the market town of Alcester.[30] In one of the few examples we found of paid ghost hunts occurring outdoors, Paranormal Playground offers events at the Rollright standing stones on the border of Oxfordshire and Warwickshire for £12.50 per ticket.

Our searches quickly demonstrated that Stratford-on-Avon was not an anomaly. Ghost tourism is thriving across Britain.

The Problem of Halloween

As might be expected, enthusiasm for all things spooky peaks around Halloween. Starting in October, a number of locations open haunted attractions or mazes filled with gore, animatronics, and actors jumping out at frightened customers. Hallowscream, twelve minutes outside York, offers five scary mazes from mid-October through the first few days of November. Those looking to be chased by murderous clowns can visit the Walsall Scare Maze near Birmingham. The Halloween Maze of Horrors at Smeaton Farm in Cornwall runs only on the Saturday evening closest to Halloween, but promises the 'scariest 15 minutes of your life!'[31] While such attractions often draw upon local folklore in composing their scares, they are fundamentally different from standard ghost tours and ghost hunts that thrive on perceived authenticity.

Many ghost walks and ghost hunts are only available during the spooky season. For example, Hoghton Tower in Lancashire has ghost tours around Halloween, where 'you will be told about the ghostly happenings from across the centuries', but offers no ghost-related activities the remainder of the year.[32] Bolsover Castle (Chesterfield), Fulham Palace (Hammersmith), Bruce Castle (Haringey), and the

Ham House Gardens (Richmond upon Thames) are some of the other historic estates that leverage their ghost lore from mid-October to early November but focus upon other events the remainder of the year. The arts centre in Boston, Lincolnshire, offers 'The Boston Ghost Walk' the week around Halloween, and Stockton-on-Tees provides the 'Halloween Spooky Walk' the weekend before.

In most places, Halloween-time ghost walks and ghost hunts are in addition to events available at other times of the year.[33] But ten LTLAs *only* had ghost tourism available around Halloween.[34] Given our interest in regular availability, we did not count an area as having ghost tourism without evidence that events occurred outside of the Halloween window. In a similar vein, we also did not count an area as having ghost tourism if there was no evidence of *future* availability. If a location had hosted ghost hunts in the past, but we could find no future events scheduled, we erred on the side of caution and did not include them as having regularly available ghost tourism.

A Marketplace of Ghosts

As of November 2023, 36 per cent of LTLAs (115 out of the 318) across England and Wales had at least one ghost walk available to tourists. One-hundred and eighty-eight (59 per cent) had at least one ghost hunt available. The true prevalence of ghost tourism in England and Wales becomes even more apparent when the data are considered in another way. We looked at which LTLAs had a ghost walk only, a ghost hunt only, both types of ghost tourism, or nothing at all. In other words, what is the likelihood that, in any given LTLA in England and Wales, one will encounter *any* form of ghost tourism? Figure 4.1 shows the breakdown of aggregate levels of ghost tourism across the LTLAs.

The most common ghost tourism configuration we found was areas that had ghost hunts available but no ghost walks (34.6 per cent). During our research, it became clear that ghost hunts can thrive in out-of-the-way places, away from other tourist attractions, provided they have a sufficiently notorious and famous haunted location.[35] Potential customers will travel farther to the extent that the location has been featured in books, movies, podcasts or, ideally, shows like *Most Haunted*. Consider a decommissioned nuclear bunker that sits just outside the small village of Kelvedon Hatch. The bunker is open for daytime tours, but there is little else to attract tourists to the area, and nothing going on in the evening; but, over time, Kelvedon Hatch bunker has developed a reputation as a haunted location, with claims of malevolent spirits and poltergeist activity. That reputation was cemented when *Most Haunted* filmed a 2009 episode in the bunker, and, as might be expected, the cast experienced significant ghostly activity. The village of Kelvedon Hatch does not have enough tourist traffic to support a regular ghost walk, but five different companies offer late-night ghost hunts at the bunker. If the necessary ghost lore exists, ghost hunts can provide a revenue-generating opportunity in otherwise quiet locations.

The rarest ghost tourism configuration we found was an area that had a ghost walk, but no ghost hunt. Less than 12 per cent (37) of places had this configuration.

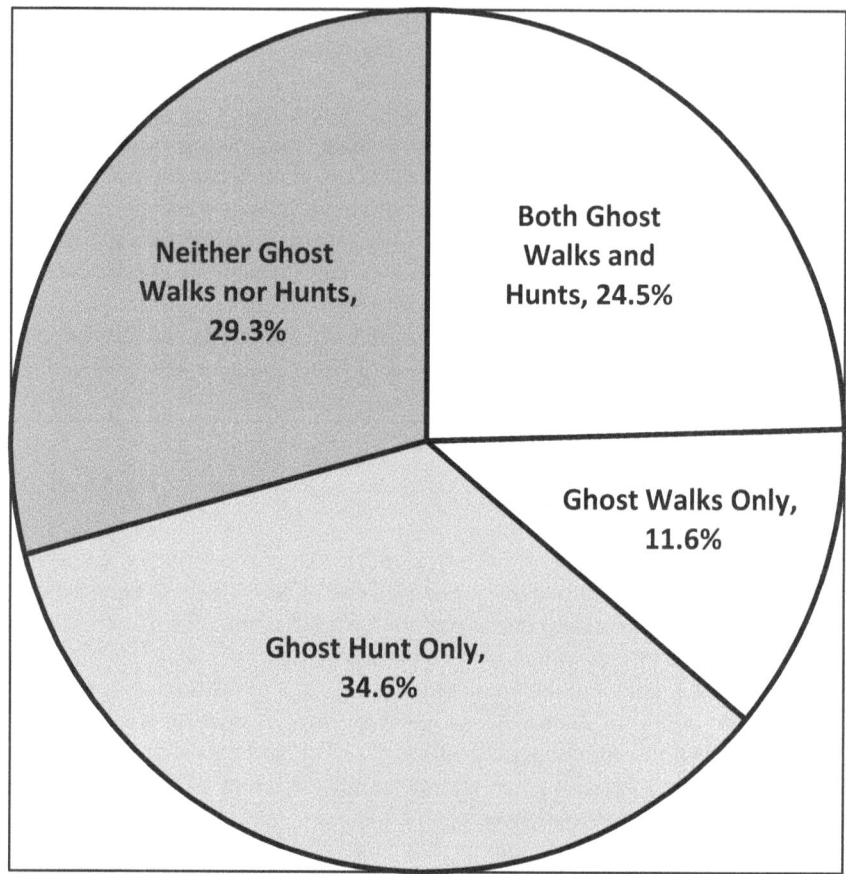

Figure 4.1 Percentage of LTLAs with regular ghost tourism available (November 2023).

One-fourth (24.5 per cent) of LTLAs had both forms of ghost tourism. The fact that most ghost walks take place in the same general areas as ghost hunts suggests a synergistic relationship between them, wherein the haunted locations needed for a ghost hunt provide the stories and stops needed by a ghost walk. Figure 4.2 provides a map of the availability of ghost tourism across England and Wales.

Less than one-third of the LTLAs (29.2 per cent) had no ghost tourism available. Taken together, these findings indicate that an individual dropped into a random location in England or Wales is more likely than not to find ghost tourism readily available.

Twenty Minutes from a Ghost

What of those who find themselves in an area bereft of ghost tourism? How far would they have to travel to find a ghost hunt or ghost walk? We closely examined

Figure 4.2 Map of ghost tourism in England and Wales.

the ninety-three areas in England and Wales that did not have any regular ghost tourism. For each, we calculated the distance in driving minutes one must travel to reach the closest ghost tourism event. For example, we could find no ghost tourism in Blaby, Leicestershire. But from the centre of Blaby it takes only eighteen minutes to reach a ghost hunt in Belgrave Hall in the Leicester district, home to a ghostly Victorian lady and the spirits of children. Twenty-four minutes away from Blaby is the Haunted Antiques Research Centre, which also hosts regular ghost hunts.[36]

The worst place to live, if one judges such matters based on the availability of ghost tourism, would be the Isles of Scilly. This cluster of islands twenty-eight miles off the southern coast of Cornwall had a total population of only 2,281 as of 2022 and no regular ghost tourism we could find. Reaching the closest such opportunity, at Penzance on the mainland, requires a flight or ferry: a time investment of at least a couple of hours.

If we remove the unique circumstance of the Isles of Scilly from consideration, the longest a person must travel to reach a ghost event in England and Wales is thirty-three minutes. Neither Reigate and Banstead in Surrey nor Kirklees had any regular, paid ghost tourism that we could locate. From either of these LTLAs, one must travel thirty-three minutes to find such activities. Thirty-three minutes from Reigate and Banstead is the Barn Theatre in Oxted that has regular ghost hunts.[37] There are ghost hunts at Bolling Hall in Bradford, which is thirty-three minutes from the centre of Kirklees. The shortest travel time was the five minutes required to reach a ghost hunt at the Avenue House in Finchley from the ghost-deficient Hertsmere, Hertfordshire.[38] Overall, in England and Wales, the average travel time, in minutes, for someone whose area does not have ghost tourism to reach the nearest such opportunity is only 21.4 minutes.

Ghostly Business as Usual

Although there exists no previous data with which to compare our findings, we were still surprised at the relative health of ghost tourism in England and Wales. Ghost tourism opportunities are available in more areas than they are not and are never far away from the consumer, regardless of location.

Nesting ghost businesses within LTLAs also allowed us to link other relevant data about local communities to determine which characteristics of locations make ghost tourism more or less viable. We drew upon the 2021 Census and the Subnational Indicators dataset (September 2023) to look at how an area's relative levels of employment, income, education, age, population density, rural/urban populations, ethnic diversity, religious diversity, internet availability, and the prevalence of entertainment and accommodation/hospitality industries might predict the presence of ghost tourism.[39]

For example, if an area is characterized by a more highly educated population, on average, is it more or less likely to have ghost tourism available? In the case of education, the answer is no. The average level of education in an LTLA was not a statistically significant predictor of the presence of ghost tourism. There were several factors that were predictive of various forms of ghost tourism, however.

Consider areas that have only *ghost hunts*, but no ghost walks. As we have noted, ghost hunts are a form of destination tourism, meaning people will travel specifically to engage in the activity. Theoretically, ghost hunts should be able to survive and even thrive in out-of-the-way places. Our data support this conclusion. Areas that are characterized by 26 per cent to 80 per cent of their populations living in rural areas are much more likely to have ghost hunts available than more urban areas. These findings suggest that the best place to start a ghost hunt business would be at a location that is rural, but reasonably close to a population centre. Unfortunately, we also found that areas with ghost hunts tended to be characterized by populations with lower levels of income and higher levels of unemployment. As discussed in Chapter 2, an abundance of theory and research within the social sciences has argued that people who are relatively deprived and on the margins of society may seek comfort in the supernatural. However, research that has found support for the marginalization hypothesis has focused upon data at the individual level, rather than the characteristics of the local area. Our findings provide some evidence that deprived *communities* also tend to favour supernatural businesses.

Given that *ghost walks* require some sort of town, village, or city centre in which to conduct said walk and multiple 'haunted' stops along the way, we were surprised to find that such businesses are not necessarily clustered in urban centres. The percentage of the population living in urban settings was not predictive of the presence of ghost walks being the only form of ghost tourism in that community. Indeed, ghost walks are most common in areas that have lower population densities. Further, places that *only* offer ghost walks tend to be characterized by a younger population on average and more people working in the entertainment industry. It is likely that these are also characteristics of coastal towns, which often feature ghost walks as part of the night-time economy.

Consistent across our analyses was the finding that ghost tourism thrives in areas where the median pay is lower. Indeed, someone who seeks the best chance of encountering both forms of ghost tourism should look for an area with certain features. Places that have both ghost hunts and ghost walks available tend to be characterized by more rural populations. A village or town surrounded by rural areas will be the most likely to support both hunts and walks. To the extent that an area is characterized by a younger average population and, again, by lower median pay, ghost hunts and walks are more likely. Ghost tourism also requires places for people to stay, so when an area is characterized by a larger number of people in the accommodation/hospitality industries, there are usually greater opportunities for ghost-related tourism.

'A Globally Renowned Scottish Brand'

While ghost tourism events are thriving and easy to locate across Britain, they are but one part of a larger *paranormal* experience economy.[40] Britain is rife with opportunities for paranormal tourism unrelated to ghosts. On any given evening, psychics and mediums entertain audiences in hotels across the Isles. MBS fairs and UFO conferences are also visible throughout the year. Rendlesham Forest, the site of a famous UFO sighting in 1980, has a UFO trail tourists can walk.[41] The magic-curious can visit the Museum of Witchcraft and Magic in Boscastle. Wiltshire provides a ghost walk and several ghost tours for visitors, but also offers the Crop Circle Visitor Centre & Exhibition. If one also considers stone circles such as Avebury and Stonehenge, purported faerie forts and the many towns and pubs that make use of the Black Shuck legend, paranormal spending opportunities abound. But to see the best example of the transformation of the paranormal into commerce, we must return to Loch Ness.

Photo 4.1 Nessieland exhibit

Scotland is well populated with its own ghosts and fae, but as we have seen, it is perhaps best known for its resident monster.[42] Around the banks of Loch Ness, there is also a diverse and segmented marketplace for Nessie. Depending on the report, the monster pumps around £30–40 million into the local economy per year.[43] At the bottom of this market sits homespun entrepreneur Steve Feltham, busking hand-crafted Nessie models from his booth on Dores Beach. Every gift shop in the environs (and far beyond) supplements its income by selling Nessie products of a seemingly endless variety. Some shops, such as Loch Ness Gifts in Drumnadrochit, are almost entirely devoted to the beast, selling everything from Nessie Christmas ornaments to Loch Ness Monster condoms, both in store and online. Sitting somewhere in the middle of the pecking order are competing boat tour operators offering cruises around the loch replete with stories of the beast.

Located close to one another in Drumnadrochit are two of the largest attractions devoted to the monster: Nessieland and the Loch Ness Centre. Nessieland is the distinctly less professional of the two, with online reviews decrying aging displays and tacky merchandise. Its 'Adventure Playground' consists of fibreglass plesiosaur models for children to climb upon and a closed minigolf. The 'Nessie Caves' are a series of cramped, crowded rooms filled with text-heavy informational plaques, stuffed animals and even more fibreglass creatures (see Photo 4.1).

One room has been transformed into a tribute to the area's other major tourist draw, the *Outlander* book series, concerning a World War II nurse who travels through time to 1743 Scotland. Curiously, an old video of Nessie hunters combing the Loch plays in a continuous loop on a television at the centre of the 'Outlander Inspired Exhibition'.

If Nessieland has seen better days, the Loch Ness Centre & Exhibition signifies the new era of Nessie as a commercial commodity. First opened in May of 1980, the exhibition has recently become the target of major investment.[44] The Centre is housed in the former home of the Drumnadrochit Hotel, which itself has strong ties to the Loch Ness Monster. On 14 April 1933, then-manager of the hotel, Mrs Aldie Mackay claimed to have spotted a 'whale-like' creature in the loch. When a story about her experience appeared in the *Inverness Courier* on 2 May 1933, Nessie's career as an undiscovered lake monster officially began.[45] Soon after the Loch Ness Centre opened, local lake monster expert Adrian Shine affiliated his Loch Ness Project with the Centre and began storing his materials there. Shine became the de facto face of the Loch Ness Centre & Exhibition over time, appearing in numerous documentaries and television shows. For the next forty-three years, the Centre operated as a key stop on the itinerary of a Loch Ness tourist.

In January of 2023, a York-based company named Continuum Attractions entered into a long-term lease with the owners to modernize the Centre & Exhibition. Continuum develops 'immersive experiences', which include limited-run shows, such as 'Star Wars: Secrets of the Empire', which ran in London from 2017 to 2018. Its holdings also include long-term leasing/operation agreements including 'The Coronation Street Experience' that allows fans of the show to tour its sets, and attractions entirely owned by Continuum, such as 'York's Chocolate Story' and a tour of underground areas of Edinburgh, 'The Real Mary's King Close'. On their website, Continuum announced their takeover of the Centre, noting that it was prompted by Nessie's economic power:

> Continuum Attractions has a new long-term lease on the iconic Highland tourism site, The Loch Ness Centre and Exhibition. Investing £1.5 million into

its refurbishment, Continuum are transforming the attraction into one that will engage, entertain and inform guests, focusing on telling the globally renowned story behind the legend of Loch Ness.

Together, Loch Ness and the legend of Nessie, is a globally renowned Scottish brand. Now visitors to the Highlands can explore how the real stories of Loch Ness and its Monster are more fascinating and engaging than any myth. At Scotland's new Loch Ness Centre, visitors from around the world will discover why in this majestic Highlands location this old former Scottish Hotel became the epicentre of true stories and the in-depth research. Over time and even today those quests continue to bring a legend to life; and helped inspire a must-see visitor experience.[46]

The Centre & Exhibition closed for six months in 2023 as Continuum completed its refurbishments. After it reopened, we visited the Centre to see how it had changed. Before this upgrade, tourists would walk through a series of rooms with information on the characteristics of the loch itself, folklore and myth, theories about the monster's identity, and famous sightings. The information was presented with a combination of props, relics from the hunt for Nessie, placards, and videos. The type of material presented does not seem appreciably different with the infusion of Continuum's resources. Rather, the changes concern the style of presentation, which has become more in line with modern tourist attractions.

Upon purchasing a ticket, customers wait in a holding room for their starting time. In the centre of the holding room are cases with pieces of Nessie memorabilia. This included an ashtray made from a hippopotamus foot, used by big game hunter Marmaduke Wetherell to fake Nessie footprints in 1933. There was a miniature skeleton of a plesiosaur, a helmet used by a diver who had once searched the loch for the beast, and a stone purporting to show ancient glyphs of a Nessie-like creature. After a couple of minutes in this room, an employee told the assembled group that it was time to begin. He pulled back a book on a bookshelf, which revealed a secret passage that the guide pointed us through.[47]

The first two rooms were dominated by large video screens. Short films would start once the group had entered. The first room, 'This Majestic Place', explained how the loch formed over time. It discussed continental drift and the dinosaurs, with a comet dramatically plummeting to Earth to destroy them. We saw the climate cooling and then warming, causing massive glaciers to melt, flooding the glens and forming the loch. The presentation finished by discussing how new creatures arose to populate the land, including deer and otter, and speculated that perhaps something else appeared as well. In the second room 'Myths & Legends', a cartoon displayed the myths and folklore about monsters and faeries in the loch. It spoke of the temperamental precursors to Nessie: the Kelpies, Selkies, and fae, and recounted the dramatic tale of St Columba, an Irish abbot and missionary who used prayer to stop a watery beast from attacking a fellow monk he had ordered to swim across the loch in AD 565.[48]

The first two rooms were not entirely different from the previous incarnation of the Centre. The information presented was very similar, but the screens were larger, and the animation more professional.

The next room, 'People & Stories', was dramatically different. Every surface, except for the floor, contained moving images. The front wall was entirely taken up with a large screen that displayed a hotel bar and a bartender casually wiping his glasses as we walked in. The left wall had screens that displayed a window looking out onto the loch. A collection of screens of different sizes made up the right-hand wall. These switched between different news clippings and talking heads. In the centre of the room were two round tables and some chairs.

After a few moments of sitting at the table, the bartender on screen looked up and acted surprised to see the gathered crowd. He welcomed us to the Drumnadrochit Hotel. Soon thereafter, a woman walked past the 'window' to our left and entered the front screen/bar. The actress was portraying Aldie Mackay, who excitedly told of her sighting of a beast in the water. Another actor sitting behind her overhears a recounting of the tale, as the May 1933 story from the *Inverness Courier* appeared onscreen. A whirlwind of activity ensued as the bartender recounted the history of the major encounters that followed Mackay's sighting. Actors walked in and out of the 'bar' and by the 'window' on the left as they entered and exited. The screens on the right continually rotated content. One screen might show an eyewitness sketch, photo, or video of Nessie, another a witness telling their story, another a newspaper article.

At times, all the screens were used to tell a singular narrative. For example, an actor playing the big game hunter Marmaduke Wetherell initially appeared in the left-hand 'window' peering through binoculars, a monkey perched on his shoulder. Marmaduke then entered the front screen/bar and told those assembled that he had just found Nessie's footprints. Another actor informed Marmaduke that a hippo's foot had been found, and Marmaduke comically ran off screen. As all this was happening to the left and front, the right-hand screens supplemented the tale. One showed an image of the actual Marmaduke (with a monkey on his shoulder), another a photo of the hippo foot, and others newspaper stories about the affair.

Over the next few minutes, we learned about key pieces of Nessie evidence such as the famous surgeon's photo (see Chapter 2) and videos taken by the late Loch Ness investigator Tim Dinsdale.[49] After this whirlwind of information and images, the bartender informed us that it was time to move on to the next room.

After a visit to the 'Waters of the Loch' room that discussed the loch's currents, lack of visibility, and the animals known to live within and around, we moved to the penultimate room, 'The Search for the Truth'. The *John Murray*, a pontoon boat fitted with sonar that Adrian Shine developed to help hunt for the beast, dominated the space. As we looked at the boat, Shine himself greeted the crowd from a screen to our right. He spoke of many possible explanations for Nessie. Some cases are hoaxes, he said. Others stem from the misidentification of boat wakes or floating logs. The loch's environment is not suitable for large catfish or sturgeon to live and breed, he argued, nor is there evidence of large eels in the loch. DNA samples taken from the soil have never shown any reptile DNA, refuting the idea of a remnant plesiosaur. In the end, Shine left it open as to what the monster might be, if anything, as we were prompted to move on.

The final room, 'The Debate', attempts to summarize what has been presented. The same bartender who appeared in the third room reappeared on the front screen. He reminded the group of some of the key pieces of Nessie evidence and introduced Steve Feltham, who talked about his sightings and recounted some of the many theories about the beast. In the centre of the room were, again, two tables with chairs about them. The tables were divided into three sections, each of which contained three buttons. In a section titled 'I see Nonsense' were buttons labelled 'Aliens', 'Hoaxes' and 'Imagined'. Under 'I see Possibilities' were buttons for 'boat wakes', 'wind patterns' and 'logs'. Finally, the 'I see Nessie' included 'seal', 'big fish' and 'plesiosaur'. The bartender informed the group that we had ten seconds to choose our preferred explanation for Nessie. Once time was up, we were presented with the results from all the visitors to date. At the time of this visit (11 October 2023), the most popular category was 'I see Nessie', with 46 per cent of visitors having chosen one of its three options. Twenty-nine per cent of respondents chose an option under 'I see Possibilities', and 25 per cent selected an 'I see Nonsense' option. The most popular option under 'I see Nessie' was that the sightings are due to a plesiosaur roaming the Loch Ness.[50]

Naturally, the tour ended with visitors funnelled into a gift shop. The items for sale confirmed that, despite the careful and cautious presentation of alternative theories, the romantic notion of a dinosaur swimming about the loch maintains its hold upon the public. There were no stuffed catfish or toy logs for sale in the gift shop. There *were* hundreds of options for purchasing something emblazoned with a multi-humped, reptile-like beast. Every book, piece of candy, stuffed animal, figurine, and garment somehow represented the 'globally renowned Scottish brand' of a long, snakelike neck peeking from the water.

The Paranormal Tourists

British tabloid the *Daily Star* recently ran a provocative headline proclaiming that the 'UK is "running out of ghosts" as old spirits dying off, paranormal expert says'.[51] Enthusiasts need not worry though, as we suspect that the spirit of capitalism will ensure the continual recurrence of ghosts and other forms of popular paranormal tourism.

Our empirical examinations of paranormal tourism indicate a healthy marketplace. Ghost tourism is readily available to any interested parties across England and Wales. Larger operations, such as Continuum Attractions, are willing to invest large sums of money into paranormal projects that were formerly local labours of love. But how many people have actually engaged in these popular forms of paranormal tourism? And how much interest is there among the public in engaging in these activities in the future?

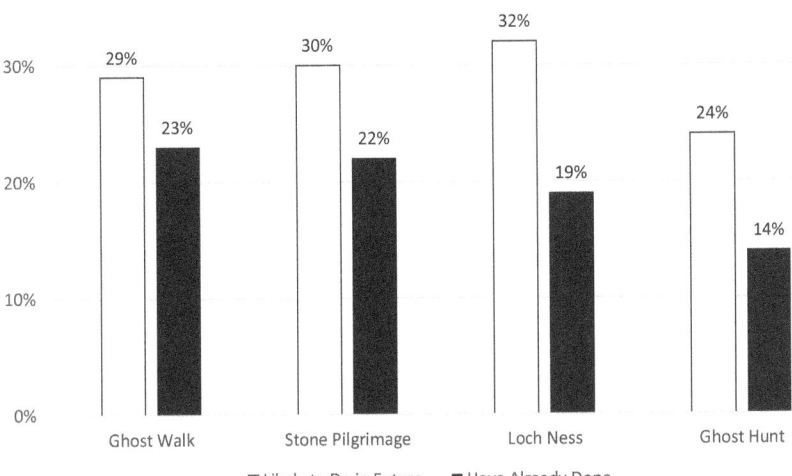

Figure 4.3 Percentage in the UK who have already done or plan to do paranormal tourism activities.

In addition to examining the 'supply' of paranormal tourism, another means by which to gauge the health of the paranormal tourism sector is to look at 'demand' by asking potential consumers their level of interest in engaging in paranormal activities. In April of 2024, we partnered with IPSOS-Mori UK to do just that. We asked a random sample of 2,000 British adults (England, Wales, Scotland, and Northern Ireland) if they have engaged in various forms of paranormal tourism in the past. We asked if they have visited Loch Ness, at least partially due to interest in the Loch Ness Monster, if they have paid to attend a ghost hunt at a haunted location, if they have paid to take a ghost walk, and/or if they have visited a stone circle, such as at Avebury or Wiltshire for spiritual reasons (see Figure 4.3).

Just under half of people in the UK (45 per cent) report that they have already done at least one of these paranormal tourist activities. Ghost walks were the most common form of paranormal tourism reported, with 23 per cent reporting having taken a guided ghost walk. A similar percentage reported visiting stone circles (22 per cent) and Loch Ness (19 per cent). The more intensive form of spirit pursuit, ghost hunting was slightly less popular, with 14 per cent of people in the UK reporting that they had paid for a ghost hunt in the past. However, since the UK has an adult population of around fifty-four million people, this still means that approximately 7.5 million people (14 per cent) have paid to attend a ghost hunt.[52]

Further, there is great interest going forward. Over half of our respondents (53 per cent) are hoping to engage in at least one of these activities in the future. Nessie tourism leads the way, with nearly one-third (32 per cent) of the public reporting that they would like to visit Loch Ness for a cryptozoological excursion. Three out of ten reported (30 per cent) wanting to make a spiritual pilgrimage to megaliths. Nearly one-third (29 per cent) plan to go on a guided ghost walk in the future. Around one out of four (24 per cent) reported that they would be willing to pay to go on a ghost hunt.

Our data suggests that experiential paranormal tourist activities are thriving. There is an ample supply of opportunities available, and the demand is also there. Substantial numbers of the British public have already engaged with the paranormal, and even more intend to do so in the future. Tabloid headlines aside, it seems that spirits – as well as cryptids, spiritual stone quests, and myriad other paranormal tourist pursuits – are in no danger of disappearing.

Why Paranormal Tourism?

Our ethnographic, spatial and survey research all suggest that paranormal tourism in Britain has a bright future. But wherein lies its appeal for the consumer? Previous work has suggested several possible explanations.

Sociologist Max Weber argued that one of the outcomes of modernization would be secularization, a decline in belief in religious and spiritual concepts.[53] This 'disenchantment' of the world would mean that the spiritual meaning undergirding social spaces would fade, leaving a landscape devoid of magic.[54] Typically, discussions of Weber's predictions focus upon the decline of organized religion and, indeed, many contemporary social scientists have thoroughly documented such a decline in the Western world, particularly in Britain. But these declines in organized religion have not led to the disenchantment of the world – not by a long shot.

Paranormal tourism represents a modern-day re-enchantment of the world, providing a sense of wonder and mystery, channelled through a consumerist and individualist framework.[55] For those who have stepped away from organized religion, a ghost hunt can create its own sense of community and ritual, as a group dives into the transcendent together.[56] Travel to places with paranormal associations, such as 30 East Drive, Loch Ness, or Avebury, is itself a form of contemporary, postmodern pilgrimage.[57]

While some of the appeal of paranormal tourism may be associated with its ties to the sacred, it is also bolstered by its connections to earthly matters (the profane). Some scholars have noted a resemblance between paranormal tourism and gambling. When tourists pay money to participate in a ghost hunt or purchase a ticket to a cruise of Loch Ness, they understand there is no guarantee of experiencing a ghost or sighting Nessie. Rather, the customer is paying for the *chance* to encounter something extraordinary.[58] The thrill of gambling is also about possibility and anticipation. Someone who has lost all of their coins at the slot machine does not attempt to sue the casino; perhaps next time, the jackpot will appear. In a similar vein, if the ghosts are not 'active' this evening, perhaps one will have better luck the next time, or perhaps Nessie popped her head above water when people were looking in another direction.[59]

Weber's contemporary, sociologist Émile Durkheim, also speculated about the future of religion. Durkheim predicted a 'cult of the individual'. Religion, he argued, was destined to transform itself, rather than disappear.[60] As society becomes less formally religious in character, he argued, the individual will come to be viewed as a sacred, religious object.[61]

In this context, the increasing availability and prevalence of paranormal tourism make perfect sense. Although British society may be increasingly secularized from traditional, organized religion, spiritual pursuits have transformed into privatized, commodified endeavours. Spiritual practices that borrow from a wide array of traditions are now available for channelling the sacred through late capitalist consumerism.[62] Consequently, paranormal tourism is perfectly suited for thriving in late modernity – and you won't have to travel far to find it.

Chapter 5

AROUND IN CIRCLES

The Power of (Enchanted) Place

Surrounded by gently sloping fields of green wheat, we surveyed the scene. 'Well, I think we've found the middle of nowhere', Chris commented as our car slowly headed westward over a dirt track. We pulled up to what appeared to be a rough intersection connecting a number of fields. To the south, a perilous-looking path wound its way upward toward the Roundway White Horse, while to the southwest, Oliver's Castle – an ordinary-looking hill that is actually an Iron Age Hillfort – sat high above the landscape. Everything was precisely what might be expected from the picturesque Wiltshire countryside.

Over a distant hill, some anonymous-looking buildings hid a tractor that was busily making its way back and forth across the horizon. 'You reckon that's the farmer?' Joseph asked. 'Probably', Tom replied. 'But I don't think the website says that we *can't* come in this one', he added hopefully.

We had come to this otherwise anonymous field on the outskirts of the market town of Devizes to see a recently reported crop circle.

A crop circle is an area of flattened crop that is arranged into a geometric pattern, often involving a formation of circles. Usually occurring in rape, barley and wheat fields, the crop is not cut or mown. Instead, it is laid down against the ground as if it has been curled, but not broken, from the base of the stem. Formations usually appear overnight, typically without witnesses to their formation.

The Crop Circle Exhibition and Centre (CCEC), also outside of Devizes, maintains a list of the latest discovered circles on its website.[1] For each of them, it also provides Google map directions and information on whether there is public access to the circle. The report on the CCEC website suggested a rather magnificent formation, with somewhat concentric circles forming a target or bulls-eye type of design, and an outer ring with attached triangles at the cardinal positions. Photos on the website provide images from several different angles (see Photo 5.1).[2]

As it turns out, finding a crop circle at ground level is not as easy as you might think. As we walked up the dirt track, we tried to peer through the small breaks in the thick hedgerow. But it was difficult to see anything, as the track was a couple of feet lower than the field and the wheat floated in the wind at eye level. 'It must

Photo 5.1 Crop circle in Roundway Down, Wiltshire, 2023.

be here somewhere', said Tom looking deeply into the map on his phone. 'What's that?', Joseph murmured as he peered into the middle distance.

As we continued to wander, it was just possible to make out a break in what otherwise appeared to be a continuous sheet of green stretching up the hill. 'Is that it?' Joseph asked hesitantly. 'Dunno, could be', Tom answered, as he scanned for a way into the field. 'I think we'll need to go back, we'll never get through here'.

Coming back around the hedgerow and into the wheat field, Chris marched his way determinedly up the path made by the tractor, trying to brush back the wheat that reached out in the wind. 'That's it! You can see the edge of it – look!' shouted Tom, pointing hopefully into the field. 'It goes around there, see?'

Some yards ahead, Chris turned southward and increased his speed down what appeared to be a flattened avenue in the wheat. It quickly opened into a wider area of yellowing wheat clinging to the floor. He exclaimed with a smile: 'Well, we've travelled 5,000 miles, and this is it: our first crop circle!'

To be certain, crop circles are far more exciting from above and from a distance. We quickly tired of wandering about in rows of wheat on a hot day and retreated to our car. But what may fail to captivate on the ground has certainly become an impressive phenomenon in Britain.

Some enthusiasts argue that crop circles have a long history, often pointing to a report submitted to *Nature* in July of 1880. It describes how John Capron visited a neighbour's farm to find 'a field of standing wheat considerably knocked about, not as an entirety, but in patches forming, as viewed from a distance, circular spots'.[3] Capron suggested that cyclonic winds had produced the circles. A 1678 pamphlet, *The Mowing Devil*, provided a more sinister, and supernatural, explanation. It tells the story of a Hertfordshire farmer angered by the price a farmworker demanded to mow his field. He said that he would rather that the 'Devil himself should Mow

5. Around in Circles

Photo 5.2 Tom explores a crop circle.

his Oats' than pay the worker.[4] After witnessing his field aflame that evening, the farmer awoke to find his oats perfectly mowed.

We have found it quite common for modern paranormal enthusiasts to seek historical records that suggest that their phenomenon of interest is not simply a modern invention. This includes claims that the Loch Ness Monster can be found in myths of the water horse or that medieval art depicts flying saucers. But, for certain, the modern crop circle mystery can be traced to the 1980s, where there was an exponential increase in the number of circles reported around England, and Wiltshire in particular.[5] Pat Delgado and Colin Andrew's 1989 book, *Circular Evidence*, documented this explosion, solidifying the reputation of crop circles as a major, modern mystery. Some cold water was tossed onto that mystery in 1991, however, when Doug Bower and Dave Chorley of Southampton confessed to having created more than 200 circles since the 1970s using nothing more than ropes and boards.[6]

More than thirty years on from this confession, belief in crop circles remains persistent in Britain. We asked respondents to CASPAR, 2021, if they think that 'crop circles are created by non-human forces or energies' (see Figure 5.1).

To be certain, there was considerable scepticism amongst our respondents. More than one-third (35.6 per cent) are entirely sceptical of non-human origins for crop circles, whilst more than another third (36.1 per cent) think it is 'probably not true'. Yet nearly one-third of our respondents are willing to give crop circles a hearing. Only 7 per cent think that it is 'definitely true' that crop circles have a supernatural origin, but another 21 per cent think the statement is 'probably

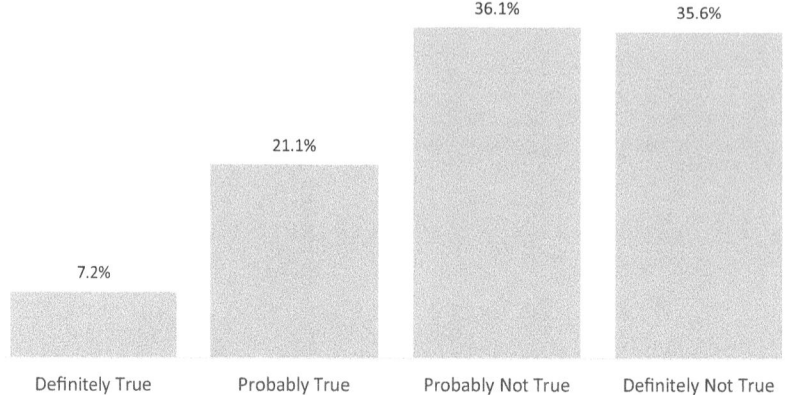

Figure 5.1 Crop circles are created by nonhuman forces or energies (CASPAR, 2021).

true'. In a full model predicting belief in crop circles using our standard sociodemographic and religious characteristics, the strongest predictors were, in order of strength: conventional religious beliefs (positive), religious practice (negative), living in the West Midlands (negative), identifying as white (positive), being Muslim (negative), claiming intensive religious experiences (positive), being maritally separated (positive), having children (positive), and being a woman (positive). By far the strongest predictor was a person's level of conventional, religious belief. We will return to the issue of how religion interacts with the paranormal in Chapter 7.

If the British public is largely sceptical of crop circles, enthusiasts were less impressed by the confessions of Bower and Chorley. Delgado and Andrews dismissed the notion that crop circles could be entirely explained by hoaxing. They argued that hoaxed circles can be easily identified by their rough shapes and broken crops, while 'the real circles are objects of beauty, precision and mysterious detail'.[7] Throughout their book, Delgado and Andrews suggest that paranormal forces are at work. Andrews claims that alarms went off and clocks stopped in his home when he brought back a soil sample from a 1986 crop circle in Childrey, Wantage.[8] The authors report equipment malfunctions, strange noises and a wildly spinning compass while visiting circles.[9]

Early crop circles were just that, circles; often one, but sometimes several together, or concentric in formation. In the early 1990s, more complex designs began to appear, which enthusiasts labelled 'pictograms'.[10] For example, on the 12th of July in 1990, the East Field Pictogram appeared outside the village of Alton Barnes near Devizes. Nearly 600 feet in length, it consisted of circles, rings, bars and shapes that looked like keys. It became especially famous after being featured on the cover of Led Zeppelin's 1990 collection, *Remasters*. Modern crop circles consist of a bewildering variety of fractals, spirals, cubes, triangles and even faces and birds, suggesting that the spherical appellation does not well apply anymore.[11]

The Crop Circle Visitor Centre and Exhibition

Crop circles have been reported from all over the world, with many examples from the United States, the Netherlands, Germany, Australia, and Indonesia. However, the majority of formations appear in Southern England, particularly in Wiltshire.[12] Consequently, it has become the home of crop circle tourism. Several companies offer crop circle-related tours to the area, with 'crop circle season' typically following the farming calendar, beginning in the latter parts of April, and continuing until crops are harvested toward the end of August. For example, Stonehenge Tours offers its *Weird Wiltshire Day Trip* in July and August:

> Join us for a 'Magical Mystery Tour' at the height of the crop circle season, and explore this amazing mystery for yourself. This exclusive tour will be led by a local Wiltshire tour expert who has access to the information network that provides breaking news on the latest formation so we set off in search of new crop circles within hours of them forming, when their energy is strongest.[13]

After our hot walk through a crop circle, we drove out to rural Wiltshire to get a better sense of the crop circle subculture. The spiritual home of this subculture is 'the Barge Inn at Honeystreet' – a public house located outside the village of Pewsey, just a few miles south of Marlborough. The pub was formerly owned by Adrian Potts, who after meeting a number of crop circle enthusiasts (a.k.a. 'croppies'), invited them to use his pub as a meeting space. As interest in the phenomena grew, so did the centrality of the Barge Inn. It soon became a hub for curiosity seekers interested in the circles.[14] Potts commissioned the artist Vince Palmer to paint crop circle murals in the pub as a lasting reminder to the local heritage of the area. We dutifully stopped at the Barge Inn for drinks, admiring the murals.

We next visited the nearby Crop Circle Visitor Centre & Exhibition, run by Monique Klinkenbergh, with whom we had arranged a tour and high tea. Originally from the Netherlands, Monique gave up her position as an editor in the fashion world to devote all of her time to crop circle research. Crop circles are a global phenomenon, she told us, but because Wiltshire is the global epicentre, situating the visitor centre here was the only real option.

Monique is often consulted for news stories about the latest crop circles. In her public role as an expert, she provided us with a range of factual information about crop formations. While doing so, she was studiously non-committal about choosing a favoured explanation. A clear example is a quote from her in a BBC News story about crop circles: 'There is definitely a mystery going on, but its [sic] very hard to label the source, whether it is extra-terrestrial, paranormal or just nature.'[15] As we would find out, this non-committal pluralism and general openness to different perspectives on crop circles was a key feature of Monique's approach to the subject.

In addition to Monique, two 'croppies' were in attendance at the Visitor Centre: Jill (pseudonym) and Austen Lynn. Jill told us she is a long-time local enthusiast who moved to the area with her husband decades ago to follow their interest in crop circles. She first camped at the Barge Inn, then lived on a canal boat for a while and now considers the hills of Wiltshire to be her physical and spiritual home. She had extensive personal knowledge of and intensive experiences within different crop circles over a number of years.

Austen is an oft-seen, friendly presence in the crop circle community. This particular day he was dressed in a muumuu adorned with yoga symbols and wore a large crystal around his neck. We asked Austen about his most recent visit to a crop circle, and he reported visiting one earlier that morning. He said that other people had been out there intentionally trying to destroy the crop circle, using trained dogs to trample the patterns and attack the drone that was attempting to get aerial footage.

Austen preferred a narrative of governmental and economic elites trying to keep the public from knowing the truth about crop circles. It was readily apparent that crop circles fit into a larger conspiratorial worldview for him. Despite his suspicions about the government, he was a very affable, free-spirited character, who was (perhaps ironically) very quick to trust and happy to divulge his ideas and theories about the formations.

Epistemic Pluralism

The Exhibition portion of the Visitor Centre has two floors. The downstairs contains a timeline and pictures of important events in the history of crop circles, while the upstairs contains many specific displays. They cover various aspects of the phenomena, such as discerning real from hoaxed crop circles, examples of academic research conducted on the topic, and videos of famous crop circle footage.

Of particular interest were the plethora of theories on offer about the phenomena, all of which were presented as possibilities. One display summarized these theories, it included faeries and demons, cyclonic whirlwinds, electrically charged whirlwinds, UFOs, sound frequencies, hoaxers, mating animals, Gaia theory, morphic resonance, light phenomena, spirits, nature itself, laser technology, the human mind, time traveling and, in case anything was missed, a 'mysterious force'. Notably, the display showed no favouritism, leaving the preferred theory to the discretion of visitors.

When we asked Monique about which explanation she personally prefers, she shaded toward a magical perspective, while also incorporating other possibilities:

> I'm personally more into the paranormal than the extraterrestrial. I will not exclude the extraterrestrial. They might be connected, those two, for some reason. So, I, uh, I just don't know. You know, there's one theory all researchers agree on … which is, it looks like something, we just don't know, picks up our thoughts and presents them in the fields. So to say it in one line. We have many, many events like this. We also experiment with it, like doing meditation asking for a certain design. So basically your thoughts are presented in the field, manifested in the field.

As a case in point, she relayed a personal experience where she saw a dead bird on the ground in a particular shape. Later that morning, a crop circle featuring a bird with that shape was found.

Our attempts to get Monique to choose a personal favourite theory for crop circles were unsuccessful; she remained as non-committal as the displays in the exhibition. For example, in terms of what is actually making the crop circles, Monique suggested a non-specific spiritual force, but one that might presumably be understood by science, at least in the distant future.

> Some call it spirits. It is a mysterious force, which we don't see, but it's there. And there's just not a name for it. It's called paranormal. And it could be all kind of things. And, yeah. Yeah, it's about seeing or witnessing things that can't be explained – yet – by science.

She continued:

> So, and that's my only thought, that it is a combination of many things. Like a part could be nature, a part paranormal, a part extraterrestrial. Also the fact that it's here in Wiltshire, where you have those energy lines crossing each other. We have the largest water aquifers. Water seems to be involved in the whole ... So it's not just nature. Not just – I think it's a combination of all kinds of things. But definitely it's, um, 'high strangeness'. Lots of things going on ... Some say it's the work of God. What is God? Is God the universe? I don't know. And, angels, yeah, could be. I mean in theory, everything could, could be the case. But to get science interested, that's the difficult part.

At an intuitive level, Monique also seemed to recognize that crop circles lay in an uncertain place between science and conventional religion. She claimed to know of scientists who believe in the supernatural origin of crop circles but keep their views secret for fear of ridicule and stigma. She also told of her encounters with people who believe that crop circles are the work of supernatural evil.

Monique: Back in the old days they thought it was the work of the devil, or the faeries, or whatever.
Chris: Do you ever have, um, conventionally religious people come in and make those sorts of claims?
Monique: Yeah, all the time. Yep.

The Edges of Knowledge

Being rejected by both mainstream science and organized religion, crop circles, like all forms of the paranormal, represent stigmatized knowledge.[16] That is, mainstream institutions penalize those who trade in such knowledge by branding them as hoaxers, kooks, heretics or, perhaps, even dangerous. This is not to say that it is all peace and love within the subculture. *Inside* the world of crop circle believers and enthusiasts, arguments erupt over theories and one's knowledge of key pieces of evidence may be challenged. 'It's a difficult, a complex community', Monique told us. Her hesitance to voice a pet theory, either in person or in the Centre is also strategic. 'That's why I decided, you know, to show only the facts. And let people come decide for themselves'.

While there was a perceived openness at the Crop Circle Centre & Exhibition, we did notice a strong tendency towards supernatural explanations. This reflects a process that we frequently encountered in paranormal subcultures, whereby believers use rhetorical practices that frame themselves as sceptical first, until they are won over by hard evidence. In practice, however, it is nearly always the inverse, in that the paranormalist's pre-existing beliefs frame the phenomena in question as real, until definitively proven otherwise. This positioning of oneself as sceptical is critical though, as it allows believers to first establish themselves as *not* being credulous, before then expressing belief. This 'para-scepticism' is an effort to 'get out in front' of the stigma of accepting the supernatural and to avoid being labelled as overly credulous. These kinds of para-scepticism operate as an interactional disclaimer, helping to anticipate and avoid the penalties of expressing stigmatized knowledge.[17]

An important example of this para-scepticism in practice occurred during our conversations with Monique and Jill about a crop circle known as 'The Galaxy'. This formation, which appeared on Milk Hill outside of Devizes in August of 2001, depicts a galaxy formation, with 409 individual circles arranged in sixfold spiral arms. With a diameter in excess of 700 feet, it was impressive indeed. Monique and Jill rejected the idea of The Galaxy being a hoax because of the perceived difficulty of creating the formation:

Monique: For example, this one is really, we can't explain this one. It happened for a fact on a very rainy night. Also when there was no light of the moon or stars or whatever. This is four football fields. 409 circles. The Galaxy, it has been called. It was huge. Jill was in there. Jill, you were in The Galaxy?

Jill: I was yeah. That morning.

Monique: Tell them. I wasn't there on the scene.

Jill: Yeah. We know that night it was absolutely dripping down with rain. Really, really wet. And there was someone camping up on top of Milk Hill, right near where the formation came. He saw absolutely nothing. Heard nothing. But in the morning, it was there. And it was so large, that when you went into it you couldn't find the way out. People have truly been lost in there. It was on, you know Milk Hill, in places, some of the fields, you couldn't see the other side it was so large. 409 circles. I think that's the most impressive.

Monique: Yes, absolutely. To get an idea, so this is a person sitting (showing picture). So if you have all those facts together. Rainy night. People camping out didn't see anything.

Jill: I mean there would be muddy footprints. You know, leading into it. There was nothing. No, no sort of, clue that it had been hoaxed, at all. But in those days we weren't, sort of, we were looking for it, but there was not as much hoaxing going on. The energies were much purer, I think. Shall we say. It was quite extraordinary. And it's one that I always point to when people are a little bit sceptical because, you know, I don't think anyone could have done that. And my husband's a surveyor and he maps out, you know charts out things, and he said, 'there's no way it could be done in that short space of time, in the dark as well'. You know?

Monique also noted that 'there was £100,000 offered if they could replicate that one [The Galaxy]. And no one came forward'. These exchanges show the importance of this particular formation in establishing the wider epistemological validity of crop circles and also how first-hand experiences of specific sites confer subcultural status for enthusiasts.[18]

Edges of Experience

Once the formation known as The Galaxy had been rhetorically established as not of human origin, Jill then proceeded to note place-based magical elements related to the event.

> It was just the sheer complexity and the size that's overwhelming. Never seen anything like it before. And the actual area is magical anyway. Do you know Milk Hill a'tall? It's a magical area. It sits right on the, it was, the formation was right on the top. So you've got a vista of, everywhere, haven't you? Up on top of Milk Hill. I haven't got a book to show you, but there's a series of hills that… I'll show you on here (points to map). This is the top of the hill. Then all along for 13 miles is what we call the 'goddess hill line'. And some books actually show you the goddess lying, in the landscape. So the energy from that, that's what people feel.

Here we can clearly see the role of localized place and its accompanying mythology, with Milk Hill acting as a sacralized landscape. These landscapes naturally lend themselves to claims of place-based magic. Once crop circles appear, it is easy to understand how these sites become 'temporary temples' for intensive spiritual experiences.[18]

Jill reported having many intensive paranormal experiences within crop circles, including multiple instances of levitation.

Chris: There's a mention here of a crop circle with an alien face. Is that pictured here somewhere?
Monique: On the timeline? You mean the two that made an alien face?
Jill: Oh, there it is, there.

Chris:	I see. That almost looks like a human face.
Jill:	It's much more complicated than ours. That's very interesting. I actually levitated in that one. On the third eye.
Tom:	Whoa.
Jill:	Yeah, I took off, and I actually got a bit scared. I put my hands down and I was off the ground.
Tom:	You levitated in the middle?
Jill:	I did, yeah.

Jill was not the only croppie on hand at the Exhibition Centre who claimed to have intensive spiritual experiences when visiting crop circles. Austen also told us about some extraordinary sensory experiences while visiting formations. Indeed, crop circle enthusiasts will often claim spiritual and paranormal experiences related to the formations. This includes precognition, out-of-body experiences, and miraculous healing. Spiritual experiences are important touchstones in the lives and narratives of those who devote themselves to crop circles. These experiences function as a form of social capital among croppies.

Mystery is the Key

Many croppies, including Monique and Jill, cite curiosity and mystery as their primary motivations for continuing to devote time and energy to the topic.[19]

Monique:	I remember last week, it was like the excitement of maybe I'll find something. And you do everything for it. It wasn't, in the end. But I mean, you just have to try.
Jill:	You still have the excitement, don't you?
Monique:	So, you know, those are the things that keep me going, because I have this moment of thinking, 'What am I doing? Where is this leading?' But if it happens to you, something like that. Having a curious mind, you just, you just go on.

The thrill of chasing new knowledge, as well as spiritual experiences, keeps croppies motivated. Here we see the mix of *discovery* – investigating the mystery – and *enlightenment* – spiritual beliefs and experiences – that animate the crop circle subculture. Although crop circles shade more toward magical enchantment, they also retain a strong discovery element, as people pursue their own research into the mysterious formations.

(Culture) Mapping Crop Circles

This straddling of enlightenment/discovery and connection to other forms of paranormalism is also evident in our survey data. As discussed in Chapter 3, we found that the paranormal beliefs of our respondents to CASPAR tended to cluster into four major categories: Aliens, Earth Mysteries, Cryptids, and Magic & Spirits. What the clustering means is that people who believe in one item in a cluster were more likely to believe *in another* item in that cluster compared to something outside of it. For example, a person who believes in visitations from aliens in Earth's past is more likely to believe that aliens are visiting Earth now, much more so than they are to believe in the existence of Big Cats. However, there were two paranormal beliefs that sat apart and did not neatly cluster with any other beliefs. One was the belief in faeries. The other was crop circles, suggesting that the mysterious formations play a unique role in the British paranormal ecosystem. Figure 5.2 plots the relationship amongst paranormal beliefs to present a visual representation of this clustering and the relationships between beliefs.

The circles (often referred to as nodes) represent the type of belief, and the lines represent the relative connections between them. The thickness of the line indicates the strength of the relationship, while the nature of the line tells us whether the relationship is positive or negative (unbroken lines are positive). The shading of the node indicates which dimension the node belongs to, while the position denotes its centrality. This is an estimation of its connectivity to other elements, so those on the edges of the network have less connectivity than those in the middle.

Both the faeries and crop circle items are centrally positioned within the network. This is because they have many connections within the network. The faeries item (number 18) bridges the Cryptid and Magic & Spirits clusters. It shares notable relationships with curses and psychics, while also relating to Alien Big

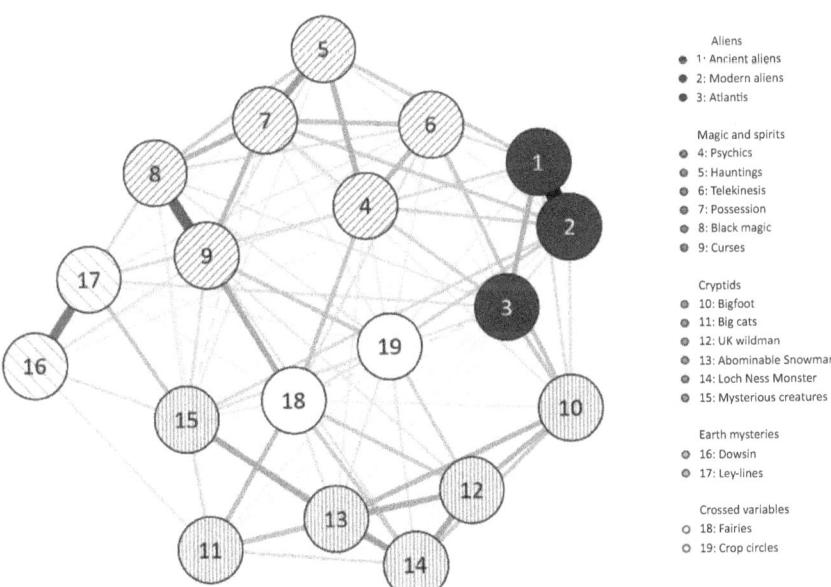

Figure 5.2 Mapping paranormal beliefs.

Cats, the UK Wildman and the Abominable Snowman. This makes a lot of sense. Some people believe that faeries are spiritual in nature, while others consider them to have a more corporeal existence.

Belief in crop circles (item 19) is even more diverse in its connections to other beliefs. It shares significant connections with modern aliens, the Loch Ness Monster, the UK Wildman, the Abominable Snowman, psychics, curses, faeries, telekinesis, black magic and ley lines.[20] Given the diversity of theories we found on display at the Crop Circle Visitor Centre & Exhibition, this is not too surprising. Belief in crop circles acts as a gateway to and a bridge across other paranormal beliefs.

A Night of Crop Circling

The epistemological pluralism of the crop circle subculture was also evident in events such as those sometimes held at Coronation Hall, a small venue in the village of Alton Barnes, outside of Devizes. Not only is it home to the Crop Circle Visitor Centre & Exhibition, but it also sits at the bottom of Milk Hill where the Galaxy formation appeared. We visited the hall when it was host to 'A Night of Crop Circling', an annual conference organized by Roeland Beljon and Nancy Polet. The lineup featured well-known crop circle enthusiasts with a diverse range of perspectives on the phenomena, including Roeland Beljon, Kathy Mingo, Miles Johnston, Bart Uytterthaegen, Barry Reynolds and Austen Lynn.

By the time the event started, the hall was around three-quarters full, with between eighty and hundred people in attendance. On the stage, a woman played a piano quietly before switching to a harp. The crowd was building, and people continued to talk excitedly. Apart from two people, the audience was entirely white, and mainly older or middle-aged. Listening to the conversations, there appeared to be quite a large Dutch contingent. The front two rows were reserved for the speakers and people associated with the organizers. Just before the event was due to start, Monique Klinkenbergh made her way into the hall. Clearly dressed for the occasion and reflective of her high status in the subculture, there was a hushed tone and people saying, 'oh, Monique's here', as she very visibly stood at the front of the hall talking to someone.

Kicking things off with a testimonial about spiritual experiences related to crop circles, Roeland Beljon focused his talk on a collective spiritual experience that he and some fellow croppies had the previous year. On this occasion, eight croppies visited a new circle in late July. When they arrived, they meditated for a while before taking samples, making pictures and playing a harp. The circle itself, Roeland told us, resembled an owl. Unfortunately, they were not there long before a farmer came and asked them to leave – but, Roeland said, the manifestations continued. As they made their way around Wiltshire and down to Glastonbury, they continued to see owls. They saw owl symbology in campsites, car parks, public walls and grocery stores. The synchronicities, Roeland told us, were difficult to miss. And although he doesn't know what all of this means, he tells us that they must be significant.

The next speaker, Kathy Mingo, also focused upon the spiritual aspects of crop circles. Kathy told us that she was going to channel the consciousness of each heavenly body. She suggested that her information comes from the unified field of consciousness that exists all around us. Kathy's capacity for channelling awakens pathways of light where everything is accelerated and where consciousness is condensed. We are all 'light beings', she told us, and crop circles are the language 'of the Divine creative'.

Kathy's language was dense, heavy and full of jargon. Although grammatically secure – the sentences had recognizable form – the content was impenetrable and divorced from conventional, shared meaning. There were clear, if unreferenced, echoes of Helena Blavatsky, Edgar Cayce, and Richard Bucke's 'Cosmic Consciousness', all of which conform to religious scholar Wouter Hanegraaff's definition of 'esotericism' as a personal revelation of cosmic significance.[21]

Kathy showed us a picture of the owl crop circle from last year that Roeland had detailed in his previous talk. In yet another synchronicity, she told us that she experienced similar things, as she saw a white owl right in the middle of the road when visiting crop circles after the event. For her, this is all evidence of the cosmic consciousness. She suggested that these synchronicities had brought us to tonight's event. Showing an allegiance to an enlightenment (rather than discovery) perspective on crop circles, she said that it does not matter whether crop circles are man-made or not.[22] She's 'not invested in that'. Instead, she's interested in channelling the consciousness of these places. Her talk about crop circles featured, among other things, Atlantis, chakras, the divine feminine, holographic vibration, photonic spectrum frequency, Enoch, Tiamat, Hephestus and, for good measure, the Kuiper Belt.

With a decided shift in focus and perspective, Miles Johnston was next. A long-time UFO researcher and organizer of the Bases Project,[23] Johnston's talk was more of a history of his work within the UFOlogy subculture – and a heavy allusion to *something* was a feature of Johnston's presentation style. In some respects, he was both loud and brash, but he also appeared sincere. He used the collective 'we' to seemingly indicate a level of support, while using 'they' with specific emphasis to refer to anyone and anything he was attempting to denigrate. This was usually some conflation of the military, government and alien races. Everything was a platform to articulate a prescient threat or danger – and the central danger for Johnson was that the government was working with 'non-human' agents for the benefit of those alien beings.

In terms of the substantive content of his claims about UFOs and aliens, Johnston discussed conspiracy theories involving the government, as well as globalist groups such as the Illuminati and the United Nations. He talked about the stories of super soldiers (discussed in Chapter 6) and diverse alien races. There was a clear air of paranoia to Johnston's worldview, although in all other respects he appeared to be a relatively mundane middle-aged man. He would later claim that his talk that night was deliberately suppressed and that he was physically attacked for trying to bring a nearby UFO sighting in Marlborough to light.

Continuing the UFO theme, the next speaker was Bart Uytterhaegen, director of the Belgian UFO Network. He cut a more formal look, dressed in suit, and reported that 'I study the files', meaning paranormal reports. In relation to crop circles, he said he looks for 'biophysical anomalies' as a means of proving their non-human origins. He stated that there are many crop circles that are not man-made and that UFOs are also real. He's searching for proof: 'that's what I do.' Similarly, his talk made use of several references to scientific topics, including 'growth rates', 'DNA frequencies' and 'photo plates', although he also claimed that crop circles are giving us a 'blueprint' for an 'anti-gravity device'.

Pushing further into amateur science was the next presenter, Barry Reynolds, who utilized 'Advanced Google Earth' as a tool to assist his discoveries. His talk consisted of overlaying historical crop circles on the landscape, 'so we can see where they are in relation to each other' without the impact of time. He called this 'location analysis'. He began with a field in Sussex, not far from Brighton. He talked about 'geometric centres' and 'the common underlying geometry'. He told us that some crop circle designs might not 'look right' at first or simply appear messy. However, they may still contain 'hidden geometry'. Indeed, this software can help make sense of these designs. Reynolds then showed us an example of this in practice, superimposing a diagram on what appears to be a poorly executed crop circle to show how, in fact, it is all part of 'the design'. Reynolds openly stated that this is a work in development. The problem for him now is to find out *why* the pattern is significant – and the pattern must have meaning, otherwise, why would it exist?

The evening shifted back to a focus upon enlightenment spirituality for the final talk by Austen Lynn, who we had spoken with at the Crop Circle Visitor Centre & Exhibition. Austen's talk concerned the connection between crop circles and ancient Druidic myths about Silbury Hill. He told us that the hill is actually a Faraday Cage that protects spiritual beings within it. He then showed us some pictures of these beings that people have seen around the hill. The pictures showed the outlines of two luminous figures against the backdrop of the hill; one was in black and white, while the other was bathed in green and yellow.

Moving on, he then told of another hill that is 'on an alignment with Silbury Hill', where a crop circle appeared twelve years ago. Walking toward the site, he noticed that there was a weather anomaly where a storm appeared to be accumulating, but without rain or noise. So, he got his camera out and began to take pictures, thinking that the lightning would illuminate the nearby windmill. He showed us photographs of lightning striking behind the windmill; 'ooo', the crowd hummed. Then he displayed an image of 'a plasma discharge event', which showed a circle of lightning. He told us the plasma resembled petroglyphs that can be found in several ancient sites.

He then looked again at the image and started to zoom in on the light. 'Love dwells in light', he intoned. Austen flicked to a slide that focused on a specific part of the image; 'and if you zoom in again …'. This time, the audience gasped. 'Beings', he said. 'Plasmoids … from the constellation Cygnus Swan, which is in alignment with the centre of our galaxy'. 'These are electrical lifeforms', he continued, 'that possibly predate the entire physical universe'. 'They are electrical beings, so they don't need physical matter to exist … they are creator beings, if you like'. 'One of them', he highlights, 'sort of looks like they're waving – "hello!" – while the other looks quite pregnant. You know, the Goddess is always pregnant, always giving birth, every second of every day – creating all of this for us'. Having successfully found God(dess) in the grain, the evening soon concluded.

Earth Mysteries: Stone Circles, Sacred Geometry and Megalithic Science

Crop circles are not the only geometric patterns that are of interest to paranormal enthusiasts – and both Barry Reynolds and Austen Lynn drew on features in the wider landscape for inspiration. Indeed, stone circles and other ancient structures are also a source of great fascination to some paranormal groups, and much attention is directed toward understanding their mysterious purposes.

The megalithic community is an overarching term for a loose network of individuals who are interested in the nature and purpose of megaliths, which means 'large stone' in Latin. Megaliths are prehistoric structures or monuments that are constructed from large stones. Perhaps the best-known example in Britain is the stone circle known as Stonehenge. However, there are many different types of megalithic structures, ranging from a single monolith to complex arrangements of stone, Earth, and landscape. There are also a great many of them. In the UK, for instance, Aubrey Burl's gazetteer lists 508 stone circles in Scotland, 316 in England, 156 in Northern Ireland, and 81 in Wales.[24] While stone circles are probably the most well-known type of megaliths in Britain, barrows, cairns, and hillforts are also common, while the Rudston monolith in the East Riding of Yorkshire measures 7.3 metres in height.

Megaliths are not limited to Britain, with sites like the Pyramids, the Nazca lines, Teotihuacán and Carnac attracting considerable interest from the community. To be clear, our interest is in the paranormal aspects of the community. Not all people who are interested in structures like 'stone circles' accept the more extraordinary claims that can be found at megalithic events. However, many certainly do have more extraordinary interests in the relationships that exist between ley lines, dowsing, Earth energies, sacred geometry, the advanced intelligence of ancient civilizations and the wider cosmos.

Perhaps the most prominent personality in the megalithic movement today is Graham Hancock. Well-known in paranormal circles since the publication of *Fingerprints of the Gods*, Hancock became a pop culture sensation with the release of the big-budget Netflix series *Ancient Apocalypse* in 2022. Recording over twenty-five million viewing hours across the world in its first week – second only to *The Crown* in viewership – the series argued that the origins of ancient agriculture, architecture and astronomy could be found in a single, advanced civilization.[25] This civilization was later largely destroyed in an Ice Age cataclysm, but its survivors seeded knowledge throughout the ancient world.

While *Ancient Apocalypse* was understandably decried as pseudoscientific by critics, one of whom called it 'the most dangerous show on television', Hancock actually avoided discussing his more esoteric beliefs in the series.[26] In *The Mars*

Mystery, Hancock argues that an ancient civilization on Mars was *also* destroyed in a cataclysm. The much-disputed 'face' on Mars, he speculates, could be part of a complex of megaliths that bear resemblance to The Sphinx and pyramids.[27] Other works include his ideas about how psychedelics can produce an expanded consciousness and profound visions. In *Supernatural: Meetings with the Ancient Teachers of Mankind*, Hancock reports his travels to the Amazon rainforest to meet with shamans and partake in the hallucinogen Ayahuasca. During the resultant visions, Hancock reports meeting otherworldly beings, drawings of which he includes in *Supernatural*.[28] He concludes that ancient cave paintings of animal-human hybrids depict supernatural beings from other dimensions that ancient shamans communed with via psychedelics.

Three focal ideas appear in much of Hancock's work that are also reflected in, and taken from, the wider megalithic community: metrology, geometry, and astronomy. *Metrology* is the study of measurement. An established field of science, it is generally concerned with the definition of measurement units, how measurement units are used in practice and the value of measurement. Members of the megalithic community posit various and unique units of measurement that they claim explain (or reveal) similarities between different ancient structures and the connections between those structures and the cosmos. One of the most popular of these was proposed by Alexander Thom, a professor of engineering at Oxford. Thom surveyed hundreds of megalithic sites around Britain and reached the conclusion that ancient builders had utilized a common unit of length, about 2.72 feet, which he labelled the 'megalithic yard'.[29]

While *geometry* is broadly concerned with shapes, angles and dimensions, 'sacred geometry' is more specifically concerned with the idea that there is a universal language of the cosmos that is expressed through particular geometric shapes and geological alignments, as reflected in megaliths such as Stonehenge. The late John Michell is arguably the predominant modern figure in sacred geometry. He argued in books such as *The View Over Atlantis* and *How the World Is Made* that ancient civilizations had privileged access to such knowledge and were capable of harnessing its spiritual energy. This knowledge is thought to be encoded within megalithic structures and stone circles.[30]

The third pillar of the megalithic community is astronomy, inasmuch as there is thought to be cosmological significance to the measurement and geometry of megaliths. Some suggest that megalithic structures were designed to reflect some aspect of the stars. For example, Egyptian author Robert Bauval argued that the positioning of the pyramids of Giza reflected the astrological alignment of Orion's Belt.[31] Often, these astronomical arguments veer into the realm of ancient astronaut theories, arguing that the designs of the pyramids and other structures reflect an advanced intelligence that is cosmological in origin.

The result of all this effort is an often bewildering array of assumptions, some of them physical, some of them metaphysical. Archaeological sites are mapped; distances are measured; measurements are converted into a seemingly exhausting array of units and ratios; lines and angles are drawn; and points and grid positions are compared. With this number of variables in play, it is virtually impossible for a dedicated proponent to *fail* to find coincidental relationships in megalithic structures or between megaliths and the stars. If one unit of measurement does not work, try another. If a particular constellation fails to map to an ancient monument, choose another – and given the range of options, it is always possible to try another angle.

As we found in our time with croppies, once a pattern is found it takes on a nearly invincible significance. That is to say, if a pattern has been found, it must have meaning. Otherwise, why would it exist? From there, any number of paranormal ideas can then be interwoven. Examples that we saw during our fieldwork included: ancient mysteries, aliens, Earth energies, psychic revelations, second sight, cosmic frequencies, dowsing, ley lines, and intelligent plasma. There is also a distinct branch of the megalithic community that is devoted to the search for evidence of giants.

If this wasn't enough to exhaust the casual reader, the delivery of these ideas generally involves presenting the audience with so much material, at such speed, that it: (a) makes the evidence seem overwhelming; (b) is often very difficult to keep up with the argument; and (c) would take a huge amount of time to process analytically. All of this forces the audience to intuit their reaction to the material being presented. This effectively splits people into those who are receptive to megalithic science and those who are not.

The relationship between the megalithic community and conventional science is also of interest: it is ambivalent at best and adversarial at worst. People with an interest in sacred geometries and megalithic science often see themselves as thinking and acting outside of conventional paradigms – which usually means scientific research. This is undoubtedly true; they do operate outside of the scientific community. For many, this is perceived to be a virtue rather than a disadvantage and the more prominent members will actively promote this 'outsider' status. Like John Michell before him, Graham Hancock seemingly takes every opportunity to denigrate science as being narrow in scope, restrictive in practice, and self-serving in nature. The scientific community has typically responded by rejecting Hancock as something of an 'autodidact', promoting dangerous pseudoscience. Unsurprisingly, Hancock has denied such claims.

However, as a journalist and author, Hancock is entirely dependent on scientific discoveries – and he frequently reports on them in his writing. Indeed, his books are largely based on the reinterpretation of extant evidence, while his website is full of references to discoveries published in mainstream scientific journals.

As evidence of this ambivalent relationship, we attended one event that showcased the recent work of a bona fide archaeologist who had spent his career in academia. Despite many of the earlier presentations being overtly critical of academia, the academic received thunderous applause when he finished his talk. He was later mobbed by people wanting to talk to him.

It is possible to make some general estimations about levels of belief in the ideas that comprise the megalith community. In the first instance, we might expect the two core elements of our Earth mysteries dimension to be fundamental to such a community. Both dowsing and ley lines incorporate the idea that there are energies associated with the Earth that can be either detected (by dowsing rods) or are realized in 'ley lines'.

To be clear, it is possible that some people believe in dowsing without holding any other paranormal belief. It is also possible to understand 'ley lines' as being nothing more than a system of ancient roads that connected sites of significance. However, more prosaic interpretations become increasingly unlikely when we combine them with other paranormal items. Ideas around Earth energies share an affinity with other paranormal ideas and experiences. This includes the idea of a race of aliens who helped to create ancient monuments, such as Stonehenge and the Avebury stones, as well as those people who visit such monuments for spiritual reasons. Indeed, in our survey, 40.6 per cent of people believed in the possibility of ley lines and 46 per cent in dowsing, while 14.2 per cent demonstrated sympathy with the idea of 'ancient aliens', and 10.9 per cent of people reported they had visited an ancient monument for spiritual reasons. When people have visited an ancient monument for a spiritual reason, it is likely to be highly indicative of wider belief in mysteries related to 'Earth energies'.

We can build a more detailed picture of these relationships. Figure 5.3 visualizes the relationships that exist between each of these beliefs.[32] The size of the circle shows the relative strength of the relationship, with the shading representing the

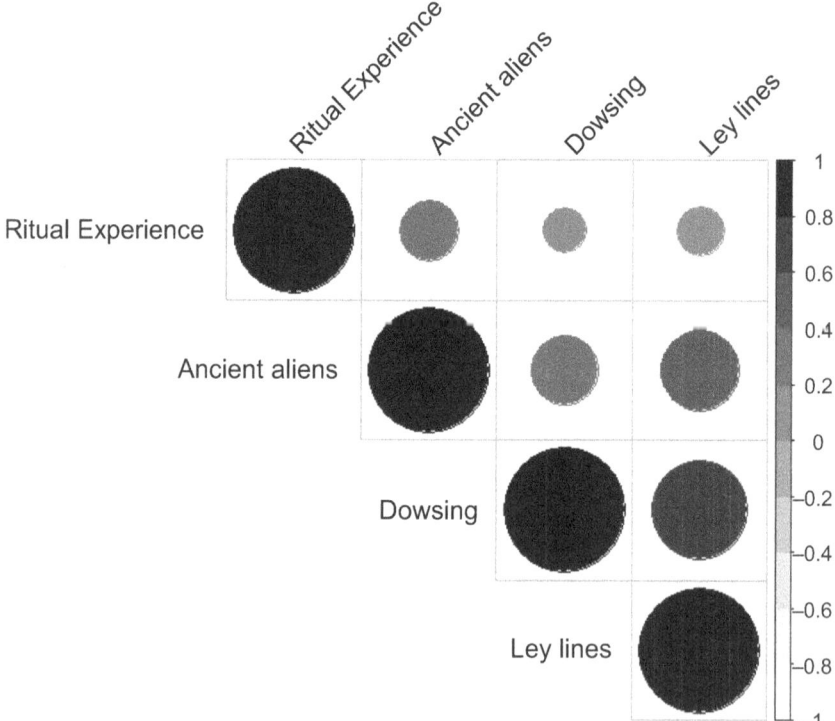

Figure 5.3 Correlogram of beliefs and experiences associated with Earth Mysteries.

direction (darker shades are positive). Beyond the four large circles that act as a point of reference to show a 'perfect' relationship, belief in dowsing and ley lines share the strongest relationship, closely followed by the relationship between ancient aliens and ley lines and then dowsing. Again, this is not entirely surprising given that there is a strand of belief known as 'orthoteny' that suggests alien spacecraft use energy lines as a way of navigating around the Earth.[33] It is also notable that the relationship between ancient aliens and having a ritual experience at an ancient monument is larger than it is for either dowsing or ley lines.

What is clear from both our survey and fieldwork is that the megalithic community has developed a pluralistic belief system that allows for unique combinations of paranormal beliefs. It is an extraordinarily flexible strategy for finding meaningful patterns underlying ancient sites.

A Pilgrimage to Avebury

The village of Avebury is situated in the Wiltshire countryside, just a few miles north of Alton Barnes. The UNESCO World Heritage site is home to the largest megalithic stone circle in Britain and one of the largest in the world. The monument consists of a henge (measuring 374 metres in diametre), an outer circle of as many as 98 stones, some of which measure over 4 metres in height, and two inner circles, named the south circle and the north circle. However, the henge and its circles are a part of a larger prehistoric landscape that also includes West Kennet Long Barrow, Windmill Hill and Silbury Hill.

Avebury is just an hour from Heathrow, but it feels incredibly secluded. The small dips, furrows and the circular embankment would almost act as a shield to the outside world, if it were not for its position on the crest of a chalk hill that looks out over the rest of the undulations that surround Wiltshire. On a sunny autumn day, Tom visited the monument to join a tour of the site led by Andrew Collins.

Collins is a celebrity within the megalithic, and wider paranormal, communities. He is the author of books that are as dense and multi-faceted as anything produced by Hancock and has made several appearances on shows such as *Ancient Aliens* espousing his theories. In his works, Collins posits, among other things, that early humans were influenced by an advanced, elite group called the Swiderians and that North America was once populated by a race of giants that were produced by the intermixing of Denisovians and humans.[34]

As I (Tom) arrived, a few people were milling around, and I joined some of them next to the National Trust caravan in the car park. Slowly, a few more people appeared and started to congregate. After a few minutes, Andrew Collins appeared, dressed in a new black duffel coat, a warm black hat and some heavy-duty walking boots. The gathered are immediately enthusiastic, and Collins explains to those assembled what is going to happen for the next four hours. He tells the group that we are going to visit the Avebury stones 'quadrant by quadrant'. He is going to pick out significant stones for us and 'tell us their story – and perhaps some of the stories that surround them'.

He begins with a discussion of the ancient ritual sites of Gobekli Tepi and Karahan Tepi located in Turkey.[35] He tells us that the people of Avebury moved through Turkey and Eastern Europe, arriving in Great Britain sometime in 5,000 BC. 'They' then start building 'big time' through Anglesey, Callenish in Scotland, Yorkshire, and, of course, Avebury. This is also a special place, he claimed, and the people who built it recognized this fact. It is a place of UFO activity, strange lights, and 'time slips' – 'and they were aware of this, the builders, that's why the monuments were put here in 3000 BC'. He thinks there were three stones put here first, 'in the line with the rise of the moon at its mostly northerly'. It is immediately clear, if nothing else, that Collins is an accomplished storyteller who can seamlessly weave several different ideas into a single narrative.

Collins then goes on to talk about the acoustic properties of the Avebury circle. 'The stones', he suggests, 'seem to respond to sounds'. Without stopping for much of an explanation, he then tells us that Avebury 'is a place of the dead', where veneration took place. This 'was not for the common folk', he suggests. Instead, 'they were contacting the dead, quite literally'.

As we passed one of the stones, there was a man meditating quietly. He barely notices as we pass by. Collins begins another monologue. This time it is about the Cygnus constellation. This is a direct reference to his own work, in which he argues for 'the influence of the Cygnus constellation on the minds of our Neolithic ancestors'.[36] He then said something about a 'megalithic computer' that I struggled to follow.

Try as I might, there is always a point at these events where you realize that you have no idea what the speaker is talking about. There was not a 'eureka' moment, as such, just a realization that I had lost the thread of what was being said and why. Collins is an excellent speaker, and it is possible to stay with him for quite a time, but his continual merging of several different esoteric ideas and controversial notions of the past eventually became overwhelming.

We made our way across the road to stand next to another circle. Collins talks about why he thinks they built the circle here: 'What you feel about these places is as good as anything you might read in a book', he proclaims. 'You feel the truth when you're inside these circles. You intuit the truth when you are here'. Here we can see how sacralized landscapes lend themselves to enlightenment practices and experiences. They allow individuals to locate themselves within wider spatial locations and deep time, particularly in relation to the history of humanity. This helps to create a sense of spiritual magnitude – which is exactly what Collins is suggesting.

He then returned to the subject of UFOs and the number of sightings that have occurred in the area – hundreds of thousands of them, he claimed. Again placing Avebury as a place of cosmic significance, he told us about the 'Earth lights' that he had seen in the circle. Collins suggested that such lights manifest from the Earth and are actually 'plasma' that 'seems to be intelligent'. This energy might be able to open portals to other dimensions to give us access to higher forms of life, he adds, further extending the spiritual magnitude of the place.

Collins then tells the group that it is time to have a 'group med' around one of the Stones. We were about to go on a psychic quest.

Psychic Questing

Emerging in the late 1970s, psychic questing is the attempt to utilize psychic information for a shared purpose. Andrew Collins is generally credited with having coined the term and has written various books on the subject, most notably, *The Sword and the Stone* (1982), *The Black Alchemist* (1988), *The Seventh Sword* (1992), and *The Second Coming* (1993). Graham Phillips, however, is widely credited as writing the 'classic' text – *The Green Stone* (1984) – which was followed by *The Eye of the Fire* (1988). Both were co-written with Martin Keatman. [37]

Collins's website defines psychic questing as 'the use of dreams, visions and intuitive leads to find hidden artefacts, explore landscape mysteries, or solve historical enigmas'.[38] It draws on the principles of 'chaos magick' and is deliberately pluralistic in its use of all types of religious doctrine, deities and symbols. It includes a heavy focus on clairvoyance and extrasensory perception.

Psychic questing usually begins with a group meditation, where individual messages or visions received during the session are then discussed amongst the group to see where points of confluence might be found and pursued. These 'clues' might be physical locations, shared meanings or things perceived to have a symbolic connection. Once resonance is found and agreed upon by the group, the point of the quest is to then follow those clues. In some cases, this might involve chasing around the country to investigate a particularly prescient vision. In other cases, it might simply involve focusing the psychic energy of the group on something they have discovered about themselves.

Collins began today's quest by telling us to close our eyes and imagine that we were breathing out smoky light. As we breathe in, we will take in a white light, he told us. Slowly, that white light will replace the smoky light that we expel. As the white light builds around us, it will form a ball in the middle of the group that will get bigger and bigger. When the white light envelopes us, Collins tells us, light will shoot out toward the edges of the stone circle, connecting with the individual stones and growing bigger and bigger within them. Collins then tells us to take a minute to think about what images we might 'see' in the circle.

Soon, Collins brought us back. We are to breathe in the white light, pulling it back from the edges of the circle, back to the group, and back into ourselves. He instructed us to 'in our own time', 'come back to this place'. Once everyone had 'returned', he began to talk about what we saw in our visions. Collins reported that he saw something of a funeral procession moving through the circle, perhaps a burial ritual. In his vision, there was a woman at the procession's centre, and he speculated that it may have been the ancient Goddess 'Tara'.[39]

A woman in the group suggested that she also saw a divine Goddess, with women dancing all around. Another man saw a black dog, while someone else saw white dogs in the sky. Yet another participant reported filaments of light erupting from the stones.

After listening to these accounts, Collins told us that if we had enough time we could look for patterns in the images and visions to find 'shared points of reference'.

We could then use these to continue the quest, and, Collins suggested, perhaps do things like 'dig up magical objects'.

The Sacralized Landscape

While megalithic structures might be more of a permanent feature of the British landscape than the more short-lived crop circles, they are both surrounded by uncertainty in terms of creation and meaning. Their inherent mystery provides places that inspire fascination, speculation, and sometimes, even levitation among devotees. The crop circles, stone circles, white horses, and hill giants of Britain have created a sacralized landscape wherein one need not travel far to find a place layered with spiritual meaning.

Part of the appeal of Earth mysteries as conceptualized in modern paranormal subcultures is that they cross many boundaries, allowing for wide and diverse appeal. As we have discussed throughout this book, we have found two major forms of paranormalism: discovery and enlightenment. Discovery paranormalism focuses upon the collection of evidence and facts in the hopes of demonstrating the reality of heretofore unexplained phenomena. As such, discovery leans towards the pseudoscientific end of the paranormal spectrum. Enlightenment paranormalism eschews concerns about evidence that an outsider might find convincing and is, rather, concerned with personal enrichment. Enlightenment focuses upon the psychic and magical and, therefore, leans into the more spiritual end of paranormalism.

Both forms are easily found, and often combined, in the enchanted world of croppies and megalith enthusiasts. Croppies easily shift between discussions of the manner in which the crops have been flattened – and how this proves they could not have been made by humans – to stories of psychic and visionary experiences within the formations. The dense works of Graham Hancock are stuffed with astronomical charts, historical references and enough measurements to induce a headache, yet inevitably drift into the realm of otherworldly beings and alternate dimensions. Andrew Collins was as comfortable discussing the measurements of Gobekli Tepe and the pyramids of Giza as he was leading us on a psychic quest to discover a goddess. Within both the subcultures of croppies and megalithomaniacs, we find a thorough integration of spiritual practices and related intensive spiritual experiences with the oft-impenetrable rhetoric of pseudoscience.

Further, both communities are wide-ranging in their incorporation of other paranormal phenomena. Crop circle enthusiasts frequently reference the work of the megalithic community and vice versa. Both subcultures then freely combine these interests with notions of ancient aliens, Atlantis, other dimensions and spirits, to name but a few. In this way, sacralized landscapes allow for the synthesis of enlightenment and discovery through emplacement, as well as temporal connections that inspire mystery and wonder. In the case of megaliths, a connection to deep human history and the cosmos becomes tangible and real. In the case of crop circles, a more temporary and time-bound form of enchanted place takes hold, inevitably to be erased with degradation and the inevitable changing of seasons. This too connects believers to the mysteries of consciousness and the cosmos.

For some, these mysteries of the cosmos extend still further, to questions of alien life, intelligence, visitation and abduction. As a result, our journey into the realms of the paranormal next takes us into the bewildering world of UFOs.

Chapter 6

MYSTERIOUS UNIVERSE

High Strangeness

On a warm summer morning, after driving up a couple of hours from Sheffield, we arrived in Filey, a seaside town of about 7,000 people northeast of York. We made our way through streets lined with pubs, chippies, and toy and gift shops and found a parking spot near a golf course. The car park was bubbling with holidaymakers unpacking towels, windbreakers, and buckets and spades in preparation for a day of relaxation on the beach.

Unlike most visitors to Filey, we were not on holiday. Instead, we had come to interview Russell Kellett, a controversial figure within the UFO community. We found our way to his home on a side street where Russ warmly greeted us, offered tea and motioned toward his living room. Before long, he was telling us about his first UFO encounter.

At four years old, Russ peered out his bedroom window one evening and saw something enter the family garden. It was dressed in a grey-silver suit and wearing what looked to a young Russ like a 'space helmet'. At first, he assumed this merely was the dustbin man coming to collect the rubbish but then thought, 'Whoa! Why's the dustbin man got a helmet on?'[1] Russ waved at the figure. It waved back. The odd figure then retreated from the garden, shuffling backwards. It entered a small craft that 'juddered from side-to-side, and went up [until] it went out of view'. Now sixty years of age, the incident is something that Russ has never forgotten. 'It were a bit odd', he joked dryly, in his distinctive Yorkshire accent.

Perhaps this childhood experience was the origin of Kellett's longtime interest in the paranormal. It is hard to say for certain, since he reports recovering more memories over time. What is clear, however, is that the 'dustbin man' encounter was but one part of what would become a lifelong pursuit. Russ has been active in several UFO clubs over the years, including the Flying Saucer Bureau, the International UFO Network, and the British UFO Hunters. He even set up his own online paranormal magazine in the early 2000s (now defunct) and a UFO hotline where people could report unusual experiences. He has authored two books, one about his own UFO experiences and another concerning a purported UFO crash in Wales called the 'Berwyn Mountains Incident'.[2]

What makes Russ controversial within the UFO community is not his childhood encounter, nor his dedication to paranormal investigation. Rather, it is the additional claims he also makes about his lifetime of alien abductions, namely that he was trained to fight as a time-traveling 'super soldier' in an intergalactic conflict. During these experiences he has encountered an astounding variety of alien species and even suggested that he saw pop star Robbie Williams aboard a spacecraft during one of his missions.[3]

While some people believe in a particular paranormal phenomenon while avoiding others, Russ contrasts sharply with those who narrowly focus on UFOs. His super soldier narrative is both highly idiosyncratic and syncretic, freely drawing upon and combining ideas from different paranormal domains. Outside of UFOs, Russ has investigated haunted houses, crop circles, and even 'the beast of Ryedale' – an alien big cat sighted roaming the North Yorkshire Moors. Russ's eclectic mix of ideas points to a key theme in the future of the paranormal: an increase in unifying narratives that stitch together multiple topics and interests.[4]

In this chapter we compare and contrast Russell Kellett's beliefs with another entrepreneur who has become a prominent figure within the UFO/paranormal community, David Icke. We examine the challenges faced by those who present paranormal narratives that combine themes from across different realms and explore which features of the paranormal promote popularity. We also investigate the potential market for these syncretic narratives by examining patterns in the consumption of paranormal media in Britain. Who reads paranormal books, watches related television shows and attends conferences? Are there differences in people who merely dip a toe into UFOs and those with more diverse interests? To explore these questions, we begin with the story that Russ told us in his front room in Filey before exploring the wider marketplace for idiosyncratic paranormal narratives that create entire, alternative worldviews.

E. T. Rider

Russ grew up in and around Bingley, a market town near Bradford. After leaving school, he went to work for a company that produced overalls for people working in heavy industry – 'the old miners, old steelworkers, ya know, sort of like old garagers'. By this time, he had also developed an interest in motorbikes and spent much of his spare time tinkering with his Suzuki trail bike, which he later replaced with a scooter, and then a 'chopper'. It was while riding his 'chopper' in the summer of 1980 that he had an unusual experience.

Russ had ridden to Druid's Altar, a local beauty spot that overlooks the main road that runs through Bingley. He was sitting on a rock meditating when he realized the evening was closing in. Russ had work the next day, so he set off for home. Towards the bottom of Altar Lane, he came across what he could 'only describe as a tunnel'. It was 'damp' and 'diffused', and there was 'a dull light inside'.

6. Mysterious Universe

The next thing, I've gone through it. And I'm sat in this dentist chair … with these things walking around. I didn't know they were walking around at first, until I looked right up and then I sees 'em. I thought, "ah, flippin heck", sort of like, and me heart sank, ya know? And one of them came behind us and shook me head forward, and there were a bit of a pain in the back of me neck.

Russ would later clarify what 'these things' were:

They're like Nosferatu, more or less. Sort of like pointed ears. And their eyes are wide, with uh, sometimes, like, a dark dot, sometimes a lighter dot, in the middle. Um, and they're like, massive. They're, ya know sort of like, they're not skinny, they're sort of like got big chests, and they're slim … And they're telepathic, for one thing.

This incident would be the first of many experiences he had with the tall, white and bald aliens (TWBAs). At first glance, it might appear that these were similar to many classic UFO abduction tales that include reports of experimentation by aliens as the motivating factor. But Russ's story is quite different. He claims that he was recruited into an elite fighting force gathered to repel attacks on the 'Nosferatu' planet by other aliens. The TWBAs had resorted to recruiting humans 'to fight alongside them'.

In fact, Russ said that some humans are particularly well-suited to the parameters of this conflict:

Now, as daft as it may sound, some of their best fighters are the women from this planet. And they take the women from this planet because of one thing. And that is, the females from Earth are more telepathic than the males. And, [the humans are] keeping [the TWBAs] alive at the moment. Because … some of the good telepaths can sense these alien races coming through their – you can call it like a teleportation system. So they can tell where [the alien enemies are] teleporting on their planet, and 15 minutes before they get there, they can sense it.

In addition to fighting in a telepathic unit, Russ also operated in what he terms 'a scout unit'. Here he learned to handle alien technology directly.

[W]hen you're using your weapons against the Dragos, and the Reptilians, mostly you use what you would call a sound weapon … But also underneath, they have a laser cannon. So that you could, basically, you know, fire at anything else. You know, because, the sound weapon, when it hits one of these dragon races, and the reptiles, they sort of like, implode. If you see what I mean? It sort of like implodes, and um, basically sucks them – I don't know how or why – but it sucks 'em inwards.

This quote suggests another key difference between Russ's narrative and the popular abduction tales of the twentieth century, a dramatically expanded cosmology. The earliest abduction tales reported by people like Betty and Barney Hill and collected by abduction researcher Budd Hopkins focused on the 'Greys': diminutive, grey-skinned entities with large black eyes.[5] Over time, abduction tales have expanded to include taller grey beings, giant praying mantises, bipedal 'Reptilians' (more on them later), the Nordic space brothers of the contactee tales of the 1950s, and many others. Russ's encounters include the greys (short and tall) and the reptilians and human-like aliens, but he also adds a host of other colourful beings to the pantheon. There are the 'Dragos' mentioned above, whom he describes as 'half-human, half-dragon' creatures. There are also creatures that look like the greys, except that they are blue. On one mission to a planet with a gigantic pyramid, he met several ten-foot-tall aliens that reminded him of Egyptian pharaohs. One had a bull's head. Another was human-like, with long black hair. A third 'was strange colour, almost red in skin tone, with a horse's head'.[6]

These more atypical elements of his story have brought Russ into conflict with some members of the UFO community. 'I don't want anything to do with them', Russ tells us. 'Liars. Cheats'. He explained that his experiences were simply too challenging for many.

Unifying Theories of the Paranormal

During our research, we have often listened to 'unifying theories of the paranormal'. These are individual belief systems that combine multiple elements of the paranormal into a unifying theory, usually in the form of an overarching narrative that is connected to intensive personal experiences. The distinctive characteristic of these unifying theories is linking multiple paranormal domains of belief and experience into a discrete narrative structure. It is also true to say that the more successful versions of these narratives are only *relatively* novel in respect to their audiences.[7] Russ alluded to the fact that the novelty of his claims made them challenging to many people. But that very novelty also attracted attention.

Social scientists use the term 'syncretism' to refer to this process of blending ideas from different traditions into new combinations and forms.[8] This process can occur at different levels of organization.[9] For example, religious groups and movements might incorporate elements of other belief systems into their doctrines over time, such as the fairly recent addition of extraterrestrial gods and lost civilizations into the neo-Pagan movement.[10] Individuals can also create their own, idiosyncratic belief systems that draw upon multiple religious traditions, as well as less organized systems such as the paranormal. In our time studying the paranormal, it was not uncommon to meet people who believe that both Jesus and Buddha are divine extraterrestrials who have visited the Earth or that a race of aliens from the planet Nibiru is responsible for charging the Earth with spiritual energy.

Certain cultural conditions are favourable to such syncretic combinations. To the extent that a local culture encourages ideological openness and is not

Photo 6.1 A horse-headed 'Egyptian Pharaoh' alien encountered by Russell Kellett.

dominated by an exclusivist set of religious beliefs, individuals are relatively freer to experiment with creative combinations. As we will discuss more in the next chapter, strict, organized religious groups often discourage experimentation outside of their doctrinal boundaries. But rapidly declining rates of affiliation with organized religion in Britain create a context wherein syncretic combinations are becoming increasingly likely.

Russ provides a window into such syncretic belief systems. He combines multiple elements of paranormal belief and experience into a single overarching theory with a unifying narrative that explains his intensive, anomalous experiences. He pushes back against those who want to narrowly focus on one aspect of the paranormal, such as just UFOs. For instance, Russ told us that when he investigates any local case of reported anomalous experiences, he runs through a wide-ranging list of possible explanations:

> Listen to this, right, yeah? This is what they say, is that when you're lookin' at UFOs, you're looking at that phenomena. And you've got to discount any other paranormal activity surrounding it. Why? Because, the thing is, if you've gone to an area, you asked all the questions. You know, like for instance, about the area. Is there any military? Any naval, or whatever buildings? Any underground buildings? Right, yeah? Has anything ever been on that land before military? Has there ever been anything on that land going back in history? Any battles? And, you know, any famous battles? Ya know what I mean? And then, has anything ever been seen there? Anything religiously? Ya know sort of like, religious beliefs and what-have-you? Has any ghosts been seen there? Any ley lines? Anything been seen of a cryptozoology nature? Like werewolves? Ya know, Bigfoot?

This is not to say that such narratives unify *all* of someone's beliefs into a single structure. The Beast of Ryedale, for example, nor his interest in ghosts are a direct part of Russ's super soldier experiences; however, they are certainly components of a larger supernatural worldview that allows for their existence. Russ's narrative contains tacit beliefs about the nature and existence of alien races, visitation and abduction, as well as intergalactic interaction *and* conflict, not to mention the existence of telepathy and advanced technologies such as teleportation and time travel. This belief system is highly syncretic in that it resonates with elements across many paranormal subcultures and is simultaneously highly idiosyncratic in that it combines these beliefs in a way that is unique and personalized.

Not *entirely* unique, however. Even the most idiosyncratic combinations usually draw upon related ideas present in popular culture and subcultures. The idea that Earth governments are in league with (or defending against) alien races has been part of the UFO subculture for years and produced the term 'exopolitics'.[11] The more specific idea of 'super soldiers' is also not without precedence. A number of people around the world have reported similar experiences. Stephen Chua (Singapore), Jean Charles Moyen (France), Corey Goode (United States), and Tony Rodrigues (United States) can all be found making guest appearances on podcasts and TV shows talking about their extraterrestrial combat experiences.[12] Outside of Russ, however, people reporting 'super soldier' experiences in the UK are still quite rare, and we are only aware of two other high-profile examples.[13]

None of this 'borrowing' is to suggest that Russ is inventing his story or just copying ideas for personal gain. Russ is engaging and genuine, and someone who is simply trying to convey his honest views about the existence of aliens and his own experiences with them. Any monetary gain that Russ has made from his

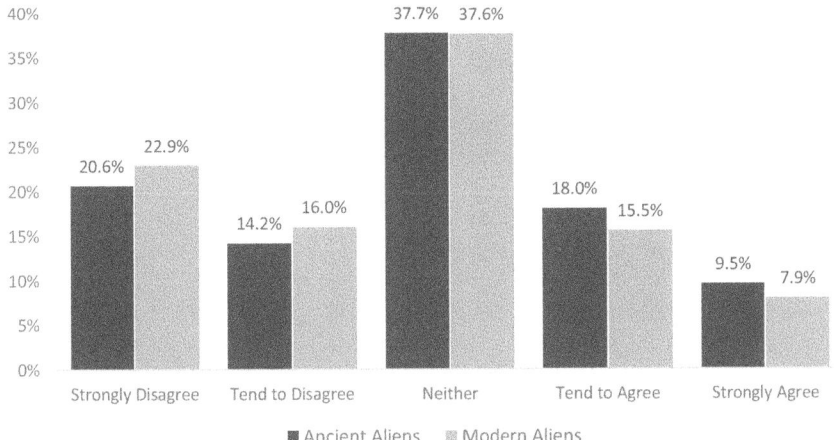

Figure 6.1 Belief in ancient and modern alien visitations (CASPAR, 2021).

story is also negligible at best. His work on the paranormal is a passion project, the outgrowth of a lifetime of intensive experiences, paranormal practices and investigations.

In some ways, Russ's tales might seem an easy sell to some, in that he can draw upon considerable belief in extraterrestrials in Britain (see Figure 6.1). Just over one-fourth (27.5 per cent) of CASPAR respondents either tend to agree or strongly agree that aliens 'have visited the Earth in our ancient past'. Likewise, nearly one-fourth (23.4 per cent) tend to agree or strongly agree that aliens 'have visited the Earth in modern times'.

With such robust belief in aliens, one would think that Russ's stories would find a large audience. The problem is that aliens are but one part of a complicated, multifaceted belief system needed to buy into Russ's worldview. His alien super soldier narrative is dependent upon several supporting ideas – such as telekinesis, psychic powers and time travel. Each element needs acceptance before a final assessment can be made about the whole. At any point, the rejection of one of the elements threatens belief in the entire *system*. In this way, Russ presents a theory of the paranormal that is both unifying and totalizing.

To these ends, although specific beliefs in the paranormal are common, holding multiple beliefs is less so. People might generally think one or two paranormal ideas are credible but become much more sceptical of the paranormal as a multifaceted phenomenon. This is demonstrated in Figure 6.2.

We asked respondents about eighteen different paranormal beliefs, including our two alien items and belief in psychic powers, hauntings, Bigfoot, telekinesis, faeries, crop circles, big cats in Britain, the UK Wildman, the Yeti, Nessie, black magic, dowsing, ley lines, mysterious creatures and curses.[14]

About one-fifth of our respondents were complete sceptics (21.7 per cent), rejecting all eighteen paranormal beliefs. As the number of paranormal beliefs increases, the number of believers decreases. About 11 per cent of our respondents

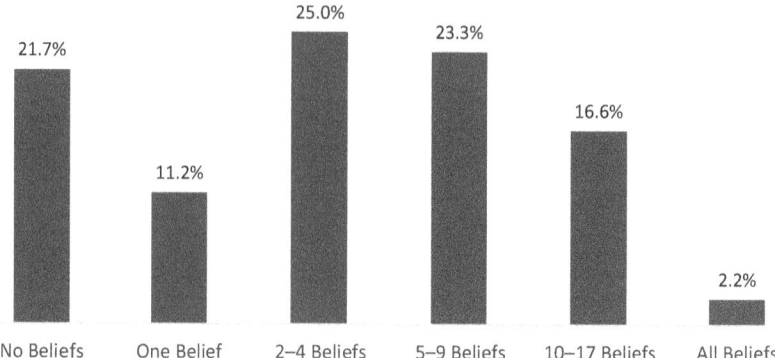

Figure 6.2 Paranormal beliefs in Britain, by number held (CASPAR, 2021).

were paranormal particularists, believing in one paranormal subject but rejecting all others. About one-fourth of our respondents found two to four elements of the paranormal credible. This drops to about 23 per cent for those who believe in five to nine elements and under 17 per cent for ten to seventeen elements. Only a small number (2.2 per cent) of our respondents accepted all eighteen paranormal beliefs.

This means that while single beliefs in the paranormal are quite common, multiple, simultaneous beliefs are less so. Thus, syncretic paranormal belief systems – such as the one that Russ presents – are likely to encounter initial resistance. Unifying and totalizing theorists like Russ become the paranormal fringe or part of a fringe subculture. However, those who develop such novel combinations also point us towards key themes in the future of paranormal belief systems. We can see such a process by considering another 'unifying theory of the paranormal' – the Reptilian hypothesis.

David Icke and the Reptilians

David Icke has spent most of his life in the public eye. Born in 1952, he retired as a footballer due to rheumatoid arthritis at the age of just twenty-one. He then began a career in sports broadcasting, and following some very high-profile jobs with the BBC, he developed a considerable interest in alternative therapies and green politics.

During a 1990 tour for his book on green politics, *It Doesn't Have to Be Like This*, Icke felt 'guided' by an unseen presence in his hotel room to explore spiritual matters.[15] This experience ultimately led him to visit the late psychic healer Betty Shine several times. He was impressed when Shine correctly predicted that one of his cats would soon develop diarrhoea, but the visits quickly turned towards more spiritual matters. Shine claimed to be contacted psychically by a 'being of immense power' named Wang. It seems Wang was in the presence of Socrates, who had this to say about Icke's future:

He is a healer who is here to heal the earth, and he will be world-famous. He will face enormous opposition, but we will always be there to protect him. He is still a child spiritually, but he will be given spiritual riches. Sometimes he will say things and wonder where they came from. They will be our words. Knowledge will be put into his mind, and at other times he will be led to knowledge.[16]

Icke seemed to take this message to heart. On an April 1991 episode of the BBC talk show *Wogan*, he proclaimed himself the 'son of God' and warned that Britain would soon be destroyed by tidal waves and floods.[17] At the time, Icke was subject to considerable ridicule, but it did not abate his enthusiasm. He is now the author of over twenty books and a major shareholder in the subscription channel 'Ickonic Media', which offers an 'alternative media platform that brings you uncensored, unbiased and unique information'.[18]

In the fall of 2023, we had the opportunity to attend one of Icke's talks during what was being billed as 'the secret tour'. It was 'secret' inasmuch as the venue of the talk was not disclosed until a few hours before it was due to start. Icke would later reveal that several venues had cancelled previous appearances due to public pressure. Indeed, in 2022 he was also banned from the Schengen Area of the European Union for a period of two years as a potential threat to public order because of statements he had made about the Covid-19 pandemic.[19] The ruling effectively prevented him from travelling in twenty-seven countries across Europe. Twitter had already 'banned him for life' in 2020, for similar reasons.[20]

The 'secret' venue turned out to be the function suite of a grill restaurant in a suburb of Leeds. Holding around 600 people, it was close to a sell-out. Icke appeared to have something of a white, upper working-class/lower middle-class audience, with a relatively equal gender balance. Many people accompanied friends on what appeared to be a Friday night out, and they were generally smartly dressed, ranging in age from around thirty years upward. Icke clearly has a dedicated fan base.

Although the talk was being recorded for streaming on his Ickonic media platform, the stated purpose of the tour was to promote his new book *The Dream*, and his talk mostly followed its content.[21] Icke's argument had three components. The first concerned the nature of perception. The second detailed the organization of a 'global cult'. The final part examined how and why our experiences are orchestrated by this shadowy cult.

'If You Control Perception, You Control Behaviour'

Around 6.00 pm, an energetic Icke took the stage to a round of enthusiastic applause, wearing a dark button-down shirt and black trousers. He began with a brief but humorous autobiographical narrative – which included his own spiritual awakening – discussed above. At points, Icke sounded like a motivational speaker. At others he presented himself as a studious and wide-ranging scholar who draws on all manner of material to support his argument. This included scientists, popular philosophy, and cultural icons and products. At the same time, he frequently used non-specific 'others' to emphasize his argument. 'They sell us our dreams', he says. 'They are trying to control our uniqueness'. We are given 'bubbles of perception', 'that imprison human life'. While the audience continued to clap enthusiastically, he said, 'it's all about perception', and continued, 'it's all about controlling and hijacking that perception, because if you control perception, you control behaviour, and if you control behaviour, you control society'.[22]

His argument in these respects amounted to an exploration of the difference between seeing and perceiving, with the aim of demonstrating that what we 'see' is dependent on what we 'know'. Unfortunately, Icke suggested, what we 'know' is little more than a 'hoax'. This is because our knowledge is based on a limited range of ideas and concepts that are learned and subsequently reinforced by any number of social and political institutions.

Up to this point, much of what Icke says does not appear to be *that* controversial. There is a long tradition within philosophy called phenomenology that discusses how our subjective experiences are influenced, and even structured, by wider social contexts. These networks of language and interpretation are termed 'plausibility structures'.[23] That is to say, we need to have some cultural points of reference in order to interpret what we 'see', and those points of interpretation are provided through pre-existing ideas necessarily contained in language and society more generally. Similarly, there is a long tradition in Marxist thought that suggests that consciousness is structured by social and economic circumstances.[24] A central purpose of Marxism is to emancipate people from such 'false consciousness'. Of course, many might disagree with these ideas and Icke himself does not acknowledge them, not least because he takes every possible opportunity to denigrate academia as an institution. This is perhaps because some academics have paid considerable attention to Icke's place within the wider world of New Age thought and conspiracy subcultures.[25]

However, Icke goes beyond these ideas in one key respect. He positions himself as revealing 'hidden knowledge' – what might be termed 'conspiratorial Gnosticism'. This is one of the key psychological and social attractions of belief systems such as Icke's. Conspiratorial Gnosticism provides a revelatory lens for understanding a complex world while also positioning believers as ideologically (and therefore culturally) superior to those who are unable to perceive such truths.[26] In other words, the exclusivity and scarcity of holding conspiratorial beliefs make people *feel* special.

A Conspiracy of Reptiles?

The second phase of Icke's presentation was dedicated to the question: 'How is this hoax orchestrated?' The answer was notably more controversial. 'It is a global cult', Icke tells us, a network of secret societies that is 'fiercely compartmentalised'.

Icke used the analogy of 'a spider's web' to explain this conspiracy. Each concentric layer represents a collection of groups and organizations that support an insidious agenda. The closest to the centre are secret societies – 'the New World

Order', 'the Bilderberg Foundation' and 'the Royals' – with the next layer operating to protect and insulate these groups. These are people like the Rosicrucians and other esoteric organizations. The next layer consists of global organizations, like the World Economic Forum, which are then supported by nation-state governments, NGOs, think tanks, and 'big pharma'.

This prompted a discussion about the Covid vaccine, which had previously gotten Icke into trouble. He played a montage of politicians talking about the response to Covid and received much approval from the audience, who very loudly jeered Boris Johnson, Bill Gates, and King Charles.

'But what about that spider?' Icke then asked. This is where things began to take a distinctly otherworldly turn. It is a 'non-human force', Icke suggests, that is 'operating in this reality'. Indeed, 'we are being manipulated from the unseen'. This nonhuman force can interact with the third and fourth dimensions, Icke proclaimed, 'so we need to enter the fifth dimension to go beyond the manipulation'.

While the third dimension is where we perceive our physical reality, Icke tells us that the fourth dimension is where we see ghosts and other 'paranormal' activity. He emphasized the word 'paranormal' as if it were quite silly and also suggested that 'a ghost is just visual interference'. But the fourth dimension – a term he used interchangeably with 'the Astral realm' – also includes those demonic Gods that 'the ancients talked about'. He then offered some anthropological material about different Gods from around the world and argued that they are actually the same 'astral entities that are running this show'.[27] These ancient societies, he tells us, are 'talking about the same thing, but with different names ... and the common themes are amazing'.

Icke then showed a slide that appeared to depict a Satanic ritual and asked rhetorically 'why are the cultists doing rituals to these Astral Gods?' Although he didn't provide a direct answer, he followed with 'reptilians are common ... but they are not the only form', 'and many people have told me exactly the same story'. Icke then talked about the Jeffrey Epstein case. He was a shapeshifter, according to Icke. 'The reptilian brain is about survival', he continued: it is impulsive, aggressive, and has 'an anti-human agenda'.

Icke has been developing the idea of a race of reptilian shapeshifters controlling humanity from the shadows since the publication of his book *The Biggest Secret* in 1999.[28] Sometimes referred to as the 'Babylonian Brotherhood', sometimes 'the Illuminati', this nefarious cabal includes Queen Elizabeth II (and the rest of the royal family), former Prime Minister Ted Heath, the Rockefellers and Rothschilds, and all of the presidents of the United States of America.

As surprising as it may seem, none of this is particularly new. Scholars have documented a long history of claims of reptilian bipeds in both fiction and New Age thought.[29] Icke actually acknowledges this lack of novelty in his books and, indeed, uses the history of notions of reptilians and the wider ancient astronaut literature as evidence for his claims. For example, Icke frequently discusses the work of Zecharia Sitchin.[30] In books such as *The 12th Planet*, the late Sitchin argued that the 'Anunnaki', a race of aliens from a planet named Nibiru, had created the human race to help them mine for gold.[31] While Sitchin described the Anunnaki as humanoid, not reptilian, Icke still utilizes his work, arguing that while Sitchin mostly got things right, some of his interpretations are 'extremely questionable'.[32] Icke also finds meaning in popular media that includes depictions of reptilians, being particularly impressed with the American television series *V*:

> [T]he closest any movie has come to the truth is the American television series of the 1980s called *V*. It tells of a reptile extraterrestrial race who take over the world by looking like humans. The film depicts the reptiles as being covered in some sort of latex skin, which is not how it works in reality, but the theme of the series is right on the button and a foretaste of things to come; unless we wake up fast.[33]

Claims of secretive, devil-worshipping cults also have a very long history, and any number of groups, including the Waldensians, Cathars, Jews, and early Christians, have been accused of such activities.[34] But while several scholars have documented the development of the cultural *idea* of a 'Brotherhood,' Icke simply embraces such work as evidence for his claims.[35] Any reference to reptilians, whether academic, non-academic, or in popular culture are a glimpse of the truth for Icke. Only by 'connecting the dots' between them is it possible to see the full picture – and it was time for him to connect those dots for us.

'The Dream'

'Next step down the rabbit hole,' Icke said, before moving on to the final element of his talk. 'Our reality is a simulation,' he announced, which he called the 'Matrix'. The architecture of this simulation is designed by non-human forces to hijack human perception: 'They are deluding the population about the reality that they think that they are experiencing,' he said. 'The laws of physics are the rules of the game,' he told us, because there is nothing outside those laws. 'Our reality is actually defined by algorithms,' Icke continued at pace. Fractals, Fibonacci, the golden ratio, and pi are all 'key codes in the simulation   that's why they keep recurring'. 'Scientists are beginning to recognise this,' he continued, 'and so they should. I've been telling them for years!' The audience laughed approvingly.

On display throughout the talk was Icke's freeform syncretism. He continually presents ideas from other scholars, even if their ideas do not directly support his. As with his references to Sitchin, he takes what he needs and ignores the rest. He discussed Immanuel Velikovsky's claims that the formation of the universe is best understood via electromagnetism rather than gravity. He then showed a video montage of people being scared/surprised by virtual reality devices. 'The body is an operating system to be manipulated,' he announces to some approval. Then, seemingly unable to resist the subject, Icke once again discussed Covid. The Moderna (Covid) vaccine 'is designed to alter the operating system' he said to thunderous applause.

He then introduced Robert Monroe's idea of 'loosh,' a form of energy purportedly given off by beings when faced with emotion or conflict. A self-proclaimed astral traveller from the 1950s, Monroe's book *Far Journeys* included a long allegory about a group called the 'collectors' who were attempting to farm loosh from beings in a garden.[36] Icke then linked this idea of farming energy to the Archons of Gnosticism and Manichaeism, before suggesting that humans are the energy source. Our evil alien controllers are 'feeding off our energy', he said, and the simulation in which we are trapped 'keeps us in the state of low vibrational energy that they need'.

What to do about all of this, exactly, was less clearly articulated. Icke seemed to be falling back on some well-worn ideas about seeing beyond our material existence and going beyond the astral realm, largely to escape 'the Matrix'. He called this destination '5D'. His book suggested a similar sort of idea to that of 'awakening' or 'ascension' that are common in a number of New Age philosophies.

Indeed, this part of Icke's talk also resonated strongly with Helena Blavatsky's theosophical movement in at least four ways.[37] First, Icke assumes the existence of higher beings, both in the form of his own spirit guides and 'the non-human force'. Second, Icke references hierarchical planes of existence that he refers to in the form of the third, fourth, and fifth dimensions. Third, Icke's idea that 'we are all one consciousness' echoes theosophical conceits about the unity of humanity and the recognition of an integral whole that pervades all life. Finally, the search for the inner truth and wisdom that Icke associates with the fifth dimension is very similar to theosophical ideas of transcendence.[38]

In his discussions of the Matrix, Icke was also not shy in referencing the film of the same name. Indeed, Icke's central argument in his book *The Dream* is that life as we know it is actually a simulation.[39] We might think that we are alive, experiencing life as it happens, but we are just hooked up to a computer programme. This is all perpetuated by the 'non-human'/reptilian entities, who are farming our energy for their own needs. The only solution, as far as it goes, is to free ourselves from our earthly bodies and transcend our material and astral existence.

Diminishing Returns or Alternative Entry Points?

In Leeds, Icke presented a bewildering (to us at least) mix of Sitchin, Velikovsky, UFOs, ancient aliens, Theosophy, secret societies, pseudoscience, astral travel and many other topics – and it was all built upon a bedrock of conspiracy theories and pop culture references. This eclectic mix of theories, disciplines and beliefs is a source of strength for Icke and to the audience it suggests that 'evidence' is to be found everywhere.[40]

However, as discussed above, such syncretic belief systems face a key challenge: an apparent requirement to hold multiple different beliefs at once. For example, belief in extraterrestrials would seem a necessary condition for accepting either Kellett's or Icke's narratives. Without aliens, neither story 'works' and the entire system collapses. Consequently, both theories might be subject to the diminishing returns associated with multiple beliefs. Our survey allows us to examine this issue directly.

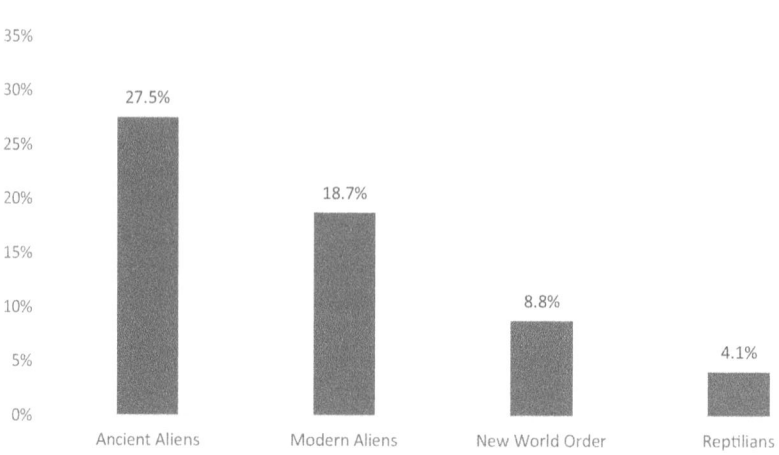

Figure 6.3 Additive belief in components of David Icke's narrative (CASPAR, 2021).

While it also includes many others, the Icke narrative contains four key elements. He argues that aliens have been on Earth for millennia and also that they are here now. Further, he claims that these aliens have orchestrated a sinister conspiracy to control our governments, in effect creating a New World Order. And finally, Icke identifies these aliens specifically as 'reptilians'. As noted above, our survey asked respondents if they agree that aliens have visited Earth in our past, and if they agree that aliens are here now (see Figure 6.1). We also asked respondents to CASPAR if they think 'A group known as the New World Order are planning to eventually rule the world through an autonomous world government, which would replace sovereign government'. Jumping directly into the world of Icke, we also asked if 'the world is controlled by a group of elite reptilian humanoids'.

In Figure 6.3, we display the percentages of the population that simultaneously believe in combinations of these items. The most popular of these beliefs is the notion that aliens have visited Earth in our ancient past. With over one-fourth (27.5 per cent) believing, it is the most accessible entry point into Icke's world.

Numbers quickly reduce once we require combinations of beliefs. Just under 19 per cent of the UK population believes in the existence of aliens in both the past and present. Once we also require belief in a New World Order conspiracy, levels drop much more; just around 9 per cent of people in the UK believe in all three. Only about 4 per cent of the UK population believes in reptilians *and* all three other beliefs. In other words, just over one in twenty-five people in the UK hold the requisite, simultaneous beliefs necessary for holistic belief in Icke's grand narrative. Of course, this does not mean that all of those 4.1 per cent will believe in Icke's particular reptilian narrative, but it does provide insight into his *potential* customers. In absolute numbers, this suggests that Icke's potential market in the UK is capped at a little over 1.6 million adults.[41] That is a substantial market to be certain, but we have reasons to suspect that this is not, in fact, Icke's upper bound.

Within both paranormal and conspiracy subcultures there is a strong emphasis on 'free thinking', wherein individuals use a wide range of texts and discourses to create idiosyncratic interpretations of similar events.[42] This gives paranormalists the cognitive flexibility to reject some parts of a unifying theory of the paranormal while still finding value in the rest. As sociologists Jaron Harambam and Stef Aupers note in their study of Icke, his wide-ranging narrative can attract 'distinctly different audiences' who can choose to 'decode' Icke's theories differently depending upon their own identity and interests.[43]

This is a phenomenon that we encountered several times in our fieldwork. For instance, at a UFO and Spirituality event we attended, we listened to a talk by an 'esoteric astrologer' who spoke at length about the consciousness of the Moon, and how he used it in his astrological practice. During the talk, the astrologer noted that Icke has claimed that the Moon is an ancient spaceship constructed by extraterrestrials as a means of transportation. 'I don't agree with him on everything', the speaker told us, 'you need to pick and choose what fits for you. You have to take out the gold – whatever you think is relevant *for you*'.

So, rather than decreasing the likelihood of belief, increasing the number of elements within a unifying theory may actually increase the potential size of an audience, allowing everyone to find *something* they like. Indeed, if we assume that people need only to believe in one or more of the core components, the picture changes considerably. While only 4 per cent of UK citizens believe in *all* the components of Icke's theory of the universe, more than two in five (44 per cent) believe in *at least* one of them.

Not everyone who believes in the possibility of extraterrestrial visitation will be interested in what Icke has to say; however, *some* people who believe in these things *might* be, particularly when they find resonance with other areas of his narrative. Icke's combination of (folk) biology, psychology, anthropology, physics, astronomy, archaeology, and history, all overlaid with elements of science fiction, global politics, banking and finance, paranormalism, and Gnosticism (and even this list is not exhaustive) provides lots of potential points of entry for different kinds of people.

A Tale of Two Unifying Theorists

There are several similarities between Russell Kellett and David Icke. Both present unifying theories of the paranormal that have extraterrestrials at the core. And both have long histories of creating content, across a wide range of media, for paranormal audiences to consume. Russ had his first paranormal website in the early 2000s and organized a number of events for like-minded enthusiasts. Today, he has a regular YouTube show – 'UFO Paranormal' – in which he interviews guests about all manner of topics. He also has another YouTube channel called 'Flying Saucer Television', which he uses to upload footage of anomalous objects in the sky. He has written two books and makes regular appearances in the print media talking about his discoveries. David Icke also uses many different platforms to deliver his content – he is the author of numerous books, gives frequent live presentations and has developed his own media platform to deliver content.

However, from a financial perspective, Icke is clearly the more successful of the two. During our time with him, Russ complained that he has trouble making ends meet and makes little money from his platforms. After our interview, Russ asked if one of us (Chris) would join him on a live stream show. So far as we could tell, the livestream viewing audience only consisted of the other two coauthors. Icke, in contrast has a successful streaming service of his own under the 'Ickonic' brand that rebroadcasts his many live performances and provides original television programming. His chat forum has over 20,000 users. In 2023, Ickonic Enterprises Limited – which largely deals with the publication side of his business – had a total equity of £325,000.[44] Ickonic Media Group, on the other hand, had a turnover of £277,571 in 2022, with a total equity of £153,118.[45]

Undoubtedly, a significant part of media success is unpredictable. One must be at the right place at the right time and, frankly, have a bit of luck. But there are some other factors that have also contributed to Kellett's and Icke's differences in fortune.

First, Icke's worldview is much more expansive than Kellett's. While Russ combines notions of time travel and psychic powers into his super soldier narrative, it is still largely a UFO story, and so it is unlikely to attract anyone not passionate about extraterrestrials. Aliens are a key component of Icke's unifying theory too, but they are combined with a heady mix of out-of-body experiences, psychic phenomena, alternative history, Gnosticism, claims that we live in a simulation and, importantly, a host of conspiracy theories. There is, of course, an implicit conspiracy implied by Kellett's claims of UFO crash retrievals and government projects with aliens, but Icke has a conspiracy for *everyone* – allegations that 5G towers cause Covid-19, 9/11 truther claims, secret societies, the JFK assassination, underground pedophile rings and many others.

Icke is a pioneer of a new form of spirituality that blends New Age belief systems with conspiracy theories that has been labelled *conspirituality*. The two key elements of conspirituality are the belief in a secret group that is controlling the world and the belief that humanity is undergoing some sort of 'paradigm shift' that may allow us to break free of that control.[46] Icke provides not only different paranormal entry points but also multiple pathways for those whose main interest is in conspiracies.

Another key difference between Icke's and Kellett's unifying theories is that Icke's vision is more easily divisible into discrete pieces. In an individualistic spiritual marketplace, ideas and products that can be extracted from their larger context and then easily syncretized with other views will have far greater public appeal. Icke provides something of a conspiritual buffet for those interested in conspiracies and/or aliens. There is something for the alien believer and the Covid-19 denier equally, and a person need not believe in both to appreciate Icke's views on one or the other. In other words, the paranormal worldview Icke sells to the public is *unifying but divisible*. In contrast, Kellett's worldview is *unifying and totalizing*. It is difficult to accept ideas about being a super soldier in an intergalactic war without accepting at least most of the other premises Kellett advocates about time travel, multiple alien races, and a multitude of other fantastical beliefs, which are needed to make sense of Russ's stories about extraterrestrial contact. In this sense, unifying theories of the paranormal that are nonetheless divisible, easily consumable, and readily available for further syncretism have a greater likelihood of being adopted by larger audiences. In contrast, unifying theories that are totalizing will have less breadth of appeal.

Further, Icke possesses a level of charismatic authority that Kellett does not. We do not use *charisma* here in the popular sense; Russ is quite affable, charming, and interesting. Rather, sociologist Max Weber argues that charisma describes the special qualities that some leaders possess that render them capable of influencing large numbers of people. Charisma is not inherent to the individual but an ephemeral property of the *social relationship* a leader has with their followers. Followers confer charisma upon a leader because they *perceive* him or her as exceptional in some way.[47]

Icke possesses this mysterious, charismatic authority. Certainly, his celebrity status as a former athlete gave him a head start in terms of garnering attention, but he has demonstrated a remarkable resilience, always bouncing back from public humiliations that would have ended others' careers. He uses such setbacks to denigrate those who might be critical of his ideas, encouraging his audience to move beyond even what he terms 'the alternative media' and our 'bubbles of perception'. Further, Icke is an impressive public speaker. Erudite and entertaining, he has a seemingly natural touch for both pace and delivery, and he displays a great talent for weaving ideas and traditions together. None of this is easy to do. Indeed, other scholars who have attended Icke's lectures have noted his connection with the audience and his ineffable charisma.[48]

The Conspiritual Marketplace

David Icke and Russell Kellett are far from the only people in the UK developing paranormal content for wider consumption. During our fieldwork, we learned about the many different ways that people engage with the paranormal. This includes the different types of content enthusiasts and professionals are creating but also the different platforms that potential customers use to consume that material.

To better understand the potential market for the unifying narratives espoused by Kellett, Icke, and others, we asked the respondents to CASPAR several questions about their media habits with regards to the paranormal. We asked if respondents had ever watched TV series, documentaries, or online videos about ghosts, aliens, cryptids, or psychic phenomena. We also asked if they had ever read a non-fiction book, consulted a website, or otherwise researched these same four subjects. Finally, we asked if respondents had ever engaged directly with someone about ghosts, aliens, cryptids, or psychic phenomena at a talk, online conference, or in a community/forum (see Figure 6.4).

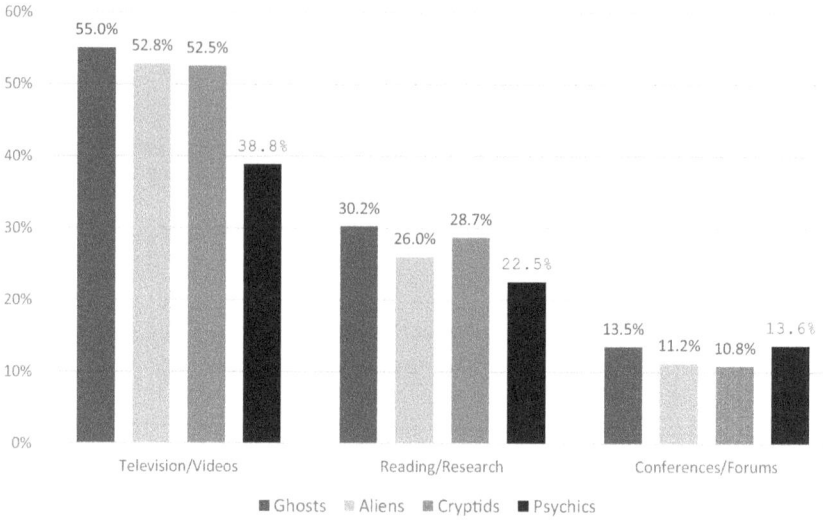

Figure 6.4 Consumption of paranormal media, by type (CASPAR, 2021).

Clearly these forms of consumption differ in terms of the effort and level of engagement required. Watching a television show or video is passive entertainment that can be done anonymously in one's own home. With the relative lack of effort and increasing prevalence of paranormal-related television shows, it is not particularly surprising that this was the most popular form of consumption. Over half the people surveyed had seen TV series, documentaries, or online videos that involved ghosts, aliens, or cryptids, and over one-third had viewed psychic-themed content.

Next was the 'reading & research' category, with over one-fourth of respondents having read a non-fiction book, website, or researched ghosts, aliens or cryptids. Over 20 per cent reported reading about psychic content. While psychic content was the least popular in terms of television and reading, it was the most popular form of content in terms of forums, closely followed by ghosts. However, interacting with people on forums or at conferences was the least popular form of consumption more generally, with each content category recording under 15 per cent. Notably, this is still around one in seven people. In many ways, these results follow more general trends in the consumption of cultural content. Most people watch television, quite a lot but fewer people read books, and fewer still engage with other people at events or on online platforms.

The types of unifying paranormal theories put forth by Icke and others, however, require more than an interest in consuming material about *one type* of phenomena. Someone who is only interested in ghosts or only cares about cryptids seems an unlikely match for the heady syncretism of Icke. Indeed, we do find a healthy amount of diverse interests amongst paranormal consumers and a general willingness to engage with multiple different paranormal topics (see Figure 6.5).

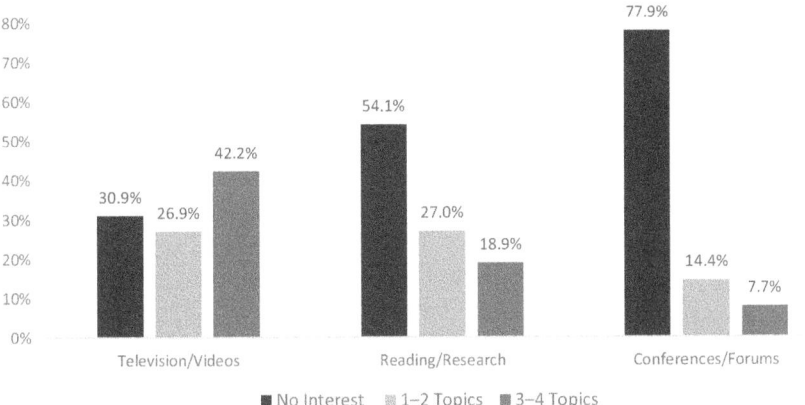

Figure 6.5 Consumption of multiple paranormal topics by media type (CASPAR, 2021).

Over 40 per cent of the survey respondents had watched TV shows or videos about at least three of the four topics; some combination of ghosts, aliens, monsters, or psychic phenomena (or all four). As we find with general consumption patterns, the more effort required from the consumer, the less likely they are to engage. Nevertheless, a little less than one-fifth (18.9 per cent) of people in the UK have read books or otherwise researched three or four paranormal subjects, and nearly 8 per cent have engaged with people about three or four paranormal subjects at conferences or on forums.

Given that there is substantial syncretism in the consumption of paranormal media, we examined exactly *who* is likely to explore the tendency towards believing in multiple things simultaneously. We conducted a series of analyses where we determined which demographic characteristics tend to be associated with consuming all types of media about multiple paranormal topics. We combined this with an examination of who tends to hold a greater number of paranormal beliefs. Given the strong focus upon conspiracy within David Icke's unifying theory of the paranormal, we elected to also examine who tends to hold a variety of conspiracy-oriented beliefs (see Table 6.1).

CASPAR 2021 asked eighteen different questions about conspiracy theories. We asked our respondents if they believed in conspiracies related to the New World Order, the JFK assassination, the suppression of technologies that could result in lower-cost energy, the storage of alien bodies or spacecraft at Area 51 in Nevada, the recovery of a flying saucer from Roswell, New Mexico, in 1947, elite reptilians controlling the world, and a flat Earth. We also asked the extent to which respondents agreed or disagreed that the UK government, in particular, was concealing what it knew about aliens visiting the Earth, the 9/11 attacks, global warming, the Holocaust, the death of Princess Diana, the Illuminati, the origin of the AIDS virus and QAnon. We also explored conspiracies specifically related to the Covid-19 virus, asking how strongly respondents agree or disagree that

Table 6.1 The Syncretists (CASPAR, 2021)

	Syncretic Paranormal Beliefs	Syncretic Conspiracy Beliefs	Syncretic Paranormal Consumption
Age		Younger	Younger
Income	Lower	Lower	
Work status		Working	Working
Education	Lower	Lower	
Marital status	Not single, separated	Not single, separated	
Race	Non-White		
Religious affiliation	Catholic, 'Other' religions	Catholic, 'Other' religions	'Other' religions
Church attendance			Lower
Biblical literalism	Less literal		More literal
Spiritual	Higher	Higher	Higher

Covid-19 was used as a pretext to insert microchips into people, that the epidemic was exaggerated, that the pharmaceutical industry was involved in the spread of Covid-19 and finally, whether there was a link between 5G technology and Covid-19. A final item deserves further explanation. We asked respondents if they believed the UK government was covering up the 'Anglesey Crash'. There is no such conspiracy.[49] Rather, by inserting this item we can gauge someone's general predilection for believing a purported conspiracy, even when presented with it for the first time.[50] For the record, 15 per cent of respondents believed in an Anglesey Crash conspiracy, demonstrating a relatively high baseline willingness to believe in governmental conspiracies.

We combined these conspiracy items into an overall index.[51] The higher a person scored on the measure of syncretic conspiracy beliefs, the more conspiracies they believed in, with a higher degree of certainty. We then conducted a series of analyses to predict syncretic paranormal beliefs, syncretic conspiracy beliefs and syncretic paranormal media consumption using predictive models that included gender, age, income, education, marital status, race/ethnicity, work status and social grade. We also determined if there were regional differences and examined the potential role of organized religion by asking about religious affiliation, frequency of religious service attendance and the extent to which a respondent takes the Bible 'literally'. Finally, we included a question that asks if respondents consider themselves 'spiritual'.

Table 6.1 displays the personal characteristics that were statistically significant predictors, controlling for the other items. For example, when it comes to predicting how many paranormal beliefs one holds, we find that the higher one's level of income and education, the lower their average number of paranormal beliefs. The same was true for the number of conspiracy beliefs a person holds. Put another way, the less education one has achieved and the lower their level of income, the more wide-ranging their paranormal and conspiracy-oriented beliefs will be. This does lend some credence to marginalization theories hypothesizing that those on the margins of society may drift towards alternative beliefs (see Chapter 2). There were several other similarities between those who hold more paranormal beliefs and more conspiracy beliefs. People who are either maritally separated or in some relationship status other than single (e.g., divorced, married, or widowed) tended to be higher in conspiratorialism and paranormalism. For religious affiliation, those who said they were Catholic or members of an 'other' religion (not one of the major religious traditions in the UK) had higher levels of belief in conspiracies and the paranormal.

While we have previously discussed how women tend to hold higher levels of belief in paranormal topics related to psychic phenomena and ghosts (see Chapter 1), when we consider all paranormal beliefs together, women are no more or less syncretic in their paranormal beliefs than men. Similarly, age is strongly related to belief in ghosts, with younger people reporting more belief (see Chapter 3), but again, when it comes to the sheer number of paranormal beliefs a person holds, age is not a factor. Younger people do, however, tend to be more conspiracy-oriented.

Those who consume multiple paranormal topics from more types of media have a slightly different profile. As with the conspiracy-oriented, younger people tend to consume more paranormal media. People who say they are currently working full-time also tend to be more conspiracy-oriented and consume more paranormal media.

In a religious sense, the consumers look slightly different. While being Catholic is predictive of holding many paranormal and conspiracy beliefs, it does not predict media consumption. Being a member of an 'other', non-mainstream religion is a characteristic associated with higher scores across the three domains. Paranormal media consumers, interestingly and unlike the other two outcomes, tended to be people who take the Bible more literally but also attend less frequently; in other words, they have a tendency towards being disaffected from religious institutions while also remaining strong believers in the supernatural.

However, there is one characteristic that is shared across the three models. People who describe themselves as 'spiritual' in orientation hold a significantly higher number of paranormal beliefs. On average, a person who describes themselves as spiritual believes in four more paranormal topics than a person who does not. A spiritual person is also more prone to conspiracy, holding on average two more conspiracy beliefs than a non-spiritual person. In a similar vein, the spiritual people in our sample engage in more diverse paranormal media consumption, with a 59 per cent higher score on this measure than people who do not describe themselves as spiritual.[52] Further, all three outcomes were significantly correlated with one another. Put another way, one of the strongest predictors of how many conspiracy beliefs someone holds is how many paranormal beliefs they hold and how much they consume paranormal media about different topics and vice versa.[53]

About two in five respondents (41.3 per cent) considered themselves moderately or very spiritual in orientation. These same people are more likely than others to hold idiosyncratic, syncretic combinations of paranormal and conspiracy beliefs, and to pursue those varied beliefs by consuming a variety of different media. Clearly not all of these people will accept a particular unifying theory such as Kellett's or Icke's. But if nothing else, the growing number of unifying theories about the paranormal that are being promoted by enterprising individuals gives target audiences the impression that there could be *something* to what they have to say. Paranormal entrepreneurs have a substantial *potential* market to work with, and as we will discuss in the next chapter, we expect these spiritual orientations to continue growing as conventional religion recedes.

Chapter 7

THE DEVIL'S BARGAIN

Angels and Aliens

What is the difference between an angel and an alien? In one sense, very little. Angels are understood to be spiritual entities with the ability to break into the material world and communicate with humans. The aliens encountered by Russ Kellett and others similarly have the power to intrude upon the physical world, with abilities that border on the mystical. But angels and aliens belong to very different cultural frameworks relative to each other. Angels reside within the framework of conventional religion.[1] Aliens 'live' in the paranormal realm. This distinction highlights an interesting issue, one that confused social scientists for many years. What is the relationship between conventional religion and the paranormal? If someone believes in conventional religious ideas, such as angels, does that make them more or less likely to believe in ghosts? Or, perhaps, does religion make no difference at all in a secularizing society?

In this chapter we discuss the *bounded affinity* between organized religion and the paranormal.[2] In general, religious and paranormal supernatural beliefs and experiences are often quite similar, and people who believe in or experience one kind of supernaturalism tend to be open to other kinds of supernaturalism; however, this innate affinity is restricted when organized religious groups attempt to limit their members' participation in competing forms of supernaturalism. In other words, if an individual is actively involved in an organized religion, then the positive connection between religious and paranormal supernaturalism will be suppressed. But if an individual is *not* actively involved in an exclusive, conventional religion, then the positive connection between religious and paranormal supernaturalism will be amplified. We will demonstrate this dynamic using data from our survey of the UK.

Further complicating the relationship between the paranormal and religion is the fact that paranormal beliefs occasionally morph into organizational forms that closely resemble conventional religion. The paranormal consists of a large, diverse pool of sometimes novel, sometimes merely out-of-fashion supernatural concepts, cultural frameworks, and ritual practices. In the right circumstances, this can sometimes spawn new religious movements (NRMs). An example of this is the many NRMs that have been founded based on beliefs about aliens and extraterrestrial contact. This includes groups such as Unarius, Raëlism, Heaven's Gate, and Scientology. To better understand the porous boundaries between religion and the paranormal, we must return to the realm of UFOs once again, by visiting one such group, the Aetherius Society, as well as the wider contactee movement from which it originated.

Space Brothers

During the 1950s, religion and the paranormal intersected extensively within the proto-religious 'contactee' movement. Most histories trace the origins of these movements to the claims of George Adamski, a self-proclaimed philosopher. On November 20, 1952, Adamski and several associates travelled to a barren area near Desert Center, California, where they claimed to have witnessed a large cigar-shaped, silver object pass overhead. Adamski moved away from the remainder of the group to approach a smaller craft that descended from the larger ship. Near this craft, Adamski met a male, human-like alien who communicated that he was from Venus. Thus began an extended series of interactions with friendly 'space brothers'. In a series of books, *Flying Saucers Have Landed* (1953), *Inside the Spaceships* (1955), and *Flying Saucers Farewell* (1961), Adamski outlined a new theology wherein extraterrestrials had been visiting Earth for centuries, and Jesus Christ and all the biblical angels were actually aliens.

Adamski's tales spawned many imitators, most of whom repeated this melding of ideas from the dawning of the space age with those from long-established religious traditions. For example, Orfeo Angelucci met with aliens near Burbank, California, and learned that Jesus Christ was an entity born of the Sun. Venusians told George Van Tassel of Landers, California, that Mother Mary was an extraterrestrial sent to Earth pregnant with the baby Jesus.[3] Where contactees sometimes differed was in the nature of their communication with the aliens. George Adamski claimed in-person, face-to-face meetings with the aliens. Others claimed to be the present incarnations of beings that had lived previous lives on other planets. Still others 'channelled' extraterrestrial entities or otherwise engaged in telepathic communication with them.[4]

The Aetherius Society

London taxi driver George King was a high-profile example of the latter, although he would eventually claim the former as well. In 1954 he received a telepathic message from extraterrestrials, eventually establishing regular, mental contact with a Venusian named Aetherius. King developed a theology that combined syncretic New Age religion with benevolent aliens and formed 'the first UFO religion', the Aetherius Society, in the mid-1950s.[5] The Aetherius Society is 'an international spiritual organisation dedicated to spreading, and acting upon, the teachings of advanced extraterrestrial intelligences'.[6] King's own cosmic status was cemented on July 23, 1958, when he was granted an in-person meeting with 'Master Jesus' atop Holdstone Down in Devonshire. There, Jesus stood and channelled 'spiritual power' into Holdstone Down, transforming it into a holy mountain.[7]

The Aetherius Society is an insightful example of how paranormal beliefs and experiences can be transformed into formal religious organizations and NRMs. To explore how this transformation occurs, we studied the group's sacred texts, newsletters, internal documents, and public records about their finances and business dealings. We also attended talks by the group at several MBS fairs, as well as taking part in the fiftieth anniversary of Operation Prayer Power – one of the group's central pilgrimages and rituals – held annually on Holdstone Down.

Prepare Yourself!

George King was raised in a Christian household but also dabbled extensively in occult practices, and over time developed an interest in Eastern philosophies. In his 40s, he started to practice yoga intensively and began to explore his psychic capacity, to the point where he received an interplanetary message while washing the dishes in his Maida Vale flat: 'Prepare yourself! You are to become the voice of Interplanetary parliament'.[8] The Cosmic Masters would also give King a new name – 'Mental Channel No. 1'.

King soon started to receive regular telepathic messages from Aetherius, who lived on Venus, and two other beings named Mars Sector 6 and Mars Sector 8. Aetherius was a representative of 'the Interplanetary Governmental System' who had been instructed to guide humans back toward 'the ancient wisdom', and to prepare for the coming of the next Master – whose arrival was understood to depend on there being enough people ready to receive him.[9] King also claimed that four other beings – Shri Krishna, the Lord Buddha, Master Jesus, and Lao Tsu – had previously descended to Earth to support the mission of Aetherius. Unlike some other UFO religions of the era, King would (wisely) not predict a specific date by which the next Master would appear. Instead, the focus of the Society would be on helping humanity negotiate any disasters it may face until there was sufficient physical and spiritual capacity to receive the new Master.

As with other contactees, King attempted to straddle the boundaries between conventional religion and mysticism.[10] The group is a regular presence at MBS fairs, taking stalls and offering workshops at events we attended. A 1980 issue of the Aetherius Society's newsletter discussed Dr. King's and the group's attendance at the fifth annual MBS festival, back in June 1980:

> The Aetherius Society occupied a large, eye-catching stand, the main theme of which was Holistic Healing. The Aetherius Society's Teachings were displayed along one side of the stand; the second side consisted of Pendulum/Kinesiology diagnosis and health food products, whilst the third side was a demonstration

area for the Radionic Pendulum, which attracted crowds of people throughout the Festival.[11]

If one foot of the Aetherius Society is dipped in the waters of the psychic realm, its other foot steps into the eschatological pool of major, organized religions. As did other contactees of the 1950s, George King incorporated Christian concepts into his cosmology. But King took a further, more audacious step and claimed the endorsement of Jesus Christ himself for his book *The Twelve Blessings*.[12]

King's messages also attempted to syncretize ideas from other established religions, especially Hinduism, Buddhism, and Taoism. More directly, King updated and expanded upon the mysticism of Helena Blavatsky's Theosophy by effectively moving the (previously Tibetan) Masters into outer space.[13] The messages delivered via King's trance-state channelling 'developed a doctrine which synthesized Theosophy with flying-saucer lore, yoga, tantrism, homeopathy, radionics, and various other elements derived from the contemporary cultic milieu'.[14]

King died in 1997, and the organization is now built around the veneration of him, with no one new claiming the title of Master.[15] The group is now primarily focused on studying the existing revelations provided by King and faithfully conducting the rituals laid out in his writings. We were fortunate enough to attend one of those rituals: 'Operation Prayer Power'.

Operation Prayer Power

Rising to a summit of 349 metres above the edge of the Bristol Channel, Holdstone Down is an isolated knoll that lies to the east of Combe Martin. It slopes up and down across the horizon, covered in hues of brown heather. The paths that trail into the distance are usually only inhabited with solitary dog walkers and occasional ramblers making their way around the coastal path.

We are here because Holdstone Down holds a special significance for the Aetherius Society. At midnight on July 23rd, 1958, George King claimed to have met Master Jesus, in person, on top of the knoll.[16] This represented some of the closest contact that King claimed with the Masters and set into motion the group's transition into a full-fledged religious movement.[17] Specifically, this meeting spurred a new development in King's messages, evolving from the initial stages of revelation into the establishment of key ritual practices for the group. Two practices are of particular importance in this regard. First is the identification of sacred mountains, which established specific sites for pilgrimages and rituals. Holdstone Down is one of nineteen 'holy' mountains recognized by the group.[18] Second is the development of the group's central collective ritual practice – 'charging sessions' – which are intended to replenish 'radionic batteries' with psychic energy.

Devised in 1973 by George King, the goal of Operation Prayer Power is to gather psychic energy into a spiritual battery so that 'uplifting and Healing' energy could be directed to suffering parts of the world.[19] King argued that spiritual energy is a tangible force that can be collected, stored, and used, much like electricity. This means that humanity can effectively save up spiritual energy for use at particular points of need, or as the Aetherius Society suggests, 'to help heal the world'.[20] King noted that crystals, pyramids, and gold have long been held to have some capacity to channel this energy, so he invented 'a radionic machine' that could be used specifically to contain and direct it. This machine is composed of a portable 'spiritual power battery' that stores the energy and a 'spiritual energy radiator' that can draw off the stored energy and release it to specific targets – such as an area threatened by war or a natural disaster. The overarching goal of Operation Prayer Power is to create and store 'spiritual energy' so that it can be utilized to alleviate suffering on Earth.

An issue of the group's newsletter describes such a release of energy that occurred on October 11, 1980, directed towards Algeria, which had recently suffered an earthquake, and Iran and Iraq, which were in the midst of conflict:

> Altogether, we released 1,063 Prayer Hours from our Batteries, all of which was sent to Algeria. But this was not the only manipulation that went on, for the Great White Brotherhood also impregnated the Iran-Iraq areas with Their Prayer Energy. Thus it was that two outstanding trouble spots in the world were given mass Spiritual Healing and help during this same manipulation.[21]

The Aetherius Society graciously agreed to let us attend the fiftieth anniversary of Operation Prayer Power, atop Holdstone Down.

And so, shortly before noon on 25 June 2023, we pulled to the side of the road at the bottom of the down and exited our car. As we made our way to the bottom of the trail, we were approached by three people who made camp there: 'Are you here for the pilgrimage?' 'Yes', we replied in unison, before they immediately responded: 'Have you been before?' We told them it was our first time and were quickly given a sizable book for free: *Realize Your Inner Potential*.[22] 'Then you'll need this', one said to us. 'Turn to page 149; that's the mantra we'll be using today. See you up there!'

The path to the top is the type of rocky trail typical of British coastal walks, although this particular view was completely unencumbered by hedgerows or fauna. Somewhere on the top of the down, it was possible to make out figures moving around, and as we got closer, we heard the hum of excited activity over the frequent gush of windswept heather. A woman dressed in a denim jacket, jeans, and a waterproof coat danced her way up the path before us, while over to the left, other people made slower progress up the path to the south. The excitable hum grew louder as we approached the top of the path, and soon we saw a large group in the process of organizing at the head of Holdstone Down.

We did a quick count and estimated around 120 people in attendance. Although the majority here were white, the composition of the group was relatively diverse in terms of ethnicity. Some had clearly travelled from the North American, African, and Indian subcontinents. The group was generally on the older side of middle age, but not exclusively so. There were a number of people who appeared to be in their thirties. There were no children present. Many of the attendees were wearing mid- to high-range outdoor gear and certainly presented themselves as (at least) middle class. Indeed, the inaccessibility of Holdstone Down means that private transport was a necessity, and the relative remoteness of the location required a certain level of mobility. A member pointed us to a pile of rocks marking where Master Jesus stood to charge the holy mountain. It lies next to the summit of four paths that cross the down.

'If you're new, then go that way', shouted a well-coiffured gentleman. He pointed to the other side of the stone pile, and we duly followed his instruction. As the wind whipped around us, the coiffured gentleman raised his megaphone and shouted the instruction to turn to page 149 of the book we had been given at the bottom of the path. The text provided a particularly detailed instruction on how to pronounce a mantra that would be used during the ceremony, and there appeared to be about twenty of us who were new to the ceremony. He then began to give us very specific instructions about the mantra and stressed the seriousness of performing the practice correctly:

> We are going to recite a mantra. The mantra should only be given by a master of yoga. I am not a master of yoga, hence the mantra is transferred to you … Please don't share this mantra with anyone else. When you say the mantra, please always finish it, even if you finish it silently. Please treat it with the utmost reverence. The more reverence you treat it with, the greater power it will have.

In addition to these general instructions, the leaders paced newcomers through extensive training on precisely how to pronounce the mantra, as well as leading some impromptu practice sessions.

After being released from mantra rehearsal, we were quickly swept up by a man in a green faux-down jacket. He pointed us towards an area where the remainder of those present were gathering in a circle. He told us to 'fill the circle' and informed us 'there can't be any gaps'. Each of us were guided to different openings in the circle, and he continued to usher others. Although seemingly mundane, the proper management of ritual participants' bodies in a given space is a vital component of generating effective rituals.[23] Creating a tight, cohesive formation rather than allowing people to straggle has an overall positive effect on people's experiences of ritual activity.

The circle was organized around the prayer battery, a light blue box standing on top of an old, wooden-frame tripod that had been lashed to the ground with some bright white guide ropes. At the front of the box, there was a short, white rod pointing out over the channel. The exact contents of the box are a mystery, but King provided some basic information:

> The Battery is encased in a small oblong container measuring 8 ½" by 6 ½" by 6 ½." It is an extremely well made piece of equipment which was designed by our Founded-President, Sir George King, many years ago. The Battery is able to contain Spiritual Energy invoked by Prayer, without any leakage, until it is discharged.[24]

In an Aetherius Society podcast recorded shortly before the Holdstone Down event, Richard Lawrence, the central leader of the group since King's death, explained that the battery is composed of crystals: '[T]his battery ... is filled with tiny crystals and the crystals are key in holding that energy, this great powerful prayer energy'.[25]

Two people were attaching a belt around the battery and the tripod to help secure it against the gusting wind. Under the tripod were two transparent boxes weighed down with a stone. Within the upper box sat an upright book – King's personal copy of his own text: *The Twelve Blessings*.

Once everyone was in place, Lawrence began to lead those assembled through visualization techniques. He asked us to imagine a light moving down through us to meet violet flames that erupt from underneath us. Afterward, he told us to move into the prayer position and for the crowd to raise their hands, open-palmed, in front of them. Lawrence noted that, 'The Master is here with us today'. He then asked everyone to gather even more tightly into two rows around the prayer battery.

Lawrence then began to recite the mantra into the megaphone, shouting above the wind. The crowd immediately joined in. Three group members gathered in a line in front of the battery. As the group chanted, the man in front of the battery assumed a pose that resembled an aggressive-looking martial arts stance. His left hand was raised, with his thumb and index finger touching to form a ring. His right hand was positioned upright in front of the battery, which now had the back plate removed to reveal a white board inside. The recitations by the prayer team sounded akin to a Pentecostal prayer, beseeching the divine to infuse its cosmic energy into the battery. Each pray-er did this for about a minute, then circled to the back of the line of three. The next person in line then stepped up to channel the group's collective energy into the battery. Lawrence continued to drive the chanting, waving his free hand in time with the mantra like a choir director.

To the left of the battery, a woman sat at a table, holding a stopwatch and a clipboard. Each time there was a change at the front of the prayer line, she pressed a button on the stopwatch. Elsewhere, as the ritual continued, the man in the green jacket patrolled around the circle. He corrected some people in their chanting method, and more generally seemed to be policing the proper execution of the ritual. As it turns out, the man in the green coat was playing the role of 'Prayer Director'. His job was to assess the *quality* of the energy being created by the circle and then report back to the timekeeper.

The goal is to gather high-quality spiritual energy, which the group ranks into categories. It was unclear exactly how the group graded the spiritual energy produced, but the aim was clear. The gold standard is AA+ energy, but this is only rarely achieved. More achievable, if still rare, is A+ spiritual energy, which is indicative of an 'absolutely superb' prayer team that is pouring their entire heart and soul into the endeavour.[26] Category A is more common, indicating a 'lower frequency of Spiritual Energy, but one of great value for use in mass Healing'.[27] Lower than level A is problematic. Energy graded as 'Category B' should be 'seldom put into our Prayer Power Batteries', according to King, who provided a special admonishment to those who did so with impunity:

If a Prayer Team Member is found to be putting consistent Category B Energy into the Battery, that person is taken off the Prayer Team and given classes to teach him or her to be a better prayer. [28]

If the level of energy is considered sufficient for storage, the timekeeper performs a calculation wherein they determine the 'Prayer Hours' collected in the battery by multiplying the seconds that each pray-er spent in front of the battery, multiplied by the number of participants.[29] The perceived quality of the prayer increases or reduces the final calculation. As an Aetherius newsletter instructs, Category A energy produces a bonus:

> When the prayer is A Category and the Mantra Team is giving ... the backing which they should, in other words, the Mantra is really good, in rhythm and has a *full expression of love and feeling behind it*, then it is equivalent to having 5 more people in the session. In other words, if with the prayer you have 40 people in the session, you add 5 more, making 45 people in that session.[30]

The process of prayer and calculations lasted for over fifteen minutes. Once complete, the lid was placed back on the battery. Richard Lawrence moved to the front and told those assembled that George King had conducted similar operations at Lake Powell, in Arizona, fifty years prior.[31] He then announced that a contingent of Aetherius members from the United States had brought a jar of sand from Lake Powell. An older man and woman came forward holding a jar.

The couple opened the jar and poured its sand under the base of the tripod with great reverence. After doing so, they read a prayer, revealing the depths of veneration the group holds for King as their divine prophet and Master:

> Our consciousness will expand, and with ever-growing determination and skill, we will spread and uphold the precious spiritual monument he has given to our world. Oh, wonderous Brahma, blessed is his immanence, Sir George King, for all that he has done for mankind in his lifetime. An almighty Para Brahma, blessed is his great cosmic avatar for what he is now. George, your divine will be done.

After this brief interlude, the group moved into the second (of five) prayer sessions for the day, with the goal of adding as much energy to the prayer battery as possible.

The members of Aetherius were uniformly welcoming and kind throughout, and the gathering had the feeling of a reunion of old friends. At the same time, they were, to a person, very serious and sincere in their efforts to charge the prayer battery. In doing so, they hoped to help humanity.

From Paranormal Experiences to Religious Movements

Most contactee-based groups lacked long-term stability, and in this regard, George King managed to create the 'most important and successful' of the contactee movements from the mid-twentieth century.[32] The Aetherius Society was successful where other UFO-based NRMs failed, for several reasons.

First, the most successful religions incorporate group rituals designed to bind members together by congregating people in physical space, generating a common mood and focus, and facilitating rhythmic bodily coordination.[33] To the extent that a group produces emotionally engaging collective rituals, participants will be more likely to accept the ideology of the group, make strong in-group social ties, personally identify with the collective, venerate group symbols, and seek out future group interactions. By establishing guidelines for stable ritual traditions, King provided the movement with structure and stability, as well as unifying practices that would help recharge the group's emotional energy (and prayer battery). Notably, the group actively monitors their rituals to ensure full and proper participation, going so far as to quantify the amount and quality of psychic power generated by their performance. The Aetherius Society takes more literally than most groups the idea of using rituals to generate collective energy.

Further, the effectiveness of rituals is enhanced to the extent that they help create sacred objects and beliefs for participants.[34] This was evident in the group's handling of the prayer battery itself. The radionic battery was always treated as a sacred object, being handled with extreme caution and following careful prohibitions to prevent profanation. Only a designated person with white gloves on was allowed to touch it. They would open the front cover of the battery before the rituals began, and when the prayers were not actively in session, the battery was always re-covered with a sliding, protective cover. At one point there was some misty rain, and a member covered the top of the prayer battery with an umbrella. The taboo against touching or mishandling the battery was clear evidence of its status as a sacred object – the literal focus of the group's collective energy. As foundational sociologist Émile Durkheim noted, 'The sacred thing is, par excellence, that which the profane must not and cannot touch with impunity.'[35]

The longevity of the Aetherius Society is also partly due to King taking advantage of the porous boundaries between conventional religion and the paranormal. Sociologist of religion Rodney Stark argued that individuals are motivated to maintain as much of their existing 'cultural capital' as possible when shopping for a new religion.[36] In other words, the more of your current beliefs, cultural practices, and personal identity you can retain – rather than being forced to lose all of this accrued 'capital' – the more likely you will be to convert to an (otherwise) novel religion.

Therefore, NRMs find greater success to the extent that they incorporate concepts from existing conventional religions in their culture of operation. For example, a seeker who grew up in a Christian household is likely to find the Mormons more attractive than the Hare Krishnas. Joining the latter requires someone to entirely disregard the Bible they have grown up with. Joining the Latter-day Saints requires the learning of new texts and doctrine (e.g. the *Book of Mormon*), but also still utilizes the Old and New Testaments as sacred texts. The Aetherius Society certainly provides something novel in its early focus upon extraterrestrials.[37] But by incorporating Jesus as a cosmic Master from Venus into its theology, someone who has drifted from Christianity can explore new ideas without entirely abandoning the notion that Jesus was divine.

Religious movements often fail when their initial, charismatic leader passes on.[38] Clearly the Aetherius Society has not replaced George King. The group remains focused upon studying the teachings of its dear, departed leader. But the group has managed to transform King's ideas into stabilized ritual practices and a hierarchical organization that successfully 'routinised' King's charismatic mysticism.[39] Aetherius developed the tightest organization and most explicitly religious structure of all the UFO religions developed at the time.[40]

None of this is to say that the Aetherius Society is shaking up the British religious landscape; however, the group is stable and relatively well-positioned for its long-term future in terms of properties and resources. They have locations in Los Angeles, Fulham, Chelsea, and Barnsley and small branches in many other places. The Society is also reported to own a cottage called 'King's House' (formerly 'The Pier House') in Inverfarigaig, on the southern shore of Loch Ness. The group, however, is not particularly concerned with expansion. They do not openly ask for donations or resource contributions. They also have an incredibly light touch – almost blasé – in terms of missionary zeal. The group is too small, however, to register on the UK National Census, with its members placed into a catchall 'other' category.[41]

Whatever its future, the Aetherius Society provides an informative example of how the paranormal can sometimes be fashioned into an organized religion. At least as long as there is a charismatic mystic who can persuasively channel alien beings and then establish effective and carefully managed collective rituals. But this is only one of the many ways that religion and the paranormal intersect. To understand the broader relationship between the paranormal and religion, we must next examine how religious and paranormal beliefs relate to one another amongst the general public.

Religion and the Paranormal Among the British Public

The decline of organized religion in the UK, particularly Christianity, is well documented.[42] Where once the vast majority of the populace was Christian, especially as members of the Church of England, today over half of the British public reports no religious affiliation. Religious affiliation, especially Anglican membership, and religious practice, such as church attendance, have also declined sharply across younger generations. In accounts of secularization in the Western world, Britain often serves as a key example of declining levels of piety amongst the population.[43]

At the same time, scholars have noted a considerable amount of residual 'spirituality' among the public, exemplified by those who 'believe without belonging' or who partake in 'vicarious religion'.[44] For example, despite steep declines in religious affiliation and church attendance since 1970, the percentage of the British population who believe in life after death has been relatively stable across that time.⁴⁵ With so many people dropping out of organized religion, yet still believing in the afterlife, we would expect to see an increase in alternative forms of spirit belief, such as ghosts. As we outlined in Chapter 3, this is precisely what we find. In this sense, the UK is not an example of complete secularization, at least in terms of supernaturalism. Rather, it is an example of how institutional religious decline can open more cultural space for alternative forms of supernaturalism. The example of over time changes to the religious and spiritual landscape of Britain points back toward the larger questions about how mainstream religion and the paranormal interact.

As the angel or alien question we began the chapter with pointedly calls out, there is considerable overlap between the concepts, beliefs, and experiences of both religious and paranormal believers. Both make claims that go beyond what is verifiable through scientific methods. Both involve the supernatural breaking into the material world. Both can produce intensive, other-worldly experiences that overtake one's senses to produce visions, voices, and bodily possession. Based on all these affinities, many researchers reasonably hypothesized that it should only be a small step from believing in angels to believing in aliens and that believing in one should make interest and involvement in the other more likely.⁴⁶

A valid counterpoint, however, is that organized religions have long placed limits on whether their practitioners should engage in external forms of supernaturalism, such as consulting psychics, hunting ghosts, or believing in aliens. There is a perfectly rational reason for this. People only have a limited amount of attention, time, and money. To the extent that I am spending my finite resources on psychics, there is less to put into the proverbial offering plate. More formally, religious organizations that place restrictions on participants' levels of investment in other supernatural endeavours are able to screen out 'free riders' (weak members) and correspondingly increase the sense of investment and commitment from those who remain in the organizations.⁴⁷ Because of these cultural boundaries enforced by organized religions, many researchers reasonably surmised that religion and the paranormal constituted separate cultural spheres. Therefore, believing in one should make interest and involvement in the other less likely.⁴⁸

It has proven difficult to determine whether religion promotes (the small step hypothesis) or deters (the separate spheres hypothesis) paranormal beliefs, because of a two-fold problem. First, early empirical assessments of whether religiosity was positively or negatively correlated with paranormalism were mixed, weak, and inconsistent.⁴⁹ Second, each of these ideas about how religion and the paranormal intersect gets a key aspect of these dynamics correct, while also necessarily missing the important point highlighted by the competing hypothesis. As a result, the connections between conventional religion and paranormalism were misunderstood for quite a long time.

On an empirical level, two improvements were needed to make sense of the complex dynamics at play. First, if conventional religiosity is assessed with only a single measure, then nonlinear analytic techniques are necessary to capture a curvilinear pattern between overall religiosity and paranormalism.⁵⁰ Second, and more preferably, multiple measures of religiosity that assess *different aspects* of conventional religiosity (e.g., practice, beliefs, and experiences) allow for a more nuanced assessment of which aspects of religiosity are related to paranormalism, both positively and negatively. Specifically, religious supernatural beliefs and experiences tend to be positively related to paranormal beliefs and experiences, while conventional religious practices tend to be negatively related to paranormalism. By separating religiosity into its different components, the complex relationship between religion and the paranormal becomes clearer.[51]

On a conceptual level, we can synthesize the parts of both the small step and separate spheres theories that are correct. We called this 'bounded affinity theory' because of the natural affinity and similarities between the supernatural beliefs and experiences found in both organized religions and the paranormal; however, this typical affinity is bounded when organized religions enforce supernatural exclusivism on their members. In other words, when people are not actively participating in exclusivist, organized religions, it is indeed only a small step between angels and ghosts (or any other paranormal and religious phenomena). In contrast, when people are actively participating in exclusivist religions, these connections will be restricted, and thus religious and paranormal ideas remain in separate cultural spheres, with little overlap. Further, in the case of fundamentalist and orthodox religious groups, there is often an openly hostile stance taken toward the paranormal, with alternative forms of spirituality being labelled as 'satanic' and 'evil'.

To see some of the different ways that religious (and secular) identities relate to paranormalism, we can look at the average number of paranormal beliefs (out of eighteen possible) and experiences (out of nine possible) for people who identify with different religious traditions in the UK. Figure 7.1 shows the average level of paranormal beliefs and experiences for people who reported that they were Anglican, Protestant, Catholic, Muslim, atheist, agnostic or religious 'none', and members of 'other' religions (comprised mainly of non-Western and alternative religious traditions). Church of England members and Protestants had similar average numbers of paranormal beliefs (5.3 and 5.4, respectively), while Catholics and Muslims reported a slightly higher average number of paranormal beliefs (6.7 and 6.8, respectively). Agnostics (3.7) and especially atheists (3.0) reported the lowest average levels of paranormal belief. By far the highest average was found among members of non-mainstream religious traditions (9.2 paranormal beliefs on average).[52] A similar pattern occurs for the average number of paranormal experiences, with atheists and agnostics reporting the lowest averages (1.3 and 1.8, respectively), followed by Protestants (2.0), Anglicans (2.1), and Catholics (2.2). Members of non-mainstream religious traditions reported by far the highest average number of paranormal experiences (3.8).

Although informative, using religious identity as the lone measure of religiosity only gets us so far. To see the complex ways that religion and the paranormal intersect at the population level requires using multiple measures of religion designed to assess the different components of religiosity. Of particular importance are having distinct measures of religious practices (such as attending religious services), supernatural beliefs (such as in God, heaven, and hell), and intensive

7. The Devil's Bargain

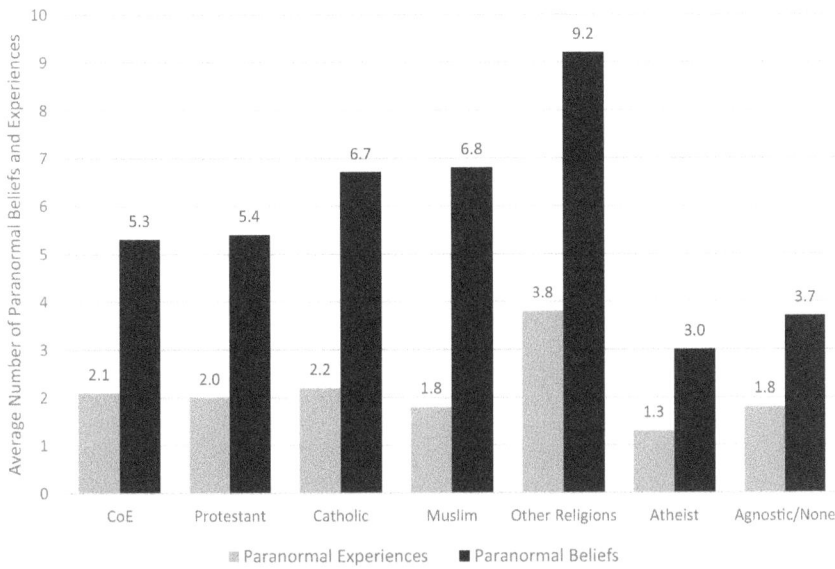

Figure 7.1 Average number of paranormal beliefs and experiences by religious identity.

experiences (such as hearing voices or being miraculously healed). By including multiple questions about different dimensions of religiosity on our survey, we were able to examine how each aspect of religiosity independently relates to paranormal beliefs and experiences among the British public.

To assess religious practice and commitment to organized religion, we asked people how often they attended religious services, how often they prayed privately, and the extent to which they considered themselves a 'religious person'. To measure religious supernatural beliefs, we asked about levels of belief in Satan, heaven, hell, purgatory, Armageddon, the rapture, angels, and demons. To measure intensive religious experiences, we asked people whether they had ever experienced a miraculous physical healing, spoken in tongues, felt called by God to do something, heard the voice of God, been in a state of religious ecstasy, or felt filled with religious spirit. For each dimension of religiosity – practice, belief, and experience – we created a summary scale combining the individual questions into a composite measure. For this assessment, our outcomes of interest were a summary scale of eighteen paranormal beliefs (including aliens, psychics, hauntings, Bigfoot, Atlantis, and telekinesis) and a summary scale of eleven paranormal experiences (including visiting a psychic, seeing a ghost, living in a haunted house, and witnessing a UFO).[53]

As seen in Figures 7.3 and 7.4, when we account for the effects of religious practices, beliefs, and experiences *simultaneously* for predicting levels of paranormal beliefs and experiences, the oppositional effects of different dimensions of religiosity are revealed. Religious practice strongly and *negatively* predicts paranormal beliefs and experiences. In contrast, supernatural religious

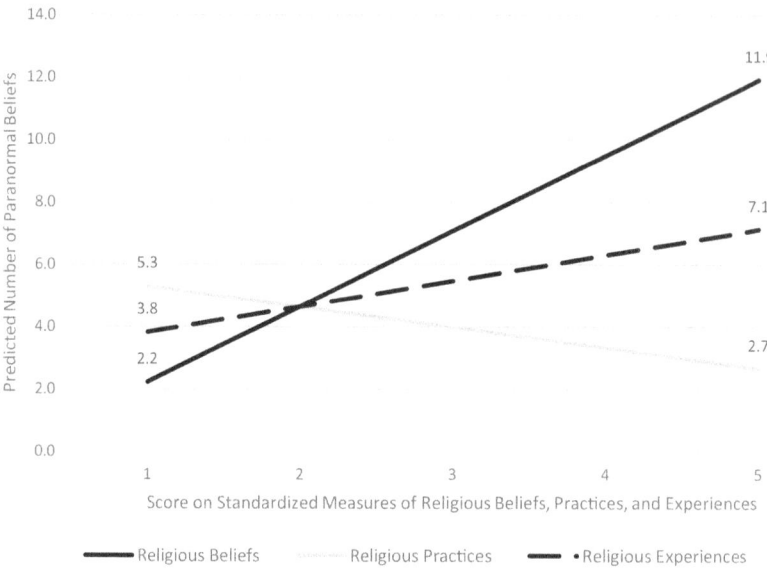

Figure 7.2 Number of predicted paranormal beliefs by levels of religious belief, practice and experience.

beliefs and intensive religious experiences are both strongly and *positively* predictive of paranormal beliefs and experiences. This is the most important basic dynamic outlined by bounded affinity theory – that religious supernatural beliefs and experiences are positively related to paranormalism, but only in isolation from active, conventional religious affiliation and practice, which leads to less paranormalism due to the bounding imposed by group exclusivity.[54]

When measures of different dimensions of religiosity are not available, the general pattern observed between conventional religiosity and paranormalism is curvilinear, such that people who are *moderately* religious have the highest average levels of paranormalism. We can see this in a basic way by looking at people on the survey who reported that they considered themselves a 'spiritual person' but not a 'religious person'. People who identify as 'spiritual but not religious' reported an average of 3.6 paranormal experiences (out of nine), compared to 2.7 for those who said they were both religious and spiritual.[55] People who reported being neither spiritual nor religious reported an average of only 1.1 paranormal experiences.

To further investigate the curvilinear pattern between overall levels of religiosity and paranormalism using the CASPAR data, we created a composite measure of religiosity that combined religious practice, beliefs, and experiences together.[56] As seen in Figure 7.4, the pattern is indeed nonlinear; however, the relationship is not 'rainbow-shaped', as seen in data from other countries, such as the United States and Italy.[57] Instead, there is a general positive relationship, with a ceiling effect.[58] This is an interesting difference and suggests that in a more secularized context such as the UK, there is, overall, a more positive relationship

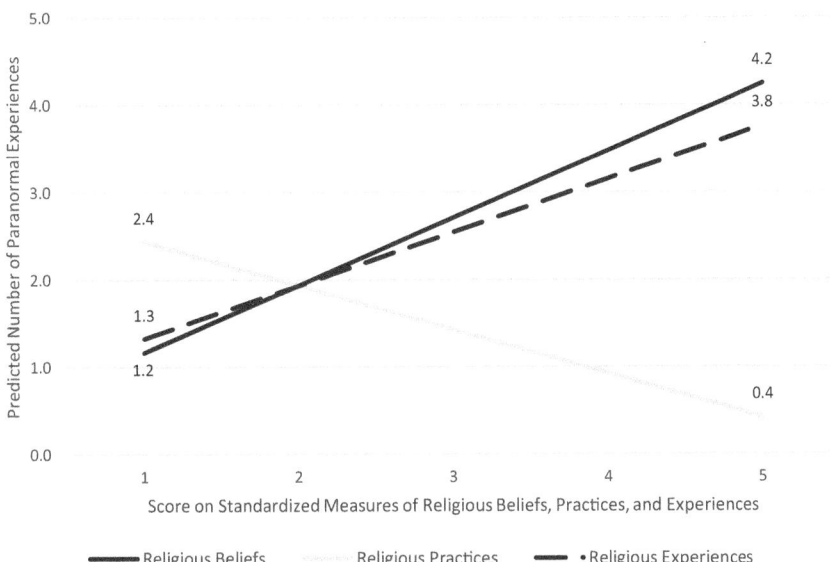

Figure 7.3 Predicted number of paranormal experiences by levels of religious belief, practice and experience.

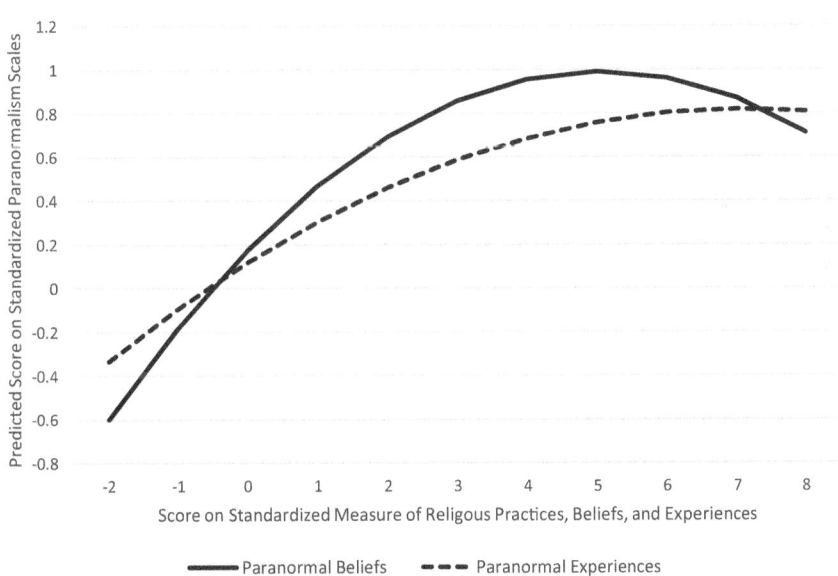

Figure 7.4 Curvilinear relationship between composite measure of religion and paranormalism.

between religion and the paranormal. In contrast, in a location such as the United States, the higher end of overall religiosity is occupied mostly by devout and often fundamentalist Christians. Similarly, in a location such as Italy, the high end of a religiosity measure will be anchored mostly by devout Catholics. This suggests that in cultural contexts with greater levels of societal secularization, declining organized religion, and lower levels of the population associated with fundamentalism/orthodoxy, a more overall positive relationship between religion and the paranormal may flourish, in contrast to the 'bell curve' dynamic found between conventional religiosity and paranormalism documented in more devout religious contexts. If Britain continues on its current path towards secularization, religion and the paranormal may increasingly occupy overlapping cultural niches.

To get a more descriptive understanding of how the boundaries between religion and the paranormal can become more porous as organized religion wanes, it is helpful to consider an example of this overlap in greater depth. For this, we turn to a long-standing religious site that has recently become a hub for tourism about conspiracy theories involving the Holy Grail, Freemasons, and the bloodline of Jesus Christ.

Rosslyn Chapel

The notes, in prelude, ROSLIN! to a blank
Of silence, how it thrilled thy sumptuous roof,
Pillars, and arches, – not in vain time-proof,
Though Christian rites be wanting! From what bank
Came those live herbs? by what hand were they sown
Where dew falls not, where rain-drops seem unknown?
Yet in the Temple they a friendly niche
Share with their sculptured fellows, that, green-grown,
Copy their beauty more and more, and preach,
Though mute, of all things blending into one.
~William Wordsworth, 'Composed in Roslin Chapel during a Storm' (1831)[59]

An important consequence of the bounded affinity between religion and the paranormal is that if organized religion weakens – as has happened throughout the Western world, including in the UK – the previously rigid boundaries between religion and paranormalism will also weaken. To illustrate this trend, we end by considering the case of Rosslyn Chapel, just outside of Edinburgh, which is 'perhaps the most infamous medieval church in the British Isles'.[60]

Since its original construction, Rosslyn Chapel has undergone many cycles of destruction and restoration, obscuring much of the original surfaces that remain.[61] This cryptic and hidden dimension of the site only enhances its modern allure. Originally a Catholic church, the chapel is currently an Anglican place of worship. More notable than its official religious history, however, is the centrality of the chapel to a number of prominent conspiracy theories about the Knights Templar and Freemasonry. These claims were widely popularized by their prominent use in the narrative of *The Da Vinci Code*, which became one of the best-selling novels of all time, with over eighty million copies sold.[62]

The chapel is the site of the unveiling of the great mysteries of the story and is dramatically lauded as '*symbology heaven*' because 'every surface in the chapel had been carved with symbols – Christian cruciforms, Jewish stars, Masonic seals, Templar crosses, cornucopias, pyramids, astrological signs, plants, vegetables, pentacles, and roses'.[63] It is hard to imagine a better marketing promotion for New Age syncretists or conspiracy-minded mystery buffs.

Indeed, in 2005 the Baylor Religion Survey, a nationally representative sample of the United States collected just two years after *The Da Vinci Code* was released, found that 29 per cent of Americans had read Dan Brown's thriller. Readers of the book were disproportionately likely to be Catholic, members of non-mainstream religions, and women. Notably, they were also less likely to have high levels of conventional religious practice and were especially unlikely to take the Bible literally.[64] Using these same data, we found that having higher levels of paranormal belief lead to a higher likelihood of reading the book. Figure 7.5 shows the predicted probability of reading *The Da Vinci Code* across levels of religiosity (including biblical literalism) and paranormal beliefs. It is clear that the book does *not* appeal to the conventionally religious but rather to those with alternative forms of spirituality.[65] Put simply, the more conventionally religious respondents were, the less likely they were to have read the book. In contrast, the more interested in the paranormal people were, the more likely they were to have read it. If deciding which of your friends will enjoy a gift related to *The Da Vinci Code*, best to pick that friend who is not very religious, or who is very interested in the paranormal, or ideally, both.

Conspiratorial ideas about Rosslyn Chapel were further popularized and diffused when Tom Hanks brought 'symbologist' and protagonist Robert Langdon to life in a trilogy of films based on Brown's books that garnered 1.5 billion dollars in worldwide box office returns.

Rather than spurn these conspiratorial connections, Rosslyn Chapel has embraced its 'alternate history' and become a tourist destination. Tourism at the chapel increased from around 10,000 visitors per year when it first opened to the public in 1995 to over 180,000 visitors in 2017, following a boon from the popularity of *The Da Vinci Code*.[66] In this case then, a site for organized religion has embraced the paranormal through the proverbial back (vault) door, and it is the paranormal rather than religious dimensions of the site that have made it into a popular tourist attraction.

Although one can easily explore Rosslyn Chapel vicariously via an endless number of online videos, blog posts, and breathless interpretations of its history and secrets, nothing compares to first-hand experience.[67] So to get a better sense of why Rosslyn has become a dark tourism hub, I (Chris) decided to visit the chapel and see why it inspires so many artistic renderings and creative (if conspiratorial) narratives.

My first visit to the chapel was in the winter, along with a colleague, and despite being a cold January day, there were still a number of visitors.[68] We were driven to

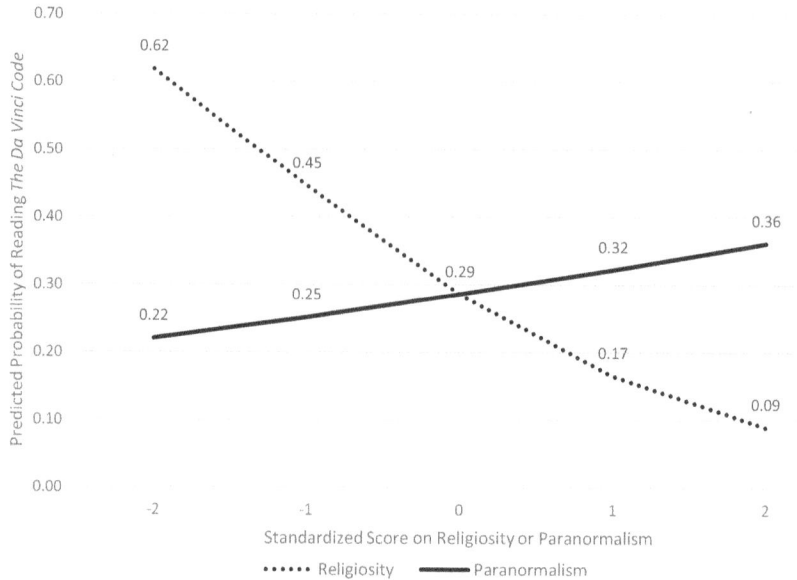

Figure 7.5 Predicted probability of reading *The Da Vinci Code*.

the chapel by our extremely friendly taxi driver, Rolf White, who, as it turns out, had quite a personal interest in the chapel.[69] He had noticed the sharp increase in tourism in the wake of *The Da Vinci Code*. He said that during the summer the area is very busy and that a nearby restaurant still serves the 'Da Vinci sandwich'.

To get to the chapel, tourists walk in through a new, modern visitor centre that contains a gift shop and café. Gift shops are a good indicator of how a location feels about its legends. The Rosslyn Chapel gift shop leans entirely into its mysteries and lore. There were no Dan Brown books on display, but they did have pins of Masonic iconography, the Green Man and many other cryptic symbols. For books, they had everything from serious histories of the chapel to more speculative works touting various theories or those attempting to summarize all of them.

The back door of the visitor centre led to the grounds where the chapel stood. After walking around the exterior taking pictures, we walked into the chapel through a large door. What is instantly striking about the interior is how it could serve as a repository for *any* mystery. Every surface seems to have a different face, carving, or shape. In one direction there will be cryptids; in another a collection of angels. Some of the pillars were plain, others decorated with swirls or patterns. In numerous places (over a hundred, according to guides), there are carvings of the face of the Green Man. Mysterious carvings, symbols, and words abound. Mysterious crucifixes and scores of unknown acronyms adorn nearly every surface. While talking to a docent named Helen, I noticed a Masonic compass carved in the column next to us.

I asked Helen how many of the people who come to visit were there simply to view a stunning chapel versus those visiting based on reading Dan Brown's novels or watching shows such as *Ancient Aliens*. She said, 'most people are here because of *The Da Vinci Code* or because of something they have read online or seen on a show'. In the winter, she said that a slightly higher percentage of folks come for historical or religious reasons (i.e., not for the conspiracies), but that in the summer it is 'mostly about the mysteries'. She noted that the Freemasons have much to do with the lore of the place and that many of the 'graffiti' are marks made by Masonic workers, pointing out some grimacing faces carved in the stone above where we stood. She said that these were likely carved by Masons who were 'having a laugh' by adding funny faces of their friends.

Near the front of the church/nave were many other interesting carvings, such as one of Lucifer (an angel hanging upside-down, bound in ropes), and a procession of skeletons atop an architectural curve. There is an evocative carving of the Dansen Macabre (Dance of Death) thought to depict the message that death always wins in the end. In the front of the church were steep steps leading down to the vault, which features heavily in *The Da Vinci Code*. Near the front of the vault was a stained-glass window of the transfiguration of Christ (added in 1954) and an altar, with a pillow for kneeling. Facing towards the stained-glass window there were two openings. About midway along the wall on the right was a red door that was closed and roped off. I immediately wondered what reaction this engendered from conspiracy-oriented visitors.

I asked Helen if she ever had people believe that *she* is part of the conspiracy. She said it happens all the time. People will assume that she knows more than she is telling and ask where the entrance to the large vault is under the church. Sometimes, visitors become too passionate or emphatic and accuse Helen of being part of a cover-up. She has heard many times before: 'You are not gonna tell me the truth – you are in on it'. When this happens, she gets the senior staff or the historian from the visitor centre to come over to deal with the person. Not surprisingly, Helen also frequently has to listen to pet personal theories from visitors. There is an ornate pillar at the front of the church that some believe held/holds the Holy Grail. One man told her that there is no way the Grail would be in that pillar, as it would be 'too obvious'. Instead, he identified another, plainer pillar at the other end of the church as the Grail's probable location.[70]

In front of the pews in the main chapel sits an altar, draped in white. As it turns out, Rosslyn is not merely a conspiracy hub but also an active church, with services every Sunday in the Scottish Episcopal tradition. The idea of an active church in such a 'mysterious' location and site for alternative spirituality was fascinating to me, so I decided to return to the chapel for services during a follow-up visit later that fall.

I once again reached out to Rolf for a ride, and he enthusiastically agreed to not only drive me to the chapel but also to attend the services with me. He picked me up in front of my hotel in Edinburgh, dressed in a tartan kilt and a sweater with a dress shirt underneath. We made the approximately thirty-minute drive and parked near the visitor centre.

Shortly before the 10.30 am start time, Rolf and I found seats in a back pew. Because the chapel is fairly small, the total maximum occupancy of the church would only be about forty. There were around thirty congregants present when the service started, not including the officiants. I cannot be sure what percentage were regular attenders, but certainly not all. For example, we chatted with an older man next to us who said he was just there to see the chapel. Unprompted, he mentioned being a big fan of Dan Brown. The congregation seems entirely comfortable with the pagan imagery in the chapel. A small section that offered children's activities at the back of the church had crayons and colouring sheets for a Green Man and a dragon.

As the service started, two officiants led the priest towards the altar. The first man to walk down had a visible earring, a sign that we were not amongst the Evangelicals. Once the service started, one could have been anywhere. There was no acknowledgment or rejection of the setting or any conspiracy theories related to Rosslyn. It was a standard, progressive, liturgical, Christian service. The priest's sermon lasted barely six minutes. He started by mentioning recent events in the Israel–Hamas War. What I thought might turn into a fiery defence of Israel, or perhaps a call for peace, turned out to be neither. Rather, the sermon turned into a call to find the good in life, even when times are hard. Near the end of the sermon, he reiterated that when events such as those happening in the Holy Land or global warming challenge us, we must try to rejoice in the blessing of our life and the good things we have, while also trying to do our part in helping people in bad situations.

After some hymns, we joined in the dismissal. The service had lasted from 10.30 until 11.20. We mingled a bit and walked out. I shook hands with the priest, who was extremely friendly. He asked where we were visiting from and how we were enjoying our time in Scotland. He did not ask us why we were there.

Regardless, this was a church that was unashamed of the history and lore of Rosslyn Chapel, as evidenced by the children's materials. Further, there were several moveable informational stands that provided details about the various Masonic and pagan markings throughout the church, which were not removed for the service. There were flyers in various locations that were for visitors of the chapel for other reasons, such as 'Welcome to Rosslyn Chapel: Explore the Mystery'. These were also left out during the church service. Not that we would have expected the church to cleanse itself of these pagan connections, but it does stand in pointed contrast to how horrified a conservative Christian would feel about this amicable relationship between the church and the 'occult'.

A useful way to think about religious groups and organizations – particularly those that are part of long-established and conventional traditions – is to examine how much tension they are in with their surrounding cultural environment.[71] Are they calling for a rejection of the world and other religions/viewpoints (high tension), or are they accepting of the outside world (low tension)? In all, the mainstream religious aspects of Rosslyn Chapel and its congregation could be characterized as very low tension. This allows it to exist in harmony with the New Age and conspiratorial elements of the site and to operate as a functioning congregation that welcomes irregular visitors who are more interested in *The Da Vinci Code* or other popular narratives about the chapel. This is an example of how mainstream religion and the paranormal can peaceably coexist, but only when traditional religion has relaxed its expectations of exclusivity and reduced its tension with 'the world'.

In terms of Rosslyn itself, it is the ultimate Rorschach test. The uses of Rosslyn for conspiracy theories and literary narratives necessarily involve interpretations of the myriad mysterious symbols in the chapel. All of the various stories about Rosslyn point to specific carvings. What is not apparent until you visit the site is how reductionistic and selective many of these narratives are, relative to the sheer number of symbols on display. In every section of the chapel is *everything* – angels, a Green Man, Masonic markings, crosses, and more. It is a rich tapestry of diverse symbols that can serve as fodder for any conspiracy, if only one has 'eyes to see it'.

Two ideas that are particularly useful for understanding the contemporary popularity of Rosslyn Chapel are mediatization and conspiratorial Gnosticism. Regarding mediatization, the success of *The Da Vinci Code* and its related films has completely changed the nature of Rosslyn as a tourist destination.[72] Indeed, Dan Brown's novel is 'now the dominant lens through which this fascinating medieval church is viewed and understood'.[73] Not only did popular media drive exponentially more tourists to the site, but populist media in the form of visitor-generated social media content have furthered the 'viral' cultural currency of the site.[74] Because of the open nature of the interpretations people can make about the chapel, it provides an ideal site for endless mediatized tourism.

As we noted with reference to David Icke, conspiratorial Gnosticism is a framework for understanding the nature and appeal of 'conspiracy theories' as a form of 'hidden knowledge'.[75] Uncovering and holding what is perceived as secret knowledge is immensely appealing, as it sets one apart by revealing the true nature of things, while others remain unaware. This is foundational to the psychological appeal of conspiracy theories (and many religions). Likewise, secrecy is a key component of esotericism, which infuses narratives about Rosslyn, and invites readers, viewers, and tourists to participate actively in unravelling its mysteries.[76] The richness and diversity of symbols throughout the site allow people to narrate their own stories about Rosslyn, and the endless mediatization of the chapel provides ample material that can be integrated into a wide variety of perspectives, ranging from far-right conspiracies to the progressive New Age.[77] The mysterious, gnostic, and participatory nature of the chapel invites people to make their own meaning and use it however they see fit.

Unbounded Affinity Between Religion and the Paranormal

Together, the findings from our survey along with more in-depth case studies of the Aetherius Society and Rosslyn Chapel show some of the interesting and complex connections between organized religion and the paranormal. We can see how paranormalism can be formalized and codified into new religions; how population dynamics between organized religion and diffuse supernaturalism are complexly intertwined; and how secularization opens up physical and cultural space for the paranormal to thrive.

The Aetherius Society shows how paranormal beliefs and experiences can be ritualized and codified into a stable, long-lasting religious organization. At the population level, the data from CASPAR show how the bounded affinity between religion and the paranormal is expressed through negative connections to religious practice, but positive connections to religious beliefs and experiences. Rosslyn Chapel shows how organized religion, when weakened from societal and organizational secularization, may welcome paranormal connections, because it has become 'good for business'. Collectively, these examples show that there is always a reciprocal dynamic between organized religion and that which is labelled culturally as paranormal. These dynamics are complex but also understandable. They flow both ways, with paranormal subcultures sometimes morphing into organized religions, and organized religions taking varying positions – ranging from welcoming to condemning – toward alternative forms of supernaturalism. Most of all, the connections between religion and the paranormal are malleable and enduring, even in, or perhaps especially in secularized contexts. Barring a surprise resurgence of Christianity in Britain, current trends suggest that as the nation continues to move away from organized religion, more and more citizens will adopt, develop, and maintain idiosyncratic combinations of supernatural beliefs and practices that include paranormalism.

CONCLUSION

The (Eternal) Return of Nobody

As the reader will recall, one of the most dramatic events of our evening at 30 East Drive in Pontefract occurred when we joined the Retford Ghost Hunters in an upstairs bedroom. The Retford Ghost Hunters (RGH) team had set up a laptop running software called the 'Alice Box' in an attempt to communicate with the dreaded Black Monk of Pontefract. Trevor and Will of RGH would ask questions of the spirits. The Alice Box would, on occasion, display a word on the laptop's screen, which Trevor would read aloud. Over the next few minutes, we saw 'can appear', 'figurine', 'ropes' and several other terms displayed. 'Can appear', produced a little excitement. Was the Monk ready to show himself?

The Monk seemed ready to talk. Suddenly, the Alice Box beeped and displayed 'I'm Nobody'. This produced much enthusiasm online, with 'Mr. Nobody' being one of the early nicknames for the Black Monk. The online audience excitedly commented to one another and informed RGH members of the importance of the phrase. It seemed we had made contact. But if we have learned anything throughout our research, it is that the paranormal is never simple. The 'I'm Nobody' incident was more complicated than it first appeared.

In the aftermath of our time at 30 East Drive, we downloaded copies of the Alice Box for PC/Windows to investigate further and ran it several times.[1] In one experiment, we let the program run for half an hour. Words appeared, and sometimes a two-word phrase. Sometimes the words appeared quickly, sometimes with longer pauses in between. In all, fifty-five words/phrases were presented in the thirty minutes. Here is one sequence of five words that appeared closely together:

SAM
COMPARE
LATE
LED
BRIDLE

Curious, we explored the program a bit more and found that these words came from a preset list of over 2,000 installed with the PC version of the program. 'SAM', 'BRIDLE', 'LED' and the other fifty-two words from the session were all on that list. But 'I'm Nobody' is not on that word list. It could not have appeared at 30 East Drive unless RHG had purposefully added it to the word bank.

Lest sceptical readers cry 'fraud!' and assume that the Retford Ghost Hunters were trying to trick us, this is common practice for users of the Alice Box. The creator of the program argues that spirits (somehow) manipulate its operations to 'swing the pendulum of probability towards a particular, purposefully chosen, entry in the pool'.[2] From this perspective, it makes sense to insert terms into the word list that might resonate with spirits. So for RGH, it was important to add 'I'm Nobody' to their list, *so that the Monk could choose it*. They also find it meaningful that the phrase does not always appear in their sessions at the 30 East Drive: 'Nobody was added on the 1st visit to East Drive and we have attended around 12 times now, and that is the 2nd time it has shown up on the Alice box', they told us.[3]

Indeed, the practice of adding to the Alice Box word bank is so popular that it is a selling point of the programme. As one reseller notes: 'While Alice has a pre-loaded word bank, you can easily remove phrases or add new ones of your own, for example to suit specific locations or places that you are investigating.'[4] The developer plans to add the ability for users to share their customized word banks online.[5] This experience of the Alice Box encapsulates the nature of the paranormal. For the diehard sceptic, adding situation-specific words to the list removes any potential validity such an experiment might have. For the enthusiast, failing to do so lessens the ability of spirits to communicate meaningfully.

In this sense the paranormal itself is 'nobody'. It lies in a liminal space where it is not quite anything. Some paranormal practices have a scientific veneer but would not be acceptable to a conventional scientist. Others, such as those of the Aetherius Society, inhabit a realm that is close to religion but would not be acceptable to anyone devoted to conventional religious doctrines.

And yet, the paranormal is also enormously popular in Britain. When we asked respondents to our survey about eighteen different paranormal beliefs, only a minority (21.7 per cent) were complete sceptics, rejecting all of them.[6] At the same time, only a small number (2.2 per cent) accepted all eighteen paranormal beliefs. Eleven per cent were true particularists and believed in one paranormal subject only and rejected all others. So the norm in modern Britain is not to reject the paranormal wholesale *nor* to believe in all of it. Rather, the norm is to believe in *something* paranormal, usually a combination of topics, with two-thirds of our random sample of UK citizens believing in two or more paranormal subjects.

These beliefs, of course, vary in their relative popularity (see Figure 8.1). The most common paranormal belief in Britain is that dowsing rods 'can be used to detect water, minerals and other elements that are buried underground', with more than half of respondents agreeing with this statement. Nearly half (46.2 per cent) believed that 'lines of energy, sometimes called "ley lines," connect many ancient structures and landmarks'. Rounding out the top five were believing that black

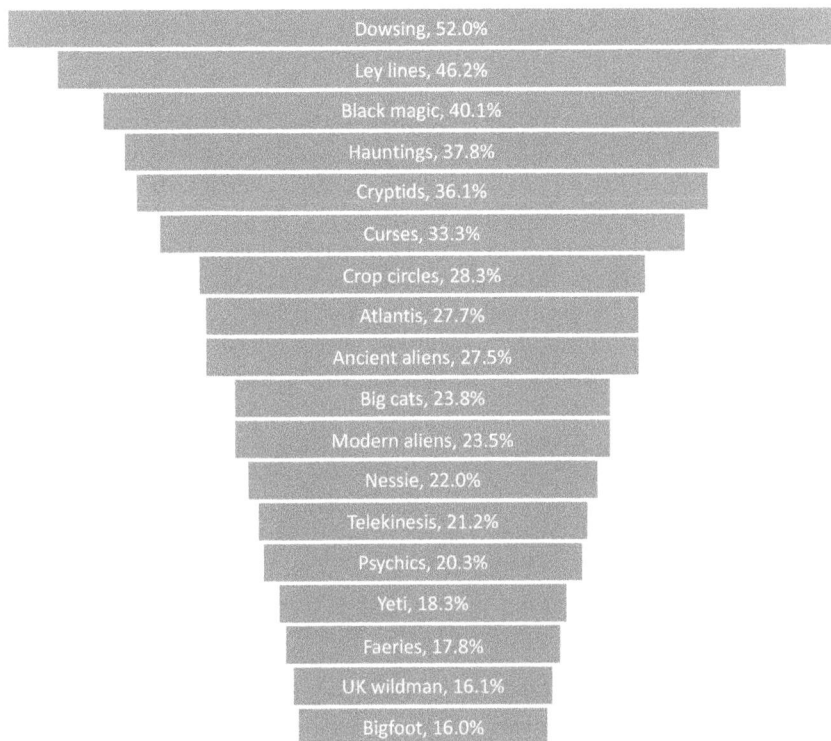

Figure 8.1 Paranormal beliefs in Britain, ranked by popularity (CASPAR, 2021).

magic exists (40.1 per cent), that places can be haunted by spirits (37.8 per cent), and that 'mysterious creatures, previously thought extinct, still inhabit this world' (36.1 per cent). Nearly all of these different paranormal beliefs were held by at least one in five respondents, with the exception of the Yeti (18.3 per cent), faeries (17.8 per cent), the UK Wildman (16.1 per cent), and Bigfoot (16 per cent).

As we discussed in Chapter 3, we do find evidence that belief in ghosts has been increasing over time. For other subjects there has not been enough systematic study to discuss growth with certainty, due to infrequent polling and changing question phrasing, making direct comparisons over time difficult. What is enormously clear, however, is that the paranormal is an important part of British life, and we do speculate that it will only increase in popularity going forward. Indeed, the very liminality of the paranormal makes it especially able to benefit from wider ongoing social trends within contemporary society. These trends include secularization and the 'subjective turn' in religion, advances in communication technologies and hyperreal religions, and the growth of the experience economy. These developments did not create the paranormal, nor did the paranormal cause them to happen. Nonetheless, the paranormal is poised to take advantage of them.

Secularization, the Subjective Turn and Diverse Supernatural Portfolios

As the shackles of organized religion have been loosened by secularization, some scholars have argued that personal religiosity has taken a 'subjective turn'.[7] Sociologists Paul Heelas and Linda Woodhead, for example, theorize that the decay of religious authority has led individuals to develop their own, idiosyncratic spiritual worldviews.[8] No longer constrained by strict religious affiliations that dictate interpretation and practice, this means that there is more room for subjectivities to emerge in what people choose to believe in and do. In a similar vein, economist Laurence Iannaccone argues that individuals are naturally motivated to hold many religious and spiritual beliefs at once, a sort of 'hedging one's bets' against having made the wrong choice. Religious organizations, on the other hand, are highly motivated to curtail outside beliefs, lest such experimentation reduce the commitment (and resource investment) of their members. But following Iannaccone's line of reasoning, if people are released from the constraints imposed by conventional religions, they will develop diverse religious 'portfolios': '[O]ne might go to confession on Sunday, consult a medium on Monday, and engage in transcendental meditation on Wednesday'.[9]

As such, religion and spirituality are becoming increasingly akin to a cafe, where someone picks and chooses what they want to consume. Of course, these choices are not limitless. But 'the menu' can be tailored in ways to suit the tastes of the individual. The paranormal flourishes in such an environment. Entrepreneurs such as David Icke can develop unified theories of the paranormal that freely take ideas and inspiration from a host of other religions, traditions, paranormal topics, and conspiracy theories, not to mention pseudoscience and alternative history. The paranormal consumer, on the other hand, is *also free* to take those parts of Icke's theory that resonate, ditch the rest, and combine this all with whatever other beliefs and practices are of personal interest.

During times of social change, paranormal ideas can be attractive simply *because* they are not typically endorsed by those in mainstream positions, or as part of conventional religions. However, while rejecting convention may be a motivating factor for some people, it is also worth making another observation about contemporary society: the sanctions for believing in many things previously thought deviant have reduced considerably among younger generations. Within a short amount of time, the stigma of being divorced has disappeared; being gay is mostly accepted and quite possible *within the Church*; there is a Wiccan shop in most towns; and Satanists are just another religion.

This is a significant change in society – but also one that can easily be taken for granted. The consequences for holding beliefs that might have previously been met with strong social and legal punishment at local, regional, and national levels have all but vanished. Therefore, it is not necessarily surprising that people are showing a greater likelihood to develop idiosyncratic combinations of beliefs, focused upon their own personal truths. The paranormal provides a wellspring of such beliefs to choose from, and the costs for incorporating them into one's spiritual worldview are minimal.

Digital Technologies and Hyper-real Religions

The second societal trend from which the paranormal is benefiting is the growth of new forms of religion that combine elements of popular culture with more traditional religious practices, a phenomenon referred to as 'hyper-real religion'.[10] The 'hyper-reality' here is a description of how lived experience and interpretation are informed and shaped by ideas that explicitly extend into the imaginary realms of popular culture. These hyperrealities largely divorce ideas and meanings from their original frames of reference and instead supplant new and sometimes quite different interpretations and practices on those ideas.[11]

Perhaps the most well-known example of a hyper-real religion is those people who, inspired by the *Star Wars* film franchise, consider themselves to be 'Jedi'. 'Jediism' is reported to be a belief system that is based on the idea of 'the Force'. This is a metaphysical power that is understood to underpin all things in the universe – and working with 'the Force' is a core concept of being a Jedi.[12] The movement came to popular attention in several national censuses in the 2000s. In the UK, for example, the 2001 census reported that 390,127 people (almost 0.8 per cent) reported themselves to be 'Jedi'.[13] These sorts of figures were repeated around the globe.[14]

To be clear, it is difficult to say how many people claimed this affiliation in jest, and it is worth stating that the 2021 census of England and Wales recorded just 1,600 'Jedi Knights'. But regardless of the apparent fall of the Jedi, sociologists have used the phenomenon to highlight how belief systems can exist within a synergistic relationship with popular culture, with both drawing influence and inspiration from each other.[15] Again, the paranormal is perfectly suited to capitalize on a tendency for people to combine media influences into personalized packages of religious and spiritual beliefs.

Paranormal television programmes, for example, are blueprints in paranormal practices, as much as they are a source of entertainment. If you want to know how to conduct a ghost hunt, you only need to watch an episode of a ghost hunting TV show like *Most Haunted*. Not only will you learn about the types of entities that you might encounter, but these programmes will also demonstrate what you need to do to detect their presence. If you have any further questions, you can simply attend regular ghost hunts or theatre shows that take place across the country.

It is true enough to say that many of the techniques used in ghost hunting TV programmes are influenced by the practices of Spiritualism that were popular in the late-nineteenth and early-twentieth centuries. But you don't need to have any knowledge of Spiritualism to participate in a séance, any more than you need to know *Star Wars* is influenced by Taoist ideas to enjoy the films.

Indeed, technological developments with respect to subscription channels like Gaia, video platforms like YouTube, and even the Facebook livestreams of the Retford Ghost Hunters further distribute and legitimate paranormal beliefs and practices. The rapid proliferation of paranormal podcasts also functions as specialist platforms through which people can explore, expand, and strengthen their subjective beliefs and experiences.

In the absence of a physically embodied congregation, the paranormal-themed channels and platforms of the (social) media world create virtual communities, through which physically dis-located and dis-connected people can learn about 'classic' cases, keep up with the latest developments, and feel part of a greater movement. As the Retford Ghost Hunters showed us at 30 East Drive, you don't need to be 'there' to feel part of a paranormal community or to participate in a paranormal activity. Just as the digital age has facilitated the spread of conspiracy theories, so too it provides an optimal environment for the expansion of paranormal subcultures, unbounded by spatial constraints.[16]

The Experience Economy

Recent years have also seen a rapid increase in the so-called experience economy. This refers to the growth in economic markets that are directed toward the creation and maintenance of memorable experiences, as opposed to simply exchanging goods and services.[17] In these markets, specific value is placed upon the conspicuous consumption of 'being there', 'doing that', and often, recording it all for reproduction on social media.

It is fair to say that we were rather stunned by the availability of businesses catering to paranormal-based experiences in Britain. Ghost hunts, past life regression, and UFO conspiracies are no longer the stuff of dedicated experts or those on the periphery of society. Instead, a bewildering array of options is available for anyone who has the money to pay. For those who wish to experience the paranormal in person, one is never more than twenty minutes from a ghost hunt or tour. Stone circles and crop circles dot the landscape. Mind Body Spirit fairs, UFO conferences, and speakers such as David Icke are never more than a few days away on the calendar. To an increasing extent, you don't even need to leave your house to experience the paranormal. Tarot readings, ghost hunts, and even exorcisms are available online at the click of a 'payment' button.

Freed from the constraining boundaries of institutional science and religion, paranormal narratives, experiences, and objects are incredibly malleable commodities. Paranormal ideas do not need to have an overarching metanarrative, make broader conceptual sense, or even be connected to a unitary sense of self. Like the rest of (Western) society, the paranormal increasingly exists as a series of advertised events where you pay for an experience and 'make your own mind up'. For sceptics and believers alike, anyone can partake in paranormal experiences and choose how to interpret them.

For the budding paranormal entrepreneur, opportunities abound. One could open a stall at a psychic fair. Lacking any widely recognized credentialing or training system, who is to say that you are not as good at contacting a guardian angel as the person at the next stall over? Or one could start a paranormal podcast or blog. Or, like the entrepreneurial Retford Ghost Hunters, livestream ghost hunts.

If one lives in a location with reputed hauntings (and most people do live close to one), or at a place such as Loch Ness with a famous monster, starting a paranormal walking tour is an option. Obviously, the ability to create a paranormal business will be subject to the same constraints as any other. One needs to advertise or otherwise find customers, and there may well already be local competition; a small village likely cannot accommodate multiple ghost tours. But there is certainly great freedom in the paranormal. You cannot copyright a lake monster's likeness any more than you can own a ghost.

With so many options available in Britain, the paranormal experience economy is akin to a vast supermarket. Just like the bread that you buy from a market, it does not particularly matter if you change your mind, move on to something new, or lose interest completely. Many of the people we met during our fieldwork had 'careers' that explored different areas of the paranormal during different times of their lives. Making these decisions and pursuing paranormal interests are now easier than ever before.

The Eternal Return

Throughout this book we have defined the paranormal *negatively*, by pointing out what it is *not* – institutional science or conventional religion. We think this negative definition is warranted because it speaks to the way paranormalism is culturally organized, and it also makes sense of the patterns we find regarding interest in and engagement with the paranormal. Paranormal beliefs and practices are more likely to thrive in economically deprived locations, among individuals of marginalized social statuses, and where organized religion has waned.

At the same time, it is also important to take account of what the paranormal is *positively*, in terms of the substantive content of these beliefs and experiences. Is there any real commonality between the tales of a monster lurking in Loch Ness, experiences of encounters with a malevolent Black Monk, and seeking out tarot divination for personal insights?

Although there are clearly differences between paranormal subcultures and their related beliefs and experiences, there are also some key commonalities. One of the most important is the centrality of recycled, remade, and reimagined narratives and experiences that draw on cultural mythology. Looking at tales of cryptic beasts that roam the countrysides, back alleys, and deep waters, we can readily see age-old myths transposed into a new form. The kelpies of old have become the lake monsters of today. The Green Man has become the British Bigfoot. When a group of ghost enthusiasts encounters a spirit, local folklore comes alive in spectral form, haunting marginalized spaces. When clients at a Mind, Body, and Spirit fair receive Reiki treatments, are these not simply the expressions of a long-held and shared spiritual need, channelled through late modern capitalism's quest for individuation via consumption? Living traditions such as divination practices or astrological beliefs also hold a trove of past ideas about these matters from which people can draw on and repurpose.

Consequently, the paranormal can thrive in contexts of secularization. When people no longer have organized religions fulfilling the human need for world-creating narratives, those needs are likely to be expressed elsewhere. Indeed, the human desire for the transcendent can be experienced through media and fandom, personal spiritual quests, or diffuse beliefs about spirituality. Perhaps through all three, as they syncretize together quite easily.

The paranormal is a repository of (currently) alternative cultural beliefs and practices, particularly those related to mythological archetypes. Stories and experiences that grip the human mind – especially in relation to mystery, magic, and the unknown – will always have their place, as humans grapple with the inherent limits of knowledge, experience, and existence. The myths of old do not necessarily look the same today, but they eternally return, beckoning the curious, the questioning, and the contrarian with the promise of mystery, insight, and adventure.

Given the current social trends towards secularization, subjective truth, digital media, and experience-based economies, we feel confident prophesying that the paranormal will not merely continue to persist; it will thrive in Britain for the foreseeable future.

NOTES

Introduction

1 As we detail in Chapter 3, the purported spirit at 30 East Drive has been well marketed by current owner Bil Bungay, see Richard Estep and Bil Bungay, *The Black Monk of Pontefract: The World's Most Violent and Relentless Poltergeist* (self-published, 2019). Online and print journalism frequently uses singular adjectives to describe the ghost. See, for example, Kara McKune, 'Pontefract House Is Home to 'Most Terrifying Ghost in UK', *Wakefield Express*, 15 October 2022.

2 30 East Drive OWNER'S PAGE. https://www.facebook.com/groups/30EastDriveOwners/.

3 Christopher Bader, Joseph O. Baker and F. Carson Mencken, *Paranormal America: Ghost Encounters, UFO Sightings, Bigfoot Hunts, and other Curiosities in Religion and Culture*, 2nd ed. (New York: NYU Press, 2017); Christopher Bader, Joseph O. Baker, L. Edward Day and C. Ann Gordon, *Fear Itself: The Causes and Consequences of Fear in America* (New York: NYU Press, 2020).

4 Michael Roskams, *Religion, England and Wales: Census 2021* (Office for National Statistics, 29 November 2022).

5 It is worth noting, however, that atheism is increasing among younger generations in the UK. So the decline in conventional religious affiliation is simultaneously fuelling a rise in *both* irreligion and paranormalism.

6 Stephen Bullivant, *Nonverts: The Making of Ex-Christian America* (New York: Oxford University Press, 2022); Paul K. McClure, 'Something Besides Monotheism: Sociotheological Boundary Work among the Spiritual, But Not Religious', *Poetics* 62 (2017): 53–65; Linda Mercadante, *Belief Without Borders: Inside the Minds of the Spiritual But Not Religious* (New York: Oxford University Press, 2014).

7 We outline our definition of paranormal at length in Chapter 1. Clearly those who believe that extraterrestrials are simply beings from another planet or that Bigfoot is merely an undiscovered ape might not agree with us classifying those entities as 'supernatural'. But because these topics are *culturally* defined as paranormal, we treat them as such for analysis.

8 Joseph O. Baker and Buster G. Smith, *American Secularism: Cultural Contours of Nonreligious Belief Systems* (New York: NYU Press, 2015); Paul Froese and Christopher Bader, *America's Four Gods: What We Say About God – & What That Says About Us* (New York: Oxford University Press, 2010); Ralph W. Hood, Peter C. Hill and W. Paul Williamson, *The Psychology of Religious Fundamentalism* (New York: Guilford Press, 2005).

9 Henry Sidgwick discusses of the Census of Hallucinations in two works: Henry Sidgwick, 'A Census of Hallucinations', *New Review* (January 1891): 52–9; Henry Sidgwick, 'Report on the Census of Hallucinations', *Proceedings of the Society for Psychical Research* 10 (1894): 25–394. An earlier attempt to document the extent of ghost sightings was conducted by Edmund Gurney and colleagues. It contained over

700 documented cases. See Edmund Gurney, F. W. H. Myers and Frank Podmore, *Phantasms of the Living* (London: Society for Psychical Research, 1886).

10 Considerable research on the psychology of paranormal belief has been conducted in the UK but among convenience samples that cannot speak to patterns among the general public. Much of this research has been focused upon the development of scales meant to measure paranormal beliefs or orientations. For reviews see Charlotte E. Dean, Shazia Akhtar, Tim M. Gale, Karen Irvine, Richard Wiseman, and Keith R. Laws, 'Development of the Paranormal and Supernatural Beliefs Scale Using Classical and Modern Test Theory', *BMC Psychology* 9, no. 1 (2021): 1–20; Kenneth Drinkwater, Andrew Denovan, Neil Dagnall and Andrew Parker, 'An Assessment of the Dimensionality and Factorial Structure of the Revised Paranormal Belief Scale', *Frontiers in Psychology* 26 (2017); Kenneth Drinkwater, Andrew Denovan, Neil Dagnall and Andrew Parker, 'The Australian Sheep-Goat Scale: An Evaluation of Factor Structure and Convergent Validity', *Frontiers in Psychology* 9 (2018); Christopher C. French and Anna Stone, *Anomalistic Psychology: Exploring Paranormal Belief and Experience* (London: Bloomsbury, 2017).

11 Erlendur Haraldsson, 'Representative National Surveys of Psychic Phenomena: Iceland, Great Britain, Sweden, USA and Gallup's Multinational Survey', *Journal of the Society for Psychical Research* 53 (1985), 145–58.

12 See Clive D. Field, 'Belief in Britain, 1939–2009', *British Religion in Numbers* (December 5, 2024). As BRIN notes, we must use caution when interpreting these numbers, as they originate from a variety of polls, which have variance in question wording and sampling techniques.

13 See Madeleine Castro, Roger Burrows and Robin Wooffitt, 'The Paranormal Is (Still) Normal: The Sociological Implications of a Survey of Paranormal Experiences in Great Britain', *Sociological Research Online* 19, no. 3 (2014): 30–44. In addition to precognition and contact with the dead, Castro et al.'s survey asked about 'mystical experiences' (feelings of being one with the universe, awareness of a presence, etc.), ESP and telepathy. Percentages reporting each type of experience were precognition (24 per cent), ESP (13 per cent), mystical experiences (12 per cent), telepathy (12 per cent), and after-death communication (10 per cent).

14 The survey was administered and collected by the marketing and polling firm IPSOS MORI UK.

15 For methodological details of the CASPAR survey, see Tom Clark, Joseph O. Baker, and Christopher D. Bader, 'Marginalized, Secularized, and Popularized? The Prevalence and Patterns of Paranormal Belief in the United Kingdom', *The Sociological Quarterly*, 66, no. 3 (2025): 612–635. https://doi.org/10.1080/00380253.2025.2461298.

16 The Association for the Scientific Study of Anomalous Phenomena, 'Welcome to ASSAP', *ASSAP*. https://www.assap.ac.uk/.

17 See David Martin and Alastair Boyd, *Nessie – the Surgeon's Photo Exposed* (East Barnet: Martin & Boyd, 1999). The book provides a detailed examination of the photograph, which concludes that 'Nessie' was a toy submarine with a monster head attached.

18 Cryptid is a term used in paranormal circles to describe a creature that is not yet recognized by science. Although by definition a cryptid could be an undiscovered grasshopper, it is generally reserved for more dramatic beasts such as Bigfoot, Mothman, and Nessie.

19 For example, interested tourists can visit the Church of All Saints and St. James in Nunnington to see the claimed tomb of Peter Loschy, who donned a suit of spiked armour to battle a dragon living on a nearby hill.
20 For an overview of the British Bigfoot, see Nick Redfern, *Wildman!* (North Devon: CFZ, 2012).
21 'UFO Trail at Rendlesham Forest', *Forestry England*, undated.
22 For example, more than one-fifth (21.6 per cent) of our respondents agree or strongly agreed that the UK Government is concealing information from the public about aliens visiting Earth.
23 John Saliba, 'The Earth Is a Dangerous Place: The Worldview of the Aetherius Society', in *The Encyclopedic Sourcebook of UFO Religions*, ed. James R. Lewis (Amherst, NY: Prometheus, 2003), 129; Scott Scribner and Gregory Wheeler, 'Cosmic Intelligences and Their Terrestrial Channel', in The *Encyclopedic Sourcebook of UFO Religions*, ed. James R. Lewis (Amherst, NY: Prometheus, 2003), 157.
24 George King, *The Twelve Blessings* (London: The Aetherius Press, 1961), 11. Jesus was sadly unavailable to endorse *Paranormal Britain*. We assume he approves, at least until we directly hear otherwise.
25 For an overview of different religious groups based around UFOs see James R. Lewis, ed., *Encyclopedic Sourcebook of UFO Religions* (Amherst, NY: Prometheus, 2003).
26 It is probably not surprising to the reader that Christian groups would claim that witchcraft is 'Satanic', but it is also common amongst conservative Christians to claim that all paranormal subjects, including UFOs, Bigfoot and ghosts are designed by Satan to draw the faithful away from biblical teachings. Some works with this perspective include Timothy Dailey, *The Paranormal Conspiracy* (Minneapolis, MN: Chosen Books, 2015); Bill Myers and David Wimbish, *The Dark Side of the Supernatural: Uncovering God's Truth* (Grand Rapids, MI: Zondervan, 2012); Ron Rhodes, *Alien Obsession* (Eugene, OR: Harvest House, 1998).

Chapter 1

1 The term *paranormal* is composed of the prefix *para* and the adjective *normal*. *Para* is of Greek origin and is variously taken to mean 'alongside, beyond; altered; contrary; irregular, abnormal'. On the other hand, *normal* is considered to be taken from the Latin *normalis*, which means 'in conformity with rule, normal'. However, the term paranormal is a relatively recent English construction. The *Oxford English Dictionary* (OED), for example, dates the first written example to 1905; however, using Ngrams, we found that the first usage of the word in English texts archived in Google books was in 1827, in the anonymously authored *Salem Witchcraft* and the Sir Walter Scott essay *On the Supernatural in Fictitious Composition*. Wider usage of the word does not occur until the 1930s.
2 There are any many companies that exist solely to promote and run such events at more regional levels – with any number of people and exhibitors in these areas wanting to offer their products, services and therapies. In 2023, for example, 'Deer Spirit Events' ran MBS wellbeing shows and psychic/wellbeing fairs in Oxfordshire, Buckinghamshire, Gloucestershire and Northants. 'White Light Events', on the other hand, concentrated on areas around the East Midlands. Moving from town to town across the summer months, these companies typically hold biweekly events in civic

centres, halls, and conference centres. Each event might attract around 60 exhibitors and perhaps as many as 1,000 visitors paying around £5 per day.
3   Colin Campbell, 'The Cult, the Cultic Milieu and Secularisation', *A Sociological Yearbook of Religion in Britain* 5 (1972): 119–36.
4   Paul Heelas and Linda Woodhead, 'The Kendal Project: Testing the "Spiritual Revolution" Thesis', *Sociology Review* 13, no. 2 (2003): 18–21; Paul Heelas and Linda Woodhead, *The Spiritual Revolution* (Oxford: Blackwell, 2005).
5   Hellas and Woodhead, 'The Kendal Project, 19.
6   Paul Heelas, *Spiritualities of Life: New Age Romanticism and Consumptive Capitalism* (Malden, MA: Blackwell, 2008).
7   Charles Fort, *The Book of the Damned* (New York: Ace Books, [1919] 1972).
8   Fort, *The Book of the Damned*, 296, capitalization in original.
9   Charles Fort, *New Lands* (New York: Boni & Liveright, 1923), 9.
10 Charles Fort, *Lo!* (New York: Claude Kendal, 1931), 31.
11 At times scientists are directly drawn into addressing religious beliefs when asked to examine evidence of a purported miracle. For example, the Shroud of Turin, which some believers think to be the burial shroud of Christ upon which his image was transferred, has been the subject of numerous scientific examinations. Even here the matter is complicated, as some such research has been funded by religious groups or commissions.
12 There are of course more liberal Christian traditions that interpret the resurrection of Jesus in purely metaphorical terms. These groups, perhaps ironically, would be much more open to allowing paranormal experimentation among members due to lower ideological strictness and exclusivity compared to more literalist traditions.
13 Ann Taves, *Fits, Trances, and Visions: Experiencing Religion and Explaining Experience from Wesley to James* (Princeton, NJ: Princeton University Press, 1999); Ann Taves, 'The Power of the Paranormal (and Extraordinary)', *History of Religions* 53, no. 2 (2013): 205–11.
14 Of course, we recognize that there are numerous tales and conspiracy theories about the recovery of downed flying saucers.
15 We have also engaged in similar pursuits in the United States and found these same trends within paranormal subcultures.
16 Andrea Molle and Christopher D. Bader, 'Paranormal Science from America to Italy: A Case of Cultural Homogenisation', in *The Ashgate Research Companion to Paranormal Cultures*, ed. Olu Jenzen and Sally R. Munt (London: Routledge, 2013).
17 Nachman Ben-Yehuda, *Deviance and Moral Boundaries* (Chicago: University of Chicago Press, 1985); Thomas F. Gieryn, *Cultural Boundaries of Science: Credibility on the Line* (Chicago: University of Chicago Press, 1999).
18 For an in-depth, autoethnographic account of tarot reading as a practice and profession, see Melissa F. Lavin, 'On Spiritualist Workers: Healing and Divining Through Tarot and the Metaphysical', *Journal of Contemporary Ethnography* 50, no. 3 (2021): 317–40.
19 Using tarot cards for the purposes of divination is a comparatively recent phenomenon. Although cards with allegorical illustrations were originally developed in the Italian courts of the fifteenth century, these were used for standard card games. While 'trump' cards appeared in the sixteenth century, it was not until the late-eighteenth century that a French occultist known as Etteilla – whose real name was Jean-Baptiste Alliette – developed a prescribed system of interpretation for

cartomancy, first using a deck of thirty-two cards, and then the more recognizable system of seventy-two cards that is still in use.

20 Similarly, there are also clearly some topics that are perceived to be 'off limits' within these workshops. At a workshop on past life regression, for example, the issue of a past life on another world was suppressed, with the suggestion that it is better to concentrate on healing rather than 'that other stuff'. Elsewhere, the issue of demons and/or possession is generally referred to along the lines of guarding against 'something else coming in'.

21 Reiki is a combination of two Japanese words 'rei' and 'ka' – which means 'universal' and 'energy', respectively.

22 There are many variations on the 'universal energy' theme. Aura, Vitalism, Odic force, Orgone, and even Vril are notable for their emergence in the nineteenth and twentieth centuries, while mana, asha, and silla, have long been associated with Polynesian, Zoroastrian, and Inuit traditions, respectively. Similarly, ideas like the Greek *pneuma* and the Latin *numen* – essentially 'life force' – are closely linked to the development of the idea of ghosts.

23 Ruth Prince and David Riches, *The New Age in Glastonbury: The Construction of Religious Movements* (New York: Berghahn, 2000), 114.

24 Karla is a pseudonym.

25 Beverly is a pseudonym.

26 Notably, believers would certainly volunteer this information, and it would be an inflection point in the reading that dictates the path of the rest of the interaction that follows. Acting in my research rather than personal capacity, however, I instead allowed the reading to continue without volunteering this information in order to see the other kinds of techniques and strategies the reader would use.

27 We can very roughly estimate the percentage of British citizens who have experienced a faith healing in an enlightenment context by making two assumptions. First, we must assume that a respondent who claims affiliation with a major organized religion experienced their faith healing within that context. We also must assume that those who report being of an 'other' religion, an atheist, or an agnostic experienced their faith healing in an enlightenment context. Under those assumptions, 2 per cent of our respondents have had an enlightenment healing experience.

28 Rodney Stark, *One True God: Historical Consequences of Monotheism* (Princeton, NJ: Princeton University Press, 2001), 102.

29 The term 'occult science' was frequently used in the Renaissance era to describe practices such as astrology, numerology, and alchemy. See Wayne Shumaker, *The Occult Sciences in the Renaissance: A Study in Intellectual Patterns* (Berkeley: University of California Press, 1972); Esprim Asprem, 'Science and the Occult' in *The Occult World*, ed. Christopher Partridge (London: Routledge, 2014).

30 Émile Durkheim, *The Elementary Forms of Religious Life*, translated by Karen E. Fields (New York: Free Press, 1995), 42, emphasis and capitalization in original. It is beyond the scope of our book to completely review the complexity and history of magic. Grappling with the paranormal is hard enough. Interested readers are pointed to two key works for starters: Owen Davies ed., *The Oxford History of Witchcraft and Magic* (Oxford: Oxford University Press, 2023); Ronald Hutton, *Pagan Britain* (London: Yale University Press, 2013).

31 There is much individual variation within these traditions regarding an explicit emphasis on magic, while others, such as pantheism, can actually conflate two very different practices. However, as a general 'rule of thumb', the religions we have listed

tend towards some type of explicitly magical practices. These census data are available from the Office of National Statistics (https://www.ons.gov.uk/census).
32 These statistics are also complicated by the fact that it is not entirely clear what people mean when they identify as 'Pagan'. Paganism can broadly be described as a 'nature-based spirituality', but it is not a highly organized movement. To name but a few, it can incorporate any number of traditions and have many different 'paths', from Green Witchcraft to the Feri Tradition, and Neo-Druidism to Discordianism.
33 Denise is a pseudonym.
34 Matthew Wood, *Possession, Power and the New Age: Ambiguities of Authority in Neoliberal Societies* (London: Rutledge University Press, 2007).
35 Jeremy Carette and Richard King, *Selling Spirituality: The Silent Takeover of Religion* (London: Routledge, 2004)
36 These models also show some limited support for marginalization theories, with education level being a significantly negative predictor of consulting psychics, while those who were martially separated or divorced were significantly more likely to consult psychics.
37 Christopher Bader, Joseph O. Baker and F. Carson Mencken, *Paranormal America*, second edn (New York: NYU Press, 2017); Kenneth Drinkwater, Kenneth, Andrew Denovan, Neil Dagnall and Andrew Parker, 'An Assessment of the Dimensionality and Factorial Structure of the Revised Paranormal Belief Scale', *Frontiers in Psychology* 26 (2017); Tony Silva, 'Masculinity, Femininity, and Reported Paranormal Beliefs', *Journal for the Scientific Study of Religion* 62, no. 3 (2023): 709–22; Tony Silva and Ashley Woody, 'Supernatural Sociology: Beliefs by Race/Ethnicity, Gender, and Education', *Socius* 8 (2022): 1–18.
38 Lavin, 'On Spiritualist Workers'.
39 Eeva Sointu and Linda Woodhead, 'Spirituality, Gender, and Expressive Selfhood', *Journal for the Scientific Study of Religion* 47, no. 2 (2008): 259–76; Linda Woodhead, 'Why So Many Women in Holistic Spirituality? A Puzzle Revisited', in *A Sociology of Spirituality*, ed. Kieran Flanagan and Peter C. Jupp (Aldershot: Ashgate, 2007).
40 On the gender gap in care seeking, see Maria I. Oliver, Nicky Pearson, Nicola Coe and David Gunnell, 'Help-Seeking Behaviour in Men and Women with Common Mental Health Problems: Cross-sectional Study', *British Journal of Psychiatry* 186 (2005): 297–301; Douglas Wendt and Kevin Shafer, 'Gender and Attitudes about Mental Health Help Seeking: Results from National Data', *Health & Social Work* 41, no. 1 (2016): e20–8.

Chapter 2

1 In 1961, Edinburgh-born biologist Ivan T. Sanderson published *Abominable Snowmen: Legend Come to Life*, in which he argued that four kinds of undiscovered ape-like creatures still roamed the planet. This work proved extremely influential to Yeti and Bigfoot belief moving forward and is cited in every popular Bigfoot book we reviewed.
2 This incident is recounted along with the sonar images on Steve Feltham's website (https://www.nessiehunter.co.uk/massive-sonar-contact-30-9-20/). Grammatical errors in original.

3 A colleague, Pete Simi, joined in this visit to see Steve Feltham. Other than Simi and a friend of Steve's who dropped by near the end of our visit, Dores Beach remained empty.
4 The claims that extraterrestrials appear in the myths, artwork and monuments of cultures throughout history are part of the larger 'ancient astronaut' hypothesis.
5 The *Madonna with Saint Giovannino* is most often attributed to Domenico Ghirlandaio; exact date unknown. It is on display at the Palazzo Vecchio in Florence. In the sky over the Madonna (to the viewer's right) is a cloud-like object radiating light. The *Annunciation* by Carlo Crivelli (1486) depicts the angel Gabriel informing Mary that she is to become the mother of the Christ child. A beam of light is striking the virgin from a cloud in the sky. See Diego Cuoghi, 'The Art of Imagining UFOs', *Skeptic* 11, no. 1 (2004): 145–8.
6 For an in-depth overview of myths, legends and the interpretation of lake monsters across cultures, see Michel Meurger and Claude Gagnon, *Lake Monster Traditions: A Cross-cultural Analysis* (London: Fortean Tomes, 1988).
7 Nessie is not universally assumed to be merely an undiscovered animal. Some authors such as the Bords posit that the Loch Ness Monster and other cryptids are supernatural beings. See Janet Bord and Colin Bord, *Alien Animals* (Harrisburg, PA: Stackpole, 1982).
8 The are several common variants of the spelling of woodwose, including wodewose and wudewasa.
9 *The Fight in the Forest* is held in the collection of the National Gallery of Art in Washington, D.C. https://www.nga.gov/collection/art-object-page.56725.html.
10 Graham J. McEwan, *Mystery Animals of Britain and Ireland* (London: Robert Hale, 1986), 155–6.
11 Hayden White, 'The Forms of Wildness: Archaeology of an Idea', in *The Wildman Within: An Image in Western Thought from the Renaissance to Romanticism*, ed. Edward Dudley and Maximillian E. Novak (Pittsburgh, PA: University of Pittsburgh Press, 2010).
12 Peter L. Thorslev, Jr., 'The Wild Man's Revenge', in *The Wildman Within: An Image in Western Thought from the Renaissance to Romanticism*, ed. Edward Dudley and Maximillian E. Novak (Pittsburgh, PA: University of Pittsburgh Press, 2010).
13 Charles K. Howard-Bury, *Mount Everest: The Reconnaissance, 1921* (New York: Longmans, Green, 1922), 141.
14 Ronald Kaulback, *Salween* (London: Hodder & Stoughton, 1983), 172–3.
15 The follow-up article was published with the title: 'The Abominable Snowman Unmasked! An Ursine "Man Friday"' in the *Illustrated London News* on 27 November 1937.
16 'Reappearance of the "Abominable Snowman"', *Illustrated London News*, 15 December 1951.
17 Michael Mcleod, *Anatomy of a Beast: Obsession and Myth on the Trail of Bigfoot* (Berkeley: University of California Press, 2009), 41.
18 A separate issue faced by those interested in the Yeti was the possibility that locals were stretching the truth about sightings in the area to encourage the income from related expeditions. See McLeod, *Anatomy of a Beast*, 39.
19 Kunzang Choden, *Bhutanese Tales of the Yeti* (Bangkok: White Lotus Press, 1997), xi.
20 For overviews of the role of mountaineers in the development of modern ideas of the Yeti, see: Joshua Blu Bluhs, *Bigfoot: The Life and Times of a Legend* (Chicago: University of Chicago Press, 2009); Mcleod, *Anatomy of a Beast*.

21 David J. Daegling, *Bigfoot Exposed: An Anthropologist Examines America's Enduring Legend* (New York: Rowan & Littlefield, 2004), 233.
22 Bord and Bord, *Alien Animals*, 154.
23 Jon Downes, 'The Big Hairy Monster of Bolam Lake', *Fortean Times* 169 (May 2003): 25.
24 Nick Redfern, *Man-Monkey: In Search of the British Bigfoot* (North Devon: CFZ, 2007); Nick Redfern, *Wildman: The Monstrous and Mysterious Saga of the 'British Bigfoot'* (North Devon: CFZ Press, 2012).
25 The episode, titled 'British Bigfoot', premiered on 4 January 2015. The episode also includes a visit to Loch Ness to look for Nessie.
26 It is common for US Bigfoot hunters to play recordings of loud, moaning howls purported to be Bigfoot or to mimic those howls themselves in hopes that a nearby creature will respond – a technique called 'call blasting'. It is also believed that Bigfoot creatures communicate with one another by knocking on trees with branches, hence the practice of banging pieces of wood together in the hopes of tricking nearby BHMs into responding.
27 Stu Neville, 'The Bigfeet of Britain', *Fortean Times* 425 (December 2002): 35–6.
28 Deborah Hatswell of Manchester is one of the most frequently interviewed British Bigfoot experts. She has her own podcast, *Deborah Hatswell BBR Investigations*, and a blog (https://debhatswell.wordpress.com/).
29 Some sample titles from the *Daily Star* tabloid include 'Bigfoot found in Cannock Chase: Footprint & claw marks "prove it"' (14 November 2021) and 'Bigfoot…The New Evidence' (28 November 2021).
30 Belief in the Yeti and British Bigfoot were significantly and highly correlated at $r = .64$ ($p < .001$).
31 With cryptids it is always complicated, but although some do indeed propose paranormal explanations, the prevailing attitude about alien big cats appears to be that they are physical creatures.
32 Bord and Bord, *Alien Animals*, 44.
33 As of this writing, Eric Ley is a member of the North Devon District Council.
34 In addition to the pilot for *Cat Hunters*, Matt Everett's Dragonfly films has produced two documentaries on ABCs, *Britain's Big Cat Mystery* (2021) and *Panthera Brittania* (2022).
35 Lisa Joyner, 'Man Spots Beast of Exmoor as "Big Cat" Seen on Dog Walk', *Country Living*, 7 January 2022.
36 A 2006 article in *The Guardian* newspaper provides an additional twenty-nine local ABC names, including the Plumstead Panther, Nottingham Lion and many other colourful monikers. Merrily Harpur, 'Seeing Is Believing: Sightings of Mystery "Big Cats" in Britain's Countryside Have Snowballed Since the 1980s, Dividing Opinion about Their Existence', *Guardian*, 21 March 2006.
37 Fiona Lang, 'The Cannich Puma', *Waithe and Wonder*, 27 August 2013. See also McEwan, *Mystery Animals of Britain and Ireland*, 44–5.
38 'Felicity the Puma'. *Inverness Museum and Art Gallery*, 17 August 2021.
39 For an outline of the various, existing theories for ABCs, see Merrily Harpur, 'As Easy as ABC: The Competing Theories', *Fortean Times* 224 (August 2007): 38–9.
40 Di Francis argues that the British Isles might be home to a species of cat that 'has evolved in isolation over thousands of years to produce a species that is unique to the British Isles'. See Di Francis, *Cat Country: Quest for the British Big Cat* (Exeter: David & Charles, 1983), 114.

41 Harpur, 'Seeing Is Believing', 2006.
42 Nick Redfern, *Three Men Seeking Monsters* (New York: Pocket Books, 2004).
43 As recently as 2006, the Big Cats in Britain research group had catalogued over sixty sightings in January alone across the UK. Mark Fraser, ed. *Big Cats in Britain Yearbook 2007* (North Devon: CFZ, 2007).
44 Email from an academic (who preferred to remain unnamed) raised in Scotland. The exact date is unknown. They simply recall that the sighting happened in the 1990s.
45 Campbell and Solomon (1972).
46 We are indebted to McEwan for his list of lough/loch monsters of Ireland and Scotland. See McEwan, *Mystery Animals of Britain and Ireland*, 206.
47 For an in-depth overview of the Owlman, see Jon Downes, *The Owlman and Others* (North Devon: CFZ, [1997] 2006).
48 Most of the 'Brentford Griffin' affair centres around Kevin Chippendale. He saw the creature twice, and a friend of his is responsible for a third sighting. Collins summarizes Chippendale's description of the beast as a 'dog with wings, dark, possibly brown in colour and with a longish muzzle'. See Andrew Collins, *The Brentford Griffin: The Truth Behind the Tales* (Essex: Earthquest Books, 1985), 35.
49 Werewolf legends appear more suspect than most, at least in terms of their provenance. The *Skeptoid* podcast failed to find a single mention of the Old Stinker prior to 2015, even though newspapers claimed it to be a 'centuries-old' legend. See Brian Dunning, 'Unmasking the Old Stinker', *Skeptoid* 804 (2 November 2021). The Shetland Museum and Archives became so exasperated by continual requests for information on ancient legends of the Wulver that it produced an article explaining it to be the 1930s invention of a folklorist named Jessie Saxby: 'No-one before Jessie had ever heard of a Shetland wolf-man'; Brian Smith, 'The Real Story Behind the Shetland Wulver', *Shetland Museum & Archives* (18 May 2021).
50 Thankfully the Fae folk are discussed in the conclusion, lest our survey of beasts become even more complicated.
51 McEwan, *Mystery Animals of Britain and Ireland*. McEwan provides an overview of Black Shuck sightings and the many names associated with the creature.
52 Norman's extensive review of Black Dog encounters and folklore includes only a few sightings from post-2000. Mark Norman, *Black Dog Folklore* (London: Troy Books, 2015).
53 'Black shuck – wagtail brewery', *Untappd* (n.d.). https://untappd.com/b/wagtail-brewery-black-shuck/134785.
54 'Black Dog', *Elgoods Brewery* (25 November 2024). https://www.elgoods-brewery.co.uk/product/black-dog/.
55 Patrick Saunders, 'Who or What Is Black Shuck?', *Norfolk Distillery* (22 July 2024). https://www.blackshuckltd.co.uk/who-or-what-is-black-shuck.
56 For example, in June, 2007, big cat researcher Neil Arnold reviewed a recent article in the *Fortean Times* by Merrily Harpur outlining theories about ABCs (Harpur, 'As Easy as ABC'). Arnold was exasperated by the inclusion of theories that suggest a supernatural origin for the cats, arguing that 'to place such animals into a realm of fantasy is complete madness'. Arnold, *Fortean Times* June 2007, 'Big Cats'.
57 For more detail on this divide within Bigfoot subcultures, see Christopher Bader and Joseph O. Baker, *Deviance Management* (Oakland: University of California Press, 2019), chapter four.
58 Mackal is a key figure in the development of 'cryptozoology' since his PhD in biology lent some credibility to the topic. In his 1976 book *The Monsters of Loch Ness*, he

argued that the 'best possible candidate is a giant, aquatic amphibian'; Roy Mackal, *The Monsters of Loch Ness* (Chicago: Swallow, 1976), 216. By a 1981 interview with the *Christian Science Monitor*, he had changed his mind; Nessie was now a zeuglodon, a long-extinct whale with an eel-like body; Clara Germani, 'Lake Champlain's "Monster": It May Be a Zeuglodon', *Christian Science Monitor*, 2 November 2021.

59 The Reverend Donald Omand conducted exorcism rites at the loch in June of 1973. See Marc Alexander, *The Man Who Exorcised the Bermuda Triangle* (New York: A.S. Barnes and Company, 1980), 73–84. Omand believed that the monster was the spectre of creatures that lived in the past.

60 Holiday (1968) posited that Nessie was a gigantic version of Tullimonstrum gregarium, more popularly known as the 'Tully monster'. The creature had a long proboscis that Holiday thought would be mistaken for a head and neck. F. W. Holiday, *The Great Orm of Loch Ness* (London: Faber & Faber, 1968).

61 In his 1973 book *The Dragon & the Disc*, Holiday reports that: 'By 1970 I had rejected the superficial view of monster phenomena – that they are just unknown animals that have somehow escaped the science net – as inadequate'. F. W. Holiday, *The Dragon & the Disc* (New York: W.W. Norton, 1973), 177.

62 Indeed, Holiday participated in the exorcism of Loch Ness. He exchanged correspondence with Reverend Omand, visited him in Devon and joined him at the exorcism on 2 June 1973. The events are recounted in chapter 7 of a book published after Holiday's death. Ted Holiday, *The Goblin Universe* (St. Paul, Minnesota: Llewellyn, 1986).

63 Tony 'Doc' Shiels, *Monstrum! A Wizard's Tale* (North Devon: CFZ, 2011).

64 Christopher Bader, Joseph O. Baker, and F. Carson Mencken, *Paranormal America*, 2nd ed. (New York: NYU Press, 2017), chapter seven.

65 Bader and Baker, *Deviance Management* discusses the stigma of paranormal beliefs at length.

66 Our paranormal belief questions utilized two different sets of response categories. Some questions used the possible responses 'strongly agree', 'agree', 'neither agree nor disagree', 'disagree', and 'strongly disagree'. We coded someone as accepting a belief if they agree or strongly agree. Other questions asked respondents if particular phenomena were 'definitely true', 'probably true', 'probably not true', or 'definitely not true'. For these items, we coded someone as accepting a belief if they thought it was probably or definitely true.

67 The average correlation between belief in the UK Wildman and other cryptids is $r = .45$. The average correlation between the UK Wildman and non-cryptid paranormal phenomena was $r = .30$.

68 Karl Marx, *Critique of Hegel's 'Philosophy of Right'* (London: Cambridge University Press, 1977).

69 Elizabeth Legerski, Marie Cornwall and Brock O'Neil, 'Changing Locus of Control: Steelworkers Adjusting to Forced Unemployment', *Social Forces* 84 (2006): 1521–38; Jerry Phares, 'Locus of Control', in *The Corsini Encyclopedia of Psychology and Behavioral Science, vol. 2*, ed. W. E. Craighead and C. B. Nemeroff (New York: John Wiley and Sons, 2001).

70 Catherine Ross and John Mirowsky, 'Households, Employment, and the Sense of Control', *Social Psychology Quarterly* 55 (2002): 217–35.

71 Joseph O. Baker, 'An Investigation of the Sociological Patterns of Prayer Frequency and Content', *Sociology of Religion* 69, no. 2 (2008): 169–85; Kenneth I. Pargament, *The Psychology of Religion and Coping: Theory Research, Practice* (New York: Guilford,

1997); Scott Schieman and Alex Bierman, 'Religious Activities and Changes in the Sense of Divine Control', *Sociology of Religion* 68, no. 4 (2007): 361–81; Scott Schieman, Kim Nguyen and Diana Elliot, 'Religiosity, Socioeconomic Status, and the Sense of Mastery', *Social Psychology Quarterly* 66, no. 3 (2003): 202–21; Scott Schieman and Gabriele Plickert, 'How Knowledge Is Power: Education and the Sense of Control', *Social Forces* 87, no. 1 (2008):153–83; Scott Schieman, Tetyana Pudrovska, Leonard I. Pearlin and Christopher G. Ellison, 'The Sense of Divine Control and Psychological Distress', *Journal for the Scientific Study of Religion* 45, no. 4 (2006): 529–49.

72 The two most commonly used scales of paranormal belief in the psychological literature are the Australian Sheep-Goat Scale (ASGS) (Michael A. Thalbourne and Peter S. Delin, 'A New Instrument for Measuring the Sheep-Goat Variables', *Journal of the Society for Psychical Research* 59 (1993): 172–86) and the Revised Paranormal Belief Scale (RPBS). See Jerome J. Tobacyk, 'A Revised Paranormal Belief Scale', *International Journal of Transpersonal Studies* 23, no. 1 (2004): 94–8; Jerome Tobacyk and Gary Milford, 'Belief in Paranormal Phenomena: Assessment Instrument Development and Implications for Personality Functioning', *Journal of Personality and Social Psychology* 44, no. 5 (1983): 1029–37. The ASGS finds that beliefs about ESP and psychokinesis cluster separately from beliefs about life after death (Drinkwater et al. 2018). The RPBS asks about a much wider variety of paranormal phenomena and includes questions about belief in God and the devil. Traditional religious beliefs loaded separately from witchcraft, psychic phenomena and others; Kenneth Drinkwater, Andrew Denovan, Neil Dagnall and Andrew Parker, 'An Assessment of the Dimensionality and Factorial Structure of the Revised Paranormal Belief Scale', *Frontiers in Psychology* 26 (2017).

73 We used Principal Axis Factoring to conduct an exploratory (followed by confirmatory) factor analysis with the eighteen paranormal questions. We split the dataset into two, with the first dataset used for the exploratory factor analysis and the second used for confirmatory factor analysis.

74 Belief in Atlantis is borderline in terms of whether it should be considered as clustering with belief in aliens. For analyses of beliefs about Atlantis and aliens done separately, see Clark et al., 'Marginalized, Secularized, and Popularized?'

75 We estimated four ordinary least squares regression models with each of our paranormal factors as a dependent variable. We only discuss the statistically significant effects here. For more detailed analyses, see Clark et al., 'Marginalized, Secularized, and Popularized?'

76 Since each factor consisted of multiple different phenomena and respondents could indicate greater or lesser degrees of certainty, someone who received a mid-range score on a factor might believe very strongly in one item and little in others, or might have moderate levels of belief in several.

77 The size of each bar is determined by the absolute value of its standardized beta in our regression analyses.

78 Robert Wuthnow, *Experimentation in American Religion* (Berkeley: University of California Press, 1978), 71.

79 Tom W. Rice, 'Believe It or Not: Religious and Other Paranormal Beliefs in the United States', *Journal for the Scientific Study of Religion* 42 (2003): 95–106.

80 Karl Marx, *Critique of Hegel's 'Philosophy of Right'*, 131.

81 Ross and Mirowsky, 'Households, Employment, and the Sense of Control'.

82. Galen Watts, Francesco Cerchiaro, and Landon Schnabel, 'The Spiritual Turn and "Feminization": Turning a Gender Lens on Spirituality', *Sociology of Religion*, 86, no. 2 (2025): 243–70. https://doi.org/10.1093/socrel/srae009.

Chapter 3

1. Owen Davies, *The Haunted: A Social History of Ghosts* (London: Palgrave Macmillan, 2007), 1.
2. Of course, there is no official register or ranking of ghostly places. Anyone can claim their home to be the most haunted in Britain, and there is no means by which to file a formal complaint.
3. The paranormal news website site Higgypop aptly described the house as an 'average looking house, on an average looking street'. Higgypop, 'Most haunted at 30 East Drive – Part One.' *Higgypop Paranormal*, 18 October 2015.
4. This quote is from the introduction to the *Most Haunted* Halloween special filmed in 2015 at 30 East Drive. Derek Hallworth (Director), 'Most Haunted Live – Halloween Special', *Most Haunted*, 31 October 2015.
5. Unless otherwise noted, our recounting of reported events at 30 East Drive that occurred prior to 1980 are summarized from Colin Wilson's chapter in *Poltergeist! A Study in Destructive Haunting*. Wilson's narrative has become definitive in outlining the early events at the site and consequently is suited to our purposes here, which is documenting the evolution of contemporary folklore about the site. See Colin Wilson, *Poltergeist!* (New York: Putnam, 1982).
6. Sarah Scholes was Jean Pritchard's mother. Her daughter and Jean's sister, Marie Kelly, lived opposite 30 East Drive. Joe Pritchard's brother and his wife, Enid, lived next door. Marie and then Enid came over to investigate the grey haze and pools of water.
7. Frustratingly, Colin Wilson does not provide a full name for 'Mr O'Donald', and future repetitions of the tale have followed suit.
8. Wilson, *Poltergeist!*, 144.
9. Michelle Hanks, *Haunted Heritage* (New York: Routledge, 2016), 17.
10. Hamlet, Act 1, Scene 5.
11. Both Eaton and Baker and Bader note the importance of *priming* (as Eaton refers to the process) or the sharing of deathlore (folklore about death) in setting the stage for a paranormal investigation. See Marc Eaton, *Sensing Spirits* (London: Routledge, 2021); Joseph O. Baker and Christopher D. Bader. 'A Social Anthropology of Ghosts in Twenty-First-Century America', *Social Compass* 61, no. 4 (2014): 569–93.
12. Eaton, *Sensing Spirits*, chapter 5, discusses the process by which participants in a ghost hunt negotiate the preferred explanation for an event.
13. In addition to Colin Wilson's scepticism about the existence of a murderous monk in *Poltergeist!*, see also Andy Evans, *Don't Look Back in Anger* (print on demand: lulu. com, 2015).
14. The ghost hunting subculture often refers to this type of haunting as an 'intelligent haunting.'
15. The ghost hunting subculture often refers to this type of haunting a 'residual haunting.'
16. In the chapter, 'The Poltergeist of the Germans' of her 1850 book *The Night-side of Nature*, Catherine Crowe notes that some haunting cases seem to have no real

purpose and to be the work of 'a mischievous imp.' For such cases, she prefers the term '*poltergeist* or racketing spectre', Catherine Crowe, *Night-Side of Nature; or, Ghosts and Ghost Seers* (Boston. B.B. Mussey, 1850), 370.
17 Wilson, *Poltergeist!*, 144.
18 Another sociologist and ethnographer, Peter Simi, joined us at 30 East Drive, and his notes also contribute to this chapter. Thanks Pete.
19 All quotes in this section are from field notes taken during the evening.
20 Clearly belief in spirits is also a common and key feature of many organized religious traditions, making belief in spirits – humanlike entities lacking physical bodies that are still able to influence the material world – one of the most common supernatural beliefs more generally.
21 Wilson, *Poltergeist!*, 150. See also Alan Murdie, 'When the Lights Went Out', *Fortean Times* 293 (October 2012): 29–37.
22 Wilson, *Poltergeist!*, 162.
23 Randall Collins, *Interaction Ritual Chains* (Princeton, NJ: Princeton University Press, 2004).
24 Durkheim, *Elementary Forms*.
25 The dowsing rod technique involves holding a thin copper rod in each hand and asking spirits to make the rods swing towards or away from one another in response to questions.
26 Sometimes ghost investigations include activities that they would themselves define as rituals, such as using magic to in some way entice ghosts, protect the group from evil spirits, or to help ghosts 'move on'.
27 Ghost hunters we have encountered often note that ghosts may choose not to manifest depending on the nature of the gathered group. For example, ghosts may not have an interest in appearing to sceptics or may be more likely to appear to people with psychic powers.
28 These are all basic outcomes of successful interactive rituals. As Collins notes, one aspect of *unsuccessful* rituals is those that are too routinized or perfunctory, so the combination of both structure and openness creates an effective and dynamic basic ritual template for ghost hunters. Collins, *Interaction Ritual Chains*.
29 Wilson, *Poltergeist!*
30 This includes, among many other strange happenings, a pair of gloves (with no visible body between them) conducting to music. Wilson, *Poltergeist!*
31 Wilson noted that there was tension between Phillip and his father Joe. Indeed, this was the reason that Phillip had stayed at home with his grandmother while the rest of the family went on holiday in Devon. Wilson, *Poltergeist!*, 165.
32 See Wilson, *Poltergeist!*, 166. Similar to how dowsers purportedly draw energy from water and ley lines, some ghost researchers claim that spirits can draw energy from moving water and damp ground.
33 Wilson, *Poltergeist!*, 171.
34 Richard Estep and Bil Bungay, *The Black Monk of Pontefract* (Independently published, 2019), 41–2.
35 Wilson, *Poltergeist!*, 164.
36 Clive D. Field, 'Belief in Ghosts and Communication with the Dead', *British Religion in Numbers*, 5 December 2024.
37 Further, as BRIN notes, responses to questions can vary depending upon the order in which they are presented.

38 Will Dahlgreen, '"Ghosts Exist", Say 1 in 3 Brits', *YouGov*, 21 October 2014; Kayleigh Lewis, 'BMG Halloween Poll', *BMG Research*, 30 October 2017.
39 David Voas and Steven Bruce, 'Religion: Identity, Behaviour and Belief Over Two Decades'. In *British Social Attitudes: The 36th Report*, ed. John Curtice, Elizabeth Clery, Jane Perry, Miranda Phillips and Nilufer Rahim (London: The National Centre for Social Research, 2019), 17–44..
40 Bungay is widely credited as the person responsible for the 'We hope it's chips' advertising campaign that was popular in the 1980s and 1990s.
41 *When the Lights Went Out* (2012), *Box Office Mojo*.
42 Quote is taken from the Wayback Machine's (https://web.archive.org/) snapshot of the 30 East Drive website taken on 13 July 2014. See '30 East Drive (Intro)', *30 East Drive | PONTEFRACT*, 13 July 2014.
43 Some narratives about the Black Monk assume he is the shade of an evil human. Others claim he is a demon.
44 Estep and Bungay, *The Black Monk of Pontefract*, 40.
45 For example, a group named Merseyside Paranormal reported that a team member had to be dragged to safety after some form of attack in the coal shed. This post is preserved on the 30 East Drive website: '30 East Drive, Merseyside Paranormal FB Post', *30 East Drive | PONTEFRACT*, n.d.
46 This quote is from the introduction to the *Most Haunted* Halloween special filmed in 2015 at 30 East Drive.
47 Karl Beattie (Director), 'Most Haunted Live – 30 East Drive, Part 2' [TV Series Episode], *Most Haunted*, 25 October 2015.
48 The show also garnered significant attention on social media, generating more than 50,000 tweets.
49 After the show, however, many viewers claimed a hoax after seeing what appeared to be a rope attached to Karl Beattie as he moved into position on the stairs. Higgypop, 'Was Karl from Most Haunted Really Dragged Upstairs by the Pontefract Poltergeist?', *Higgypop Paranormal*, 3 November 2015.
50 In Figure 3.3 we did not include data from 2004 to 2010 on the chart because for this entire range the relative popularity of the search terms was zero.
51 Of course, there are alternative explanations to ghosts when someone says that they believe it is possible to communicate with the dead. Someone may agree with this statement if they believe that through prayer they can get a message to loved ones who have died, for example.
52 The respondent categories for these two questions were 'strongly agree', 'tend to agree', 'neither agree nor disagree', 'tend to disagree', and 'strongly disagree'. For this figure the percentages represent the per cent of respondents who selected either 'tend to agree' or 'strongly agree'.
53 We asked about many paranormal experiences on our survey. Age was significantly related to only some of them. Younger people were more likely to believe that they had a dream that later came true and to report using crystals for the purposes of healing. However, age was not significantly related to believing one has seen a UFO, nor consulting a medium, fortune teller, or psychic.
54 Baker and Bader, 'A Social Anthropology of Ghosts' 569–93.
55 On age dynamics of ghost interest in the United States: Baker and Bader, 'A Social Anthropology of Ghosts'. On declining rates of organized religious affiliation and how 'believing without belonging' is highly conducive to paranormalism: Joseph O. Baker and Buster G. Smith, *American Secularism* (New York: NYU Press, 2015); Joseph O.

Baker, Christopher D. Bader and F. Carson Mencken, 'A Bounded Affinity Theory of Religion and the Paranormal', *Sociology of Religion* 77, no. 4 (2016): 334–58.
56 Karen Anderson, 'Irish Secularisation of Religious Identities', *Social Compass* 57, no. 1 (2010): 15–39; Christopher D. Bader, Joseph O. Baker and Andrea Molle, 'Countervailing Forces: Religiosity and Paranormal Belief in Italy', *Journal for the Scientific Study of Religion* 51, no. 4 (2012): 705–20, 716.
57 Of course, we recognize that simply by being present, we are still impacting a developing narrative, even if only indirectly.
58 Eaton, *Sensing Spirits*.
59 Some people joined late and others left early, so there were not 866 viewers connected all at the same time.
60 This comment included the commenter's full name. In such cases, we have deleted the name.
61 These comments are aggregated from throughout the evening.
62 We have removed comments that included full names.
63 Sometimes she was called Emily and sometimes Emma. Per one person on the livestream: 'Her name is Emily but Emma for short'.
64 Another addition to the Monk narrative is that he may have murdered many people.
65 During the evening the RGH occasionally chastised the Monk for 'keeping Emily here'.
66 The comments about Emily are interspersed with comments about what the RGH members were doing on the main feed, which we have removed here.
67 Andrea Molle and Christopher D. Bader. 'Paranormal Science from America to Italy', in *The Ashgate Research Companion to Paranormal Cultures*, ed. Olu Jenzen and Sally R. Munt (London: Routledge, 2013); Eaton, *Sensing Spirits*.
68 Baker and Bader, 'A Social Anthropology of Ghosts'; Nils Bubandt, 'A Psychology of Ghosts', *Anthropological Forum* 22, no. 1 (2012): 1–23; Shane McCorristine, *Spectres of the Self* (Cambridge University Press, 2010).

Chapter 4

1 See the respective websites to view schedules: Haunted Happenings (https://www.hauntedhappenings.co.uk); Haunted Houses UK (https://www.haunted-houses.co.uk/); and Haunted Rooms (https://www.hauntedrooms.co.uk).
2 https://www.veritasparanormaluk.com/.
3 Dancausa, Hernandez and Perez (2023) describe ghost tourism as an 'emerging area'; Genoveva Dancausa, Ricardo D. Hernandez and Lenor M. Perez. 'Motivations and Constraints for the Ghost Tourism: A Case Study in Spain'. *Leisure Sciences* 45, no. 2 (2023): 156–77. Hill (2011) describes it as a 'growth area'; Annette Hill, *Paranormal Media* (New York: Routledge, 2011), 106. Hanks (2015) paints ghost tourism as 'undeniably a growing sector of the global tourist market'; Michelle Hanks, *Haunted Heritage* (New York: Routledge, 2015), 16. However, as Houran et al. (2020) note, all such observations have been made lacking any 'verifiable metrics'; James Houran, Sharon A. Hill, Everett D. Haynes and Ursual A. Bielski, 'Paranormal Tourism', *Cornell Hospitality Quarterly* 61, no. 3 (2020): 287–311, 287.
4 See for example Kenneth Drinkwater, Brandon Massullo, Neil Dagnall, Brian Laythe, Juliette Boone and James Houran. 'Understanding Consumer Enchantment via

Paranormal Tourism', *Cornell Hospitality Quarterly* 63, no. 2 (2022): 195–215; Hanks, *Haunted Heritage*; Julian Holloway, 'Legend-Tripping in Spooky Places', *Environment and Planning D: Society and Space* 28 (2010), 618–37; Houran, Hill, Haynes and Bielski, 'Paranormal Tourism'; David Inglis and Mary Holmes, 'Highland and Other Haunts', *Annals of Tourism Research* 30, no. 1 (2003): 50–63; Carmen Pedreño-Peñalver, Irene Huertas-Valdivia and Alicia Orea-Giner, 'An Exploratory Study of the Future Paranormal Tourist Experience on Ghost Tours', *Journal of Tourism Futures* 10, no. 3 (2023): 524–38.

5   Racheal Ironside, 'The Allure of Dark Tourism', in *The Supernatural in Society, Culture and History*, ed. Dennis Waskul and Marc Eaton (Philadelphia: Temple University Press, 2018); Hill, *Paranormal Media*; Annette Hill, 'Paranormal Cultural Practices', in *The Ashgate Research Companion to Paranormal Cultures*, ed. Olu Jensen and Sally R. Munt (Surrey, England: Ashgate, 2013).

6   See Gavin Weston, Justin Woodman, Helen Cornish and Natalie Djohari, 'Spectral Cities', *Urbanities* 9, no. 2 (2019): 36–51; Also Drinkwater, Massullo, Dagnall, Laythe, Boone and Houran, 'Understanding Consumer Enchantment via Paranormal Tourism'.

7   Hanks, *Haunted Heritage*.

8   Houran, Hill, Haynes and Bielski, 'Paranormal Tourism', 303.

9   See Hanks, *Haunted Heritage*, 123–5, and Houran, Hill, Haynes and Bielski, 'Paranormal Tourism', 303, for a discussion of perceived authenticity in haunted locations.

10 As Houran, Hill, Haynes and Bielski, 'Paranormal Tourism', 289, note: 'there are neither publicly available nor firm statistics on the number of consumers or product offerings in this sector'.

11 Keith Stuart, 'Pushing Buttons', *The Guardian*, 27 September 2023.

12 According to marketing data firm Statista, in 2021 Costa, Greggs and Starbucks had a combined 5,784 locations across the UK. By 2024, combined locations had increased by approximately 11 per cent to 6,417. 'Leading coffee shop chains UK 2024', *Statista*, n.d.

13 Ironside, 'The Allure of Dark Tourism', 96. Folklorist Bill Ellis is credited with the concept of the legend trip. Bill Ellis, 'Legend Trip', in *American Folklore: An Encyclopedia*, ed. Jan Harold Brunvand (New York: Garland, 1996); Bill Ellis, 'Legend-Trips and Satanism', in *Contemporary Legend: A Reader*, edited by G. Bennet and P. Smith (New York: Routledge, 1996).

14 See Houran, Hill, Haynes and Bielski, 'Paranormal Tourism', who took a similar approach.

15 Hanks (2015) uses the same typology for ghost tourism that includes ghost walks and commercial ghost hunts. Since we are focusing on paid tourism here, we do not include the nonprofit activities of ghost clubs, as Hanks did in *Haunted Heritage*.

16 The entire Ghost Bus Tour is not spent on the bus. For example, the Edinburgh Ghost Bus Tour had customers get off the bus at St. Cuthbert's Kirkyard to learn about the grave robbers Burk and Hare and hear about a ghostly young girl who was supposed to haunt the cemetery. See https://www.theghostbustours.com/.

17 In our searches we found some castles and historic sites that offer special tours related to ghosts. Unlike ghost walks, such events are confined to a single location. Unlike ghost hunts, the events do not involve overnight stays and often do not involve the usage of paranormal equipment. For example, the Bradford Police Museum offers ghost tours where visitors can learn about its many hauntings and view photos of ghosts taken on the property. Although distinctive, such single-location ghost tours

were comparatively rare. In the numbers presented below, we group ghost tours with ghost hunts.
18 Hanks, *Haunted Heritage*, 63.
19 Quote is from Macbeth, speaking to the ghost of Banquo, in Act III, Scene IV.
20 The UK Office of National Statistics provides datasets of the LTLAs in England and Wales. For this chapter, we downloaded the most recently available. As of April 2023, there were 296 LTLAs in England, including 32 London boroughs, 36 metropolitan districts, 164 nonmetropolitan districts, 62 unitary authorities, as well as the City of London and the Isles of Scilly. There were twenty-two unitary county and county borough councils ('local authorities') in Wales.
21 'Halton Data Profile'. *Halton Borough Council*, n.d.
22 'How Life Has Changed in Southwark: Census 2021', *Office for National Statistics*, n.d.
23 Our initial searches would combine the name of the LTLA, e.g., 'Swansea' with each of the three terms 'ghost hunt', 'ghost walk' and 'ghost tour'. If we failed to find any events using these three searches, we would begin searching using the names of the towns and villages contained within the LTLA. For example, our initial searches in Tameside (near Manchester) failed to produce any ghost-related events. But upon searching areas within Tameside, 'Audenshaw ghost hunts' found regular ghost hunts at Ryecroft Hall in Audenshaw. These searches took place in November of 2023.
24 'Stratford-*on*-Avon' is intentional. The use of 'on' distinguishes the LTLA of Stratford-on-Avon from its largest town Stratford-*upon*-Avon.
25 'Ghost Walk'. Stratford Town Walk, n.d.
26 'The Sinister Side of Shakespeare's Stratford Guided Walking Tour'. *Sinister Stratford*, n.d.
27 Tudor World is located in the historic Falstaff building and is often called 'Falstaffs Museum' by companies using the space for ghost investigations.
28 Daniel Fessahaye, 'Double, Double, Toil and Trouble! Turf War Breaks Out in Shakespeare's Hometown between Rival Ghost Tours', *Daily Mail Online*, 21 July 2023.
29 'Falstaff Museum Experience Ghost Hunts', *HauntedHappenings.co.uk*, n.d.
30 Paranormal Eye UK, Haunted Happenings and Afterlife & Spooky Events had five evenings booked between them in 2024.
31 'Special Events 2024', *The Amazing Cornish Maize Maze*, n.d.
32 '8th March – Ghost Tour', *Hoghton Tower*, 27 January 2025.
33 Twenty-one of the LTLAs had Halloween-only ghost hunts or ghost walks *and* ghost tourism available at other times of year.
34 We did not find any ghost tours or ghost hunts available outside the Halloween season in Basingstoke and Deane, Boston, Central Bedfordshire, Crawley, East Hertfordshire, Haringey, Redditch, Richmond upon Thames, Woking and Wokingham.
35 Houran, Hill, Haynes, and Bielski, 'Paranormal Tourism', 303.
36 Clearly such a measure does not provide a perfect accounting of the proximity of ghost tourism. Someone who lives at the very edge of one district may be closer to a ghost hunt right over the 'border' than they are to one in their own district.
37 Reigate has a Halloween season ghost walk, but nothing that is regular that we could locate.
38 'Avenue House Ghost Hunts', *HauntedHappenings.co.uk*, n.d.
39 The Subnational Indicators dataset is provided by the Office of National Statistics. 'Subnational Indicators Dataset'. *Office for National Statistics*, 21 March 2024.
40 Holloway, 'Legend-Tripping in Spooky Places'; Pedreño-Peñalver, Huertas-Valdivia and Alicia Orea-Giner, 'An Exploratory Study of the Future Paranormal Tourist

Experience on Ghost Tours'; Daniel Wright, 'Encountering UFOs and Aliens in the Tourism Industry', *Journal of Tourism Futures* 8, no 1 (2022): 7–23.
41 'UFO Trail at Rendlesham Forest', *Forestry England*, n.d.
42 Inglis and Holmes, 'Highland and Other Haunts'.
43 A 1990 economic study by Mackay Consultants of Inverness claimed that Nessie brings £42 million into the local economy. See '"Nessie" Nets about $42 Million Per Year', United Press International, 28 May 1990. In 2018, accountant Gary Campbell claimed that data from local tourism companies allowed him to estimate that Nessie-related tourism brings in £41.7 million per year, up £11 million from four years previous. See 'Loch Ness Monster Worth Nearly £41m a Year to Scottish Economy', *Aberdeen Press and Journal*, 13 September 2018.
44 Tony Harmsworth, *Loch Ness, Nessie and Me* (Createspace, 2024).
45 As noted in Chapter 2, there was talk of Kelpies and other folkloric water beasts well before the 1930s.
46 'The Loch Ness Centre', Continuum Attractions, 11 August 2023.
47 This kind of presentation also speaks to the centrality of mysteries and perceived secret knowledge as a key draw to paranormal interest and related tourism.
48 See Adomnan of Iona, *The Life of St. Columba* (London: Penguin Classics, 1995) for a full recounting of the tale.
49 Dinsdale started investigating the loch in 1960. He ultimately wrote several books on the subject – *The Loch Ness Monster*, *The Story of the Loch Ness Monster* and *Project Water Horse*. In his first expedition to the loch, he captured video of something moving across the water that was shown during this presentation.
50 While these displays showed the percentage of visitors who chose a button under each larger category, it did not show the percentages broken down within each category – a visual bar chart, with no associated percentages, was shown for each category. Within the 'I see Nessie' category the plesiosaur option was markedly higher than other options and appeared to be about ¾ or more of those respondents.
51 Leigh Mcmanus, 'UK Is "Running Out of Ghosts" as Old Spirits Dying Off', Paranormal Expert Says', *Daily Star*, 27 May 2024.
52 'Population estimates for the UK, England, Wales, Scotland, and Northern Ireland: Mid-2022', *Office for National Statistics*, 26 March 2024.
53 Jeffrey E. Green, 'Two Meanings of Disenchantment', *Philosophy & Theology* 17, nos. 1–2 (2005), 51–84.
54 On the meanings of 'disenchantment' in Weber's writing, particularly in relation to magic, see Mario Marotta, 'A Disenchanted World', *Journal of Classical Sociology* 24, no. 3 (2023), 224–42.
55 Drinkwater and colleagues (2022) and Houran et al. (2022) have conducted interesting work wherein they suggest that ghost-related tourism is particularly able to provide a sense of 'situational enchantment'. Drinkwater, Massullo, Dagnall, Laythe, Boone and Houran, 'Understanding Consumer Enchantment via Paranormal Tourism'; James Houran, Rense Lange and Brian Laythe, 'Understanding Consumer Enchantment via Paranormal Tourism: Part II – Preliminary Rasch Validation', *Cornell Hospitality Quarterly* 63, no. 2 (2022): 216–30.
56 Some aspects of ghost tourism are remarkably similar to religious rituals, such as the holding of hands during a séance. Hill, *Paranormal Media*.
57 Hanks, *Haunted Heritage*, 26.
58 Houran, Hill, Haynes and Bielski, 'Paranormal Tourism', 304; Hill, 'Paranormal Cultural Practices', 74.

59 Charitable opinions on the part of gamblers and paranormal tourists depend, of course, on a lack of perceived fraud. If a gambler believes that the slot machines are fixed, they will not return. If ghost enthusiasts come to believe that claims are based on hoaxes, they will similarly lose interest.
60 Émile Durkheim, *The Elementary Forms of Religious Life* (New York: Free Press, 1995), 432.
61 Charles E. Marske, 'Durkheim's "Cult of the Individual" and the Moral Reconstitution of Society', *Sociological Theory* 5, no. 1 (1987): 1–14, 3.
62 On Durkheim's predictions for the 'cult of the individual' and the future of religion, see: W. S. F. Pickering, *Durkheim's Sociology of Religion* (London: Routledge, 1984), 476–99. On religion and spirituality in relation to capitalist consumption in the West, see Paul Heelas, *Spiritualities of Life* (Malden, MA: Blackwell, 2008).

Chapter 5

1 'Latest Crop Circles', *Crop Circle Access*, 29 August 2024.
2 'Crop Circle at Roundway Down', *Crop Circle Connector*, n.d.
3 John R. Capron, 'Storm Effects', *Nature* 22 (29 July 1880): 290–1.
4 'The Mowing Devil', [Pamphlet] (August 1678).
5 See Joe Nickell and John F. Fischer, 'The Crop Circle Phenomenon', *Skeptical Inquirer* 16, no. 2 (1992): 136–49.
6 Eric Gregersen, 'Crop Circle', *Encyclopædia Britannica*, 21 February 2025.
7 Pat Delgado and Colin Andrews, *Circular Evidence* (Grand Rapids, MI: Phanes Press, 1989), 155.
8 Delgado and Andrews, *Circular Evidence*, 43–4.
9 Ibid., chapter 6.
10 Monique Klinkenbergh and Andreas Müller, *Crop Circles: The Exhibition* (Pewsey: Crop Circle Centre & Exhibition, 2017), 38.
11 For example, an image named 'the dove' appeared in August of 2015 near the village of Hampton Lucy, Warwickshire. See Steve Alexander and Karen Alexander, *Crop Circle Yearbook 2015* (Hampshire: Temporary Temple Press, 2015), 22–3. In July of 2010, two crop circles appeared near Hungerford, Berkshire. Crop circle researcher Andreas Müller argues that when images of the two circles are superimposed over one another, the resulting picture resembles the Shroud of Turin. See Klinkenbergh and Müller, *Crop Circles: The Exhibition*, 46–7.
12 For example, in 1989, 233 of the 305 crop circle reports (76 per cent) collected by the Circles Effect Research Group (CERES) were found in Wiltshire. See G. Terence Meaden, 'Further News on the Circles Effect from CERES', in *Circles from the Sky*, ed. Terence Meaden (London: Souvenir Press, 1991), 126.
13 'Weird Wiltshire Day Trip 2025 – Mysterious Crop Circles'. Stonehenge Tours. n.d.
14 Joanne Moore, 'Pub Landlord Who Turned Hamlet into Croppie Mecca Dies', *Wiltshire Times*, 29 July 2020.
15 BBC, 'New Data Shows Wiltshire Has Most Crop Circles in England', *BBC News*, 22 July 2023.
16 On the concept of stigmatized knowledge and its changing relationship to mainstream discourse in the digital age, see Michael Barkun, 'Conspiracy Theories as Stigmatized Knowledge', *Diogenes* 62, nos. 3–4 (2015): 114–20.

17 On disclaimers as stigma avoidance strategy, see John P. Hewitt and Randall Stokes, 'Disclaimers', *American Sociological Review* 40, no. 1 (1976): 1–11.
18 Temporary Temples is the name of an initiative run by photographers Steve and Karen Alexander that documents and archives information about crop circles in the UK: https://temporarytemples.co.uk/.
19 'Mystery is the key' is a tagline is often used by Steve and Karen Alexander in reference to their work on crop circles.
20 Belief in crop circles is also strongly correlated with the four different scales of paranormal beliefs – aliens ($r = .53$), magic and spirits ($r = .53$), earth mysteries ($r = .51$), and cryptids ($r = .60$).
21 Wouter J. Hanegraaff, *Western Esotericism: A Guide for the Perplexed* (London: Bloomsbury, 2013); Richard M. Bucke, *Cosmic Consciousness: A Study in the Evolution of the Human Mind* (New York: E. P. Dutton, 1901).
22 Notably, however, Mingo did still use some scientistic rhetoric about cutting-edge scientific discoveries, such as the Higgs-Boson particle. At the same time, she offhandedly claimed to have discovered a new planet in our solar system called 'Matahara', so any connection to mainstream science was purely rhetorical.
23 https://thebasesproject.org/.
24 Aubrey Burl, *The Stone Circles of Britain, Ireland, and Brittany* (New Haven, CT: Yale University Press, 2000).
25 Geoff McMaster, '"Ancient Apocalypse" Is More Fiction Than Fact, Say Experts', *Folio*, 14 December 2022; Liam Mathews, Tim Surette, Allison Picurro, and Kelly Connolly, 'Netflix Top 10 Shows and Movies', *TV Guide*, 15 November, 2022.
26 Stuart Heritage, 'Ancient Apocalypse Is the Most Dangerous Show on Netflix', *The Guardian*, 23 November 2022.
27 Graham Hancock, *The Mars Mystery* (New York: Broadway Books, 1999).
28 For example, *Supernatural* features drawings made by Hancock after an ayahuasca vision that look strikingly like the grey-alien beings featured in UFO abduction narratives. Graham Hancock, *Supernatural* (London: Arrow, 2015), 319.
29 Edmund Sixsmith, 'The Megalithic Story of Professor Alexander Thom', *Significance* 6, no. 2 (2009): 94–6.
30 See John Michell, *The View Over Atlantis* (London: Garnstone Press, 1969); John Michell and Allan Brown, *How the World Is Made* (Rochester, Vermont: Inner Traditions, 2012).
31 Robert Bauval and Adrian Gilbert, *The Orion Mystery* (London: Heinemann, 1994).
32 All relationships are statistically significant at the $p < .01$ level.
33 Aimé Michel proposed that flying saucers tended to follow straight lines in their flight paths in *Flying Saucers and the Straight-Line Mystery* (New York: S.G. Phillips, 1958).
34 Andrew Collins, *Göbekli Tepe: Genesis of the Gods* (Rochester, Vermont: Bear & Company, 2014); Andrew Collins, *Denisovan Origins* (Rochester, Vermont: Bear, 2019).
35 Having previously authored a book about Gobekli Tepe in 2014, in 2024 Collins released a book about Karahan Tepe. In the text, Collins makes many references to the links between the ancient site, the Watchers and the Nephilim of the Old Testament, and the Anunnaki of Sumerian mythology. In many paranormal communities, the Anunnaki are commonly understood to be the name of the ancient alien race who helped build the monuments. See Andrew Collins, *Karahan Tepe* (Rochester, Vermont: Bear, 2024).
36 Andrew Collins, *The Cygnus Mystery* (London: Watkins Publishing, 2012).

37 Andrew Collins, *The Sword and the Stone* (Wickford: Octavo, 1982), *The Black Alchemist* (Leigh-on-Sea, Essex: ABC Books, 1988), *The Seventh Sword* (London: Century, 1991), and *The Second Coming* (London, Century: 1993). Graham Phillips and Martin Keatman, *The Green Stone* (Jersey: Neville Spearman, 1983).
38 Andrew Collins, 'What Is Psychic Questing?', *andrewcollins.com*, n.d.
39 'Tara' is a Goddess associated with Hinduism and Buddhism. See Stephan Beyer, *The Cult of Tara: Magic and Ritual in Tibet*, (Berkeley: University of California Press, 1978).

Chapter 6

1 All quotes are drawn from our field notes from an audio recorded and transcribed interview with Russell Kellett. The interview was transcribed manually by the authors to ensure accuracy of content, tone, and inflection.
2 Russell Kellett, *Alien Invasion Wales* (Self-published, 2022); Russell Kellett, *Russell Kellett Is E.T. Rider* (Self-published, 2023).
3 When asked about the story, Williams simply replied 'no comment'. Andrew Robinson and Claire Gilbody-Dickerson, 'Robbie Williams "Abducted by Aliens" Says UFO Researcher Who Saw Him on Spaceship,' *Mirror*, 18 November 2020.
4 There have long been paranormal authors who argue that all its varied manifestations might have a single origin. For example, John Keel argued that ghosts, poltergeists, monsters and UFOs might all be the works of 'ultraterrestrials'; John Keel, *The Eighth Tower* (New York: Signet, 1977).
5 John G. Fuller, *Interrupted Journey* (New York: Dial, 1966); Budd Hopkins, *Missing Time* (New York: Richard Marek, 1981).
6 Kellett, *Russell Kellett Is E.T. Rider*, 174.
7 Ideas are often more effective in terms of cognitive transmission if they are 'minimally counterintuitive', rather than overwhelmingly counterintuitive on one hand, or mundane on the other; Pascal Boyer, *Religion Explained* (New York: Basic Books, 2001).
8 On the history of syncretism, as well as some of the competing views on the topic within religious studies, see Anita M. Leopold, 'The Architecture of Syncretism', *Historical Reflections* 27, no. 3 (2001): 401–23; on its uses in anthropology, see Charles Stewart, 'Syncretism and Its Synonyms', *Diacritics* 29, no. 3 (1999): 40–62.
9 Emily Sigalow, 'Towards a Sociological Framework of Religious Syncretism in the United States', *Journal of the American Academy of Religion* 84, no. 4 (2016): 1029–55.
10 Charles Stewart, 'Relocating Syncretism in Social Science Discourse', in *Syncretism in Religion: A Reader*, ed. Anita M. Leopold and Jeppe S. Jensen (London: Equinox, 2004).
11 Michael Salla, *Exopolitics* (Tempe, AZ: Dandelion, 2004).
12 Unfortunately Stephen Chua died shortly after revealing his story, while Corey Goode has changed parts of his testimony.
13 These are James Casbolt (a.k.a Michael Prince) and Max Spiers. There are, of course, any number of individuals who report alien abductions that have telepathic dimensions. Tony Topping and Simon Parkes, for example, have made a number of appearances in the media documenting their experiences.

14 Each question was asked on a Likert scale. We counted someone as holding a belief if they chose either the 'tend to agree' or 'strongly agree' responses.
15 David Icke, *Truth Vibrations* (Dublin: Gill & MacMillian, 2014), chapter 1. Note: This edition of the book is unpaginated.
16 David Icke, *Truth Vibrations*, chapter 1.
17 Miles, Geoff (Director), 'Episode #11.49', *Wogan*. BBC One, 29 April 1991.
18 From the homepage of https://www.ickonic.com/.
19 British Broadcasting Corporation, 'David Icke: Conspiracy Theorist Banned from Netherlands', *BBC News*, 4 November 2022.
20 Marianna Spring, 'Twitter Bans David Icke Over Covid Misinformation', *BBC News*, 4 November 2020. Notably, this ban only lasted two years, when Twitter-cum-X head honcho Elon Musk re-instated Icke, along with a number of other far-right and conspiracy-minded celebrities such as Andrew Tate, Roger Stone and Michael Flynn. Kayla Gogarty, Ruby Seavey and Natalie Mathes, 'Elon Musk Is Unilaterally Reinstating Banned Twitter Accounts, Despite Assuring Civil Rights Groups and Advertisers that he Wouldn't,' *Media Matters*, 22 November 2022. https://www.mediamatters.org/twitter/elon-musk-unilaterally-reinstating-banned-twitter-accounts-despite-assuring-civil-rights.
21 David Icke, *The Dream* (Isle of Wight: David Icke Books, 2023).
22 All quotes are taken from our notes during David Icke's *Secret Tour* event in Leeds on 29 September 2023.
23 Peter L. Berger and Thomas Luckmann, *The Social Construction of Reality* (New York: Anchor Books, 1966).
24 Ron Eyerman, 'False Consciousness and Ideology in Marxist Theory', *Acta Sociologica* 24, nos. 1/2 (1981): 43–56.
25 See for example Tyson Lewis and Richard Kahn, 'The Reptoid Hypothesis', *Utopian Studies* 16, no. 1 (2005): 45–74; David Robertson, 'David Icke's Reptilian Thesis and the Development of New Age Theodicy', *International Journal for the Study of New Religions* 4 (2013): 27–47; Tara Smith, 'Esoteric Themes in David Icke's Conspiracy Theories', *Journal for the Academic Study of Religion* 30, no. 3 (2017): 281–302.
26 See Bader, Baker, Day and Gordon, *Fear Itself*, on the dynamics of conspiratorial Gnosticism as a general belief system.
27 There are some clear parallels between the quasi-religious and spiritual elements of Icke's claims about aliens and those of George King, founder of the Aetherius Society, which we detail in Chapter 7.
28 See chapter 2, 'Never Mind the Reptiles,' in David Icke, *The Biggest Secret* (Scottsdale, AZ: Bridge of Love, 1999).
29 See, for example, Michael Barkun, *A Culture of Conspiracy* (Berkely: University of California Press, 2006), who ties ideas of a reptilian conspiracy to Robert E. Howard's *Conan* series. For a discussion of the reptilian thesis in New Age thought, see Smith, 'Esoteric Themes in David Icke's Conspiracy Theories'.
30 See, for example, chapter 1 of Icke, *The Biggest Secret*.
31 Sitchin believed that Nibiru was located in an elliptical orbit between Jupiter and Mars and travelled out far beyond Pluto – hence 'the 12th planet' described in the title of his book. Zecharia Sitchin, *The 12th Planet* (New York: Avon, 1976).
32 Icke, *The Biggest Secret*, 4.
33 Ibid., 33.

34 See Norman Cohn, *Europe's Inner Demons* (Chicago: University of Chicago Press, 2001) on historical examples, or Jeffrey S. Victor, *Satanic Panic* (Chicago: Open Court Press, 1993) for a more recent hysteria about Satanism.
35 Barkun, *A Culture of Conspiracy*.
36 See Robert Monroe, *Far Journeys* (New York: Doubleday, 1985), 162–70, for the discussion of Loosh and the Collectors.
37 On the connections between theosophy and esoteric traditions, see Nicholas Goodrick-Clarke, 'Western Esoteric Traditions and Theosophy', in *Handbook of the Theosophical Current*, ed. Olav Hammer and Mikael Rothstein (Leiden: Brill, 2013).
38 On the dynamics of syncretism with Theosophy specifically, see Siv Ellen Kraft, 'To Mix of Not to Mix', *Numen* 49, no. 2 (2002): 142–77.
39 David Icke, *The Dream*.
40 For a discussion of epistemological pluralism in Icke's theories, see Jason Harambam and Stef Aupers, 'From the Unbelievable to the Undeniable', *European Journal of Cultural Studies* 24, no. 4 (2021): 990–1008.
41 As of 2023 there were approximately 40.5 million adults (18–64) in the UK.
42 Interestingly, while conspiracy theorists frequently claim to be free and critical thinkers, psychological research has found a distinct lack of critical thinking ability amongst them. See, for example, Anthony Lantian, Virginie Bagneux, Sylvain Delouvee and Nicolas Gauvrit, 'Maybe a Free Thinker but Not a Critical One', *Applied Cognitive Psychology* 35, no. 3 (2021): 674–84.
43 Harambam and Aupers, 'From the Unbelievable to the Undeniable', 990.
44 Ickonic Enterprises is now run by Icke's son, Gareth, and Icke's ex-wife.
45 Ickonic Media Group is primarily run by Icke's other son, Jaymie. Both Gareth and Jaymie regularly appear as presenters on the Ickonic Media Platform. Icke is also a director for another company – Worldwide Wakeup Limited. In 2023, it had reported net liabilities of £154,579, largely because of a payment due to (unnamed) creditors of £258,608.
46 Charlotte Ward and David Voas, 'The Emergence of Conspirituality', *Journal of Contemporary Religion* 26, no. 1 (2011): 103–21.
47 On Weber's notion of charisma, see Paul Joosse, 'Becoming a God', *Journal of Classical Sociology* 14, no. 3 (2014): 266–283; and Roy Wallis, 'The Social Construction of Charisma', *Social Compass* 29, no. 1 (1982): 25–39.
48 See, for example, Dean Ballinger and Ann Hardy, 'Conspirituality and the Web', *Journal of Contemporary Religion* 37 (2022), 1–20; Harambam and Aupers, 'From the Unbelievable to the Undeniable'.
49 Or is there?
50 Here we follow the Chapman University Survey of American Fears, which regularly includes an item that asks Americans their level of belief in the 'South Dakota crash' for a similar purpose. See Bader, Baker, Day and Gordon, *Fear Itself*.
51 The scale has relatively high internal reliability, with a Cronbach's α = .89.
52 In ANOVA analyses, spiritual people had a mean of 7.29 on the number of paranormal beliefs, while non-spiritual people had a mean of 3.35. For conspiracy belief, spiritual people had a mean of 6.1, compared to four for non-spiritual people. The media consumption measure had a mean of 4.39 for spiritual people and 2.7 for non-spiritual people. All differences in means were statistically significant ($p < .05$).
53 See Cristoffer Tidelius, 'Occulture and Other Predictors of Paranormal Practices and Experiences in Contemporary Sweden', *Nordic Journal of Religion and Society* 37, no. 1 (2024): 49–62. In the CASPAR sample, the correlation between paranormal beliefs

and conspiracy beliefs was r = .72 (p < .001). The correlation between paranormal beliefs and paranormal consumption was r = .43 (p < .001). The correlation between conspiracy beliefs and paranormal consumption was r = .35 (p < .001).

Chapter 7

1. We, of course, recognize that all of this is complicated, and that angels make appearances in the paranormal realm. For example, the idea of a guardian angel is common at MBS fairs.
2. Baker, Bader, and Mencken, 'A Bounded Affinity Theory of Religion and the Paranormal'.
3. Bader, Baker, and Mencken, *Paranormal America*, 2nd edn.
4. Roy Wallis, 'The Aetherius Society', *Sociological Review* 22, no 2 (1974): 27–44.
5. Sarah M. Pike, *New Age and Neopagan Religions in America* (New York: Columbia University Press, 2004), 72.
6. 'Overview', The Aetherius Society, 8 June 2022.
7. 'Holy Mountains', The Aetherius Society, 12 July 2024.
8. 'Dr George King', The Aetherius Society, 30 April 2024.
9. John A. Saliba, 'The World Is a Dangerous Place – The Worldview of the Aetherius Society', *Marburg Journal of Religion* 4, no. 2 (1999): 1–19, 7.
10. Mikael Rothstein, 'Hagiography and Text in the Aetherius Society', in *Sects, Cults, and New Religions*, ed. Carole M. Cusack and Danielle Kirby (New York: Routledge, 2014).
11. Aetherius Society, 'Festival for Mind * Body * Spirit 1980', *The Aetherius Society Newsletter* 19, nos. 11–14 (June/July 1980), 25. The Radionic Pendulum is a product that is still offered by the Aetherius Society. It is marketed as a tool that will help the user develop their intuitive and psychic abilities.
12. George King, *The Twelve Blessings* (London: Aetherius Press, 1961), 11–12.
13. For more detail on the Theosophical roots of Aetherius, see Rothstein, 'Hagiography and Text in the Aetherius Society'.
14. Roy Wallis, 'Ideology, Authority, and the Development of Cultic Movements', *Social Research* 41, no. 2 (1974): 299–327, 313.
15. Rothstein, 'Hagiography and Text in the Aetherius Society'.
16. George King, *Jesus Comes Again* (Hollywood, California: Aetherius Society, 1984).
17. Simon G. Smith, 'Opening a Channel to the Stars', in *UFO Religions*, ed. Christopher Partridge (New York: Routledge, 2003); Wallis, 'The Aetherius Society'.
18. According to the group, there are nine holy mountains in the British Isles, four in the United States, two in Australia, one each in New Zealand, Africa, Switzerland, and France. See 'Holy Mountains' for a list.
19. Aetherius Society, 'Healing Prayer Power Energy Sent to Algeria', *Cosmic Voice* 1, nos. 5–8 (October/November 1980).
20. 'Cosmic Seminar: The Spiritual Science of Radionics'. The Aetherius Society, 18 September 2020.
21. Ibid., all emphases and capitalization in original.
22. George King and Richard Lawrence. *Realize Your Inner Potential*, 3rd ed. (Hollywood, CA: Aetherius Press, 2016).
23. Scott Draper, *Religious Interaction Ritual* (Lanham, MD: Lexington Books, 2019).

24 George King, 'A Brief Description of Operation Prayer Power', *Cosmic Voice* 1, nos. 5–8 (1980), 14.
25 Richard Lawrence, '50 Years of Operation Prayer Power' [Audio podcast], *Aetherius Society Podcast*, 20 June 2023.
26 Aetherius Society (1979, p. 3).
27 King, 'A Brief Description of Operation Prayer Power', 14.
28 Ibid.
29 Ibid.
30 Aetherius Society. 'Great Revelations in Operation Prayer Power', *Cosmic Voice* 18, nos. 23–24 (October 1979), 3, emphasis in the original.
31 'Timeline', *The King Who Came to Earth*, 30 May 2019.
32 Smith, 'Opening a Channel to the Stars', 88.
33 On the broader theory of interaction rituals, see Randall Collins, *Interaction Ritual Chains* (Princeton, NJ: Princeton University Press, 2004). For an in-depth application of interaction ritual theory to religious rituals across a broad range of traditions, see Draper, *Religious Interaction Ritual*.
34 Émile Durkheim, *The Elementary Forms of Religious Life* (New York: Free Press, 1995).
35 Durkheim, *The Elementary Forms of Religious Life*, 38.
36 Rodney Stark, 'Why Religious Movements Succeed or Fail', *Journal of Contemporary Religion* 11, no. 2 (1996).
37 Although alien beliefs and experiences were central to George King's message and remain integral to the worldview of Aetherius members, this dimension is rather downplayed in the group's rituals and writings now. During the fiftieth anniversary of Operation Prayer Power, extraterrestrials were hardly mentioned. Instead, there was more generic discussion of spirituality related to 'higher beings', 'advanced intelligences' and 'cosmic Masters'.
38 Rodney Stark, 'Why Religious Movements Succeed or Fail'.
39 Notably, the Aetherius Society closely follows the strategy of 'traditionalising' King's charisma through organization and ritualization, rather than through choosing a prophetic successor. On the routinization of charisma into stable organizations, see Max Weber, *Economy and Society* (Berkeley: University of California Press, 2013); Trice M. Harrison and Janice M. Beyer, 'Charisma and Its Routinization in Two Social Movement Organizations', in *Research in Organizational Behavior*, ed. Barry M. Staw and L. L. Cummings (Greenwich, CT: JAI, 1986).
40 Robert S. Ellwood and Harry B. Partin, *Religious and Spiritual Groups in Modern America*, 2nd ed. (New York: Routledge, 1988), 126.
41 This, of course, assumes that an Aetherius Society member uses their open-ended response to indicate as such. Given the group's syncretic combination of Christianity, Buddhism, Hinduism, yoga, etc., some people who dabble with the group may choose a different religious identity.
42 Steve Bruce and Tony Glendinning, 'When Was Secularization', *British Journal of Sociology* 61, no. 1 (2010): 107–26; Alasdair Crockett and David Voas, 'Generations of Decline', *Journal for the Scientific Study of Religion* 45, no. 4 (2006): 567–84; Clive D. Field, *Counting Religion in Britain, 1970–2020* (Oxford: Oxford University Press, 2022).
43 Steve Bruce, 'Religion in Britain, R.I.P.', *Sociology of Religion* 62, no. 2 (2001): 191–203; Linda Woodhead, 'The Rise of "No Religion" in Britain', *Journal of the British Academy* 4 (2016): 245–61.
44 Grace Davie, *Religion in Britain* (Malden, MA: Wiley-Blackwell, 2015).

45 Clive D. Field, 'Belief in the Afterlife, 1939–2008', *British Religion in Numbers*, 5 December 2024.
46 Alan Orenstein, 'Religion and Paranormal Belief', *Journal for the Scientific Study of Religion* 41 (2002): 301–11; Tom W. Rice, 'Believe It or Not', *Journal for the Scientific Study of Religion* 42 (2003): 95–106; Robert Wuthnow, *Experimentation in American Religion* (Berkley: University of California Press, 1978).
47 Laurence R. Iannaccone, 'Sacrifice and Stigma', *Journal of Political Economy* (April 1992): 271–91.
48 Charles F. Emmons and Jeff Sobal, 'Paranormal Beliefs', *Review of Religious Research* 22 (1981): 301–12; Rodney Stark, *What Americans Really Believe* (Waco, TX: Baylor University Press, 2008).
49 Michael Donahue, 'Prevalence and Correlates of New Age Beliefs in Six Protestant Denominations', *Journal for the Scientific Study of Religion* 32 (1993): 177–84; Glenn G. Sparks, 'The Relationship between Paranormal Beliefs and Religious Beliefs', *Skeptical Inquirer* 25 (2001): 50–6; Rice, 'Believe It or Not'.
50 Joseph O. Baker and Scott Draper, 'Diverse Supernatural Portfolios: Certitude, Exclusivity, and the Curvilinear Relationship between Religiosity and Paranormal Beliefs', *Journal for the Scientific Study of Religion* 49 (2010): 413–24.
51 Here we rely on Glock and Stark's (1965) typology of the different types of religiosity. Charles Y. Glock and Rodney Stark, *Religion and Society in Tension* (Chicago, IL: Rand-McNally, 1965).
52 Within this catchall category, members of 'magical' religious traditions such as Pagans and Wiccans predictably had the highest levels of paranormal belief.
53 This pattern also holds if we examine more refined versions of the paranormal outcomes, such as using different measures for magic and spirits, Earth mysteries, cryptids, and aliens. The same patterns also hold when examining a scale of 'superstitious' beliefs as an outcome (e.g., belief in luck, charms, and fate). Overall, the general pattern is consistent when using different outcomes and closely matches patterns found in samples from other Western countries.
54 The graphical results shown are from ordinary least squares regression models controlling for employment, income, social grade, education, age, race, region, marital status, and religious identification.
55 See also Tony Glendinning, 'Religious Involvement, Conventional Christian, and Unconventional Nonmaterialist Beliefs', *Journal for the Scientific Study of Religion* 45 (2006): 585–95.
56 Each dimension was weighted equally; however, since this weights the measure toward two dimensions of religiosity that are positively related to paranormalism (belief and experience) and only one dimension that is negatively related to paranormalism (practice), we also specified models with alternative composite measures. Using a measure that equally weighted religious practice and a (pre-combined) single measure of religious beliefs and experiences together produced results nearly identical to those shown.
57 On this pattern in the United States, see Baker and Draper, 'Diverse Supernatural Portfolios'; on Italy, see Bader, Baker, and Molle, 'Countervailing Forces'.
58 For more detail on this pattern and its relative shape when predicting the different domains of paranormalism (Earth mysteries, cryptids, aliens, and magic and spirits), see Clark et al., 'Marginalized, Secularized, and Popularized?'.

59 William Wordsworth, 1831, 'Composed in Roslin Chapel During a Storm', 302, in *The Complete Poetical Works of William Wordsworth*, ed. Henry Reed (Philadelphia, PA: Troutman & Hayes, 1854).
60 Lizzie Swarbrick, 'Rosslyn Chapel', in *The Modern Memory of Military-Religious Orders*, ed. Rory MacLellan (New York: Routledge, 2022), 21.
61 Swarbrick, 'Rosslyn Chapel'.
62 Karen Heller, 'Meet the Elite Group of Authors Who Sell 100 Million Books – or 350 Million', *Independent*, 28 December 2016.
63 Dan Brown, *The Da Vinci Code* (New York: Doubleday, 2003), 434, emphasis in original.
64 Jerry Z. Park and Joseph O. Baker, 'What Would Jesus Buy: American Consumption of Religious and Spiritual Material Goods', *Journal for the Scientific Study of Religion* 46, no. 4 (2007): 501–17.
65 The model controls for standard sociodemographic characteristics, such as age, education, income, gender, and region of residence. The paranormal beliefs scale from the 2005 Baylor Religion Survey includes items on aliens, Atlantis, astrology, psychics, hauntings, and cryptids. The religiosity measure is a composite of religious attendance, prayer, salience, and biblical literalism.
66 Ian Gardner, 'Record Breaking Year for Visitors at Rosslyn Chapel', *The Official Rosslyn Chapel Website*, 18 January 2018.
67 On the extensive 'mediatisation' of Rosslyn Chapel on social media, see Maria Mansson, 'Mediatized Tourism', *Annals of Tourism Research* 38, no. 4 (2011): 1634–52.
68 Dr. Peter Simi of Chapman University.
69 https://rolfsrides.com/.
70 We're guessing this visitor was a big fan of *Indiana Jones and the Last Crusade*.
71 On tension, see Benton Johnson, 'On Church and Sect', *American Sociological Review* 28, no. 4 (1963): 539–49; William S. Bainbridge and Rodney Stark, 'Sectarian Tension', *Review of Religious Research* 22, no. 2 (1980): 105–24; Rodney Stark and William S. Bainbridge, 'Of Churches, Sects, and Cults', *Journal for the Scientific Study of Religion* 18, no. 2 (1979): 117–31.
72 David Martin-Jones, 'Film Tourism as Heritage Tourism', *New Review of Film and Television Studies* 12, no. 2 (2014): 156–77.
73 Carole M. Cusack, 'Esoteric Tourism in Scotland', in *Prophecy, Fate and Memory in the Early Medieval Celtic World*, ed. Jonathan M. Wooding and Lynette Olson (Sydney: Sydney University Press, 2020).
74 Maria Mansson, 'Mediatized Tourism'.
75 For a more extended discussion of conspiratorial Gnosticism and related analyses of belief in conspiracy theories, see Bader, Baker, Gordon, and Day, *Fear Itself*.
76 On the esotericism of Brown's novel, see Cusack, 'Esoteric Tourism in Scotland'.
77 On the uses of Rosslyn by far-right groups, see Swarbrick, 'Rosslyn Chapel'.

Conclusion

1 Alice Box is available from many resellers and in many different versions. There are apps for IOS and Android, and even a stand-alone piece of equipment that runs the program. Since it was what the ghost hunters used, we download the PC/Windows

version, which is available here: https://www.infraready.co.uk/shop/alice-box-instrumental-trans-communication-licesnse-key-free-download/.
2. 'The Alice Story'. *Alice: Home of the Alicebox Family* (undated) http://www.alicebox.co.uk/web/.
3. This quote is from a Facebook message conversation with the Retford Ghost Hunters that occurred on 3 February 2025.
4. This quote is from the product page for Alice Box on the website of *infraready* which sells a variety of ghost hunting equipment. https://www.infraready.co.uk/shop/alice-box-tablet/.
5. 'The Alice Story' (n.d.).
6. These items include belief in ancient aliens, modern alien visitations, psychic powers, hauntings, Bigfoot, telekinesis, faeries, crop circles, big cats in Britain, the UK Wildman, the Yeti, Nessie, black magic, dowsing, ley lines, mysterious creatures, and curses. Each question was asked on a Likert-type scale. We counted someone as holding a belief if they chose either the 'tend to agree' or 'strongly agree' response.
7. Philosopher Charles Taylor utilized the term 'subjective turn' to describe the modern tendency to focus more upon expressive individualism and subjective truth rather than truths prescribed by social institutions. Charles Taylor, *The Ethics of Authenticity* (Cambridge, MA: Harvard University Press, 1991); Charles Taylor, *A Secular Age* (Cambridge, MA: Harvard University Press, 2007).
8. Heelas and Woodhead, *The Spiritual Revolution*.
9. Iannaccone, 'Risk, Rationality and Religious Portfolios', 288.
10. Adam Possamai (ed.), *Handbook of Hyper-real Religions*, (Leiden: Brill, 2012).
11. A more general example of this tendency was initially highlighted by French sociologist Jean Baudrilliard, who infamously proclaimed that 'the Gulf war was not a war'. Whilst the media recycled images to make it appear as if there was conflict that could equate to 'war', Baudrillard argues that it was 'an atrocity masquerading as war'. Effectively, a media-constructed 'hyper-reality' had replaced on-the-ground reality. Jean Baudrillard, *The Gulf War Did Not Take Place* (Bloomington: Indiana University Press, 1995).
12. Adam Possamai, *Religion and Popular Culture: A Hyper-real Testament* (Brussels: Peter Lang, 2005), 72–6.
13. Teemu Taira, 'The Category of "Invented Religion": A New Opportunity for Studying Discourses on "Religion"', *Culture and Religion*, 14, no. 4 (2013): 477–93.
14. Adam Possamai and Murray Lee, 'Hyper-real Religions: Fear, Anxiety, and Late-Modern Religious Innovation', *Journal of Sociology*, 47, no. 3 (2011): 227–42.
15. See William Sims Bainbridge, *Dynamic Secularization: Information Technology and the Tension Between Religion and Science* (New York: Springer, 2017), 121–49.
16. On the elective affinities between conspiracism and the digital age, see Bader et al., *Fear Itself*; Thomas Milan Konda, *Conspiracies of Conspiracies: How Delusions Have Overrun America* (Chicago: University of Chicago Press, 2019).
17. B. Joseph Pine II and James H. Gilmore, 'The Experience Economy: Past, Present and Future', in *Handbook on the Experience Economy*, ed. Jon Sundbo and Flemming Sorensen (Cheltenham: Edward Elgar, 2013).

BIBLIOGRAPHY

'8th March – Ghost Tour'. *Hoghton Tower*, 27 January 2025. https://www.hoghtontower.co.uk/special-events/ghost-tours-2/.

'30 East Drive (Intro)'. *30 East Drive | PONTEFRACT*, 13 July 2014. Retrieved 19 October 2025 from https://web.archive.org/web/20140713220901/http://www.30eastdrive.com/introductions

'30 East Drive, Merseyside Paranormal FB Post'. *30 East Drive | PONTEFRACT*, n.d. http://www.30eastdrive.com/merseyside-paranormal-fb-post/#prettyPhoto[slides]/0/.

'The "Abominable Snowman" Unmasked! An Ursine "Man Friday."' *Illustrated London News*, 27 November 1937.

'Avenue House Ghost Hunts'. *HauntedHappenings.co.uk*, n.d. https://www.hauntedhappenings.co.uk/avenue-house/.

'Black Dog.' *Elgoods Brewery*, 25 November 2024. https://www.elgoods-brewery.co.uk/product/black-dog/.

'Black Shuck – Wagtail Brewery.' *Untappd*. Retrieved 19 October 2025 from https://untappd.com/b/wagtail-brewery-black-shuck/134785.

'Cosmic Seminar: The Spiritual Science of Radionics'. *The Aetherius Society*, 18 September 2020. https://www.aetherius.org.nz/cosmic-seminar-the-spiritual-science-of-radionics/.

'Crop Circle at Roundway Down, nr Devizes, Wiltshire. Reported 11th June 2023'. *Crop Circle Connector*, n.d. https://cropcircleconnector.com/2023/RoundwayDown/RoundwayDown2023a.html.

'Dr George King: Master of Yoga & Founder of the Aetherius Society'. *The Aetherius Society*, 30 April 2024. https://www.aetherius.org/dr-george-king/.

'Falstaff Museum Experience Ghost Hunts'. *HauntedHappenings.co.uk*, n.d. https://www.hauntedhappenings.co.uk/falstaffs/.

'Felicity the Puma.' *Inverness Museum and Art Gallery*, 17 August, 2021. https://www.highlifehighland.com/inverness-museum-and-art-gallery/felicity-the-puma/.

'Ghost Walk'. Stratford Town Walk, n.d. https://stratfordtownwalk.co.uk/ghost-walk/.

'Halton Data Profile'. *Halton Borough Council*, n.d. https://www3.halton.gov.uk/Pages/councildemocracy/CensusandStatistics/CensusandStatistics.aspx.

'Holy Mountains – Pilgrimages to These Great Spiritual Power Batteries'. *The Aetherius Society*, 12 July 2024. https://www.aetherius.org/pilgrimages-to-holy-mountains/.

'How Life Has Changed in Southwark: Census 2021'. Office for National Statistics, n.d. https://www.ons.gov.uk/visualisations/censusareachanges/E09000028.

'Latest Crop Circles'. *Crop Circle Access*, 29 August 2024. https://www.cropcircleaccess.com/latestcropcircles/.

'Leading Coffee Shop Chains UK 2024'. *Statista*, n.d. https://www.statista.com/statistics/297863/leading-coffee-shop-chains-in-the-united-kingdom-uk-store-number/.

'The Loch Ness Centre.' *Continuum Attractions*, 11 August 2023. https://www.continuumattractions.com/case_studies/the-loch-ness-centre/.

'Loch Ness Monster Worth Nearly £41m a Year to Scottish Economy'. *Aberdeen Press and Journal*, 13 September 2018.

'The Mowing Devil: Or Strange News Out of Hartford-Shire'. [Pamphlet], August 1678.

'"Nessie" Nets about $42 Million Per Year'. *United Press International*, 28 May 1990. Retrieved 19 October 2025 from https://www.upi.com/Archives/1990/05/28/Nessie-nets-about-42-million-per-year/2370643867200/.

'Overview'. *The Aetherius Society*, 8 June 2022. https://www.aetherius.org/overview/.

'Population Estimates for the UK, England, Wales, Scotland, and Northern Ireland: Mid-2022', Office for National Statistics, 26 March 2024. https://www.ons.gov.uk/peoplepopulationandcommunity/populationandmigration/populationestimates/bulletins/annualmidyearpopulationestimates/mid2022.

'The Sinister Side of Shakespeare's Stratford Guided Walking Tour'. *Sinister Stratford*, n.d. https://www.sinisterstratford.co.uk/.

'Special Events 2024'. *The Amazing Cornish Maize Maze*, n.d. https://www.amazingcornishmaizemaze.co.uk/special-events.php.

'Subnational Indicators Dataset'. Office for National Statistics, 21 March 2024. https://www.ons.gov.uk/peoplepopulationandcommunity/wellbeing/datasets/subnationalindicatorsdataset.

'Reappearance of the "Abominable Snowman"'. *Illustrated London News*, 15 December 1951.

'Timeline'. *The King Who Came to Earth*, 30 May 2019. https://drgeorgeking.org/timeline/.

'UFO Trail at Rendlesham Forest', *Forestry England*, n.d. https://www.forestryengland.uk/rendlesham-forest/ufo-trail-rendlesham-forest.

'Weird Wiltshire Day Trip 2025 – Mysterious Crop Circles'. *Stonehenge Tours*, n.d. https://www.stonehengetours.com/day-tours/weird-wiltshire-stonehenge-crop-circle-tour.

'When the Lights Went Out (2012).' Box Office Mojo. https://www.boxofficemojo.com/title/tt1743993/.

Adomnan of Iona. *The Life of St. Columba*. London: Penguin Classics, 1995.

Aetherius Society. *Some Basic Principles Included in Its Teachings*. London: Aetherius Society, 1984.

Aetherius Society. 'Great Revelations in Operation Prayer Power'. *Cosmic Voice* 18, nos. 23 and 24 (October 1979): 1–7.

Aetherius Society. 'Healing Prayer Power Energy Sent to Algeria'. *Cosmic Voice* 1, nos. 5–8 (October/November 1980): 4–5.

Aetherius Society. 'Festival for Mind * Body * Spirit 1980'. *Aetherius Society Newsletter* 19, nos. 11–14 (June/July 1980).

Alexander, Marc. *The Man Who Exorcised the Bermuda Triangle*. New York: A.S. Barnes, 1980.

Alexander, Steve, and Karen Alexander. *Crop Circle Yearbook 2015*. Hampshire: Temporary Temple Press, 2015.

Anderson, Karen. 'Irish Secularisation of Religious Identities: Evidence of an Emerging New Catholic Habitus'. *Social Compass* 57, no. 1 (2010): 15–39.

Arnold, Neil. 'Fortean Times June 2007 – "Big Cats"'. *Kent Big Cat Research*, 3 June 2007. http://kentbigcats.blogspot.com/2007/06/fortean-times-june-2007-big-cats.html.

Asprem, Esprim. 'Science and the Occult'. In: *The Occult World*, ed. Christopher Partridge, 710–19. London: Routledge, 2014.

Association for the Scientific Study of Anomalous Phenomena 'Welcome to ASSAP'. ASSAP. https://www.assap.ac.uk/.

Athens, Lonnie. 'The Self as Soliloquy'. *Sociological Quarterly* 35, no. 3 (1994): 521–32.
Bader, Christopher, and Joseph O. Baker. *Deviance Management*. Oakland: University of California Press, 2019.
Bader, Christopher, Joseph O. Baker, L. Edward Day and C. Ann Gordon. *Fear Itself: The Causes and Consequences of Fear*. New York: NYU Press, 2020.
Bader, Christopher, Joseph O. Baker, and F. Carson Mencken. *Paranormal America: Ghost Encounters, UFO Sightings, Bigfoot Hunts, and Other Curiosities in Religion and Culture*. 2nd ed. New York: NYU Press, 2017.
Bader, Christopher D., Joseph O. Baker and Andrea Molle. 'Countervailing Forces: Religiosity and Paranormal Belief in Italy'. *Journal for the Scientific Study of Religion* 51, no. 4 (2012): 705–20.
Bainbridge, William Sims. *Dynamic Secularization: Information Technology and the Tension Between Religion and Science*. New York: Springer, 2017.
Bainbridge, William S., and Rodney Stark. 'Sectarian Tension'. *Review of Religious Research* 22, no. 2 (1980): 105–24.
Baker, Joseph O. 'An Investigation of the Sociological Patterns of Prayer Frequency and Content.' *Sociology of Religion* 69, no. 2 (2008): 169–85.
Baker, Joseph O., and Buster Smith. *American Secularism: Cultural Contours of Nonreligious Belief Systems*. New York: NYU Press, 2015.
Baker, Joseph O., and Christopher D. Bader. 'A Social Anthropology of Ghosts in Twenty-First-Century America'. *Social Compass* 61, no. 4 (2014): 569–93.
Baker, Joseph O., Christopher D. Bader and F. Carson Mencken. 'A Bounded Affinity Theory of Religion and the Paranormal'. *Sociology of Religion* 77, no. 4 (2016): 334–58.
Baker, Joseph O., and Scott Draper. 'Diverse Supernatural Portfolios: Certitude, Exclusivity, and the Curvilinear Relationship between Religiosity and Paranormal Beliefs'. *Journal for the Scientific Study of Religion* 49 (2010): 413–24.
Ballinger, Dean, and Ann Hardy. 'Conspirituality and the Web: A Case Study of David Icke's Media Use'. *Journal of Contemporary Religion* 37 (2022), 1–20.
Barkun, Michael. *A Culture of Conspiracy: Apocalyptic Visions in Contemporary America*. Berkeley: University of California Press, 2006.
Barkun, Michael. 'Conspiracy Theories as Stigmatized Knowledge'. *Diogenes* 62, nos. 3–4 (2015): 114–20.
Baudrillard, Jean. *The Gulf War Did Not Take Place*. Bloomington: Indiana University Press, 1995.
Bauval, Robert, and Adrian Gilbert. *The Orion Mystery: Unlocking The Secrets of the Pyramids*. London: Heinemann, 1994.
BBC. 'New Data Shows Wiltshire Has Most Crop Circles in England'. *BBC News*, 22 July 2023. https://www.bbc.com/news/uk-england-wiltshire-66245271.
Beattie, Karl (Director). 'Most Haunted Live – 30 East Drive, Part 2' [TV Series Episode]. *Most Haunted*, 25 October 2015.
Ben-Yehuda, Nachman. *Deviance and Moral Boundaries*. Chicago: University of Chicago Press, 1985.
Beyer, Stephan. *The Cult of Tara: Magic and Ritual in Tibet*. Berkeley: University of California Press, 1978.
British Broadcasting Corporation. 'David Icke: Conspiracy Theorist Banned from Netherlands'. *BBC News*, 4 November 2022. https://www.bbc.com/news/world-europe-63511142.
Berger, Peter L. *The Sacred Canopy: Elements of a Sociological Theory of Religion*. New York: Anchor Books, 1967.

Berger, Peter L., and Thomas Luckmann. *The Social Construction of Reality: A Treatise in the Sociology of Knowledge*. New York: Anchor Books, 1996.
Blu Bluhs, Joshua. *Bigfoot: The Life and Times of a Legend*. Chicago: University of Chicago Press, 2009.
Bord, Janet, and Colin Bord. *Alien Animals*. Harrisburg, PA: Stackpole, 1982.
Borkowski, Mark. 'Macabre'. *Mark Borkowski*, 26 June 2007. https://www.markborkowski.co.uk/macabre/.
Boyer, Pascal. *Religion Explained: The Evolutionary Origins of Religious Thought*. New York: Basic Books, 2001.
Brown, Dan. *The Da Vinci Code*. New York: Doubleday, 2003.
Bruce, Steve. 'Religion in Britain, R.I.P.'. *Sociology of Religion* 62, no. 2 (2001): 191–203.
Bruce, Steve, and Tony Glendinning. 'When Was Secularization? Dating the Decline of the British Churches and Locating its Cause'. *British Journal of Sociology* 61, no. 1 (2010): 107–26.
Bubandt, Nils. 'A Psychology of Ghosts: The Regime of the Self and the Reinvention of Spirits in Indonesia and Beyond'. *Anthropological Forum* 22, no. 1 (2012): 1–23.
Bucke, Richard M. *Cosmic Consciousness: A Study in the Evolution of the Human Mind*. New York: E. P. Dutton, 1901.
Bullivant, Stephen. *Nonverts: The Making of Ex-Christian America*. New York: Oxford University Press, 2022.
Burl, Aubrey. *The Stone Circles of Britain, Ireland, and Brittany*. New Haven, CT: Yale University Press, 2000.
Campbell, Colin. 'The Cult, the Cultic Milieu and Secularisation'. *A Sociological Yearbook of Religion in Britain* 5 (1972): 119–36.
Campbell, Elizabeth, and David Solomon. *The Search for Morag*. London: Tom Stacey, 1972.
Capron, John R. 'Storm Effects'. *Nature* 22 (29 July 1880): 290–1.
Castro, Madeleine, Roger Burrows, and Robin Wooffitt. 'The Paranormal Is (Still) Normal: The Sociological Implications of a Survey of Paranormal Experiences in Great Britain'. *Sociological Research Online* 19, no. 3 (2014): 30–44.
Choden, Kunzang. *Bhutanese Tales of the Yeti*. Bangkok: White Lotus, 1997.
Clark, Tom, Joseph O. Baker, and Christopher D. Bader. 'Marginalized, Secularized, and Popularized? The Prevalence and Patterns of Paranormal Belief in the United Kingdom'. *Sociological Quarterly* 66, no. 3 (2025): 612–35. https://doi.org/10.1080/00380253.2025.2461298.
Cohn, Norman. *Europe's Inner Demons: The Demonization of Christians in Medieval Christendom*. Chicago: University of Chicago Press, 2001.
Collins, Andrew. 'What Is Psychic Questing?'. *andrewcollins.com*, n.d. https://www.andrewcollins.com/page/articles/psychicQ.htm.
Collins, Andrew. *The Brentford Griffin: The Truth Behind the Tales*. Essex: Earthquest Books, 1985.
Collins, Andrew. *The Black Alchemist*. Leigh-on-sea, Essex: ABC Books, 1988.
Collins, Andrew. *The Seventh Sword*. London: Century, 1991.
Collins, Andrew. *The Second Coming*. London: Century, 1993.
Collins, Andrew. *The Cygnus Mystery: Unlocking the Ancient Secret of Life's Origins in the Cosmos*. London: Watkins, 2012.
Collins, Andrew. *Göbekli Tepe: Genesis of the Gods*. Rochester, Vermont: Bear, 2014.
Collins, Andrew. *Denisovan Origins: Hybrid Humans, Göbekli Tepe, and the Genesis of the Giants of Ancient America*. Rochester, Vermont: Bear, 2019.

Collins, Andrew. *Karahan Tepe: Civilization of the Anunnaki and the Cosmic Origins of the Serpent of Eden*. Rochester, Vermont: Bear, 2024.
Collins, Randall. *Interaction Ritual Chains*. Princeton, NJ: Princeton University Press, 2004.
Crockett, Alasdair, and David Voas. 'Generations of Decline: Religious Change in 20th-Century Britain'. *Journal for the Scientific Study of Religion* 45, no. 4 (2006): 567–84.
Crowe, Catherine. *Night-Side of Nature or Ghosts and Ghost Seers*. Boston: B.B. Mussey, 1850.
Cunniff, Tom. *The Supernatural in Yorkshire*. Skipton: Dalesman Books, 1985.
Cuoghi, Diego. 'The Art of Imagining UFOs'. *Skeptic* 11, no. 1 (2004): 43–51.
Cusack, Carole M. 'Esoteric Tourism in Scotland: Rosslyn Chapel, *The Da Vinci Code*, and the Appeal of the "New Age"'. In: *Prophecy, Fate and Memory in the Early Medieval Celtic World*, ed. Jonathan M. Wooding and Lynette Olson, 246–69. Sydney: Sydney University Press, 2020.
Daegling, David J. *Bigfoot Exposed: An Anthropologist Examines America's Enduring Legend*. New York: Rowan & Littlefield, 2004.
Dahlgreen, Will. '"Ghosts Exist," Say 1 in 3 Brits'. *YouGov*, 21 October 2014. https://yougov.co.uk/politics/articles/10857-ghosts-exist-say-1-3-brits.
Dailey, Timothy. *The Paranormal Conspiracy: The Truth about Ghosts, Aliens and Mysterious Beings*. Minneapolis, MN: Chosen Books, 2015.
Dancausa, Genoveva, Ricardo D. Hernandez and Lenor M. Perez. 'Motivations and Constraints for the Ghost Tourism: A Case Study in Spain'. *Leisure Sciences* 45, no. 2 (2023.): 156–77.
Davie, Grace. *Religion in Britain: A Persistent Paradox*. 2nd edn. Malden, MA: Wiley-Blackwell, 2015.
Davies, Douglas. 2018. *Mormon Culture of Salvation*. New York: Routledge, 2018.
Davies, Owen. *The Haunted: A Social History of Ghosts*. London: Palgrave Macmillan, 2007.
Davies, Owen, ed. *The Oxford History of Witchcraft and Magic*. Oxford: Oxford University Press, 2023.
Dean, Charlotte. E., Shazia Akhtar, Tim M. Gale, Karen Irvine, Richard Wiseman and Keith R. Laws. 'Development of the Paranormal and Supernatural Beliefs Scale Using Classical and Modern Test Theory'. *BMC Psychology* 9, no. 1 (2021): 1–20.
Delgado, Pat, and Colin Andrews. *Circular Evidence*. Grand Rapids, MI: Phanes, 1989.
Donahue, Michael J. 'Prevalence and Correlates of New Age Beliefs in Six Protestant Denominations'. *Journal for the Scientific Study of Religion* 32 (1993): 177–84.
Downes, Jon. 'The Big Hairy Monster of Bolam Lake'. *Fortean Times* 169 (May 2003): 24–5.
Downes, Jon. *The Owlman and Others*. North Devon: CFZ Press ([1997] 2006).
Draper, Scott. *Religious Interaction Ritual: The Microsociology of the Spirit*. Lanham, MD: Lexington Books, 2019.
Drinkwater, Kenneth, Andrew Denovan, Neil Dagnall and Andrew Parker. 'An Assessment of the Dimensionality and Factorial Structure of the Revised Paranormal Belief Scale'. *Frontiers in Psychology* 8, no. 1693 (2017): 1–12. 10.3389/fpsyg.2017.01693.

Drinkwater, Kenneth, Andrew Denovan, Neil Dagnall and Andrew Parker. 'The Australian Sheep-Goat Scale: An Evaluation of Factor Structure and Convergent Validity'. *Frontiers in Psychology* 9, no. 1594 (2018): 1–14.. 10.3389/fpsyg.2018.01594.

Drinkwater, Kenneth, Brandon Massullo, Neil Dagnall, Brian Laythe, Juliette Boone and James Houran. 'Understanding Consumer Enchantment via Paranormal Tourism: Part I – Conceptual Review'. *Cornell Hospitality Quarterly* 63, no. 2 (2022): 195–215.

Dunning, Brian (Host). 'Unmasking the Old Stinker: The Hull Werewolf'. *Skeptoid* 804 (2 November 2021). https://skeptoid.com/episodes/4804.

Durkheim, Émile. *The Elementary Forms of Religious Life*, translated by Karen E. Fields. New York: Free Press, [1912] 1995.

Eaton, Marc A. '"Give Us a Sign of Your Presence": Paranormal Investigation as a Spiritual Practice'. *Sociology of Religion* 76, no. 4 (2015): 389–412.

Eaton, Marc A. *Sensing Spirits: Paranormal Investigation and the Social Construction of Ghosts*. London: Routledge, 2021.

Ellis, Bill. 'Legend Trip'. In: *American Folklore: An Encyclopedia*, ed. Jan Harold Brunvand, 438–40. New York: Garland, 1996.

Ellis, Bill. 'Legend-Trips and Satanism: Adolescents' Ostensive Tradition as 'Cult' Activity'. In: *Contemporary Legend: A Reader*, ed. G. Bennet and P. Smith, 167–86. New York: Routledge, 1996.

Ellwood, Robert S., and Harry B. Partin. *Religious and Spiritual Groups in Modern America*. 2nd edn. New York Routledge, 1988.

Emmons, Charles F., and Jeff Sobal. 'Paranormal Beliefs: Functional Alternatives to Mainstream Religion?' *Review of Religious Research* 22 (1981): 301–12.

Estep, Richard, and Bil Bungay. *The Black Monk of Pontefract: The World's Most Violent and Relentless Poltergeist*. Self-published, 2019.

Evans, Andy. *Don't Look Back in Anger*. Print on demand: lulu.com, 2015.

Eyerman, Ron. 'False Consciousness and Ideology in Marxist Theory'. *Acta Sociologica* 24, nos. 1–2 (1981): 43–56.

Fessahaye, Daniel. 'Double, Double, Toil and Trouble! Turf War Breaks Out in Shakespeare's Hometown between Rival Ghost Tours'. *Daily Mail Online*, 21 July 2023.

Field, Clive. *Religion in Great Britain, 1939-99: A Compendium of Gallup Poll Data*. Manchester: University of Manchester, 2015.

Field, Clive D. *Counting Religion in Britain, 1970–2020: Secularization in Statistical Context*. Oxford: Oxford University Press, 2022.

Field, Clive D. 'Belief in Britain, 1939–2009'. *British Religion in Numbers*, 5 December 2024. https://www.brin.ac.uk/figures/belief-in-britain-1939-2009/.

Field, Clive D. 'Belief in Ghosts and Communication with the Dead'. *British Religion in Numbers*, 5 December 2024. https://www.brin.ac.uk/figures/belief-in-britain-1939-2009/alternative-religious-belief/belief-in-ghosts-and-communication-with-the-dead/.

Field, Clive D. 'Belief in the Afterlife, 1939–2008', *British Religion in Numbers*, 5 December 2024. https://www.brin.ac.uk/figures/belief-in-britain-1939-2009/conventional-belief/belief-in-the-afterlife-1939-2008/.

Fort, Charles. *The Book of the Damned*. New York: Ace Books, [1919] 1972.

Fort, Charles. *Lo!* New York: Claude Kendal, 1931.

Fort, Charles. *New Lands*. New York: Boni & Liveright, 1923.

Francis, Di. *Cat Country: Quest for the British Big Cat*. Exeter: David & Charles, 1983.

Fraser, Mark, ed. *Big Cats in Britain Yearbook 2007*. North Devon: CFZ, 2007.

French, Christopher C., and Anna Stone. *Anomalistic Psychology: Exploring Paranormal Belief and Experience*. London: Bloomsbury, 2017.

Froese, Paul, and Christopher Bader. *America's Four Gods: What We Say About God – and What That Says About Us*. New York: Oxford University Press, 2010.

Fuller, John G. *Interrupted Journey: Two Lost Hours Aboard a Flying Saucer*. New York: Dial, 1966.

Gardner, Ian. 'Record Breaking Year for Visitors at Rosslyn Chapel', *The Official Rosslyn Chapel Website*, 18 January 2018. https://www.rosslynchapel.com/news/record-breaking-year-visitors-rosslyn-chapel/.

Germani, Clara. 'Lake Champlain's "Monster": It May be a Zeuglodon'. *Christian Science Monitor*, 2 November 2021.

Gieryn, Thomas F. 'Boundary-Work and the Demarcation of Science from Nonscience: Strains and Interests in Professionalization Ideologies of Scientists'. *American Sociological Review* 48, no. 6 (1983): 781–95.

Gieryn, Thomas F. *Cultural Boundaries of Science: Credibility on the Line*. Chicago: University of Chicago Press, 1999.

Glanvill, Joseph. *A Blow at Modern Sadducism in Some Philosophical Considerations about Witchcraft. To Which Is Added, the Relation of the Fam'd Disturbance by the Drummer, In the House of Mr. John Mompesson, with Some Reflections on Drollery and Atheisme*. London: E.C., 1668.

Glendinning, Tony. 'Religious Involvement, Conventional Christian, and Unconventional Nonmaterialist Beliefs'. *Journal for the Scientific Study of Religion* 45 (2006): 585–95.

Glock, Charles Y., and Rodney Stark. *Religion and Society in Tension*. Chicago, IL: Rand-McNally, 1965.

Goodrick-Clarke, Nicholas. 'Western Esoteric Traditions and Theosophy.' In: *Handbook of the Theosophical Current*, ed. Olav Hammer and Mikael Rothstein, 259–307. Leiden: Brill, 2013.

Green, Jeffrey E. 'Two Meanings of Disenchantment: Sociological Condition vs. Philosophical Act – Reassessing Max Weber's Thesis of the Disenchantment of the World'. *Philosophy & Theology* 17, nos. 1–2 (2005): 51–84.

Gregersen, Eric. 'Crop Circle'. *Encyclopædia Britannica*, 21 February 2025. https://www.britannica.com/art/crop-circle.

Gurney, Edmund, F. W. H. Myers and Frank Podmore. *Phantasms of the Living*. London: Society for Psychical Research, 1886.

Hallworth, Derek (Director). 'Most Haunted Live – Halloween Special' [TV Series Episode]. *Most Haunted*, 31 October 2015.

Hancock, Graham. *Fingerprints of the Gods: The Evidence of Earth's Lost Civilization*. New York: Crown Books, 1995.

Hancock, Graham. *The Mars Mystery: The Secret Connection Between Earth and the Red Planet*. New York: Broadway Books, 1999.

Hancock, Graham. *Supernatural: Meetings with the Ancient Teachers of Mankind*. London: Arrow Books, 2005.

Hanegraaff, Wouter J. *New Age Religion and Western Culture: Esotericism in the Mirror of Secular Thought*. Albany: State University of New York Press, 1998.

Hanegraaff, Wouter J. *Western Esotericism: A Guide for the Perplexed*. London: Bloomsbury, 2013.

Hanks, Michelle. *Haunted Heritage: The Cultural Politics of Ghost Tourism, Populism, and the Past*. New York: Routledge, 2016.

Harambam, Jaron, and Stef Aupers. 'From the Unbelievable to the Undeniable: Epistemological Pluralism, or How Conspiracy Theorists Legitimate Their Extraordinary Truth Claims'. *European Journal of Cultural Studies* 24, no. 4 (2021): 990–1008.

Haraldsson, Erlendur. 'Representative National Surveys of Psychic Phenomena: Iceland, Great Britain, Sweden, USA and Gallup's Multinational Survey'. *Journal of the Society for Psychical Research* 53 (1985), 145–58.

Harmsworth, Tony. *Loch Ness, Nessie and Me*. Createspace, 2024.

Harpur, Merrily. 'Seeing Is Believing: Sightings of Mystery "Big Cats" in Britain's Countryside Have Snowballed Since the 1980s, Dividing Opinion about Their Existence'. *Guardian*, 21 March 2006.

Harpur, Merrily. 'As Easy as ABC: The Competing Theories'. *Fortean Times* 224 (August 2007): 38–9.

Heelas, Paul. *Spiritualities of Life: New Age Romanticism and Consumptive Capitalism*. Malden, MA: Blackwell, 2008.

Heelas, Paul, and Linda Woodhead. 'The Kendal Project: Testing The 'Spiritual Revolution' Thesis'. *Sociology Review* 13, no. 2 (2003): 18–21.

Heelas, Paul, and Linda Woodhead. *The Spiritual Revolution*. Oxford: Blackwell, 2005.

Heller, Karen. 'Meet the Elite Group of Authors Who Sell 100 Million Books – or 350 Million', *Independent*, 28 December 2016.

Heritage, Stuart. 'Ancient Apocalypse Is the Most Dangerous Show on Netflix'. *Guardian*, 23 November 2022. https://www.theguardian.com/tv-and-radio/2022/nov/23/ancient-apocalypse-is-the-most-dangerous-show-on-netflix.

Hewitt, John P., and Randall Stokes, 'Disclaimers'. *American Sociological Review* 40, no. 1 (1976): 1–11.

Higgypop. 'Most Haunted at 30 East Drive – Part One'. *Higgypop Paranormal*, 18 October 2015. https://www.higgypop.com/news/30-east-drive-part-one/.

Higgypop. 'Was Karl from Most Haunted Really Dragged Upstairs by the Pontefract Poltergeist?.' *Higgypop Paranormal*, 3 November 2015. https://www.higgypop.com/news/karl-dragged-upstairs/.

Hill, Annette. *Paranormal Media*. New York: Routledge, 2011.

Hill, Annette. 'Paranormal Cultural Practices'. In: *The Ashgate Research Companion to Paranormal Cultures*, ed. Olu Jensen and Sally R. Munt, 65–77. Surrey, England: Ashgate, 2013.

Hood, Ralph W., Peter C. Hill and W. Paul Williamson. *The Psychology of Religious Fundamentalism*. New York: Guilford, 2005.

Holiday, F. W. *The Dragon & the Disc*. New York: W.W. Norton, 1973.

Holiday, F. W. *The Great Orm of Loch Ness*. London: Faber & Faber, 1968.

Holiday, Ted. *The Goblin Universe*. St. Paul, Minnesota: Llewellyn, 1986.

Holloway, Julian. 'Legend-Tripping in Spooky Places: Ghost Tourism and Infrastructures of Enchantment'. *Environment and Planning D: Society and Space* 28 (2010), 618–37.

Hopkins, Budd. *Missing Time: Documented Stories of People Kidnapped by UFOs and Then Returned with Their Memories Erased*. New York: Richard Marek, 1981.

Houran, James, Sharon A. Hill, Everett D. Haynes and Ursual A. Bielski. 'Paranormal Tourism: A Market Study of an Interactive Approach to Space Activation and Monetization'. *Cornell Hospitality Quarterly* 61, no.3 (2020): 287–311.

Houran, James, Rense Lange and Brian Laythe. 'Understanding Consumer Enchantment via Paranormal Tourism: Part II – Preliminary Rasch Validation'. *Cornell Hospitality Quarterly* 63, no. 2 (2022): 216–30.

Howard-Bury, Charles K. *Mount Everest: The Reconnaissance, 1921*. New York: Longmans, Green, 1922.
Hutton, Ronald. *Pagan Britain*. London: Yale University Press, 2013.
Iannaccone, Laurence R. 'Risk, Rationality and Religious Portfolios'. *Economic Inquiry* 23 (1985): 285–95.
Iannaccone, Laurence R. 'A Formal Model of Church and Sect'. *American Journal of Sociology* 94 (1988): 241–68.
Iannaccone, Laurence R. 'Sacrifice and Stigma: Reducing Free Riding in Cults, Communes and Other Collectives'. *Journal of Political Economy* (April 1992): 271–91.
Icke, David. *The Biggest Secret: The Book That Will Change the World*. Scottsdale, Arizona: Bridge of Love, 1999.
Icke, David. *Truth Vibrations: From TV Celebrity to World Visionary*. 3rd edn. Dublin: Gill & MacMillan, 2014.
Icke, David. *The Dream: The Extraordinary Revelation of Who We Are and Where We Are*. Isle of Wight: David Icke Books, 2023.
Inglis, David, and Mary Holmes. 'Highland and Other Haunts: Ghosts in Scottish Tourism'. *Annals of Tourism Research* 30, no. 1 (2003): 50–63.
Ironside, Rachael. 'The Allure of Dark Tourism: Legend Tripping and Ghost Seeking in Dark Places'. In: *The Supernatural in Society, Culture and History*, ed. Dennis Waskul and Marc Eaton, 95–115. Philadelphia, PA: Temple University Press, 2018.
Izzard, Ralph. *The Abominable Snowman Adventure*. London: Hodder & Stoughton, 1955.
Johnson, Benton. 'On Church and Sect'. *American Sociological Review* 28, no. 4 (1963): 539–49.
Joosse, Paul. 'Becoming a God: Max Weber and the Social Construction of Charisma'. *Journal of Classical Sociology* 14, no. 3 (2014): 266–83.
Joyner, Lisa. 'Man Spots Beast of Exmoor as "Big Cat" Seen on Dog Walk'. *Country Living*, 7 January 2022. https://www.countryliving.com/uk/wildlife/countryside/a38691826/beast-of-exmoor-big-cat-spotted/.
Kaulback, Ronald. *Salween*. London: Hodder & Stoughton, 1983.
Keel, John. *The Eighth Tower*. New York: Signet, 1977.
Kellett, Russell. *Alien Invasion Wales: The Berwyn Mountain UFO Cover Up*. Self-published, 2021.
Kellett, Russell. *Russell Kellett Is E.T. Rider*. Self-published, 2023.
King, George. *The Twelve Blessings: The Cosmic Concept as Given by the Master Jesus*. London: Aetherius Press, 1961.
King, George. 'A Brief Description of Operation Prayer Power'. *Cosmic Voice* 1, nos. 5–8 (1980): 14–15.
King, George. *Jesus Comes Again: A Physical Meeting with Master Jesus*. Hollywood: Aetherius Society, 1984.
King, George, with Richard Lawrence. *Realize Your Inner Potential*. 3rd edn. Hollywood: Aetherius Press, 2016.
Klinkenbergh, Monique, and Andreas Müller. *Crop Circles: The Exhibition*. Pewsey: Crop Circle Centre & Exhibition, 2017.
Konda, Thomas Milan. *Conspiracies of Conspiracies: How Delusions Have Overrun America*. Chicago: University of Chicago Press, 2019.
Kraft, Siv Ellen. '"To Mix of Not to Mix": Syncretism/Anti-syncretism in the History of Theosophy'. *Numen* 49, no. 2 (2002): 142–77.

Lang, Fiona. 'The Cannich Puma: Felicity, Alien Big Cat of the Scottish Highlands'. *Waithe and Wonder*, 27 August 2013. http://fionalang.blogspot.com/2013/08/the-cannich-puma-felicity-alien-big-cat.html.

Lantian, Anthony, Virginie Bagneux, Sylvain Delouvee and Nicolas Gauvrit. 'Maybe a Free Thinker but Not a Critical One: High Conspiracy Belief Is Associated with Low Critical Thinking Ability'. *Applied Cognitive Psychology* 35, no. 3 (2021): 674–84.

Lavin, Melissa F. 'On Spiritualist Workers: Healing and Divining Through Tarot and the Metaphysical'. *Journal of Contemporary Ethnography* 50, no. 3 (2021): 317–40.

Lawrence, Richard. '50 Years of Operation Prayer Power'. [Audio podcast]. *Aetherius Society* Podcast, 20 June 2023. Retrieved from https://www.aetherius.org/50-years-of-operation-prayer-power/.

Legerski, Elizabeth, Marie Cornwall and Brock O'Neil. 'Changing Locus of Control: Steelworkers Adjusting to Forced Unemployment'. *Social Forces* 84 (2006): 1521–38.

Leopold, Anita M. 'The Architecture of Syncretism: A Methodological Illustration of the Dynamics of Syncretism'. *Historical Reflections* 27, no. 3 (2001): 401–23.

Lewis, James R., ed. *Encyclopedic Sourcebook of UFO Religions*. Amherst, NY: Prometheus, 2003.

Lewis, Kayleigh. 'BMG Halloween Poll: A Third of Brits Believe in Ghosts, Spirits or Other Types of Paranormal Activity'. *BMG Research*, 30 October 2017.

Lewis, Tyson, and Richard Kahn. 'The Reptoid Hypothesis: Utopian and Dystopian Representational Motifs in David Icke's Alien Conspiracy Theory'. *Utopian Studies* 16, no. 1 (2005): 45–74.

Mackal, Roy. *The Monsters of Loch Ness*. Chicago: Swallow, 1976.

Mansson, Maria. 'Mediatized Tourism'. *Annals of Tourism Research* 38, no. 4 (2011): 1634–52.

Marotta, Mario. 'A Disenchanted World: Max Weber on Magic and Modernity'. *Journal of Classical Sociology* 24, no. 3 (2023), 224–42.

Marske, Charles E. 'Durkheim's "Cult of the Individual" and the Moral Reconstitution of Society'. *Sociological Theory* 5, no. 1 (1987): 1–14.

Martin, David, and Alastair Boyd. *Nessie – the Surgeon's Photo Exposed*. East Barnet: Martin & Boyd, 1999.

Martin-Jones, David. 'Film Tourism as Heritage Tourism: Scotland, Diaspora and *The Da Vinci Code* (2006)'. *New Review of Film and Television Studies* 12, no. 2 (2014): 156–77.

Marx, Karl. *Critique of Hegel's 'Philosophy of Right'*. London: Cambridge University Press, 1977.

Mathews, Liam, Tim Surette, Allison Picurro and Kelly Connolly, 'Netflix Top 10 Shows and Movies', *TV Guide*, 15 November, 2022.

McClure, Paul K. 'Something Besides Monotheism: Sociotheological Boundary Work Among the Spiritual, but Not Religious'. *Poetics* 62 (2017): 53–65.

McCorristine, Shane. *Spectres of the Self: Thinking about Ghosts and Ghost-seeing in England, 1750–1920*. New York: Cambridge University Press, 2010.

McEwan, Graham J. *Mystery Animals of Britain and Ireland*. London: Robert Hale, 1986.

McLeod, Michael. *Anatomy of a Beast: Obsession and Myth on the Trail of Bigfoot*. Berkeley: University of California Press, 2009.

McKune, Kara. 'Pontefract House Is Home to 'Most Terrifying Ghost in UK''. *Wakefield Express*, 15 October 2022.

Mcmanus, Leigh. 'UK Is "Running out of Ghosts" as Old Spirits Dying Off, Paranormal Expert Says'. *Daily Star*, 27 May 2024. https://www.dailystar.co.uk/news/latest-news/uk-running-out-ghosts-old-32900960.

McMaster, Geoff. '"*Ancient Apocalypse*" Is More Fiction than Fact, Say Experts'. *Folio*, 14 December 2022. https://www.ualberta.ca/en/folio/2022/12/ancient-apocalypse-is-more-fiction-than-fact-say-experts.html.

Meaden, G. Terence. 'Further News on the Circles Effect from CERES'. In: *Circles from the Sky*, ed. Terence Meaden, 125–31. London: Souvenir Press, 1991.

Mercadante, Linda A. *Belief Without Borders: Inside the Minds of the Spiritual But Not Religious*. New York: Oxford University Press, 2014.

Meurger, Michel, and Claude Gagnon. *Lake Monster Traditions: A Cross-cultural Analysis*. London: Fortean Tomes, 1988.

Michel, Aimé. *Flying Saucers and the Straight-Line Mystery*. New York: S.G. Phillips, 1958.

Michell, John. *The View Over Atlantis*. London: Garnstone, 1969.

Michell, John, and Allan Brown. *How the World Is Made: The Story of Creation According to Sacred Geometry*. Rochester, Vermont: Inner Traditions, 2012.

Miles, Geoff (Director). 'Episode #11.49' [TV Series Episode]. *Wogan*. BBC One, 29 April 1991.

Molle, Andrea, and Christopher D. Bader. 'Paranormal Science from America to Italy: A Case of Cultural Homogenisation'. In: *The Ashgate Research Companion to Paranormal Cultures*, ed. Olu Jenzen and Sally R. Munt, 121–38. London: Routledge, 2013.

Monroe, Robert A. *Far Journeys*. New York: Doubleday, 1985.

Moore, Joanne. 'Pub Landlord Who Turned Hamlet into Croppie Mecca Dies'. *Wiltshire Times*, 29 July 2020. https://www.wiltshiretimes.co.uk/news/18614529.publican-turned-barge-honeystreet-crop-circle-hub-dies/.

Murdie, Alan. 'When the Lights Went Out'. *Fortean Times* 293 (October 2012): 29–37.

Myers, Bill, and David Wimbish. *The Dark Side of the Supernatural: Uncovering God's Truth*. Grand Rapids, MI: Zondervan, 2012.

Neville, Stu. 'The Bigfeet of Britain'. *Fortean Times* 425 (December 2002): 30–6.

Nickell, Joe, and John F. Fischer. 'The Crop-Circle Phenomenon: An Investigative Report'. *Skeptical Inquirer* 16, no. 2 (1992): 136–49.

Norman, Mark. *Black Dog Folklore*. London: Troy Books, 2015.

Office for National Statistics. 2022. *Statistical Bulletin: Religion, England and Wales: Census 2021*. https://www.ons.gov.uk/peoplepopulationandcommunity/culturalidentity/religion/bulletins/religionenglandandwales/census2021.

Oliver, Maria I., Nicky Pearson, Nicola Coe, and David Gunnell. 'Help-Seeking Behaviour in Men and Women with Common Mental Health Problems: Cross-sectional Study'. *British Journal of Psychiatry* 186 (2005): 297–301.

Orenstein, Alan. 'Religion and Paranormal Belief'. *Journal for the Scientific Study of Religion* 41, no. 2 (2002): 301–11.

Pargament, Kenneth I. *The Psychology of Religion and Coping: Theory Research, Practice*. New York: Guilford, 1997.

Park, Jerry Z., and Joseph O. Baker. 'What Would Jesus Buy: American Consumption of Religious and Spiritual Material Goods'. *Journal for the Scientific Study of Religion* 46, no. 4 (2007): 501–17.

Pedreño-Peñalver, Carmen, Irene Huertas-Valdivia and Alicia Orea-Giner. 'An Exploratory Study of the Future Paranormal Tourist Experience on Ghost Tours'. *Journal of Tourism Futures* 10, no. 3 (2023): 524–38.

Penninston, James W., and Gary Osborn. *The Rendlesham Enigma: Book 1: Timeline*. Self-published, 2019.
Phares, Jerry. 'Locus of Control'. In: *The Corsini Encyclopedia of Psychology and Behavioral Science, vol. 2*, ed. W. E. Craighead and C. B. Nemeroff, 889–91. New York: John Wiley and Sons, 2001.
Phillips, Graham, and Martin Keatman. 1983. *The Green Stone*. Jersey: Neville Spearman, 1983.
Pickering, W. S. F. *Durkheim's Sociology of Religion: Themes and Theories*. London: Routledge, 1984.
Pike, Andrew. *The Rendlesham File: Britain's Roswell?* Pontefract: Flying Disk Press, 2017.
Pike, Sarah M. *New Age and Neopagan Religions in America*. New York: Columbia University Press, 2004.
Pine, B. Joseph II, and James H. Gilmore. 'The Experience Economy: Past, Present and Future'. In: *Handbook on the Experience Economy*, ed. Jon Sundbo and Flemming Sorensen, 21–44. Cheltenham: Edward Elgar, 2013.
Pope, Nick, John Burroughs and Jim Penninston. *Encounter in Rendlesham Forest: The Inside Story of the World's Best-Documented UFO Incident*. New York: St. Martin's Press, 2015.
Possamai, Adam. *Religion and Popular Culture: A Hyper-real Testament*. Brussels: Peter Lang, 2005.
Possamai, Adam (ed.). *Handbook of Hyper-real Religions*. Leiden: Brill, 2012.
Possamai, Adam, and Murray Lee. 'Hyper-real Religions: Fear, Anxiety, and Late-Modern Religious Innovation'. *Journal of Sociology* 47, no. 3 (2011): 227–42.
Prince, Ruth, and David Riches. *The New Age in Glastonbury: The Construction of Religious Movements*. New York: Berghahn, 2000.
Redfern, Nick. *Three Men Seeking Monsters*. New York: Pocket, 2004.
Redfern, Nick. *Man-Monkey: In Search of the British Bigfoot*. North Devon: CFZ, 2007.
Redfern, Nick. *Wildman: The Monstrous and Mysterious Saga of the 'British Bigfoot'*. North Devon: CFZ Press, 2012
Rice, Tom W. 'Believe It or Not: Religious and Other Paranormal Beliefs in the United States'. *Journal for the Scientific Study of Religion* 42, no. 1 (2003): 95–106.
Riesebrodt, Martin. '*Charisma* in Max Weber's Sociology of Religion'. *Religion* 29, no. 1 (2011): 1–14.
Rhodes, Ron. *Alien Obsession*. Eugene, OR: Harvest House, 1998.
Robertson, David. 'David Icke's Reptilian Thesis and the Development of New Age Theodicy'. *International Journal for the Study of New Religions* 4 (2013): 27–47.
Robinson, Andrew, and Claire Gilbody-Dickerson. 'Robbie Williams "Abducted by Aliens" Says UFO Researcher Who Saw Him on Spaceship'. *Mirror*, 18 November 2020. https://www.mirror.co.uk/news/weird-news/robbie-williams-abducted-aliens-says-23028275.
Roskams, Michael. *Religion, England and Wales: Census 2021*. Office for National Statistics, 29 November 2022. https://www.ons.gov.uk/peoplepopulationandcommunity/culturalidentity/religion/bulletins/religionenglandandwales/census2021.
Ross, Catherine, and John Mirowsky. 'Households, Employment, and the Sense of Control'. *Social Psychology Quarterly* 55 (2002): 217–35.
Rothstein, Mikael. 'Mahatmas in Space: The Ufological Turn and Mythological Materiality of Post-World War II Theosophy'. In: *Handbook of the Theosophical Current*, ed. Olav Hammer and Mikael, 217–36. Rothstein. Leiden: Brill, 2013.
Rothstein, Mikael. 'Hagiography and Text in the Aetherius Society. Aspects of the Social Construction of a Religious Leader'. In: *Sects, Cults, and New Religions: Critical*

Concepts in Sociology, ed. Carole M. Cusack and Danielle Kirby, 165–94. New York: Routledge, 2014.

Rothstein, Mikael. 'Rituals and Ritualization in New Religions Movements'. In: *The Oxford Handbook of New Religious Movements*, ed. James R. Lewis and Inga Tøllefsen, 335–45. New York: Oxford University Press, 2016.

Saliba, John A. 'The World Is a Dangerous Place – The Worldview of the Aetherius Society'. *Marburg Journal of Religion* 4, no. 2 (1999): 1–19.

Saliba, John A. 'The Earth Is a Dangerous Place: The Worldview of the Aetherius Society'. In: *The Encyclopedic Sourcebook of UFO Religions*, ed. James R. Lewis, 123–42. Amherst, NY: Prometheus, 2003.

Salla, Michael. *Exopolitics: Political Implications of the Extraterrestrial Presence*. Tempe, AZ: Dandelion, 2004.

Sanderson, Ivan T. *Abominable Snowmen: Legend Come to Life*. New York: Chilton, 1961.

Saunders, Patrick. 'Who or What Is Black Shuck?', *Norfolk Distillery*, 22 July 2024. https://www.blackshuckltd.co.uk/who-or-what-is-black-shuck.

Schieman, Scott, and Alex Bierman. 'Religious Activities and Changes in the Sense of Divine Control'. *Sociology of Religion* 68, no. 4 (2007): 361–81.

Schieman, Scott, Kim Nguyen and Diana Elliot. 'Religiosity, Socioeconomic Status, and the Sense of Mastery'. *Social Psychology Quarterly* 66, no. 3 (2003): 202–21.

Schieman, Scott, and Gabriele Plickert. 'How Knowledge Is Power: Education and the Sense of Control'. *Social Forces* 87, no. 1 (2008): 153–83.

Schieman, Scott, Tetyana Pudrovska, Leonard I. Pearlin and Christopher G. Ellison. 'The Sense of Divine Control and Psychological Distress: Variations by Race and Socioeconomic Status'. *Journal for the Scientific Study of Religion* 45, no. 4 (2006): 529–49.

Scribner, Scott, and Gregory Wheeler. 'Cosmic Intelligences and Their Terrestrial Channel'. In: *The Encyclopedic Sourcebook of UFO Religions*, ed. James R. Lewis, 157–71. Amherst, NY: Prometheus, 2003.

Shiels, Tony. 'Doc'. *Monstrum! A Wizard's Tale*. North Devon: CFZ Press, 2011.

Shumaker, Wayne. *The Occult Sciences in the Renaissance: A Study in Intellectual Patterns*. Berkeley: University of California Press, 1972.

Sitchin, Zecharia. *The 12th Planet*. New York: Avon, 1976.

Silva, Tony. 'Masculinity, Femininity, and Reported Paranormal Beliefs'. *Journal for the Scientific Study of Religion* 62, no. 3 (2023): 709–22.

Sidgwick, Henry. 'A Census of Hallucinations'. *The New Review* (January 1891): 52–9.

Sidgwick, Henry. 'Report on the Census of Hallucinations'. *Proceedings of the Society for Psychical Research* 26 (1894): 25–394.

Sigalow, Emily. 'Towards a Sociological Framework of Religious Syncretism in the United States'. *Journal of the American Academy of Religion* 84, no. 4 (2016): 1029–55.

Silva, Tony, and Ashley Woody. 'Supernatural Sociology: Beliefs by Race/Ethnicity, Gender, and Education'. *Socius* 8 (2022): 1–18.

Sixsmith, Edmund. 'The Megalithic Story of Professor Alexander Thom'. *Significance* 6, no. 2 (2009): 94–6.

Smith, Brian. 'The Real Story Behind the Shetland Wulver'. *Shetland Museum & Archives*, 18 May 2021. https://www.shetlandmuseumandarchives.org.uk/blog/the-real-story-behind-the-shetland-wulver.

Smith, Simon G. 'Opening a Channel to the Stars: The Origins and Development of the Aetherius Society'. In: *UFO Religions*, ed. Christopher Partridge, 84–102. New York: Routledge, 2003.

Smith, Tara Blue Moon. 'Esoteric Themes in David Icke's Conspiracy Theories'. *Journal for the Academic Study of Religion* 30, no. 3 (2017): 281–302.
Sointu, Eeva, and Linda Woodhead. 'Spirituality, Gender, and Expressive Selfhood'. *Journal for the Scientific Study of Religion* 47, no. 2 (2008): 259–76.
Sparks, Glenn G. 'The Relationship between Paranormal Beliefs and Religious Beliefs'. *Skeptical Inquirer* 25 (2001): 50–6.
Spring, Marianna. 'Twitter Bans David Icke Over Covid Misinformation'. *BBC News*, 4 November 2020. https://www.bbc.com/news/technology-54804240.
Stark, Rodney. 'Why Religious Movements Succeed or Fail: A Revised General Model'. *Journal of Contemporary Religion* 11, no. 2 (1996): 133–46.
Stark, Rodney. *One True God: Historical Consequences of Monotheism*. New Jersey: Princeton University Press, 2001.
Stark, Rodney. *What Americans Really Believe*. Waco, TX: Baylor University Press, 2008.
Stark, Rodney, and William S. Bainbridge. 'Of Churches, Sects, and Cults: Preliminary Concepts for a Theory of Religious Movements'. *Journal for the Scientific Study of Religion* 18, no. 2 (1979): 117–31.
Stewart, Charles. 'Syncretism and Its Synonyms: Reflections on Cultural Mixture'. *Diacritics* 29, no. 3 (1999): 40–62.
Stewart, Charles. 'Relocating Syncretism in Social Science Discourse'. In: *Syncretism in Religion: A Reader*, ed. Anita M. Leopold and Jeppe S. Jensen, 264–85. London: Equinox, 2004.
Storm, Jason Ānanda Josephson. *The Myth of Disenchantment: Magic, Modernity, and the Birth of the Human Sciences*. Chicago: University of Chicago Press, 2017.
Stuart, Keith. 'Pushing Buttons: Why I'm Mourning the Death of the True Arcade Game'. *Guardian*, 27 September 2023.
Swarbrick, Lizzie. 'Rosslyn Chapel: Templar Pseudo-history, 'Symbology,' and the Far-Right'. In: *The Modern Memory of Military-Religious Orders*, ed. Rory MacLellan, 21–43. New York: Routledge, 2022.
Taira, Teemu. 'The Category of "Invented Religion": A New Opportunity for Studying Discourses on "Religion"'. *Culture and Religion* 14, no. 4 (2013): 477–93.
Taves, Ann. *Fits, Trances, and Visions: Experiencing Religion and Explaining Experience from Wesley to James*. Princeton, NJ: Princeton University Press, 1999.
Taves, Ann. 'The Power of the Paranormal (and Extraordinary)'. *History of Religions* 53, no. 2 (2013): 205–11.
Taylor, Charles. *The Ethics of Authenticity*. Cambridge, MA: Harvard University Press, 1991.
Taylor, Charles. *A Secular Age*. Cambridge, MA: Harvard University Press, 2007.
Thalbourne, Michael A., and Peter S. Delin. 'A New Instrument for Measuring the Sheep-Goat Variables: Its Psychometric Properties and Factor Structure'. *Journal of the Society for Psychical Research* 59 (1993): 172–86.
30 East Drive OWNER'S PAGE. *Home* [Facebook page]. Facebook. Retrieved 5 February 2025, from https://www.facebook.com/groups/30EastDriveOwners.
Thorslev, Jr., Peter L. 'The Wild Man's Revenge'. In: *The Wildman Within: An Image in Western Thought from the Renaissance to Romanticism*, ed. Edward Dudley and Maximillian E. Novak, 281–308. Pittsburgh, PA: University of Pittsburgh Press, 2010.
Tobacyk, Jerome J. 'A Revised Paranormal Belief Scale'. *International Journal of Transpersonal Studies* 23, no. 1 (2004): 94–8.

Tobacyk, Jerome, and Gary Milford. 'Belief in Paranormal Phenomena: Assessment Instrument Development and Implications for Personality Functioning'. *Journal of Personality and Social Psychology* 44, no. 5 (1983): 1029–37.
Trice, Harrison M., and Janice M. Beyer. 'Charisma and Its Routinization in Two Social Movement Organizations'. In: *Research in Organizational Behavior*, volume 8, ed. Barry M. Staw and L. L. Cummings, 113–64. Greenwich, CT: JAI Press, 1986.
Victor, Jeffrey S. *Satanic Panic: The Creation of a Contemporary Legend*. Chicago, IL: Open Court Press, 1993.
Voas, David, and Steve Bruce. 'Religion: Identity, Behaviour and Belief over Two Decades'. In: *British Social Attitudes: The 36th Report*, ed. John Curtice, Elizabeth Clery, Jane Perry, Miranda Phillips and Nilufer Rahim, 17–44. London: National Centre for Social Research, 2019.
Wallis, Roy. 'The Aetherius Society: A Case Study in the Formation of a Mystagogic Congregation'. *Sociological Review* 22, no 2 (1974): 27–44.
Wallis, Roy. 'Ideology, Authority, and the Development of Cultic Movements'. *Social Research* 41, no. 2 (1974): 299–327.
Wallis, Roy. 'The Social Construction of Charisma'. *Social Compass* 29, no. 1 (1982): 25–39.
Ward, Charlotte, and David Voas. 'The Emergence of Conspirituality'. *Journal of Contemporary Religion* 26, no. 1 (2011): 103–21.
Warren, Larry, and Peter Robbins. *A First-Hand Account of the Rendlesham Forest UFO Incident, Its Cover-Up, and Investigation*. New York: Cosimo-on-Demand, 2005.
Weber, Max. *Economy and Society: An Outline of Interpretive Sociology*, ed. Guenther Roth and Claus Wittich. Berkeley: University of California Press, 2013.
Wendt, Douglas, and Kevin Shafer. 'Gender and Attitudes about Mental Health Help Seeking: Results from National Data'. *Health & Social Work* 41, no. 1 (2016): e20–e28.
Weston, Gavin, Justin Woodman, Helen Cornish and Natalie Djohari. 'Spectral Cities: Death and Living Memories in the Dark Tourism of British Ghost Walks'. *Urbanities* 9, no. 2 (2019): 36–51.
White, Hayden. 'The Forms of Wildness: Archaeology of an Idea' In: *The Wildman Within: An Image in Western Thought from the Renaissance to Romanticism*, ed. Edward Dudley and Maximillian E. Novak, 3–38. Pittsburgh, PA: University of Pittsburgh Press, 2010.
Wilson, Colin. *The Occult: A History*. New York: Random House, 1971.
Wilson, Colin. *Mysteries: An Investigation into the Occult, the Paranormal, and the Supernatural*. New York: G. P. Putnam, 1978.
Wilson, Colin. *Poltergeist! A Study in Destructive Haunting*. New York: Putnam, 1982.
Wood, Mathew. *Possession, Power and the New Age: Ambiguities of Authority in Neoliberal Societies*. London: Rutledge University Press, 2007.
Woodhead, Linda. 'Why So Many Women in Holistic Spirituality? A Puzzle Revisited'. In: *A Sociology of Spirituality*, ed. Kieran Flanagan and Peter C. Jupp, 115–25. Aldershot: Ashgate, 2007.
Woodhead, Linda. 'The Rise of "No Religion" in Britain: The Emergence of a New Cultural Majority'. *Journal of the British Academy* 4 (2016): 245–61.
Wright, Daniel and William Mackenzie. 'Encountering UFOs and Aliens in the Tourism Industry'. *Journal of Tourism Futures* 8, no 1 (2022): 7–23.
Wordsworth, William. 'Composed in Roslin chapel during a Storm', *Verse*. [1803]. https://verse.press/poem/composed-in-roslin-chapel-during-a-storm-5590.
Wuthnow, Robert. *Experimentation in American Religion*. Berkeley: University of California Press, 1978.

INDEX

30 East Drive 1–2, 7, 11, 55–61, 63–7, 69–74, 77–8, 80–3, 85, 88, 102, 173–4, 178

abduction/abductee 4, 10, 127, 130–2, 134
Aetherius Society, The 10, 17, 152–5, 157, 159–60, 171–2, 174
Alice Box 1–2, 57, 64–6, 70, 71, 79, 173–4
alien(s)
  ancient 33, 48, 49, 122, 123, 126, 135, 139, 141, 142, 169
  belief in 7, 10, 47, 127, 134, 135, 142, 144, 151, 161, 163
  conspiracy 117, 134, 141, 142, 144
    marketplace, the 145–7
  face 113
  modern 9, 49, 135, 142
  races 145, 160
    'Anunnaki' 139
    'Dragos' 131, 132
    'Grey's' 132
    Horse Headed 'Egyptian Pharaoh' 133
    'Reptilians' 132
    TWBAs (Tall White Bald Aliens) 131
  spacecraft 46, 123, 147
  technology 131
  visitation 2, 4, 8, 10, 47, 48, 115, 127, 132, 134, 135, 142, 143, 147, 152
Ancient Aliens (TV) 123, 169
Ancient Civilisations 2, 8, 48, 119–20
Andrew Collins 123, 125–6
  Black Alchemist, The (1988)
  Second Coming, The (1993)
  Seventh Sword, The (1992)
  Sword and the Stone, The (1982)
angels 20, 111, 151, 152, 161–3, 168, 171
asceticism 18
Astral Realm, The 139, 141
astrology 3, 14, 15, 20, 21, 23, 32, 33, 40, 120, 143, 167, 179
  Robert Bauval 120

Atlantis, *City of* 47, 48, 117, 126, 163
Atlantis Bookshop, The 31
Audience Participation Phenomena 78–83
aura(s) 4, 11, 14, 17, 19, 23, 26, 28, 36
Avebury Stone Circles 95, 101, 102, 122–124

Battery (Prayer) 154–9
Baylor Religion Survey 167
Betty Shine 136
Bible, The 17, 38, 50, 53, 148, 149, 159, 167
Big Cats (ABC's) 6, 7, 33, 42–5, 49, 51, 115, 130, 135
  'Beast of Bodmin Moor' 43
  'Beast of Buchan' 43
  'Beast of Exmoor' 43
  'Beast of Ryedale, the' 130, 134
  'Black Shuck, The' 6, 8, 45, 95
  Cotswolds Big Cat 43
  'Daimon' Cats 44–5
  'Felicity' 43
  'Surrey Puma' 43
Bigfoot 2, 6, 7, 19, 33, 40–3, 45, 49, 52, 134, 135, 163, 175
  Abominable Snowman, The 4, 6, 33, 39, 41, 49, 51, 116
  American 49
  British Bigfoot 6, 17, 19, 36, 43, 49, 179
  British Bigfoot Association, The 41
  British Bigfoot Research 41
  Irish Bigfoot Research Org, The 41
  Researchers 45
  see Wildman (UK)
  Yeti 39–42, 51, 135, 175
Black Dogs 45, 125
Black Monk of Pontefract, The 7, 54–8, 66–74, 77–85, 89, 98, 173–4, 179
  see also 'Mr. Nobody'
Blythburgh Church 6–8, 45
Book of the Damned, The (Charles Fort) 16
Bounded Affinity Theory 151, 162, 164, 166, 171, 172

British Religion in Numbers (BRIN) 3, 68, 69

CASPAR (Chapman and Sheffield Paranormal and Religion Survey) 3–4, 33, 38, 42, 50, 52, 62, 69, 74–6, 83, 107–8, 135–6, 142, 145–8, 164, 172, 175
 and IPSOS-Mori UK 101
 see also survey data
 see data analysis
Cat Country (Di Francis) 43–4
Centre for Fortean Zoology of Devon 41
Census, UK (2001–21) 2, 29–30, 86, 94, 177
 Table 1.1 30
channelling 5, 14, 15, 25, 103, 117
Colin Wilson 73, 81, 83
 Mysteries: An Investigation into the Occult, the Paranormal, and the Supernatural (1978) 67
 Poltergeist! A Study in Destructive Haunting (1981) 67
 The Occult: A History (1971) 67
Conspiracy Theories 4, 9, 11, 110, 117, 137–44, 147–9, 166–71, 176, 178
Continuum Attractions 97–8, 100
cosmic consciousness 117
Covid-19 Pandemic 137, 139, 140, 144, 147–8
crop circles 4, 6, 8–9, 47–9, 105–19, 126, 130, 135, 178
 '*A Night of Crop Circling*' 116
 Barge Inn, The 109–10
 Crop Circle Exhibition and Centre, The (CCEC) 105, 109–11, 114, 116, 118
 'croppies' 4, 126
  Austen Lynn 109–14, 116, 118–19
  Barry Reynolds 116, 119
  Bart Uytterthaegen 116
  Kathy Mingo 116, 117
  Monique Klinkenbergh 109–14, 116
  Roeland Beljon 116
 Circular Evidence (Delgado and Andrew) 1989 107, 108
 Doug Bower and Dave Chorley 107, 108
 Milk Hill 112, 113, 116
 '*The Galaxy*' 112–13, 116
 Silbury Hill 118, 123
 The Mowing Devil (1678) 106

Cryptids
 see Big Cats (ABC's)
 Belief in 7, 19, 44, 45, 47, 50–3, 115
 see Bigfoot
 Each-Uisge 38
 see faeries
 'Green Children of Woolpit' 8
 Griffin 44
 Kelpie 38, 98, 179
 see Loch Ness
 Owlman 44
 Selkie 98
 Werewolves 44
  Cannock Chase Werewolf 6, 44
  'Old Stinker of Hull' 44, 189
  Shetland Wulver 45, 189
'Cultic Milieu' 15, 34, 154
cults 103, 137–40
curses 4, 47, 49, 51, 115–16, 135

Dangerous Wild Animals Act (1976) 43
data analysis (CASPAR)
 age 7, 51, 54–5, 74, 76, 77, 82, 95, 148–9, 160, 176
 education 32, 36, 47–9, 51–3, 74, 94, 148
 ethnic identity/minorities 47, 48, 49, 53, 94
 see gender
 marital status 32, 49, 50, 74, 108, 148–9
 religious affiliation/identity 2, 53, 69, 77, 148–9, 160, 164, 176
 socio-economic class 32, 47–9, 52–3, 74, 94–5, 137, 148, 156
David Daegling 40
David Icke 9–10, 130, 136–50, 171, 176, 178
 Biggest Secret, The (1999) 139
 The Dream (2023) 140–1
 '*Ickonic Media*' 137
 It Doesn't Have to Be Like This (1990) 136
Da Vinci Code, The (Dan Brown) 11, 167–71
demonic/demons 6, 40, 47, 55, 58–9, 66, 82, 83, 110, 139, 163
Devil, The 4, 10, 17, 20, 45, 106, 111, 140, 169

Devizes, Wiltshire 105, 108, 112, 116
Discovery *Paranormalism* 6, 18–19, 32–36, 49–51, 54, 114, 117, 126
divination 17, 19-20, 23–4, 29, 42, 179
  see tarot
  see astrology
dowsing 47–9, 63, 119, 121–3, 135, 174

earth mysteries 7, 48, 115, 119, 121–2, 126
economies
  experience 95, 175, 178–80
  night-time 86, 95
  see Marketplace, The 'Paranormal'
EMF meters 63, 87, 90
Émile Durkheim 29, 63, 103, 159
energy(ies)
  earth 31, 107–9, 111, 113, 119–24, 132, 174
  incompatible 35
  'Loosh' 140–1
  magical 113
  negative 14, 17, 25–8, 64
  positive 13, 26–8, 63, 64
  psychic 6, 58–9, 61–2, 66, 67, 82, 125, 159
  spiritual 81–3, 154–9
  universal 25–7
Enlightenment *Paranormalism* 6, 13, 18–25, 28–9, 32–6, 49, 51, 54, 114, 117–18, 24, 126
epistemic pluralism 110, 116, 123, 125
'Esotericism' (Wouter Hanegraaff) 117
E.S.P. (Extra Sensory Perception) 15, 19, 53, 125
Exmoor National Park 43
'exopolitics' 134
extraterrestrial(s)
  see aliens

faeries 4, 8, 47, 48–9, 95–6, 98, 110–11, 115, 135, 175
fortune tellers 23, 32–3, 49, 51
Freemasons 166, 168–71
F. W. Holiday 45–6
  Dragon & the Disc, The (1973) 46
  Orm of Loch Ness, The (1968) 45

gender 7, 31–4, 48, 49, 51–4, 108, 137, 148
George Adamski 152

Flying Saucers Farewell (1961) 152
Flying Saucers Have Landed (1953) 152
Inside the Spaceships (1955) 152
George King 10, 152–6, 159, 160
  see Aetherius Society, The
  Master Jesus 154, 155
  The Twelve Blessings (1958) 10, 154, 157
ghost(s)
  belief in 2–5, 7, 8, 13, 47–55, 68–9, 74, 76–7, 82, 149, 175
  see Black Monk of Pontefract, The
  'Emily/Emma' 81
  hauntings 7, 17, 55–8, 60, 67, 70, 74, 79, 83, 86, 135, 163, 179
  hunters/investigators 1, 6, 7, 19, 46–7, 55–64, 73, 81, 85, 173–4, 177–8
  see also Retford Ghost Hunters
  see 'Mr Nobody'
  tourism 85–94, 100
  tours
    Haunted Happenings 85
    Haunted Houses UK 85
    Haunted Rooms 85
    JDH Books Paranormal 85
    Veritas Paranormal 85
  walks (hunts) 8, 55, 87–95, 101–2, 177, 178
  'Sinister Side of Stratford Walking Tour' 89
  Stratford Ghost Walk 89
Gigantopithecus 40, 45
  Bernard Heuvelmans 39
Gnosticism 141–4
  conspiratorial 138, 171
god 2, 4, 11, 17, 48, 50, 53, 111, 137, 162–3
Godalming, Surrey 43
Graham Hancock 121, 123, 126
  Fingerprints of the Gods (1995) 119
  The Mars Mystery (1999) 119–20
  Supernatural: Meetings with the Ancient Teachers of Mankind (2005) 120
Graham Phillips and Martin Keatman
  Eye of the Fire, The (1988) 125
  Green Stone, The (1984) 125
Green Man, The 168, 170–1, 179

Halloween 90–1
healing
  acupuncture and massage 25

aura(s) 4, 11, 14, 17, 19, 23, 26, 28, 36
  crystal 5, 13–14, 25–9, 32, 33, 155, 157
  faith 29
  hypnotherapy 24, 32
  Reiki 13–14, 22, 25–6, 28, 179
  shamanic 6, 12–13, 26–7
  spiritual 25, 155
Helena Blavatsky 117, 141, 154
hoax(ing) 37, 40, 43, 46, 58, 99–100, 108, 110–13, 138
'Holographic Energetic Structuring' 13
Holdstone Down, Devonshire 153–7
Holy Grail, The 166, 169
horoscopes 25, 32

Janet and Colin Bord (1981) 40

Karl Marx 47, 53
  Marxism 138
Kelvedon Hatch 91
Kendal Project, The 15–16
Knights Templar 166

idiosyncratic *belief* 9, 14, 16, 27–8, 130, 132, 134, 143, 145, 149, 172, 176
illuminate 117, 138–9, 147
Inverness Museum and Art Gallery 43

'Legend Tripping' 87
ley lines 4, 8, 47–8, 116, 119, 121–3, 134–5, 174
livestreaming 77–81, 83, 137, 144
Loch Ness
  Aldie Mackay 99
  Dores Beach 36–7, 97
  Drumnadrochit 36, 97, 99
  see F. W. Holiday
  Loch Ness Centre 8, 36, 97–100
  Marmaduke Wetherell 98, 99
  Monster (Nessie) 2, 4–8, 17, 19, 35–8, 42–7, 49, 51, 96–102, 107, 116, 135, 179
  Nessieland 36, 96, 97
  Nessie Tourism 101–2
  Ronald Mackenzie 35–7
  see Steven Feltham
  Tim Dinsdale 99
levitation 113–14, 126
London MBS Festival (2023) 13, 153

Lower Tier Local Authorities (LTLA's) 88–94

magic
  ancestral 15
  Black 15, 47, 49, 51, 116, 135, 174–5
  chaos 15, 125
  elemental 30–1
  place-based 113, 117
  runic 20, 30
  and spirits 7, 49, 51–4, 115
  Thelemic 15
  White 15
Man-Monkey (Nick Redfern, 2007) 41
Marginalization Hypothesis 7, 48, 53, 148–9
marketplace, The '*Paranormal*' 16, 24–5, 30–2, 34, 36, 91, 96–100, 103, 130, 142–7, 178
Max Weber 102–3, 145
mediums 1, 3, 6, 14, 17, 19, 23–5, 29, 33, 95, 176
mediatization 171
megaliths 102, 119–21, 123, 126
  Alexander Thom 120
Monstrum! A Wizard's Tale (Anthony 'Doc' Shiels) 46
Migoi (Kunzang Choden) 40
  lhaende 40
Mind Body Spirit (MBS) Fairs/Events 6, 13–14, 17–20, 23–6, 28–31, 34, 95, 153, 179
Most Haunted (TV) 73, 80, 83, 91, 177
  Yvette Fielding 55, 71, 73
Mount Everest (Expeditions) 39–40
  Charles Kenneth Howard-Bury, Lt Col (1921–2)
  Edmund Hilary, Sir (1960)
  Eric Shipton (1951)
  Francis S. Smythe (1937)
  Ralph Izzard (1954)
  Ronald Kaulback (1935–6)
'Mr. Nobody' 1, 4, 7, 11, 62–6, 71, 79–80, 83, 173–4
  see also Black Monk of Pontefract
mysticism 8, 15, 18, 30, 53, 153–4, 160

'Necrophonic' (app) 71
New Age 6, 8, 13, 15, 30, 32, 138–9, 141, 144, 152, 167, 170–1

Nibiru (planet) 132, 139
NRMs (New Religious Movements) 151–3, 159

occult 6, 13, 15, 20, 29–31, 67, 153, 170
'Operation Prayer Power' 10, 153–7
'orbs' 81–2
Ouija Board 4, 63, 75–6, 90

paranormal
  belief
    see aliens
    see cryptids
    clusters 36, 43, 48–9, 51, 53, 115
    religious intersection 160–6, 170–2
    see ghosts
    see idiosyncratic
    see syncretism
    scepticism 174
    unifying theory 9, 130, 132, 135–6, 143–7, 150
  consumer 8, 24, 32, 88, 94, 101–3, 146–9, 176
  In the media 7, 41, 130, 134
  particularism 46–7, 174
  pilgrimage 9, 63, 101, 102, 153–5
  see subcultures
  tourism 4–5, 7–8, 11, 38, 83, 95–103
    dark 86, 167–8, 171
    see also ghost
    see also Loch Ness
    see also Crop Circle
past-life regression 4, 14–15, 24, 178
phenomenology 138
podcasts 36, 91, 134, 157, 177–8
Pritchards, The 56, 57, 61, 62, 67, 70, 81
  Diane 62–3
  Phillip 58, 67
profiling 50–4
psychic quest(ing) 125–6
psychics 6, 13–15, 18, 19, 23–5, 29, 32, 47, 51, 95, 115, 135, 136
  see also fortune tellers
  see also mediums

religion(s)
  agnostic 49, 51, 82, 83, 162
  alien/UFO 151, 152
    see Aetherius Society, The
  Raëlism 17, 152
  scientology 152
  atheist 49, 51–3, 162–3
  Catholic 49, 52–3, 148–9, 162–3, 166–7
  Christianity 2, 10, 16–17, 20, 39, 59, 140, 153–4, 159–60, 166–7, 170, 172
    conventional 2, 4, 9–11, 15–16, 48, 53, 69, 77, 82, 108, 111, 133, 151, 153, 159, 161–7, 174, 176, 179
    decline of 2, 10–11, 68–9, 77, 82, 102–3, 133, 150, 160–1, 166
  Diverse Religious Portfolios 176
  fundamentalist 164, 166
  'hyper-real' 177
  Jedi 177
  Jesus Christ 10, 12, 16–17, 152–3, 154, 159–60, 166, 169
  'magical' 29, 30, 31, 34
    Pagan(ism) 29–32, 132, 170
    Satanism 10, 29–30, 176
    Wicca 29–31, 176
  Muslim 49, 108, 162–3
  Protestant 29, 49, 53, 162–3
  secularism 11, 16, 82–3, 102–3, 151, 160–2, 164–6, 172, 175–6, 180
  Theosophy 141, 154, 203–4
Rendlesham Forest 8, 95
reptilian(s) 9, 131–2, 136, 139–42, 147
Retford Ghost Hunters 1, 6, 7, 59–66, 70–1, 77–80, 173–4, 177–8
  Livestream (RGH) 77–81
  Rachel Parsons 59–60, 77–8
rituals 15, 29, 31, 63–4, 77, 82, 139, 151–60
Robin Hood 27
Rosslyn Chapel 10–11, 166–72
Russell Kellett 9–10, 129–34, 141, 143–5, 150, 151
  'UFO Paranormal' and 'Flying Saucer Television' (YouTube) 143

'Sacred Geometry' 8, 119–20
scepticism 41, 67, 107
  'para-scepticism' 112
science 6, 16–19, 26, 29, 43, 111, 118–20, 178
  astronomy 120, 143

metrology 120
pseudoscience 18, 19, 119, 121, 126, 176
social 3, 95, 102, 132, 151
Separate Spheres Hypothesis 161–2
shamanic
   see healing
Small Step Hypothesis 53, 161–2
Social Attitudes Survey (BSAS) 69
social media 1, 24, 77, 85, 87, 171, 177–8
Spirit Box 63–4, 88
   see also Alice Box
'spirituality' 8, 15, 33–4, 54, 68, 143, 160, 162, 167, 169, 176
   'conspirituality' 144, 150
   spiritualism 6, 177
St Columba 98
Steven Feltham 35–7, 46, 96, 100
Stone Circles 8–9, 55, 95, 101, 119–20, 126, 178
   see also Avebury
   see also Megaliths
Stonehenge 8, 95, 119–20, 122
subcultures 4–5, 15–16, 86, 112–14, 126, 134, 138, 143, 172, 178–9
'Subjective turn' 175–6
supernatural(ism) 6, 12, 15, 17, 47, 48, 107, 172
'Super Soldiers' 117, 130–1, 134–5, 144
survey data (CASPAR) 3–5, 8–10, 23, 25, 29, 32, 41, 44, 47, 48, 53, 69, 74, 77, 83, 114–16, 122–3, 141–2, 146–7, 151, 163–4, 171, 174
symbology 19–23, 39, 110, 116, 125, 159, 167–171
syncretism 2, 9, 82, 130, 132–134, 136, 140–1, 145–9, 152, 180

tarot (cartomancy) 4, 6, 14, 19–23, 25, 29, 31–3, 178–9
   Rider-Waite Tarot Deck 21–2
tasseography 20, 30
telekinesis 15, 47, 49, 116, 135, 163
telepathy 3, 15, 17, 134, 152
Three Pillars of
   Psychic (MBS) Fair, The
      see Divination
      see Healing
      see Magic

British Cryptids
   see Loch Ness
   see Bigfoot
   see Big Cats (ABC's)
Tom Cunnif 67, 69, 83
Tudor World Museum, The 89, 90

U.F.O.('s)
   see also abduction/abductees
   see also alien(s)
   Anglesey Crash Conspiracy 148
   'Berwyn Mountains Incident' 129
   community 129–30, 132
      British UFO Hunters 129
      Flying Saucer Bureau 129
      International UFO Network 129
   conferences 4, 95, 130, 178
   see conspiracy theories
   encounter(s) 5, 47, 129, 132
   flying saucers 3, 10, 19, 38, 107, 152
   researchers 38, 47, 117
      Bart Uytterhaegen 117–18
      Budd Hopkins 132
      Miles Johnston 117
      Bases Project, the
      see Russell Kellet

V (TV) 1980s 140
View Over Atlantis and How the World Is Made, The (John Mitchel) 120

'Wang' (god) 136–7
When the Lights Went Out (Film) Pat Holden/Bil Bungay 69–70, 73, 83
White Horse
   Roundway 105
   Uffington 8
witchcraft 30–1, 48, 95
Wildman (UK) 4, 6–7, 38–42, 47, 49, 116, 135, 175
   Nant Gwynant Valley, Wales 39
   Ogof y Gwr Blewog or 'Cave of the Hairy Man' 39
   The Fight in the Forest, Hans Burgkmair (I, c. 1500/1503) 39
workshops/talks 5, 14, 23–4, 26–31, 137–41, 158

Zecharia Sitchin 139